MW00985009

ANGER TREATMENT FOR PEOPLE WITH DEVELOPMENTAL DISABILITIES

ANGER TREATMENT FOR PEOPLE WITH DEVELOPMENTAL DISABILITIES
A THEORY, EVIDENCE AND MANUAL BASED APPROACH

John L. Taylor
Northumbria University, Newcastle upon Tyne and
Northgate and Prudhoe NHS Trust, Northumberland, UK

Raymond W. Novaco
University of California, Irvine, USA

John Wiley & Sons, Ltd

Copyright © 2005   John Wiley & Sons Ltd, The Atrium, Southern Gate, Chichester,
West Sussex PO19 8SQ, England

Telephone   (+44) 1243 779777

Email (for orders and customer service enquiries): cs-books@wiley.co.uk
Visit our Home Page on www.wiley.com

All Rights Reserved. No part of this publication may be reproduced, stored in a retrieval system or transmitted in
any form or by any means, electronic, mechanical, photocopying, recording, scanning or otherwise, except under
the terms of the Copyright, Designs and Patents Act 1988 or under the terms of a licence issued by the Copyright
Licensing Agency Ltd, 90 Tottenham Court Road, London W1T 4LP, UK, without the permission in writing of
the Publisher. Requests to the Publisher should be addressed to the Permissions Department, John Wiley & Sons
Ltd, The Atrium, Southern Gate, Chichester, West Sussex PO19 8SQ, England, or emailed to
permreq@wiley.co.uk, or faxed to (+44) 1243 770620.

Designations used by companies to distinguish their products are often claimed as trademarks. All brand
names and product names used in this book are trade names, service marks, trademarks or registered trademarks
of their respective owners. The Publisher is not associated with any product or vendor mentioned in this book.

This publication is designed to provide accurate and authoritative information in regard to the subject matter
covered. It is sold on the understanding that the Publisher is not engaged in rendering professional services. If
professional advice or other expert assistance is required, the services of a competent professional should be
sought.

Other Wiley Editorial Offices

John Wiley & Sons Inc., 111 River Street, Hoboken, NJ 07030, USA

Jossey-Bass, 989 Market Street, San Francisco, CA 94103-1741, USA

Wiley-VCH Verlag GmbH, Boschstr. 12, D-69469 Weinheim, Germany

John Wiley & Sons Australia Ltd, 33 Park Road, Milton, Queensland 4064, Australia

John Wiley & Sons (Asia) Pte Ltd, 2 Clementi Loop #02-01, Jin Xing Distripark, Singapore 129809

John Wiley & Sons Canada Ltd, 22 Worcester Road, Etobicoke, Ontario, Canada M9W 1L1

Wiley also publishes its books in a variety of electronic formats. Some content that appears in print may not
be available in electronic books.

Library of Congress Cataloguing-in-Publication Data

Taylor, John L. (John Lionel), 1961–
    Anger treatment for people with developmental disabilities : a theory, evidence, and
manual based approach / John L. Taylor, Raymond W. Novaco.
        p.   cm.
    Includes bibliographical references and index.
    ISBN-13 978-0-470-87004-4 – 978-0-470-87005-1

    1. Developmentally disabled – Rehabilitation.   2. Anger – Treatment.
3. Aggressiveness – Treatment.   4. Cognitive therapy.   I. Novaco, Raymond W.   II. Title.
HV1570 .T39   2005
616.85′820651 – dc22   2004027108

British Library Cataloguing in Publication Data

A catalogue record for this book is available from the British Library

ISBN-13 978-0-470-87004-4 (hbk) 978-0-470-87005-1 (pbk)

Typeset in 10/12pt Times and Helvetica by TechBooks, New Delhi, India

JLT   To Caroline, Olivia and Alexander for their patience and support throughout.

RWN   To my mother, Mary Theresa Novaco, whose fortitude, feisty spirit, and independence continue to be a source of inspiration.

CONTENTS

ABOUT THE AUTHORS

John L. Taylor is Professor of Developmental Disability Psychology, Northumbria University, Newcastle upon Tyne; Head of Psychological Therapies and Research and Consultant Clinical Psychologist, Northgate and Prudhoe NHS Trust, Northumberland, UK. Since qualifying as a clinical psychologist from Edinburgh University, John Taylor has worked mainly in developmental disability and forensic services in community, medium secure, special hospital and prison settings in the UK. In 1999 he received a Department of Health Sir Kenneth Calman Bursary Award to develop his research interests in the area of anger treatment. In recent years he has published work related to his clinical research interests in assessment and treatment of offenders with developmental disabilities in a range of research and professional journals. He is currently Chair of the British Psychological Society's Faculty for Forensic Clinical Psychology and the Learning Disability Steering Group of the NHS National Forensic Mental Health Research and Development Programme.

Raymond W. Novaco is Professor of Psychology and Social Behavior, University of California, Irvine, USA. Cognitive-behavioural therapy for anger was pioneered by Ray Novaco, for which he received the Best Contribution Award in 1978 from the International Society for Research on Aggression. Funded by the MacArthur Foundation Research Network on Mental Health and the Law in 1991–1993, he developed new procedures for anger assessment for use with mentally disordered persons, which are here being extended to the developmental disabilities domain. He received the Distinguished Contributions to Psychology Award from the California Psychological Association in 2000. In addition to being programme consultant for the Northgate Hospital anger project, he serves as Research Consultant to The State Hospital in Scotland and for many years served on the Advisory Board of Atascadero State Hospital in California.

CONTRIBUTORS

Bruce T. Gillmer is Consultant Clinical Psychologist and Head of Forensic Psychology Division, Northgate and Prudhoe NHS Trust, Northumberland, UK.

Alison Robertson is Consultant Clinical Psychologist, Northgate and Prudhoe NHS Trust, Northumberland; and Honorary Clinical Lecturer, University of Newcastle, Newcastle upon Tyne, UK.

FOREWORD

In the late 1980s and early 1990s, deinstitutionalization was in full swing. Most institutions had rehabilitation and community integration policies with large-scale relocation projects to move people with developmental disabilities into local communities. With the success of these policies and projects came the normal problems of community living. A number of individuals began to be referred back to services because of problems with anger and aggression. It was immediately apparent that behaviour modification programmes and behaviour therapy programmes that had previously been employed in institutions would not always, or indeed often, be feasible in these less controlled settings. At that time, a number of us were thankful for the theoretical analysis of anger and aggression that had been developed by Ray Novaco and that had such practical extensions for treatment. In this way, fledgling anger management programmes developed for individuals with intellectual disabilities. These programmes allowed the personal development of anger control techniques that relied to a much lesser extent on behavioural contingencies and to a greater extent on cognitive control and self-restraint. Since that time, it has become clear, to a significant extent through the work of John Taylor, that anger and aggression are serious problems for this client group and that it has important repercussions for policies, staff and services. John has written elsewhere, and will also review the information in this book, that the effect of client anger on staff morale, self-esteem, and absenteeism is considerable. It is crucial that clients themselves are allowed to develop personal abilities which will enable them to control their own emotions so that they can go about their daily business more effectively in communities, with friends, with family, and at home.

These issues are not merely for philosophical enquiry or academic interest, they are vital to people's lives and it is for these reasons that this book is not only of the utmost practical importance but also timely. John Taylor and Ray Novaco have written a knowledgeable, erudite, and practical text. They review the historical routes of thinking on anger, tracing developments from the eighteenth century to the present day. Their summaries of the way in which different psychological theories have considered anger will be of interest both to the newcomer to the field and to those of us who have worked in the area for some time. They also make careful evaluation of recent research and the effectiveness of individual treatment methods. The greatest value of this book, however, is obviously the extent and detail of the treatment protocols. I have often said in the past that one of the most difficult treatments to conduct and one that requires a high level of skill is the treatment of individuals who are angry. When doing this work, I am always aware that there is a potential for the individual who I am treating to become angry during the session. Treatment therefore requires a good level of clinical skill and knowledge. The background information, research reviews, assessment protocols, and treatment techniques that are all detailed in this text contribute significantly to enabling us all to become technically equipped to deal with this difficult treatment group. Typically for John and Ray and their attention to detail, they have provided specific chapters on applications with women, and supervision and support of therapists, ably written by Alison Robertson and Bruce Gillmer respectively.

Not only does this book summarize the available information on anger, anger treatment, and people with intellectual disabilities, it enables the individual who has general experience in the field of intellectual disabilities to embark on a well-validated assessment and treatment programme that will be of crucial relevance to their clients. It also marks a significant theoretical advance in the field of anger and anger control. It represents *the state of the art* in anger treatment for individuals with developmental disabilities and I would expect to see a significant effect from this text on the development of treatment services. I certainly hope that it promotes a greater understanding of why our clients (and ourselves) get angry and promotes greater access to treatment.

Bill Lindsay
November 2004

PREFACE

While anger is a normal human emotion and can have a number of positive functions, it is closely associated with aggression, psychological distress and physical ill-health. Thus, anger and associated aggression can carry heavy costs for individuals and for health and social care systems concerned with providing treatment and support to clients with chronic anger control problems. The societal as well as the psychological interest in anger control have a fascinating historical background, which we present in our opening chapter.

The Northgate Anger Treatment Project was established in the male forensic services of Northgate and Prudhoe NHS Trust, a specialist learning disability service located in the North-East of England. The great majority of patients in the forensic services have offending or quasi-offending histories. That is, they have been convicted of carrying out particular offences, or they have well-documented histories of behaviours that, for a variety of reasons, have not been processed through the criminal justice system, but have placed the individual at risk of becoming a convicted offender. The major offence categories for this population at Northgate Hospital are violent offences, sex offences, and fire-setting offences. Many patients have convictions or documented histories of offending behaviour in more than one of these categories.

Given the forensic histories of this population, the Trust's Department of Psychological Therapies and Research has designed, developed and implemented offence-specific assessment and intervention programmes aimed at reducing the risk of future offending behaviour and thereby facilitating rehabilitation of patients from in-patient hospital services to community-based facilities. Based on the 'what works' meta-analysis literature concerning recidivism rates for offenders, sex offender and fire-setter treatment programmes have been developed and implemented with reference to number of key principles (McGuire, 1995, 2002). This has involved the development of treatment interventions that are cognitive-behavioural in nature, are responsive to the learning needs of clients, focus on the criminogenic aspects of the clients presenting problems, take into account the level of risk presented by clients, and attend to issues of programme integrity. Based on the evidence available for non-developmentally disabled (mainly adolescent) offenders, it has been suggested that interventions incorporating these principles are likely to be more effective than those that do not, and could reduce recidivism rates significantly. The development of the anger treatment procedures within a 'what works' framework is described further in Chapter 7.

The issue of programme integrity is central in delivering successful psychological intervention programmes. In order to avoid threats to integrity, interventions need to be based on sound theoretical frameworks that have empirical evidence to support them. The therapists implementing the interventions need to be well trained in both theory and delivery aspects, and the use of manualized protocols to guide the delivery of interventions is an important factor. Therapist training, along with supervision, support and other process issues, are discussed in depth by Bruce Gillmer in Chapter 10.

In addition to the offence-related reasons for developing an anger treatment approach for patients in the Trust's forensic services, given the association between anger and a range of psychological conditions and poor general health, it was anticipated that by helping patients with their anger problems, their general psychological and physical well-being would be improved and they could be more amenable to, and have additional resources to cope with, the demands of other offence-specific treatments, e.g. group-based sex offender therapy. Further, many patients are willing to discuss temper control problems early in their rehabilitation, compared with, for example, sexual aggression. Therefore, by beginning with a problem that has salience for the patient and is relatively unthreatening, therapeutic relationships and trust can be built that facilitate more offence-focused work at a later stage. In this way anger treatment can be viewed as adjunctive therapy rather than as a stand-alone encapsulated procedure. A guiding framework for anger dysregulation and cognitive behavioural anger treatment is set out in Chapter 2.

When psychotherapeutic approaches have been made available to people with develop-mental disability and emotional problems, too frequently they have been applied without reference to empirically-based research. When treatment has been ineffective, there has been a tendency to attribute this to the characteristics of the clients with disability, rather than to the limitations of treatment techniques (or the therapists delivering them). In Chapter 4, the lack of evidence for effective psychological therapies for emotional and mental health problems among people with developmental disabilities is discussed.

Taking into account these factors and influences, the Northgate Anger Treatment Project aimed to achieve two main goals within the Trust's forensic services. First, to investigate the nature, scope, and patient needs in relation to anger control problems. This was to be done through a service-wide anger assessment study, the results of which are described in Chapter 6. Second, the effectiveness of a cognitive-behavioural anger treatment de-veloped specifically for this population was evaluated in several concatenated controlled outcome studies. The methods, design, procedures, and results of these studies are de-scribed in considerable detail in Chapters 5 and 7. Most importantly, included in this book is the anger treatment protocol that we have constructed and implemented. Chap-ter 8 contains the six-session treatment preparatory phase, and Chapter 9 is the 12-session treatment phase. Handout/exercise sheets used to support the delivery of the treatment pro-tocol are also provided as Appendices, and online at our dedicated website www.wiley. com/go/angertreatment

While the focus of the Northgate Anger Treatment Project has been on people with of-fending and quasi-offending histories, the underlying theoretical framework, principles, and procedures, and the results of the supporting empirical studies apply equally to people with developmental disabilities with anger control problems but who have not necessarily come into contact with the criminal justice system and those who live in less secure, supervised, and non-institutional settings. Our belief is that if these approaches can be effective and can benefit clients with chronic, deep-rooted anger problems often associated with significant histories of neglect and abuse, then they can be at least as effective and potentially beneficial to clients with less severe problems. However, this is an empirical question that requires further investigation and enquiry.

Similarly, the assessment and treatment approaches presented in this volume have been developed with men with developmental disabilities. It would be remiss to assume that women with developmental disabilities experience anger in the same way as their male counterparts, or that their response to treatment will be the same in all respects. For these reasons the Anger Treatment Project has been extended to the women residing in the Northgate forensic services. In Chapter 11, Alison Robertson describes the anger assessment and treatment studies that have been conducted with this population and sets this within the context of gender-specific issues relating to the experience and expression of anger.

Finally, we need to explain to readers the reasons for our choice of terminology in the title of this volume and to describe the client population with whom we are concerned. In the United Kingdom the term 'learning disability' is commonly used to describe people characterized as: (1) having significant sub-average general intellectual functioning as measured on standard individual intelligence test; (2) having more difficulties in functioning in two or more specified areas of adaptive behaviour than would be expected, taking into account age and cultural context; and (3) having experienced the onset of this disability before the age of 18 years. These criteria are broadly those included in the *International Classification of Diseases* (ICD-10; World Health Organization, 1992), the *Diagnostic and Statistical Manual of Mental Disorders* (DSM-IV; American Psychiatric Association, 1994) and the American Association on Mental Retardation (AAMR) diagnostic classification systems. The terms 'mental retardation' and 'intellectual disability' are commonly used in North America and Australia respectively to refer to the same syndrome.

One reason for attempting to define disability is to have descriptive terms that help communities of interest to communicate about phenomena in such ways that convey shared understanding and meaning. For this reason the term 'developmental disability' is used throughout this volume to describe the participants involved in the development of the anger assessment and treatment procedures presented. It refers to the definition given in the United States Developmental Disabilities Assistance and Bill of Rights Act (2000) and is a broad concept covering the equivalent terms of mental retardation, learning disability, and intellectual disability commonly used in North America, the United Kingdom, and Australia, respectively. In general terms, developmental disability means a severe, chronic disability of an individual that: (1) is attributable to a mental or physical impairment or combination of mental and physical impairments; (2) is manifested before the individual attains the age of 22 years; (3) is likely to continue indefinitely; and (4) results in substantial functional limitations in three or more areas of major life activity.

In addition to learning disability, the concept includes other conditions that do not necessarily involve significant sub-average intellectual functioning such as autism, epilepsy, and some other neurological conditions. The definition of developmental disability also focuses on functional limitations and life-long support needs that should be individually planned and co-ordinated. The assessed levels of intellectual functioning of the participants involved in the treatment and research programme described in this volume, and the inclusion of people with conditions other than learning disability, mean that the term developmental disability provides the best description of the population involved in these studies. However, in describing research conducted by others in a range of settings across a number of continents, whenever appropriate, and when it makes sense to do so, the terms used by authors in their reports to describe the participants involved in their studies are used.

John L. Taylor
Raymond W. Novaco
October 2004

There is a dedicated website for this book at www.wiley.com/go/angertreatment, containing the handout exercise sheets from the Appendix. These are available to readers to view and download.

ACKNOWLEDGEMENTS

In addition to the Northgate Anger Treatment Project core team, comprising Professor John Taylor, consultant clinical psychologist, Professor Ray Novaco, programme consultant and advisor, Dr Bruce Gillmer, consultant clinical psychologist, Ian Thorne, forensic psychologist and Alison Robertson, consultant clinical psychologist, a large number of colleagues have contributed to this work in many different ways in the past five years, and we extend to them our considerable gratitude.

Claire Guinan and Nicola Street worked steadfastly as research assistant psychologists on the assessment and outcome study phases of the project. More recently Sarah Matthews, Danielle Wilson, and Sherley Tordoff, research assistants, have skilfully managed and maintained the programme databases.

Our Forensic Psychology Division colleagues, Melanie McKenna, chartered forensic psychologist, Sam Bainbridge, senior occupational therapist, and Kirsty Lowe, consultant clinical psychologist, have treated a number of patients as part of the development of the intervention as a routine clinical programme in the service. A host of assistant psychologists working in the department for fixed periods have collected and collated assessment data *and* delivered the treatment protocol to clients. These include Ginny Avery, Tracy Belshaw, Helen Clothier, Louise Dixon, Andrew Dunn, Jennifer Lane, Sarah Richardson, Angela Simcox, Nicola Street, Pauline Summerfield, Rachel Turnbull, Angela Watson, and Danielle Wilson. A number of trainee clinical psychologists from the University of Newcastle Doctorate in Clinical Psychology programme have also been involved in the delivery of the treatment as part of their placement experience in the department, including Debra Hall, Lene Rasmusen, Jennifer Gracie, Tom Christodoulides, and Vicki Grahame.

Our nursing colleagues, with direction and leadership from Paul Thornton, forensic services manager, and Graham English, forensic nursing programme co-ordinator, have provided unstinting support for the programme in terms of completion of endless informant-rated measures, support for individual patients engaged in anger treatment and implementation of maintenance programmes. Our psychiatrist colleagues, led by Professor Gregory O'Brien, clinical lead for forensic services, have also provided a good deal of support and encouragement throughout. The Executive Directors of Northgate and Prudhoe NHS Trust, particularly Dr Anthony Perini, medical director, have facilitated this development and provided the financial support without which it could not have taken place.

Our department secretaries, Pat Blakely and Wendy Hart, have been willing helpers in terms of preparation of materials and reports for the anger treatment project. Many thanks also to Sherley Tordoff for proof reading the manuscript and references, and for collecting new data regarding the maintenance of anger treatment gains.

We especially thank our colleagues and collaborators Dr Bruce Gillmer and Alison Robertson for contributing important chapters concerning therapist training, supervision, and the treatment process and anger treatment for women with developmental disabilities, respectively. At John Wiley & Sons Lesley Valerio and Dr Vivien Ward, and more recently Gillian Leslie, Claire Ruston, and Ruth Graham have been supportive, helpful, and considerate during the production of this book. But finally, and most importantly, we are grateful to and deeply thank our patients and clients (past and present) who involved themselves in this project and gave permission for the results of their assessments and treatments to be collated and used to evaluate this new treatment approach.

ANGER AND AGGRESSION: CONCEPTUAL BACKGROUND AND HISTORICAL PERSPECTIVE

OVERVIEW

An efficacious approach to anger treatment must be grounded in a coherent view of anger and how this normal emotion can become 'disordered'. Anger is a captivating, unsettling, and oddly satisfying emotion. Activated in our surround, it commands attention and alertness for potential danger. Triggered within us, it provides empowerment yet can otherwise be cause for apprehension or shame. Anger is embedded in our hard-wiring for survival and perseverance. In response to oppressive circumstances, its expression is often tension-relieving. Recurrent anger, however, adversely affects emotional and physical health and is disruptive of social relationships that sustain personal well-being. Overridingly salient, perhaps, is anger's linguistic, symbolic, and empirical connection to aggression, which impels societies to seek remedies for its control.

Anger is indeed a perplexing emotion, and there is a multi-level ambivalence about its control. It is part of the human fabric and the diversity of personality, often garnering delight as well as disapproval. As a subjective experience, it curiously has self-serving qualities that can carry a gratifying aura, particularly in the service of retaliation. Thus, we do appreciate its functionality, but nevertheless recognize its commonly troublesome products. Precisely because it is associated with subjective distress, detrimental effects on personal relationships, health impairments, and the manifold harmful consequences of aggressive behaviour, interest in anger control prevails as a human welfare and societal concern.

Providing clinical interventions for persons having recurrent anger problems is a challenging enterprise. This turbulent emotion, ubiquitous in everyday life, is a feature of a wide range of disorders encountered by mental health and social service professionals in diverse settings. It is commonly observed in various personality, psychosomatic, and conduct disorders, in schizophrenia, in bipolar mood disorders, in organic cognitive disorders, in impulse control dysfunctions, and in a variety of conditions resulting from trauma. The central characteristic of anger in the broad context of clinical problems is that it is 'dysregulated' – its activation, expression, and ongoing experience occur without appropriate

Anger Treatment for People with Developmental Disabilities by J. L. Taylor and R. W. Novaco.
Copyright © 2005 John Wiley & Sons, Ltd.

controls. Alternatively stated, in such clinical conditions, there is a substantial incongruence between anger engagement and the requirements for optimal functioning, both in the short term and in the long term.

For persons with developmental disabilities, their life circumstances and psychosocial experiences, from childhood onward, are conducive to the activation of anger. Moreover, the environmental settings in which many reside are intrinsically constraining and limited in satisfaction. Recurrent thwarting of physical, emotional, and interpersonal needs can easily activate anger; cognitive functioning deficits readily impair effective coping with frustrating or aversive events; and impoverished support systems curtail problem-solving options. For decades, however, a prime treatment target for persons with developmental disabilities has been their 'challenging behaviour', which focuses away from internal emotional distress. As was so aptly stated by Blunden and Allen, 'very few intervention plans actually teach people with learning difficulties socially acceptable ways of expressing anger or frustration, and challenging behaviour may be the one way in which people in such circumstances can exert control over the way in which they live' (1987, p. 39).

Because anger is a common precursor of aggressive behaviour, it can be unsettling for mental health professionals to engage as a treatment focus, regardless of its salience as a clinical need. Because seriously angry people tend to be treatment-avoidant, engaging them in the therapeutic enterprise is often hard-going. Efforts to achieve clinical change are challenged by the adaptive functions of anger as a normal emotion and by its ties to symbolic structures having high personal, familial, and social group relevance. Anger routines have identity attachment qualities and are not easily relinquished. The oppositional nature of many high-anger clients results from anger being entrenched in personal identity, derivative of traumatic life history, associated with personality or mental disorder, and unmitigated by soothing social influences. Intellectual functioning deficits clearly add to the challenges of anger regulation from the standpoint of both clients and those who seek to help them therapeutically.

In this book, we address the assessment of anger and the provision of anger treatment for persons with developmental disabilities. Our approach is cognitive-behavioural in orientation, and while it is grounded in an extensive clinical research project with hospitalized forensic patients, the proffered content and overview are more broadly based. Our attention to anger is mindful of the entanglements of the clinical problem in this client population – namely, the conjunction of developmental disability, impoverished family background, early conduct difficulties, substance use, serious offence history, institutionalization, re-offending, amalgamative emotional distress, and recurrent challenging behaviour for mental health care staff. Innovations and evidence in the existing literature point to achievements in the assessment and treatment of persons having such multi-layered difficulties in regulating anger and aggressive behaviour, and this bodes well for extensions to clients with less severe anger problems and less resource impairment.

THE SOCIETAL CALL FOR ANGER CONTROL

Proscriptions for anger control have been plentiful since classical philosophers sought rational control over the emotions, which were then understood as passions that seized the personality, disturbed judgement, and imperilled behaviour. Pre-dating the Greek and Roman Stoics were Buddhist teachings about the path to enlightenment, seeking to train the mind to gain inner strength. Anger control has been a vexing issue addressed in disparate ways by Buddhists, Stoic philosophers, Psalmists, Scholastics, philosophers of the European Enlightenment, Jonathan Swift, American colonists, Victorians, Existentialists, early North American psychology, Dr Spock, Dale Carnegie, sensitivity trainers, Zen masters, and psychodynamic and cognitive-behavioural therapists, to name an assortment of promulgators.

Interest in anger control gained prominence in recent decades both in the general culture of Western societies and in broad clinical psychology literature. In many countries, the call for 'anger management' is commonly encountered in news/entertainment media, as well as in directives from social gatekeepers seeking to rectify someone's troublesome behaviour. In the popular press, road rage metastasized into air rage, cinema rage, golf rage, rink rage, surf rage, trolley rage, and royal rage. Anger management became a frequent prescription given by judicial officers, school administrators, mental health system directors, and prison and probation authorities. Its diffusion is exemplified by the many self-help tradebooks written by clinical practitioners, the subtitles of which reflect the quest for wellness through anger control (e.g., Carter, 2003; Colbert, 2003; Cullen & Freeman-Longo, 1995; Davies, 2000; Harbin, 2000; McKay, Rogers, & McKay, 1989). Advances in academic research and in evidence-based psychological treatment provided the springboard for the societal consciousness-raising, which has now included a Hollywood production on the topic. Perhaps it is too cynical to state that anger problems are commonly trivialized, but it seems fair to conclude that, unless serious violence is involved, anger therapy is viewed with less gravitas than therapy for depression.

The designated recipients of real-life anger interventions have been highly diverse in problem condition, e.g., domestic violence perpetrators, traffic offenders, children with conduct problems, quarrelsome neighbours, explosive felons, and persons with various psychiatric disorders being offered anger management as supplementary care. Anger treatment gains for clients having a wide range of clinical disorders have been reported in case studies and multiple baseline studies, which will be presented later. In contrast, a great many recipients of anger treatment in controlled studies have been college student volunteers, which unfortunately results in such studies with quasi-clinical clients receiving disproportionate attention in meta-analyses. As six meta-analyses have now been published (Beck & Fernandez, 1998; Del Vecchio & O'Leary, 2004; DiGuiseppe & Tafrate, 2003; Edmondson & Conger, 1996; Sukhodolsky, Kassinove, & Gorman, 2004; Tafrate, 1995), there oddly may be more meta-analyses of anger treatment than the number of high quality clinical trials justify.

The call for 'anger management' has perhaps been far too prevalent, and those ready to be proficiently responsive far too few. Nevertheless, mental health professionals in many service delivery domains have now become familiar with client anger problems and have explored diverse approaches to improving their clinical care capacity in this regard. Dissemination of programmes has occurred in schools, clinics, hospitals, and prisons, especially of cognitive-behaviour therapy (CBT) interventions, implemented with varying degrees of systematization. As reviewed by Taylor (2002a), anger treatment also took hold in the field of intellectual disabilities, including CBT, as well as other modalities. Because the general procedures of CBT are relatively accessible, attempts to apply this mode of treatment to anger can easily miss important elements of this therapeutic approach, from the clinical problem formulation, to the complexities of cognitive restructuring, and to the details of stress inoculation work with provocation hierarchies. To facilitate improvements in service provision, this book presents a full anger assessment and treatment protocol, buttressed by clinical material and procedural tools to enable effective implementation for persons with developmental disabilities.

As an important backdrop, the historical context of psychological interventions for anger will be broadly overviewed to cultivate a differentiated understanding of the anger construct. Being versed in the conceptual complexities will foster adeptness in assessment of anger problems and provide a firmer grasp of core elements of CBT anger treatment. Implementation of the anger treatment ultimately requires proficient flexibility and nuances in protocol application. One must 'breathe life' into a treatment manual (Kendall, Chu, Gifford, Hayes, & Nauta, 1998). An enriched understanding of anger and aggression provides a grounding for the identification of anger problem dimensions, points of leverage, and treatment avenues.

AN ENCAPSULATED HISTORY

Early psychology

Since the writings of Charles Darwin, William James, and Walter B. Cannon, anger has been viewed in terms of the engagement of the organism's survival systems in response to threat and the interplay of cognitive, physiological, and behavioural components. It is an elementary Darwinian notion that the adaptive value of a characteristic is entailed by its fitness for the environment (Darwin, 1859); if the environment changes, that characteristic may lose its adaptive value, and the organism must adjust. Thus, the activation of anger may usefully serve to engage aggression in combat and to overcome fear, but, in non-combat environments (and even in combat ones), anger is often maladaptive. Many theories of emotion have enlarged upon the Darwinian view of emotions as reactions to basic survival problems created by the environment and upon Cannon's (1915) idea that internal changes prepare the body for fight or flight behaviour. These core ideas are exemplified in Plutchik (1980), as well as in Lazarus (1968). From Cannon to Lang (1995), emotion has commonly been viewed as an action disposition. As well, emotional expression is understood to have communicative value, which Darwin (1872) recognized and which has received extensive research attention from Ekman (2003), Izard (1977), and others.

Anger was prominently addressed by Darwin (1872), both throughout that volume and in a chapter detailing its vicissitudes (i.e., defiance, indignation, rage, and hatred). However, anger had long been the subject of scholarship in philosophical writings, from the classicists, such as Aristotle and Seneca, through Augustine, Aquinas, Hobbes, Spinosa, Nietzsche, and Sartre – to do some leapfrogging over time. To summarize the work of philosophers on anger would be a daunting task, and on the classicists there is a masterful book by Harris (2001) and a splendid edited volume by Braund and Most (2003). Regarding intellectual ancestry highly pertinent to what is presented in this book, it should be noted that a conception of anger as a product of threat perceptions, as having confirmatory bias characteristics, as being primed by aversive precursors, and as having social distancing effects can be found in the writings of Lucius Seneca (44/1817), who was Nero's tutor and is perhaps the first anger scholar.

In the field of psychology, G. Stanley Hall's (1899) important monograph sought to move us beyond the predominantly philosophical analyses that prevailed at that time. To this end, he distributed a questionnaire in a national mailing that produced 2,184 returns. His questionnaire asked for descriptions of sensations, symptoms, overt acts, mental correlators, cognitive constructions, and palliatives associated with anger reactions. He distilled the responses into various content categories: causes, physical manifestations, 'vents', reactions, control, and treatment. Despite Hall's rich account, no programmatic work followed. In the ensuing decades, there was a peppering of diary studies of anger experiences (cf. Novaco, 1986), some introspection experimentation (e.g., Richardson, 1918), and some prescient clinical writings in the nascent field of psychosomatic medicine (e.g., Alexander, 1939; Miller, 1939; Saul, 1939) that called attention to the relationship of anger to blood pressure. No paradigm for research came to the fore, nor was there a prevailing conceptual framework – anger had no conceptual salience for Freud and his followers. Hall (1915) asserted that every Freudian mechanism applies to anger as well as to sexuality, yet anger remained neglected.

As there is no better metaphor for anger than hot fluid in a container, it is surprising that interest in anger and blood pressure slipped into abeyance until a burst of laboratory research occurred in the 1950s (e.g., Ax, 1953; Funkenstein, King, & Drolette, 1954; Oken, 1960; Schacter, 1957). There was dormancy again until the important field research of Harburg and his colleagues (Harburg et al., 1973; Harburg, Blakelock, & Roeper, 1979) on anger and essential hypertension, which importantly highlighted person–environment interactive variables and provided impetus for the study of anger as a public health issue. These clusters of research on anger and cardiovascular processes and disease are noteworthy – while developments in several areas of psychology have fuelled our contemporary interest, it was especially research in health psychology that served to spur attention to anger that had merely flickered since Hall's (1899) effort to advance psychological work on this subject.

Nascent aggression research

Research on aggression in personality and social psychology was substantial following the famous *Frustration and Aggression* monograph (Dollard, Doob, Miller, Mowrer, & Sears, 1939). Oddly, this body of research, for the most part, ignored anger; indeed, the word 'anger' is virtually absent in Dollard et al. (1939), appearing rarely and only incidentally, as in a footnote that refers to a diary study monograph by Goodenough (1931). In accounting for the activation of aggression, Dollard et al. relied on the term 'instigation', a hypothetical internal motivational state, rather than give attention to anger. The empirical agenda of experimental psychology in observable events resulted in a preference for the study of aggressive behaviour over the emotion of anger, which was seemingly more elusive and unsuitable for the positivistic programme.

Frustration was understood by Dollard et al. as a measurable goal-blocking – its intensity was seen to vary with the importance of the goals ('strength of the goal response'), the degree of interference with the goal response, and the number of response sequences frustrated. Its empirical locus was outside the person. The inherent ambiguity of the term, which certainly connotes an internal state, and the over-generality of its application ultimately weighed against its utility in accounting for aggression. As Buss stated, 'It is difficult to imagine a behaviour sequence in which some drive is not suffering interference, especially when security and comfort are included as drives' (1966, p. 153). Pertinent to later cognitive appraisal formulations of the dynamics of anger and aggression, research by Pastore (1952) and Cohen (1955) had shown that the experience of frustration did not uniformly provoke aggression but that the 'arbitrariness' of frustrations was an important mediating factor.

The landmark book by Buss (1961) did indeed given attention to anger (e.g., a chapter on anger physiology), but being strongly inclined toward positivism (Buss defined aggression as 'a response that delivers noxious stimuli to another organism', ibid. p. 1), he did not designate anger as an antecedent to aggression. In was Berkowitz (1962), in his important book, who argued for giving greater focus to anger as the emotional response mediator of frustration–aggression relationships. He used 'anger' in lieu of 'instigation to aggression' and asserted that it would be profitable now to consider this emotional state as the mediating condition. For example, one of his distinguished students, Geen (1968) later showed that when frustration is personalized or is exacerbated by insult, the resulting anger and aggression are proportionately greater. Oddly, although Berkowitz (1962) argued for the value of anger as a central mediating variable, he gave relatively little attention to it in the remainder of the book after his discussion of frustration–aggression propositions. In subsequent decades, Berkowitz also changed his view of the role of anger as a determinant of aggression, instead asserting that 'negative affect' was the central mediator (Berkowitz, 1990, 1993).

In the experimental laboratory research that evolved from the frustration–aggression hypothesis (see also, Feshbach, 1964, 1971), as well as the development of social learning theory (Bandura, 1973), the pre-ordained focal topic was aggression, and anger remained a secondary subject. Feshbach's approach to aggression also reflected the positivistic bias that excluded anger as a primary research topic. He asserted that 'aggressive drive', an intervening variable specified in Hullian terms (a mediating response-drive stimulus), motivated aggressive behaviour. He distinguished anger from aggressive drive, which was said to be facilitated by anger. Thus, the motivation for aggression was ascribed to a hypothetical condition having no organismic or phenomenological referents, which thereby diverted attention away from internal states. Simarly, Bandura's (1973) social learning theory analysis relegated anger to a secondary position of importance. He adopted a general arousal model in accounting for the disposition for aggression, asserting that any source of emotional arousal would increase its probability, and while he certainly incorporated anger in his pioneering book, it had no featured status. In this genre of research, attention given to anger in experimental psychology occurred predominately with regard to it being a laboratory precondition manipulated to instigate aggression. In the aggression theories of Berkowitz, Feshbach, and Bandura, respectfully, anger arousal is assigned response-energizing, response-motivating, and response-activating functions. Anger was viewed in each of their theories as an emotional response that facilitates aggression, rather than as a necessary condition, which remains the standard position among aggression scholars.

We will return to mainstream aggression research after first discussing psychoanalytic writings and some important concepts that it has bequeathed pertinent to our understanding of anger and its regulation.

Psychoanalytical theory

The heuristic source of the frustration–aggression hypothesis was psychoanalytic theory, but anger was a sparse topic in psychoanalytic writings (cf. Novaco, 1986). Freud, in his many works, never provided a coherent view of anger. Menninger (1938), one of Freud's primary exponents, presented many clinical and journalistic stories of persons who 'boil over with rage' and later asserted that the human child 'usually begins his life in anger' (Menninger, 1942); but he did not give explicit attention to anger and rarely used the word in his books. Similarly, the treatise on aggression by Hartmann, Kris, and Loewenstein (1949) virtually omits the word 'anger' – it appears in one incidental comment in describing hypothetical behaviour of a child. Their concern was with the integration of libido and aggression, and their conjectures were consonant with the frustration–aggression hypothesis. Anna Freud's (1949) article on aggression in that same volume (originally a paper presented at the Royal Society of Medicine in 1947) had emotional development in its title, but the word 'anger' does not appear anywhere in the text. She too was preoccupied with the fusion of the libidinal and aggressive instincts. For example, in describing pathological aggressiveness of young children who had distressed family backgrounds, who had been exposed to war, or who had been in institutions or camps, she states: 'Closer observation shows that the pathological factor in the cases is not to be found in the aggressive tendencies themselves, but in the lack of fusion between them and libidinal (erotic) urges' (ibid., p. 41). For her, the pathology was located in the blocking of emotional libidinal development due to impaired object relations. It is as if anger was a triviality.

Among the psychoanalytic writers who thought that Freud overemphasized libidinal frustration in the etiology of the neuroses was Horney (1939) who conjectured that hostile impulses toward parents may be aroused in the child in many ways, including lack of respect, injustice, unreasonable demands, unreliability, coercion, and manipulation. It is not surprising, then, that in the camp of psychoanalysis, it was one of her disciples, Rubin (1969), who gave anger top billing. Rubin's book was written in colloquial style. He advocated an outlook on anger that recognized its normality. However, he was preoccupied with the blocking, freezing, twisting, subverting, or otherwise 'perverting' of anger and hence leaned a bit far in the ventilationist direction. His overstating of the adaptive value of anger expression is readily seen in the 103 questions he puts forward at the book's end to prod the reader towards a healthier outlook on anger.

The first psychoanalytic authors to grant anger some priority were Redl and Wineman (1951, 1952), whose theoretical framework for their work with children posited an impulse system and control system hydraulic model, within which disorders of anger were understood in terms of breakdowns in the control system. Despite the cogency of their work, anger remained an undiscovered topic in psychoanalytic writings. Crocker's (1955) lengthy case study of a highly aggressive 13-year-old boy, with 'severe temper tantrums', which was published in the flagship journal, *The Psychoanalytic Study of the Child*, was approached in formulation and in treatment in terms of ego mastery of libidinal development – indeed, to an astounding degree. Saul's *The Hostile Mind*, (1956), in effect picks up where Freud (1930) had left off in *Civilization and Its Discontents*, viewing 'hostility' as the motivating force for human destructiveness – essentially, by-passing anger. There are many examples of the inattention to anger by psychoanalytic scholars in the decades after Freud. In Rochlin's (1973) scholarly book that examines aggression as viewed by psychoanalytic theory, the vantage point is narcissism – anger is not indexed and is sparsely mentioned. Bowlby's (1969, 1973) treatment of the subject is sparse. In his first volume on attachment, he briefly touches on anger in commenting about the reification of 'feeling' terms in discussing appraisal processes; in his second volume, it occupies a very small proportion of the text, despite its inclusion in the book's subtitle. Bowlby saw anger as functional when it served to fortify attachment bonds and dysfunctional when it weakened them.

As noted above, Rubin's (1969) book was an exception, being fully devoted to anger, and this is also the case for Madow (1972). However, as he himself says, 'no attempt is made in this book to distinguish between "aggression," "hostility," "rage," "resentment," and "anger"' (ibid., p. x). Madow's chapter on the *causes* of anger rests on frustrations of the pleasure principle and the societal demands for its surrender, and his analysis of societal violence turns on frustrations associated with deprivation and competition. The more recent book, *Rage*, by the psychoanalyst, Eigen (2002), describing case studies of psychoanalytic therapy, is near-tabloid in presentation and offers no conceptual framework.

Psychoanalytic theory gave scant attention to anger, but it was the inspiration for the frustration–aggression hypothesis, which in turn was the springboard for a wealth of research on human aggressive behaviour. Even psychoanalytic concepts, such as catharsis and repressed anger/hostility, which have been mired in empirical controversy far too complicated to address here, have influenced our understanding of anger and aggression, if only in being foci of debate and empirical investigation.

THE EMERGENCE OF ANGER IN PSYCHOLOGICAL RESEARCH

The post-FA field

In the decades after the frustration-aggression monograph, anger was for the most part an incidental topic in studies of human aggression. Berkowitz (1962) had flagged up the value of anger for this genre of research, but he gave it little coverage. Even Geen, one of Berkowitz's top intellectual offspring, who found significance for anger in the study on types of frustration noted earlier (Geen, 1968), soon thereafter was pursuing a general arousal model in accounting for aggressive behaviour (Geen & O'Neal, 1969), minimizing the relevance of anger. In the well-regarded book on aggression by Johnson (1972), anger is not in the subject index, and he gives it sparse treatment in two paragraphs of the book. In his chapter on the 'Control of Aggression', the word 'anger' is not to be found. In was in this historical context that Novaco (1975, 1976) argued for the importance of anger and anger control as subject matter, as it was paradoxically much discussed colloquially but rarely studied scientifically.

Several prominent aggression researchers (namely, Hokanson, 1961a, 1961b; Konecni, 1975a, 1975b; Zillmann, 1971; Zillmann & Bryant, 1974) did give anger a highlighted focus. It has centrality in Konecni's model of aggressive behaviour and in Hokanson's research on the physiology of catharsis. With the exception of their work, and that of Zillmann on arousal states, anger's status in aggression research through the 1970s was that of a nearly inconsequential phenomenon. There is a somewhat parallel situation in contemporary research on violence risk factors for psychiatric patients, as anger is just beginning to be identified as an important dynamic variable, as will be discussed in Chapter 6 concerning anger assessment.

Zillmann has contributed importantly to our understanding of the anger–aggression relationship (see especially Zillmann, 1979, 1988), and his key discovery was that of 'excitation transfer' effects (Zillmann, 1971). This idea and phenomenon are that arousal ('excitation') residues from a prior activating event can combine with arousal activated by some present event, thus transferring the undissipated arousal to that present event. This transfer then enhances or intensifies the experience of anger and the potentiation of aggressive behaviour, when cognitively guided by cues of anger/aggression. Transfer effects are not conjectured to occur when the residual arousal is attributed to non-provocation sources. In a series of studies (see also Zillmann, Katcher, & Milavsky, 1972) involving physiological and behavioural measures, but no explicit anger measure (observation of anger came in debriefing interviews), he and his colleagues found that arousal residues from prior, non-provocation sources (physical exercise or erotic films) intensified subsequent aggression in the context of anger provocation. To put it simply, and to paraphrase Zillmann and Bryant (1974), someone who is already aroused 'blows their top' more readily than someone who is not already aroused.

Zillmann's excitation transfer concept is important because it provides a theoretical and empirical base for understanding how exposure to stressors, both acute and ambient, can predispose the person to respond angrily when faced with a minor provocation. For persons with developmental disabilities, the sequential experience or accumulation of aversive events can easily occur. When problems, conflicts, or disappointments remain unresolved due to resource limitations, the arousal residue can amplify anger in response to a subsequent thwarting. This concept highlights the need for arousal reduction techniques as part of a therapeutic programme.

Studies of anger in the fields of emotion and stress

A major boost to the study of anger occurred through the ascendancy of emotion in the agenda of psychological research, and the scholarship of Averill (1982, 1983) was particularly important. Great pioneers in the field of psychology, William James (1890) and Walter B. Cannon (1915), had given attention to anger in their efforts to understanding psychophysiology and emotion as an action impulse, but its relevance was subsidiary to concern with general principles. With the advent of behaviourism, from Watson to Skinner, anger was generally off the radar, being a within-the-skin subjective phenomenon. The behaviouristic emphasis that characterized the work that flowed from the frustration–aggression hypothesis, as discussed above, bypassed anger as emotion.

Following the seminal work by Hall (1899), about which the reader might now have even greater appreciation, there were a number of self-report diary studies done with college students, including that of Gates (1926) with women in New York (Barnard College), Stratton (1926, 1927) with males and females in California (Berkeley), Meltzer (1933) with males and females in Oregon, and Anastasi, Cohen, and Spatz (1948) with Barnard College women. A much more intensive investigation, which concerned young children, was reported in a very fine monograph by Goodenough (1931). These studies were conducted to ascertain normative patterns of anger, but the research samples were limited in generalizability (cf. Novaco, 1986, for a review of this body of research). Averill's (1983) work would correct that shortcoming.

Two other notable exceptions to the anger research dearth decades, and which incorporated sample variation, were the little known studies by Landis, Ferrall, and Page (1936) and by McKellar (1948, 1949). Landis et al. were inspired by Stratton's (1926) research, (rudimentary as it was) relating anger to disease, and they conducted a questionnaire study (anger and fear) with both college students and hospitalized psychiatric patients in New York. Relevant to points that will be addressed in our chapter on the assessment of anger, the college students reported higher anger than did the psychiatric patients, and female patients reported

more anger than did male patients. Landis et al. also found that anger significantly correlated with the number of physical diseases among the psychiatric patients, but not among
the students. McKellar (1948) conducted both an introspective study (as did Richardson,
1918), with himself as subject over 47 days, and questionnaire studies with adult education
students in the London area. This was followed by a multi-stage interviewing study with
male soldiers and female college students (McKellar, 1949). He was insightful about the
complexities of anger and its activating conditions, and he asserted that 'behaviourist and
operationist type' methods were insufficient for the study of anger and aggression, 'in view
of the frequency of the non-expression of experienced anger' (1948, p. 155).

To be sure, there was substantial psychological scholarship on emotion (e.g., Cannon,
1931; Gray, 1935; Hebb, 1946; Leeper, 1948; Wechsler, 1925; Zangwill, 1948), but that work
addressed the subject generically, as theorists struggled to define and demarcate emotion,
emotional experiences, and emotion-driven behaviour. Anger would be mentioned, but not
given a concerted focus. Later emotion theorists, especially Izard (1977), certainly featured
anger, but his research, and that of other prominent theorists (e.g., Ekman, Friesen, &
Ancoli, 1980; Plutchik, 1980) primarily concerned facial expressions. Tomkins (1963)
virtually ignored anger; also, the term appears in only a few lines in the book by Mandler
(1975) on the psychology of emotion and stress.

The field of human stress offered another potential avenue for anger research, particularly
given the bridge provided by Lazarus (1966, 1967), most centrality with regard to the
concepts of threat, appraisal, and coping, which interfaced with the study of emotion. Arnold
(1960) had already proffered the appraisal concept in the emotion field, as pertaining to what
she called the 'estimative system' involved with the experience of emotional states and the
impulse to action. However, in the stress field, the affective state that received most attention
was anxiety, and rarely anger. Even in the book by Lazarus and Folkman (1984), anger is a
sparse topic. It is astounding that in the field of posttraumatic stress disorder (PTSD), anger
has been given little priority (see Novaco & Chemtob, 1998) despite its phenomenological
salience in PTSD and its demonstrable empirical relevance, particularly for combat-related
PTSD (Novaco & Chemtob, 2002). Nevertheless, in the 1970s, stress emerged as a rubric
under which a wide variety of adaptation-related phenomena were investigated.

Psychological approaches to stress, as compared to those in the medical field, gave
considerable emphasis to cognitive mediational processes and had a person–environment
interactive focus. The research and theorizing done by Lazarus and his students, most
notably Averill (1973), as well as by others, such as Glass and Singer (1972), strongly drove
the cognitive mediation theme that became a core focus of research on anger and on the
development of cognitive-behavioural interventions for anger problems (Novaco, 1975). As
well, cognitive-behavioural pioneers, particular Meichenbaum (1977), laid the groundwork
for the refinement of anger treatment and the formulation of the stress inoculation approach
(Meichenbaum & Novaco, 1978). In was in this sea of influences that Novaco (1979) put
forward a perspective on the cognitive regulation of anger and stress, and first implemented
the stress inoculation approach for anger problems (Novaco, 1977a, 1977b).

The significance of Averill's (1982, 1983) work in advancing anger research and theory is unmistakable. He conducted multiple community and college sample studies that
mapped normative data on various components of anger episodes, including background
conditions, targets, objectives, intensity, duration, perceptions, continuing reactions, and
also responses to the anger of others. Beyond his exceptional studies of the 'everyday experience of anger', he set forth a theory of anger that differs markedly from other thinking

in the field. As a social constructivist, he views anger as a socially constituted syndrome – a transitory social role governed by social rules. His constructivist viewpoint emphasizes the idea that the meaning and function of emotions are primarily determined by the social systems in which they occur and of which they are an integral part. Emotions are interpreted as passions, rather than actions, i.e., as something that happens to one, rather than something that one does. He articulated this analysis with relevant biological and psychological systems, and his scholarly book covered historical, philosophical, legal, and scientific literature.

However, Averill's view of anger does not inform us about anger from the standpoint of maladjustment or psychopathology. That is, the elements of his perspective do not provide for understanding of anger as *psychological disturbance*. Nor is there direction for remedies for anger-related disorders. Only a few pages in his book are concerned with problematic anger. His intention was instead to emphasize the positive or functional aspects of anger within social systems, being quite inclined to see anger as a form of problem solving.

In the past decade or so there have been a number of autobiographical recall and questionnaire studies, which will be discussed in Chapter 6 on anger assessment.

Anger in health psychology

Emotion garnered broad attention in psychological research and theory in the 1980s (e.g., Frijda, 1986, 1988; Lazarus, 1982; Ortony, Clore, & Collins, 1988; Russell, 1991; Zajonc, 1984), and, in parallel, enthusiasm for the study of anger grew strongly, especially in conjunction with cardiovascular diseases. Research on anger and cardiovascular disease was bountiful, as reflected in the publication of a number of academic books (Chesney & Rosenman, 1985; Friedman, 1992; Johnson, 1990; Johnson, Gentry, & Julius, 1992; Siegman & Smith, 1994), as well as ones for lay readers (e.g. Williams & Williams, 1993). Among the seminal works were the book by Friedman and Rosenman (1974) and the study by Barefoot, Dahlstrom, and Williams (1982) that linked coronary heart disease incidence and mortality among physicians to their hostility scale scores obtained during medical school admissions testing.

In this genre of research, the differentiation between anger and hostility was often muddled, including in a major review by Miller, Smith, Turner, Guijarro, and Hallet (1996). Nevertheless, anger was featured prominently in research programmes pertaining to hypertension and coronary artery disease (see, Diamond, 1982; Dembroski, MacDougall, Williams, Haney, & Blumenthal, 1985; Siegman, 1994). Current research has differentiated the anger and hostility constructs, and in their review of psychosocial risk factors, Strike and Steptoe (2004) state that anger shows a more consistent relationship to coronary artery disease. This is confirmed by the mortality data for men in a large sample prospective study by Eaker, Sullivan, Kelly-Hayes, D'Agostino, and Benjamin (2004) and by the fascinating study by Rosenberg et al. (2001) concerning facial expressions related to ischemia.

It is curious that enthusiasm for the study of anger was so enhanced by its identification with medical disorders. After all, people have been dying as a result of anger and hostility for a rather long time. Mostly, they died from externally caused tissue damage inflicted by anger-induced uncivilized behaviour, as opposed to anger-induced internal disease processes. There had always been numerous interpersonal and societal problems that result from this emotion and the violence that it subtends. While the general populace and community gatekeepers knew well about the lethality of unregulated anger, academic researchers did not seem to get intrigued until it was established that desirable clientele, such as corporate executives, had anger problems. Once amenable to assessment and treatment in medico-laboratory settings, anger's popularity as a research topic grew exponentially. Setting any cynicism aside, it was all to the good that anger received such focus, not the least because heart disease was identified as the 'number one killer', with close to a million deaths per year in the United States (cf. Kannel et al. 1986). It also presents a vulnerability for other physical illness (Suinn, 2001).

It had long been known that anger is accompanied by heightened cardiovascular arousal, which acts as the mechanism that translates personality and behaviour into cardiovascular disease processes (Siegman and Smith, 1994). Dr John Hunter, a famous eighteenth-century British surgeon, is often quoted as having once remarked, 'My life is in the hands of any rascal that chooses to annoy me . . . ' and, he died suddenly while attending a hospital board meeting (Jenkins, 1978). Indeed, the famous Professor William Osler, in his Lumleian Lectures on angina pectoris stated that 'Many instances of slight anginal attacks are brought on by anger, worry, or sudden shock; and while in individual cases they may be serious, yet the cause is rather easier to avoid . . . though John Hunter neither thought so, nor found it so' (1910, p. 974). This intuition and expert medical opinion long preceded the landmark research by Barefoot et al. (1982) on the association of hostility assessed in medical school with physician mortality 25 years later, but with that study the physician death toll became scientific news.

The link between anger proneness and coronary heart disease (CHD) is empirically robust (e.g., Kneip et al., 1993; Krantz, Contrada, Hill, & Friedler, 1988; Williams, Nieto, Sanford, & Tyroler, 2001). In the study of 12,986 men and women by Williams et al. (2000), the multivariate adjusted risk ratio for CHD was 2.2 for high versus low anger. High anger in early adulthood was found by Chang, Ford, Meoni, Wang, and Klag (2002), in a follow-up study of 1,055 men since medical school, to have a relative risk ratio of 3.5 for CHD and 6.4 for a myocardial infarction. However, a large sample prospective study by Eaker et al. (2004) found trait anger to be predictive of atrial fibrillation and mortality in men but not in women.

With regard to hypertension, Johnson et al. (1992) stated that the preponderance of evidence indicates that the suppression of anger is characteristic of hypertensive patients. Although the meta-analysis by Suls, Wan, and Costa (1995) on resting blood pressure found the effect to be small and variable, the meta-analysis on ambulatory blood pressure by Schum, Jorgensen, Verhaeghen, Sauro, and Thibodeau (2003) concluded that not expressing anger was related to elevated diastolic pressure. In a study of over 4,300 men and women in Japan, Ohira et al. (2002) reported that Japanese men who do not express their anger have an increased risk of high blood pressure. Thus, the hypothesis proffered by Alexander (1939) seems to have held up.

Overall, ample scientific evidence was amassed that pointed to a robust association between anger and the deterioration of cardiovascular health. The evidence has accumulated in both epidemiological and laboratory-based research. The epidemiological studies have linked anger to heart disease and mortality, and the laboratory work has shown that anger-prone individuals react to conflict with greater increases in blood pressure and are more at risk for cardiovascular dysfunction. This body of research about such important health problems has most certainly spurred interest in anger assessment and treatment.

Contemporary clinical research: anger and violence risk

As broad-based interest mounted to find remedies for violent behaviour, attention began to be given to violence risk factors, particularly in research with psychiatric patients and forensic populations. Progressively, anger has emerged in clinical assessment and violence risk research, including with offenders having developmental disabilities (Novaco & Taylor, 2004; Taylor, 2002a). Recurrent anger and aggressive behaviour are among the most refractory problems faced by mental health treatment staff who work with criminal offenders, either in secure institutional settings or in out-patient facilities. Yet, despite anger's seemingly transparent relevance, it was a sparse subject in the book by Wykes (1994) on violence and health care professionals. In the volume on the 'neurobiology and clinical views of aggression and impulsivity' by Maes and Coccaro (1998), the word 'anger' is virtually absent. This is similarly the case for Volavka's (2002) masterful book on the neurobiology of violence, despite its extensive concern with the clinical context. While patient assaultiveness received considerable attention in institutional settings (e.g. Lion & Reid, 1983; Rice, Harris, Varney, & Quinsey, 1989), comparatively little research on assessment and intervention was devoted to anger. This lapse will be addressed further in Chapter 6 on anger assessment with regard to staff-rating scales.

In the early stages of research on the clinical prediction of violent behaviour, anger was neglected, as it was in the various research domains we have discussed. The landmark monograph by Monahan (1981) did take note of the relevance of anger, but it had not yet been included in prediction variable schemes. In Monahan's (1992) evidence review, anger studies did not appear. However, with the advent of the MacArthur Violence Risk Study (Monahan & Steadman, 1994) and the results obtained from that stellar project involving over 1,100 discharged psychiatric patients in three US metropolitan areas (Monahan et al., 2001), the empirical grounds for anger as a risk factor for psychiatric patient violence were established. This is not to say that the relevance of anger has been fully embraced, e.g., in the book by Hodgins and Muller-Isberner (2000) on violence, crime, and mental disorder, it is completely ignored. Nevertheless, there are substantial conceptual and empirical grounds for advocating the importance of anger as a risk factor for clinical populations (Novaco, 1994), and advances in anger assessment have facilitated research on anger with persons at risk for violent behaviour in various community and institutional settings, both clinical and correctional.

In the mental health field, violence is a prevalent and costly problem. Anger has been found to predict physical aggression by psychiatric patients in the community prior to hospital admission (Craig, 1982; McNeil, Eisner, & Binder, 2003), in the hospital (Novaco, 1994; Novaco & Renwick, 1998; Wang and Diamond, 1999) and subsequently in the community after discharge (Monahan et al., 2001). For persons with developmental disabilities, Novaco and Taylor (2004) found anger, as self-rated by the patients themselves, to be predictive of hospital assaultiveness, controlling for age, length of stay, IQ, violent offence, and personality variables.

Within a hospital, anger and aggression incur a great cost. High levels of direct care staff injuries have been reported in studies done in secure hospitals in the USA (Bensley et al., 1997; Carmel & Hunter, 1989), in the UK (National Audit Office, 2003), and in Australia (Cheung, Schweitzer, Tuckwell, & Crowley, 1996). Assaultive behaviour by hospital patients seriously impairs the treatment milieu, results in restrictions and diminished chances for discharge, constitutes very significant risk for harm among staff, and has considerable financial cost for the institution in workers' compensation claims and employee turnover. Reciprocally, staff expectations of being assaulted by patients may potentiate a disposition toward anger as a defence against perceived threat.

It must never be forgotten, however, that the non-isomorphism between anger and aggression leaves much to be explained with regard to violence prediction and much to be protected with regard to the human right to self-determination. Regarding the latter, one should consider the autobiography of Clifford Beers (1908), for whom anger was central to his recovery from a debilitating disorder while in a psychiatric hospital. Our approach to anger is aimed at fostering self-regulation and gives diligent attention to the psycho-social context of the person and the care-giving system.

Because anger is a common precursor of aggressive behaviour, it can be unsettling for mental health professionals in any setting to engage as a treatment focus, regardless of its problem salience. In that regard, it is the aim of this book to provide a resource for clinical practice and research concerning anger problems, especially for clients with intellectual disabilities who indeed have anger and aggression as a clinical need. That clinical need and problem salience, as well as the contextual conditions that engender and sustain it among persons with developmental disabilities, are detailed in Chapter 2.

SUMMARY

Anger is a commonly encountered clinical problem among persons served by mental health professionals in community and institutional settings. Its assessment and treatment are a challenging clinical enterprise. Anger is a feature of a wide variety of clinical disorders, and it has high relevance for persons with developmental disabilities, whose lives are often replete with frustration, unfairness, discouragement, and unsupportiveness.

Societal interest in anger control is abundant, but the assessment and treatment of anger problems should proceed with proficient understanding of anger and aggressive behaviour. The historical background of theory and research on anger has been presented, so as to foster an enriched view of this complex emotion. Being grounded in how anger has emerged as a psychological research topic across many sub-fields will facilitate comprehension of the theoretical view that is offered in the next chapter as a guiding conceptual perspective.

2

ANGER AND ITS DYSREGULATION: A GUIDING FRAMEWORK

INTRODUCTION

Therapeutic interventions for anger and theories of anger go hand-in-hand. How one construes anger and aggression strongly influences how one proceeds therapeutically. As there are many things about anger that are adaptive, even the simple declaration that someone has an anger problem can be misinformed. Individuals whose behaviour is troublesome are all too easily tagged as being in need of 'anger management', yet their difficulties and treatment needs may not at all be anger-centred.

Providing therapy for persons whose life experiences have engendered strong anger reactions and whose well-being is impaired by deficiencies in anger control requires a grounded conceptual framework. To understand clients' anger and how it adversely affects their lives, it is advantageous to have a theoretical anchoring that identifies problem dimensions, operative systems, and dynamic factors bearing on psychosocial outcomes. Knowing what to target for change, how to approach the change process, and how to make inroads regarding refractory problem areas is greatly facilitated by a theoretical scheme.

One's conception of anger demarcates what is relevant for assessment and provides for clinical problem formulation. It also orients treatment procedure and its emphasis in a particular case. Recall that the classic psychoanalytic approach, such as that of Anna Freud (1949) and of Crocker's (1955) case study with a boy having 'severe temper tantrums', focused on libidinal development, whereas that of Rubin (1969) views malaise as derivative of constraints on anger expression. In the cognitive-behavioural domain, Ellis's (1977) dominant concern is with irrational beliefs composing self-angering philosophies, which can be seen in Ford's (1991) study with violent inmates. Beck (1999) focuses on cognitive errors, cognitive distortions and automatic thoughts, as exemplified in the application of his approach to anger by Deffenbacher, Dahlen, Lynch, Morris, and Gowensmith (2000). Alternatively, consider the Skinnerian approach to the experimental analysis of behavioural, reflected in Marcus, Vollmer, Swanson, Roane, and Ringdahl (2001), which concerned aggressive behaviour by persons with developmental disabilities. Their study implemented four contingencies, examined for their effect on aggressive behaviour: (1) negative reinforcement (escape from instructional demands); (2) positive reinforcement (materials); (3) positive reinforcement (attention); and (4) no consequences/no interaction. They

Anger Treatment for People with Developmental Disabilities by J. L. Taylor and R. W. Novaco.
Copyright © 2005 John Wiley & Sons, Ltd.

concluded that 'aggression is an operant behaviour and can be assessed as such' (ibid., p. 211). Their strict behavioural orientation precludes concern with cognition, and they pay no attention to self-control or self-regulation.

Our approach is cognitive-behavioural, and it adopts a contextual perspective (Novaco, 1993a) that addresses anger's emergence within a physical, temporal, and social milieu. If one examines the assessment and treatment procedures reported in our published intervention studies with developmental disabilities patients (Taylor, Novaco, Gillmer, & Thorne, 2002; Taylor, Novaco, Gillmer, Robertson, & Thorne, in press) and given detailed presentation in this volume, one sees elaborate attention to background and aptitude factors, comorbid disorders, hospital environment conditions, and engagement of ward-level support staff. The overarching programme is a systems-level intervention, which carries added value for the person receiving the treatment, as it is being implemented in an enhanced therapeutic context. This will be evident in Chapter 10 on Therapist Training, Supervision, and Process Considerations. The treatment diffusion effects that we observed across patients (Taylor et al., in press) are indicative of this overarching systems influence.

A theoretic framework also has utility for understanding obstacles that are likely to be encountered in doing anger therapy. People with serious anger problems are often ambivalent about earnestly engaging in treatment, largely due to the value that they ascribe to anger in dealing with life's adversities. Because of the instrumental value of anger and aggression, many clients do not readily recognize the personal costs that their anger routines incur, so there may be inertia to overcome in motivating change efforts. Because of the embeddedness of anger in long-standing psychological distress, discussions about anger entail accessing many other troubled emotions, which can be most unsettling for some clients. Such issues are relevant in any setting where clients are guarded about self-disclosure and reactive to having 'treatment-needing' status, and they are salient ones in forensic settings. Getting leverage for therapeutic change can be an elusive goal, particularly when many referrals for anger treatment entail some element of coercion or may be perceived as such. As our conceptual framework incorporates generic themes pertinent to anger maintenance and modification (e.g., functionality, threat perception, self-regulation, stress coping skills, and contextuality), a therapeutic change agent can navigate the change process more efficiently by being mindful of these core themes.

'Anger management' is a workplace metaphor. However, that analogy can be bifurcated. Straightforwardly, one might think of managing anger like a troublesome problem on the shop floor. Prescriptions for job conduct from Dale Carnegie on winning friends and influencing people and later from T-group sensitivity trainers, left little room for anger. Rampages by disgruntled employees in the workplace violence script adopted so frequently in the United States, and now exported, have solidified this metaphorical vein. So has the overarching litigation-inspired need of employers to manage risks. Murderous rage-venting on school campuses has reinforced this further. 'Anger management' is thus dispensed as a prescription from various social gatekeepers to ensure tranquillity and consensus in social relations.

Alternatively, the managing of anger can be viewed as what one does with a crucial resource or asset. We are hard-wired for anger, because it has survival value. Anger is a fundamental resource not to be squandered by unnecessary activation and expenditure. In the face of adversity, it can mobilize psychological resources, energize behaviours for corrective action, and facilitate perseverance. Yet, its unmistakable link to aggressive behaviour, and its detrimental effect on physical health and social relationships render the need for its regulation not only a legitimate societal concern, but also a viable treatment target to ensure well-being. Unregulated anger does get people into trouble, and anger is, for the most part, incompatible with happiness and appreciation. High intensity anger and recurrent anger are indicative of being out of control, and this is unsettling to the angry person, as well as to others.

Persons with developmental disabilities are often referred to specialized psychological services for 'challenging behaviour'. As will be seen in Chapter 4 devoted to the evidence base on anger and aggression specific to this population, epidemiological research on three continents has found high rates of 'challenging behavior', in which aggression features prominently. People are institutionalized because of aggressive behaviour, but anger is rarely a client intake screening priority; yet Lindsay and Law (1999) reported that more than 60% of the learning disabled clients referred to a UK community-based service for challenging or offending behaviours had clinically significant anger problems.

ANGER AND AGGRESSIVE BEHAVIOUR

Anger is a negatively toned emotion, subjectively experienced as an aroused state of antagonism towards someone or something perceived to be the source of an aversive event. It is triggered or provoked situationally by events perceived to constitute deliberate harm-doing by an instigator towards oneself or towards those to whom one is endeared. Provocations usually take the form of insults, unfair treatment, or intended thwartings. Anger is prototypically experienced as a justified response to some 'wrong' that has been done. While anger is situationally triggered by acute, proximal occurrences, it is shaped and facilitated contextually by conditions affecting the cognitive, arousal, and behavioural systems that comprise anger reactions. Anger activation is centrally linked to threat perceptions and survival responding (Novaco, 2000).

As a normal human emotion, anger has considerable adaptive value, although there are socio-cultural variations in the acceptability of its expression and the form that such expression takes. In the face of adversity, it can mobilize psychological resources, energize behaviours for corrective action, and facilitate perseverance. Anger serves as a guardian to self-esteem, operates as a means of communicating negative sentiment, potentiates the ability to redress grievances, and boosts determination to overcome obstacles to our happiness and aspirations. Anger is an emotion with multiple functions (Novaco, 1976).

The relationship of anger to aggressive behaviour is that it is a significant activator of aggression and is reciprocally influenced by aggression, but it is neither necessary nor sufficient for aggression to occur (Konecni, 1975a; Novaco, 1979; Zillmann, 1979). Just because someone is angry does not mean that this person will act aggressively, and when aggression does occur, it does not mean that the person was angry to begin with. Level of anger does influence the probability of aggression, and, because anger and aggression occur in a dynamic interactional context, the occurrence of aggression will, in turn, influence the level of anger. With the exception of Berkowitz (1990, 1993), it is generally agreed that anger is an activator of aggression. Berkowitz's contrary view is that anger occurs parallel to aggression and that both are produced by 'negative affect' induced by unpleasant external events.

If Berkowitz's view was correct, the association between aggression and depression would be roughly equivalent to that between aggression and anger, and there is little real-world data to substantiate that deduction. As discussed in the previous chapter, depression and anger are often intermingled. The MacArthur study of violence risk (Monahan et al., 2001), which involved over 1,100 discharged psychiatric patients, did find post-discharge violence to be related to diagnoses of depression, but, in the analyses of violence risk factors, depression was not significant, whereas anger was significant. In the study by Novaco and Taylor (2004), which examined assaultive behaviour in the hospital by male patients with developmental disabilities, anger was significantly related to whether the person was assaultive and to the number of assaults, controlling for age, IQ, length of stay, prior violence offence, and personality measures. Although not reported in that article, we did not find any significant relationship for depression, even in zero-order correlations without covariate controls. The simple correlations between assaults in hospital and staff-rated measures of depressive symptoms were: $r = .09$ for 'withdrawal from social contacts', $r = .02$ for 'decreased energy', $r = .08$ for 'reporting feelings of emptiness', and $r = .01$ for 'statements/appearance of sadness, loneliness, unhappiness, hopelessness, or pessimism'. In contrast, the correlation of assaults with the staff-rated patient characteristic of 'has outbursts of anger' was .36; and, for a seven-item anger index for a week of observation, it was .28; and for multiple patient self-rated anger scales, the correlations exceeded .33, with several scales over .40. Numerous anger indices, staff-rated and patient-rated, were significantly related to assaults, but no depression measure was.

Anger activates aggression, but aggressive behaviour is not an automatic consequence of anger, because aggression is regulated by inhibitory mechanisms engaged by internal and external factors. Whether or not aggression occurs is a joint product or net effect of provocation and inhibitory forces. Theories of aggression (e.g., Bandura, 1983; Berkowitz, 1990, 1993; Dollard et al., 1939; Freud, 1930/1961) uniformly entail inhibitory mechanisms that include expectations of punishment for acting aggressively. People are provoked to act aggressively, but the perceived undesirable consequences of aggression serve to restrain harm-doing behaviour. This net effect of provocation and inhibition can be seen not only at the individual level of analysis but also at the aggregate level, as found in studies on job loss and violence (Catalano, Novaco, & McConnell, 1997, 2002). To understand the likelihood of aggressive behaviour, both activation and inhibition must be taken into account.

As the regulation of aggression centrally involves inhibitory control, the erosion of external and internal inhibitory controls raises the probability of harm-doing actions. That is, the occurrence of aggressive behaviour is not only a function of factors that activate ('push' and 'pull') aggression (e.g., anger, incentives, or situational cues); it also a product of factors that disinhibit ('release') aggression by lowering inhibitory control. Types of inhibitory factors are expectations of punishment, values counter to aggression, and consideration of the consequences of one's behaviour. The punitive consequences may be legal sanctions, direct retaliation, social disapproval, or self-reproach. While external punishment for aggression is codified in the social contract, it is typically the internalization of societal controls that guides civility. Socially acquired personal moral codes and self-monitoring are more pervasive regulators of aggressive behaviour than externally imposed punishments. Both societal restraints and internalized personal restraints are needed to minimize and regulate aggression. The situational attenuation or progressive erosion of these restraining factors, such as by substance abuse or by desensitization to the awfulness of violence, weakens inhibitory control, and thereby disinhibits aggression. Anger, as a key activator of aggression, is most likely to result in violence when inhibitory controls are attenuated.

Finally, in discussing the anger–aggression relationship, a distinction is often made between 'hostile' versus 'instrumental' aggression (e.g. Berkowitz, 1993). That category distinction seeks to differentiate aggressive behaviour that is enacted for the purpose of doing harm/damage to the attacked person/target, from aggression that is motivated by non-injurious goals, such as economic gain or status enhancement. This is a bogus distinction, as aggression is inherently instrumental (including being an expression of anger). Other re-labellings of this distinction, such as 'annoyance-motivated' versus 'incentive-motivated' or 'reactive' versus 'pro-active' have been offered. These bi-furcated classifications of aggression that hinge on ambiguously differentiated goal distinctions can be by-passed by simply thinking of aggression as occurring with or without anger (Novaco, 1986). Bushman and Anderson (2001) have cogently argued to pull the plug on the hostile versus instrumental dichotomy.

ANGER REGULATION

Because anger can activate aggressive behaviour, anger control is indispensable for aggression control. In addition to the detriments associated with inducing aggression, anger arousal is also problematic because it can interfere with information processing and, thereby, impair judgement and problem-solving. Recurrent anger detracts from adaptive functioning in the contexts of work, family, and social relationships. An angry person is not optimally alert, thoughtful, empathic, prudent, or appreciative. Anger is also problematic as an internal stressor, causing wear and tear on the body when recurrently activated, as reflected in its link to cardiovascular disease.

The concept of emotion regulation has gained considerable prominence in the past decade, particularly in the fields of developmental psychology, personality and social psychology, and cognitive neuroscience. The momentum building research on this subject was grounded in the work of emotion theorists such as Ekman, Frijda, and Lang that was discussed in Chapter 1. For the most part, emotion regulation theory and research have been concerned with emotion generically, as in examining regulation processes or strategies, such as suppression, reappraisal, distraction, comfort seeking, withdrawal, etc. It has not attended to the dynamic complexities of a particular emotion, such as anger. In its most elementary sense, emotion regulation is a process whereby engagement or activation of one system component modulates the state of another system component. Lang (1995), for example, conceives of emotion as controlled by appetitive and aversive motive systems in the brain, with the amygdala serving as the key site for the aversive motivation system, where anger would be located. Anger would be seen by Lang to be a product of subcortical structures related to harm avoidance and to be primed by this motivational system. Hence, the reappraisal of threat would serve to lower anger.

In the field of developmental psychology, emotion regulation theory and research are reflected in the work of Cole and Zahn-Waxler (1992), Dodge (1989), and Eisenberg and Fabes (1992) and more recently that of Campos, Frankel, and Camras (2004). Links to attachment theory can be seen in Mikulincer, Shaver, and Pereg (2003). In personality and social psychology, some exemplifications are the control process theory of Carver and Scheier (1990) and Muraven and Baumeister's (2000) view of self-control as a consumable resource. The impressive work of Gross (e.g. Gross, 1998, 2002; Gross & Oliver, 2003) has spanned the fields of cognition and emotion, social psychology, clinical psychology, and neuroscience. Given the vast expansion of the literature on this evolving field, its discussion must here be truncated.

The concept of anger regulation is not addressed systematically by existing theories of anger and aggression. Neither of the two most prominent theories of aggression, those of Bandura (1973, 1983) and Berkowitz (1990, 1993), provide explicit accounts of anger regulation. While such theories do address processes that regulate aggression, they are mostly silent about anger. Since Bandura viewed external stimuli as having anger-evoking potency though symbolic conditioning and asserted that anger can be self-generated by provocative thoughts, it can be inferred that changes in cognitive meaning systems and in rumination would be expected to have a regulatory effect on anger.

Similarly, Berkowitz's (1993) attention to regulation and control is virtually all given to aggression, only addressing anger regulation in the context of catharsis. Berkowitz (1990) claimed to address anger regulation (given the title of his article), but said surprisingly little about it, only stating that unwanted feelings activate cognitive activity that searches for coping options. That is, awareness of negative feelings prompts thoughts about causes of those feelings and considerations of how to act. His view of anger is that it is associatively linked with the 'negative affect' produced by unpleasant events. He regards anger and fear as processes that only parallel the escape and aggressive motor tendencies evoked by negative affect. For Berkowitz, thought only play a small role in the initial stages of anger evocation, as automatic association processes are dominant and govern the initial reactions. He clearly posits cognitive control of aggressive behaviour, as when conscious anticipation of punishment can suppress aggression, but for him cognition has minimal influence on the activation of anger.

As we have discussed, Bandura and Berkowitz primarily sought to understand aggressive behaviour and have treated anger as a secondary phenomenon. In contrast, Averill (1982) took anger as his focus, and his social constructivist approach to emotion conceives of anger as a transitory social role governed by social rules. His research on normative patterns of anger does not provide for an understanding of anger as a clinical problem or a condition of psychological disturbance. That is, he omits dealing with the dysregulation of anger or internal processes that provide for ongoing monitoring of anger states.

Novaco's (1994) model of anger pertains to normal and abnormal forms, conceptualizing anger as entailing three reciprocally connected domains: cognitive, arousal, and behavioural, which are linked to an environmental context. Anger is viewed as a product of: (1) the cognitive processing of environmental circumstances; (2) conjoined physiological arousal; and (3) behavioural reactions. Novaco's (1994) model mapped these domains of anger and their sub-dimensions and stipulates their reciprocal connectedness with each other and with environmental circumstances, but left regulatory systems unspecified. His subsequent work in collaboration with Chemtob (Chemtob, Novaco, Hamada, Gross, & Smith, 1997a; Novaco & Chemtob 1998, 2002) has sought to understand anger regulation in terms of threat perception in the context of PTSD. Importantly for the assessment and treatment programme presented in this volume, the cognitive, arousal, and behavioural domains serve as rubrics for identifying anger problems and for implementing the therapeutic intervention.

As the cognitive mediation of anger and the threat-sensing tendencies of high anger are central to our understanding of anger problems, these concepts require further elaboration.

ANGER, THREAT, AND COGNITIVE MEDIATION

The conception of anger as a product of threat perceptions, as having confirmatory bias characteristics, as being primed by aversive precursors, and as having social distancing effects can be found in the writings of Lucius Seneca (44/1817), who was Nero's tutor. Seneca's Stoic view of anger, though, is almost exclusively negative, and his idea of anger control is largely that of suppression. He discounted the functional value of anger and missed the principle of regulation. Seneca understood that we can make ourselves angry, that shifting our thoughts can minimize anger, and that behavioural enactments provide guidance for the course that anger runs, i.e., speaking softly will reduce anger. However, Seneca denies anger any adaptive value, and he at times confuses anger with aggression. Crucially, he missed the significance of the intensity dimension – he used the term 'moderate' for many things, but not for anger – and therefore does not come upon the theme of regulation and pivotal role of self-monitoring. As will be discussed later, the 'intensity' parameter of anger is a gateway for therapeutic change.

Humans have elaborate neuro-cognitive systems for detecting threat. Neurophysiological evidence indicates that we have a neural architecture (especially the limbic system) specialized for the processing of emotion and emotion-cognition interactions (e.g., LeDoux, 1984, 1989). The activation of the amygdala is centrally involved in detecting events as threats (Aggleton & Mishkin, 1986; McGaugh, 2003). Neurobiological mechanisms associated with amygdala involvement in aversive emotion have been addressed by Cahill and McGaugh (1990), Cahill, Roozendaal, and McGaugh (1997), and McGaugh (1995). As mentioned earlier, Lang (1995) asserts that the amygdala serves as a key site for the aversive motivational system, by which anger is primed. Regarding threat perception, associative linkages to anger have greater access, and anger is more likely when the aversive motivational system is engaged by stimuli signifying present danger or reminders of trauma. In contrast to Lang's work pointing to the aversive or avoidance motivation, the impressive work of Harmon-Jones on frontal brain activity (Harmon-Jones, 2004; Harmon-Jones & Allen, 1998; Harmon-Jones & Sigelman, 2001) has linked anger with left-prefrontal cortical activity, which has typically been associated with positive affect and approach motivation. However, the anger conditions he has studied are not traumatic ones. While it is known that the limbic system, cortical structures, and neurotransmitters such a norepinephine, serotonin, and dopamine are involved in anger activation (e.g., Anderson & Silver, 1998; Davidson, Putnam, & Larson, 2000), the neural structures and circuitry in anger dysregulation remain to be disentangled. The neurobiology of violence (e.g., Volavka, 2002) oddly seems to have progressed independently of anger, and the inevitable convergence of these research domains would seem to hold great promise for clinical application.

When threat signals are detected, higher-level cognitive reasoning elaborates this information, in what are termed appraisal processes (Lazarus, 1994; Ortony, Clore, & Collins, 1988). The perception of threat is conjoined with sympathetic nervous system activation of autonomic arousal components, such as heart rate, blood pressure, and respiration increases that prepare the body for emergency action. In addition to potentiating action, anger in such states of mobilization has adaptive value as a source of information. To others, it communicates perceived wrongdoing, threat of aggression, or intent of reprisal. Such information exchange prior to aggression can facilitate social and interpersonal negotiations towards conflict resolution. For the self, it serves as information for prioritizing and decision-making. The intensity of anger, for example, can help focus and maintain attention on relevant goals and help one estimate progress toward those goals. When pressed for a decision, anger serves as a summary affective cue that can be processed without need for elaborate analysis.

Anger is directed by attention. To get angry about something one must pay attention to it. Anger is often the result of selective attention to cues having high provocation value. A principal function of cognitive systems is to guide behaviour, and attention itself is guided by integrated cognitive structures, known as schemas, which are mental representations that incorporate rules about environment–behaviour relationships. Summary theoretical presentations on cognitive processing pertinent to anger and aggression can be found in Huesmann (1998) and Novaco and Welsh (1989), as well as Beck (1999). What receives attention is a product of the cognitive network that assigns meaning to events and the complex stimuli that configure them. Expectations guide attentional search for cues relevant to particular needs or goals. Once a repertoire of anger schemas has been developed, events (e.g., being asked a question by someone) and their characteristics (e.g., the *way* the question was asked, *when* it was asked, or *who* asked it) are encoded or interpreted as having meaning in accord with the pre-existing schema. Because of their survival function, the threat-sensing aspect of anger schemas carries urgent priority and can pre-empt other information processing.

Since the writings of the Stoic philosophers, especially Seneca (44/1817), anger has been understood to be strongly determined by personal interpretations of events. The concept of appraisal is that of interpretation, judgement, or meaning embedded in the perception of something – not as a cognitive event occurring after that something has happened. Appraisal of provocation is *in* the seeing or hearing (cf. Novaco, 1986). Appraisal, though, is an ongoing process, so various reappraisals of experience will occur and will correspondingly affect whether or not the probability of aggression is lessened, maintained, or intensified. Rumination about provoking circumstances will extend or re-vivify anger reactions. As well, the occurrence of certain thoughts can prime semantically-related ideas that are part of an anger schema. Imagined violence among hospitalized psychiatric patients was found by Grisso, Davis, Vesselinov, Appelbaum, and Monahan (2000) to be strongly related to anger and to post-discharge community violence.

Perceived malevolence is one of the most common forms of anger-inducing appraisal. When another person's behaviour is interpreted as intending to be harmful to oneself, anger and aggression schemas are activated. In turn, receiving information about mitigating circumstances (e.g., learning that the person was fatigued and working overtime) can defuse the appraisal of personal attack and promote a benign reappraisal. Perceiving malevolence pulls for anger by involving the important theme of justification, which includes the externalization of blame. When harm or injustice have been done, social norms of retaliation and retribution are engaged. Pertinent here is Averill's (1983) view of anger that it is a socially constituted syndrome or a transitory social role governed by social rules. Thus, provocation meaning and function would be determined by the social systems in which it occurs and of which it is an integral part.

Justification is a core theme in the activation of anger and aggression, being rooted in ancient religious texts, such as the Bible and the Koran, as well as classical mythologies about deities and historical accounts of the behaviour of ancient rulers. Correspondingly, anger and physical aggression are often viewed as applying a legitimate punitive response for transgression or as ways of correcting injustice. Sometimes, however, justifications are embellished so as to exonerate blame for destructive outcomes of expressed anger.

As people monitor their physical and social environment for threats to their resources or their self-esteem, as well as for opportunities to acquire more resources or esteem enhancement, they operate with expectations about how events and the behaviour of others will unfold. As discussed earlier, thwarted expectations are frustrative and can induce aggression. Further, when anger, antagonism, opposition, or annoyance is expected, this can lead to selective perception of situational cues in line with an aggressive script. Scripts serve as guides for behaviour by laying out the sequence of events that are believed likely to happen and the behaviour that one believes is appropriate (cf. Huesmann, 1998). Also, when aggression is expected to be instrumental in achieving desired outcomes, it will occur in anticipation of those rewards. When punishing consequences or retaliation are anticipated, aggression is restrained. Anger arousal provides energy for aggression script enactment, which has heightened probability when the situation has survival significance for the individual.

Linking anger to threat perception carries several implications for understanding anger dysregulation (Chemtob et al., 1997a; Novaco & Chemtob, 2002; Novaco & Welsh, 1989). Persons with high anger dispositions are highly vigilant in threat sensing and quick in response. Threat sensing is confirmation-biased – anything that could be perceived as harmful or malevolent is rapidly designated as such, and the anger responses are highly automatized. The rapid engagement of anger pre-empts alternative appraisals of the triggering event and considerations of alternative action plans. The strong arousal overrides inhibitory controls of aggressive behaviour, and the threat–anger–aggression responses forge a positive feedback loop – the more threat is perceived, the more anger and aggression; and, conversely, the more anger and aggression, the greater the readiness to perceive threat and the likelihood of new inputs that will constitute threat. Anger and aggression generate unfriendly responses from others.

Self-monitoring is centrally important for obviating or interrupting the self-confirming vicious cycle by inducing the person to detect disconfirming evidence (e.g., lack of hostile intent), consider mitigating circumstances, or reframe the episode. When anger activation is 'hot', such self-regulation is very difficult, hence our treatment procedures give extensive attention to the acquisition of self-monitoring skills.

To facilitate anger regulation, our treatment procedures strive to *disconnect anger from the threat system*. This is done first through the provision of safety, patience, and psychological space for reflection, exploration, and choice. The client's view of anger is normalized, to obviate worries about being a 'bad' or unworthy person. The therapist will acknowledge the legitimacy of the client's feelings, affirming his or her self-worth. Building trust in the therapeutic relationship is pivotal. As self-regulation hinges on knowledge, education about anger and discovery of the client's personal anger patterns or 'anger signature' are facilitated. Much is done to augment self-monitoring and to encourage the moderation of anger intensity. As tension or strain may often surface in the course of treatment, the therapist models and reinforces non-anger alternative responding so as to build replacements for the automatized angry reactions that had been the client's default coping style.

COGNITIVE-BEHAVIOURAL TREATMENT APPROACH TO ANGER CONTROL

Clinical interventions for problems of anger seek to remedy a turbulent emotion that is associated with subjective distress, detrimental effects on personal relationships, health impairments, and the manifold harmful consequences of aggressive behaviour. Anger is often entrenched in personal identity and may be derivative of a traumatic life history. While some high anger patients present with a hard exterior, they can be psychologically fragile, especially those having histories of recurrent abuse or trauma, or when abandonment and rejection have been significant life themes. As anger may be embedded with other distressed emotions and long-standing personal hardships, as occurs with developmental disabilities, accessing anger is often not straightforward.

Providing services for people having recurrent anger problems is a challenging enterprise, as engaging them in the clinical process is often hard-going. Seriously angry people appear to resist treatment, owing to the functional value of their anger routines. Howells and Day (2003), however, have turned the 'treatment resistance' notion on its head, asserting instead that the treatment engagement problem be understood as a matter of 'readiness'. They propose that readiness for anger management is affected by an array of impediments: the complexity of cases presenting with anger problems, institutional settings, client inferences about their problem, mandatory treatment, the client's personal goals, cultural differences, and gender differences bearing on responsivity to provided programmes. This analysis by Howells and Day is insightful, particularly as it removes the onus of the problem from the dispositional status of the client. In this regard, we utilize a treatment 'preparatory phase' to foster engagement, develop core competencies necessary for treatment (emotion identification, self-monitoring, communication about anger experiences, and arousal reduction), and build trust in the therapist, providing an atmosphere conducive to personal disclosure and collaboration.

The term 'anger management' has become a rubric for a variety of interventions, as well as becoming common parlance. Hence, Novaco, Ramm, and Black (2000) distinguished levels of therapeutic intervention for anger, differentiating (1) general clinical care for anger, (2) anger management, and (3) anger treatment. General clinical care for anger identifies it as a clinical need and addresses it through counselling, psychotherapeutic, and psychopharmacological provisions, including client education, support groups, and eclectic treatments, without a formal intervention structure. In contrast, 'anger management' typically refers to a structured CBT intervention, which originally was applied as an individual therapy (Novaco, 1975, where the term was coined) but now is often provided in a group mode, largely psycho-educational in format, such as occurs in court-referred or school-based programmes and in general public workshops. Such programmes typically follow a topical sequence, covering situational activators ('triggers'), how thoughts and beliefs influence anger, self-observation, relaxation techniques, problem solving and conflict resolutions strategies, and other CBT coping skills, such as calming self-statements, effective communication, and appropriate assertiveness. There is wide variation in 'anger management' programmes, which are now marketed commodities.

Anger treatment, as we present in this book, is distinguished from these other levels of intervention by its theoretical grounding, systematization, complexity, and depth of therapeutic approach. It is best provided on an individual basis and may require a preparatory phase to facilitate treatment engagement. Increased depth is associated with thoroughness of assessment, attention to core needs of the clients, greater individual tailoring to client needs, greater specialization in techniques, and the need for clinical coordination and supervision. The specialized form of CBT anger treatment that we have implemented follows a 'stress-inoculation' approach (Meichenbaum, 1985; Meichenbaum & Novaco, 1978; Novaco, 1977a), which involves therapist-guided, graded exposure to provocation stimuli to facilitate anger control. This occurs *in vitro* through imaginal and role-play provocations in the clinic, and *in vivo* through planned testing of coping skills in anger-inducing situations, as established by a hierarchy of provocation scenarios collaboratively constructed by ᴜ.ᴜ client and therapist.

Central to CBT for anger control is the idea that anger is produced by the self-appraised meaning of events and the person's resources for dealing with them, rather than by objective properties of the events. Sometimes anger occurs as a fast-triggered, reflexive response, while other times it results from deliberate attention, extended search, and conscious review. Because anger activation is viewed as intrinsically linked to perceptions of threat and injustice, anger control CBT targets the way people process information, remember their experiences, and cognitively orient to situations of stress or challenge.

As we have discussed, cognitive factors include knowledge structures, such as expectations and appraisals, that are schematically organized as mental representations about the environment–behaviour relationship entailing rules governing threatening situations. Things can have provocation value by virtue of their symbolic significance, such as social group identifiers or fighting words. Arousal or physiological factors include activation in the cardiovascular, endocrine, cortical, and limbic systems, and by tension in skeletal musculature. Neurobiological mechanisms include the amygdala, the prefrontal cortex, and serotonin. Behavioural factors include conditioned and observationally learned repertoires of anger-expressive behaviour, including aggression but also avoidance. Implicit in the cognitive labelling of anger is an inclination to act antagonistically towards the source of the provocation. However, an avoidant style of responding, as in some personality and psychosomatic disorders, can foment anger by leaving the provocation unchanged or exacerbated. Treatment targets the person's cognitive, somatic, and behavioural systems, as well as the environmental context.

The stress inoculation approach to anger treatment involves the following components:

1   client education about anger, stress, and aggression;
2   self-monitoring of anger frequency, intensity, duration, and situational triggers;
3   construction of a personal anger provocation hierarchy, created from the self-monitoring data and used for the practice and testing of coping skills;
4   arousal reduction techniques of progressive muscle relaxation, breathing-focused relaxation, and guided imagery training;
5   cognitive restructuring by altering attentional focus, adjusting expectations, modifying appraisals, and using self-instruction;
6   training behavioural coping in communication and respectful assertiveness as modelled and rehearsed with the therapist; and
7   practising the cognitive, arousal regulatory, and behavioural coping skills while visualizing and role playing progressively more intense anger-arousing scenes from the personal hierarchies.

Cognitive-behavioural anger therapy seeks enduring change. The cognitive restructuring, arousal reduction, and behavioural skills work is implemented so as to change valuations of anger/aggression routines. Because it addresses anger as embedded in aversive and traumatic life experiences, it entails the evocation of distressed emotions, i.e. fear, sadness, and shame, as well as anger. Therapeutic work centrally involves the learning of new modes of responding to cues previously evocative of anger in the context of relating to the therapist – and it periodically elicits negative sentiment on the part of the therapist to the frustrating and unappreciative behaviour of the client. Given the functionality of anger and aggression, therapeutic work must replace a client's old problematic routines with new coping skills that enhance well-being. The 'aggression replacement training' programmes of Goldstein and his colleagues (Goldstein & Keller, 1987; Goldstein, Nensen, Daleflod, & Kalt, 2004) also proceed from this premise.

A core objective in CBT anger treatment is to augment the client's self-regulatory capacity. It aims to minimize anger frequency, intensity, and duration and to moderate anger expression. It is an adjunctive treatment for a targeted clinical problem and thus is not meant to address other or more general psychotherapeutic needs. A key feature of the stress inoculation approach that we have adopted is therapist-guided progressive exposure to provocation, in conjunction with which anger-regulatory coping skills are acquired.

Cognitive-behavioural treatments of anger are varied but have been shown to have applicability to a wide range of clients. The following chapter presents a review of anger treatment effectiveness research across clinical populations. A review of anger treatment and research with developmental disabilities clients is presented in Chapter 5.

3

ANGER TREATMENT EFFECTIVENESS

INTRODUCTION

Many of the published studies involving cognitive-behavioural approaches to anger problems are based on the treatment approach developed by Novaco (1975) which utilizes a stress inoculation paradigm (Meichenbaum, 1985). The core components of this integrated treatment approach are (1) cognitive re-structuring; (2) arousal reduction; and (3) behavioural skills training. Following the initial evaluations of this approach by the treatment originator (Novaco, 1975, 1977a), some controlled studies followed this approach (for reviews see Novaco, 1997; Novaco & Jarvis, 2002). In addition, more generic cognitive-behavioural approaches were adopted (e.g., Deffenbacher, Story, Stark, Hogg & Brandon, 1987; Feindler & Ecton, 1986; Feindler, Ecton, Kingsley, & Dubey, 1986; Hazaleus & Deffenbacher, 1986).

Despite research on anger treatment efficacy still lagging behind that for anxiety and depression, there are, nonetheless, numerous studies indicating this approach, or variants of it, to be effective with a range of forensic and clinical groups, including adult and adolescent in-patients and out-patients, as well non-clinical samples, particularly student volunteers. In recent years there have been six meta-analyses of anger treatment published (Beck & Fernandez, 1998; Del Vecchio & O'Leary, 2004; DiGuiseppe & Tafrate, 2003; Edmondson & Conger, 1996; Sukhodolsky et al., 2004; Tafrate, 1995). The Sukhodolsky et al. review is devoted to anger treatment for children and adolescents and is not discussed below. The main features and results of these substantive reviews are described below.

META-ANALYTIC REVIEWS OF PSYCHOLOGICAL ANGER TREATMENT

Tafrate (1995)

Tafrate conducted a review of the effectiveness of treatment strategies for anger disorders in adults. This involved 17 studies published between 1974 and 1994, all of which involved comparisons of various forms of anger treatment against control conditions using subjective

Anger Treatment for People with Developmental Disabilities by J. L. Taylor and R. W. Novaco.
Copyright © 2005 John Wiley & Sons, Ltd.

measures of anger frequency and intensity. Only two of the 17 studies involved clinical or forensic patients as participants, the remainder being made up of samples of university undergraduates. The majority of the treatment studies (12 out of 17) used a group therapy format rather than individual treatment sessions.

The results of this meta-analysis were that for the five cognitive treatments included, the average treatment effect size was .93 which is considered large in terms of the guidelines given by Cohen (1992). Of the five cognitive treatments considered in this part of Tafrate's review, four were based on a self-instructional training model and one treatment study was based on the cognitive treatment approach of Beck (1976). In another section of the review, nine 'multicomponent' treatments were analyzed for their effect sizes. These treatments were characterized by the combination of several intervention techniques such as relaxation, self-instructional training and application training. The average treatment effect size for these combined interventions was calculated to be 1.00.

Tafrate's (1995) review suggests that cognitive and combined cognitive-behavioural treatments for anger problems are as effective as relaxation therapies and skills-based treatments. However, as the author notes, the analysis includes only a small number of studies, the majority of which involved volunteer students as subjects. Also, over half of all the studies included involved the same researcher (Deffenbacher). It is likely that the nature and scope of the anger problems experienced by forensic and clinical populations will be very different to those reported by the samples included in the majority of these studies. Therefore, the conclusions of this review should be treated with caution.

Edmondson and Conger (1996)

Edmondson and Conger aimed to improve on the Tafrate (1995) review of treatments for adults with anger problems by including studies that used behavioural measures to evaluate outcome and by taking into account the type of control group employed, and the use of follow-up studies. They identified 18 studies that met their inclusion criteria published between 1970 and 1994. Each study compared groups of 'generally angry' non-clinical adult subjects in different treatment conditions, one of which was a control condition. They purposely excluded studies that involved people under the age of 18 years, people with developmental disability, and spouse or child abusers as participants.

In order to compare the effectiveness of different anger treatments, Edmondson and Conger (1996) averaged effect sizes for different types of treatments. The treatments included were (1) relaxation; (2) cognitive; (3) cognitive-relaxation; and (4) social skills. Eight studies were dropped from this analysis due to difficulties in computing effect sizes on some of the outcome measures reported in them. Therefore, for this comparative effect size analysis only ten of the 18 studies identified in this review were used and these produced a total of 17 treatment groups.

Overall, cognitive and cognitive-relaxation treatments produced medium–large effect sizes while relaxation and social skills treatments had large effect sizes. The authors concluded that it is difficult to recommend one treatment approach over any other based on this analysis as different treatments produced large effect sizes for some aspects of anger and small effects for others. As Edmondson and Conger point out, these recommendations are tentative, as this comparative analysis is based on small numbers of treatment groups.

These groups generally had fewer than 20 subjects in them, making it difficult to detect significant between-group differences due to inadequate statistical power.

In addition to these statistical issues, Edmondson and Conger's (1996) review has a number of limitations. As in the Tafrate's (1995) review, studies involving clinical, forensic, and quasi-offender populations (such as spouse abusers) were intentionally eliminated. None of the studies included in the comparative effect size analysis involved self-referring clients with the kinds of serious anger problems that would be seen routinely by mental health and forensic services. Seven out of the ten studies included in the analysis involved the same researcher who used 'convenience' populations such as nurses or college students (Deffenbacher). Finally, all but one of the studies included used group therapy formats so there was no attempt to compare these therapies with those delivered to individuals.

Beck and Fernandez (1998)

In their survey of the literature on anger problems, Beck and Fernandez found that the great majority of anger treatment outcome studies had involved cognitive and behavioural approaches. In order to carry out a meta-analytic review that was more representative of research available on the cognitive-behavioural treatment of anger, Beck and Fernandez used broader inclusion criteria than those utilized by Tafrate (1995) and Edmondson and Conger (1996). They included published and unpublished (mainly doctoral dissertation) studies conducted between 1970 and 1995. Diverse samples of adults *and* children were included, many of which demonstrated severe anger problems associated with criminal behaviour, child and spouse abuse, delinquency, and classroom aggression.

The final sample in Beck and Fernandez's (1998) review comprised 50 studies incorporating 1,640 subjects. Eight offender, five abusive parents/spouses and 12 juvenile delinquent/clinical adolescent samples, along with one adult clinical, and one adult mental retardation sample were included in the review. The remaining 23 studies involved other samples such as school children, college students, and 'volunteers'. Only studies incorporating combination cognitive-behavioural treatments were included. Forty of the review studies used control groups and 10 utilized single group, repeated measures designs. The 50 effect sizes obtained from the studies were weighted by sample size to take into account variations in the statistical power across studies.

Beck and Fernandez found that the mean weighted effect size was .70, with the majority of study effect sizes being between .50 and .99. This is consistent with the outcomes of reviews of the effectiveness of cognitive-behavioural treatments for other affective disorders including depression and anxiety. They calculated that the average subject in a cognitive-behavioural treatment condition did better than 76% of those not receiving this type of treatment and this effect was significantly different than would be expected by chance. The authors concluded that cognitive-behavioural treatments have general utility in the clinical management of anger in a range of clinical, forensic, and delinquent populations. While the medium–large mean weighted effect size was slightly smaller than that reported for multicomponent cognitive-behavioural treatments by Tafrate (1995), the latter was based on only a small number of studies (9), did not weight effect sizes depending on statistical power, did not incorporate unpublished studies, and included just two clinical samples.

DiGuiseppe and Tafrate (2003)

DiGuiseppe and Tafrate sought to improve on previous reviews by including a larger sample of 57 studies of anger treatment involving a total of 1,841 adult participants and 92 interventions conducted between 1969 and 1998. Fifty of the studies included were between group designs with control groups; the remaining seven studies provided within-group data only. Using this larger database DiGuiseppe and Tafrate attempted to look at the influence of moderator variables on outcome and to investigate the effects of different treatments on various anger dimensions. They also looked at the durability of treatment effects by examining follow-up data.

The overall effect size for the between-group studies reviewed at post-treatment was .73 and .99 for within-group studies. These medium–large effect sizes were moderated by several variables. Dependent variables that were more conceptually related to the anger construct, e.g., anger self-reports, aggression, and hostile attitudes, produced significantly better effects than those less closely associated with anger such as self-esteem and interpersonal relationships. Little differences in effect sizes were found for different treatment types (e.g. cognitive restructuring vs. relaxation vs. behavioural skills training vs. combined). However, there were small numbers of studies that used each treatment approach, and the majority were cognitive, behavioural, or cognitive-behavioural in nature. There were indications though that use of manuals to guide interventions, treatment fidelity checks, and individual (as opposed to group) treatment formats were associated with higher effect sizes on a number of dependent variables. The average effect size at follow-up was .59 and this was related to the length of follow-up. Follow-up effect sizes remained most stable compared to post-treatment effect sizes for the conceptually relevant dependent measures of anger, aggression, and hostile attitudes.

The DiGuiseppe and Tafrate (2003) meta-analysis is a good effort at improving the information available to practitioners when making choices about anger treatments, but there are several limitations to the review. Just over 50% of the 57 studies included in the review involved non-clinical samples, often student and other convenience samples. Nineteen of the 27 studies that involved clinical populations appeared to include mental health and forensic samples (excluding developmental disabilities) with the other eight studies involving physical health (mainly cardiac) patients. Of the 19 mental health/forensic studies, just 12 were published in peer-reviewed journals – the remainder were contained in unpublished doctoral dissertations.

Del Vecchio and O'Leary (2004)

In a meta-analytic review of anger treatments for non-institutionalized adults, Del Vecchio and O'Leary found 23 studies, involving a total of 1,340 participants, conducted in outpatient settings between 1980 and 2002. The treatments included in the review were categorized into cognitive-behavioural, cognitive, relaxation, and other (e.g. counselling, social skills training) types. The authors suggest that the main benefit of their analysis over previous reviews is the inclusion of studies only if used with a standardized measure of anger (e.g. STAXI; Spielberger, 1996; NAS; Novaco, 2003) as a dependent measure and involved random allocation of subjects to treatment and control groups. The mean weighted effect sizes across the studies included in the review ranged from .61–.90. This is similar to the findings of previous reviews and lends support for the use of psychological treatment approaches for people with anger problems. There was no association found between effect size and the publication status of the study, but length of treatment appeared to have an influence with longer interventions yielding bigger effect sizes.

There were no significant differences between the effect sizes for different types of treatment, though cognitive-behavioural treatments appeared to provide solid medium–large effects for problems of anger control, expression, trait anger, and driving anger. However, the numbers of studies included in the analysis of the other treatment categories were probably too small to be confident about drawing conclusions about their impact on different types of anger problems. Other limitations of this review are that 17 out of the 23 studies included involved student participants, and 65% of the studies were conducted by the same research team. Only three of the studies involved clinical samples so that very few of the studies included individuals who had sought treatment.

COGNITIVE-BEHAVIOURAL ANGER TREATMENT FOR OFFENDERS AND PEOPLE WITH SERIOUS MENTAL DISORDERS

Controlled studies involving offenders

While the Beck and Fernandez (1998) and DiGuiseppe and Tafrate (2003) reviews indicated that cognitive-behavioural anger treatments can be effective when applied to offender and quasi-offender groups, there have been few well-designed studies of anger treatments in forensic populations, despite the proliferation of anger management programmes in prison and probation settings. Watt and Howells (1999) in Western Australia reported discouraging results for a group anger management programme of 10 two-hour sessions delivered over five weeks with violent offenders in maximum- and minimum-security prisons. Measures of anger knowledge, anger disposition, anger expression, observed aggressive behaviour, and prison misconduct showed no treatment gains for the programme participants, compared to non-equivalent wait-list controls. The non-randomness of the treatment group assignment may have been a factor in the non-significant effects, but the authors were inclined to attribute the absence of effects to motivational issues for participants and other programme delivery factors.

Eamon, Munchua, and Reddon (2001) reported on the effectiveness of an anger management programme for women inmates in a mixed (medium and minimum) security prison in Edmonton, Canada. The intervention was a group-based therapy that was delivered weekly for a total of 12 weeks. The treatment group did not show any treatment gains compared to the control group participants on self-rated measures of anger disposition, reactivity, and aggression. There was a significant improvement for the treatment group over the control group on a measure of anger control. The treatment group participants were also reported to have shown a significant reduction in the number of 'institutional charges' they received while those for the control group did not reduce significantly. The treatment conditions in this study were not balanced with regard to violent offence histories, ethnic mix, and length of stay in the prison – with the treatment group faring much worse on each of these factors which might explain the modest outcomes for this study.

Controlled studies involving people with serious mental disorders

Controlled anger treatment outcome studies involving seriously disordered adult clinical populations are also hard to locate. Stermac (1986) conducted a study with 40 in-patients remanded by the courts to a Canadian forensic facility for psychiatric assessment. The majority of study participants had a diagnosis of personality disorder and more than half had a previous psychiatric history. Subjects were randomly assigned to a psycho-educational group control condition or to an anger treatment condition in which they received six sessions of brief group therapy based on cognitive-behavioural and stress inoculation principles. Those in the anger treatment group showed significant therapeutic gains on measures of anger disposition, use of cognitive re-structuring techniques, and use of strategies to reduce self-denigration, compared with control group subjects who received an eight-session psycho-educational group intervention.

Despite being published in a premier journal, a study by Chemtob, Novaco, Hamada, and Gross (1997b) concerning very angry Vietnam War veterans suffering from severe post-traumatic stress disorder was missed by the Beck and Fernandez (1998) and DiGuiseppe and Tafrate (2003) meta-analyses. Patients in this study were randomly assigned to either cognitive-behavioural anger treatment or to routine clinical care conditions. Significant treatment effects were obtained in anger reaction and anger control in the anger treatment compared to routine clinical care, and these effects were maintained at 18-month follow-up.

Case studies and case-series reports

The reviews described above point to the effectiveness of cognitively based anger treatments as evidenced through controlled treatment trials and systematic group studies. However, these meta-analyses omit many published case studies and case series reports of cognitive-behavioural anger treatment that typically involve real patients and clients with serious clinical problems. Brief reviews of the clinical treatment studies on anger with offender populations can be found in Novaco (1997) and Novaco et al. (2000). These describe studies, in addition to that by Stermac (1986), involving offender populations that closely followed the cognitive-behavioural treatment developed by Novaco (1975, 1993b). Bornstein, Weisser, and Balleweg (1985) applied the stress inoculation paradigm with three forensic inpatients. Using a multiple baseline design they demonstrated significant anger treatment gains on measures of staff-rated behaviour, self-reported anger and evaluations of videotaped role-plays.

Howells (1989) used a similar approach in a case study with a patient with an extensive history of violent offending that had led to numerous prison sentences and psychiatric admissions. A group therapy intervention that focused on cognitive re-framing, arousal reduction through deep muscle relaxation and behavioural skills training, incorporating video feedback, was helpful in reducing his violent behaviour.

Renwick, Black, Ramm, and Novaco (1997) delivered a modified and extended version of Novaco's (1993b) anger treatment protocol to four mentally disordered offender patients in a maximum-security hospital in Scotland. The participants in this study were all men with histories of psychiatric illness including schizophrenia, personality disorder, and alcohol/substance abuse. Three of the patients also had histories of severe self-injury or suicide attempts, while all of them were chronically assaultive towards others, most particularly nursing staff. Following treatment, all four participants were judged by the therapists to have made significant clinical progress in treatment. This was most evident in improved levels of motivation and engagement, reduced sensitivity to perceived criticism and threat, and increased ability to be reflective and think more flexibly about the actions of others. Care staff, including psychiatrists, nurse key-workers, and day service staff rated all patients involved in the study to have become more tolerant of frustration, less tense, and defensive. The treatment gains made by participants in this study led to one patient being transferred into the community and another two being recommended for transfer to less secure facilities.

Anger treatment for children and adolescents

In addition to these studies involving adult offender samples that utilized treatments based on Novaco's anger treatment approach, Novaco et al. (2000) also describe a number of studies using this approach successfully with adolescent offenders. For example, Schlichter and Horan (1981) treated institutionalized aggressive adolescents using the stress inoculation approach. The treatment group showed significant treatment effects compared with a no-treatment group. There have been numerous other studies using less sophisticated versions of this treatment approach, often psycho-educational in nature, that have reported positive outcomes for example with young offenders (McDougall, Boddis, Dawson, & Hayes, 1990). More recently Sukhodolsky et al. (2004) carried out a meta-analytic review of cognitive-behavioural therapy for anger in children that included 40 controlled studies involving 1,953 children aged 7–17 years carried out between 1968 and 1997. The overall mean effect size was .67 which is in the medium range and is consistent with effects for psychotherapy for children in general and for cognitive-behavioural anger treatments for adults.

SUMMARY

In summary, across the six meta-analyses described above, anger treatments, most often cognitive-behavioural in nature, have produced medium–large effect sizes. This suggests that around 75% of those receiving anger treatment improved compared to those in control conditions. Taking these findings into account, it remains the case that more controlled studies are required with seriously disordered clinical and forensic populations and with robust multi-modal assessment designs, although there are many examples of good quality non-controlled, case series, and case study reports that point to the effectiveness of cognitive-behavioural anger treatment for people with such complex needs.

4

EMOTIONAL PROBLEMS, AGGRESSION, AND PSYCHOTHERAPY FOR PEOPLE WITH DEVELOPMENTAL DISABILITIES

INTRODUCTION

It has been noted by several clinicians and writers in the field that we know relatively little about the emotional aspects of the lives of people with developmental disability (Arthur, 1999, 2003; Benson & Ivins, 1992; Frankish, 1989, Strongman, 1985). Also, despite the increased vulnerability of people with developmental disabilities to mental health problems (Deb, Thomas, & Bright, 2001; Moss, 1999), we are unsure about the prevalence and course of these conditions in this population (Hatton, 2002; Taylor, Hatton, Dixon, & Douglas, 2004). There are a number of possible reasons for these gaps in our knowledge, including a general lack of interest in, or concern for, the needs of people seen as different, and a paucity of well-developed instruments to help with the assessment and understanding of the emotional and mental health needs of people with developmental disability (Benson & Ivins, 1992; Patel, Goldberg, & Moss, 1993; Prout, Chard, Nowak-Drabik, & Johnson, 2000). Also, providers of mental health services may be concerned about their responsibility to meet the needs of this socially excluded group if they were to better understand the emotional distress they experience.

PSYCHOTHERAPY AND PEOPLE WITH DEVELOPMENTAL DISABILITIES

Bender (1993) suggests that, among other reasons, therapists are reluctant to offer individual therapy to people with developmental disabilities as this would necessitate building close therapeutic relationships with people perceived as unattractive because of their disability. There is also a tendency to attribute any emotional difficulties presented by such individuals to their disability rather than to their emotional state or needs (Butz, Bowling, & Bliss, 2000; Hollins & Sinason, 2000). This phenomenon has been described as 'diagnostic overshadowing' by Reiss, Levitan, and Szyszko (1982). Consequently, commissioners and

Anger Treatment for People with Developmental Disabilities by J. L. Taylor and R. W. Novaco.
Copyright © 2005 John Wiley & Sons, Ltd.

providers of services are not motivated to fund and systematically develop the provision of psychological therapies for these clients (Arthur, 2003).

Assuming that there was greater interest in these people, and better instruments available to detect and describe the emotional and mental health problems experienced by people with developmental disabilities, clinicians sometimes have concerns about the effectiveness of interventions to alleviate psychological distress that have been developed with other client groups (Stenfert Kroese, 1998). Moreover, recent policy in the UK National Health Service (NHS) is that the provision of treatments must be evidence-based (Department of Health, 1999; Hall & Firth-Cozens, 2000). So what evidence regarding effectiveness is available to support the development of psychological approaches to the treatment of emotional problems in people with developmental disability? Butz et al. (2000) suggest that research on the efficacy of psychotherapy applied to this population is lacking, and recent reviews by Beail (2003), Hatton (2002), Prout and Nowak-Drabik (2003), and the Royal College of Psychiatrists (2004) would appear to support this view.

Hatton (2002) reviewed 'psychosocial interventions' for mental health problems experienced by adults with intellectual disabilities. The studies reviewed were published between 1986 and 2000, and although the term 'psychosocial interventions' was not defined, the studies included were primarily cognitive-behavioural in terms of theoretical orientation. Small numbers of case studies, case series, and group studies were reviewed regarding outcomes for mental health problems in a number of domains. Two case studies and a case series showed reduced symptoms of depression following the application of modified cognitive-behavioural interventions. Similarly, a small number of case studies and case series showed the potential of cognitive and behavioural psychotherapeutic approaches in reducing anxiety and phobic symptoms among people with intellectual disabilities. In terms of psychosis, just one single case study was reported as helping a man with intellectual disabilities manage his hallucinations more effectively. The picture for cognitive behavioural interventions for the management of anger in this population is slightly better according to Hatton (2002), with three case studies/case series, two uncontrolled trials of group intervention, and a small wait-list controlled trial reporting improvements following treatment.

Hatton (2002) cites five uncontrolled studies of cognitive-behavioural interventions by Lindsay and colleagues that reported some success in improving attitudes and behaviours associated with sexual aggression in men with intellectual disabilities (e.g. Lindsay & Smith, 1998). Just one single case study was available to provide evidence for the utility of cognitive-behavioural therapy in treating fire-setting behaviour in a man with mild intellectual disabilities. Two uncontrolled open trials were cited as providing some limited evidence that psychodynamic psychotherapy can be helpful in reducing behaviour problems shown by clients with intellectual disabilities.

From his review Hatton (2002) concluded that there is only limited evidence that psychosocial interventions can be helpful in ameliorating the mental health problems experienced by people with mild intellectual disabilities, but there is need for more practice-based evidence to support the increasing use of these approaches with this population.

In their evaluation of the effectiveness of psychotherapy with people with mental retardation, Prout and Nowak-Drabik (2003) reviewed 92 studies published over a 30-year period between 1968 and 1998. They provided a clear definition of what constituted psychotherapy for inclusion in the review. Using a reasonably robust method for sorting and rating the papers included in their evaluation, they identified just nine reports that met the criteria and provided sufficient information to be used in a meta-analysis of treatment effectiveness.

Most of these studies involved behavioural psychotherapy and they yielded a mean effect size of 1.01. The pool of 92 studies was rated by 'experts' with regard to outcome and effectiveness. The studies in this pool involved behavioural (33%), cognitive-behavioural (13%), analytic/dynamic (15%), humanistic/person-centred (2%), and 'other' (37%) types of psychotherapy. The overall mean outcome rating indicated 'significant' change among study participants, and the mean rating for effectiveness suggested 'moderate'–'significant' benefits to clients from the interventions.

Exploratory analyses suggested that published studies, individual treatment and behaviourally orientated therapies yielded higher outcome and effectiveness ratings. Prout and Nowak-Drabik (2003) concluded from their analysis that psychotherapy for people with mental retardation produces moderate outcomes and benefits for clients. Although many of the studies included in the review lacked methodological rigour, the authors suggested that psychotherapeutic interventions should be more frequently considered in treatment plans for these clients.

In a commentary comparing cognitive-behavioural and psychodynamic psychotherapy outcome research in the developmental disabilities field, Beail (2003) reviewed 'self-management' approaches, cognitive therapy, and psychodynamic psychotherapy studies. Numerous case studies, case series, and a small number of uncontrolled group studies concerning self-management approaches, especially in the forensic intellectual disability field were identified. Only a few attempts at controlled studies were cited – two studies in the area of problem-solving reported mixed results in terms of outcome, and three studies in the anger management field produced significant improvements on the outcome measures used.

Although the literature pertaining to cognitive-behavioural self-management approaches reviewed by Beail (2003) is quite limited, this is contrasted with that available for psychodynamic psychotherapy with this client group. Four pre-post treatment open trials of psychodynamic psychotherapy are reported that were successful in reducing behavioural and offending problems among people with developmental disabilities, and there was some indication that these effects were maintained at long-term follow-up. Very little literature was available to support the use of cognitive therapy as means of targeting distorted cognitions that underpin problem behaviour, attitudes and emotional distress in this population.

Beail (2003) concluded that the evidence base for cognitive-behavioural psychotherapy had progressed a little in the previous five or six years, but more than that for psychodynamic psychotherapy. However, the paucity and quality of the outcome research in this area are such that claims for the effectiveness of these types of interventions can only be tentative. The potential of these emerging therapies warrant more thorough evaluation using more robust methodologies – although logistical problems may be an obstacle to better research designs with sufficient size and power to detect treatment effects.

In a report focusing on the use of psychotherapy with people with learning disabilities, the Royal College of Psychiatrists (2004) briefly reviewed the evidence base for the effectiveness of psychological treatments with this client group. The report suggests that the lack of good quality research evidence to support the use of psychological therapies with this population is, in part, due to intellectual disability having been used routinely as an exclusion criterion from efficacy research. The available, albeit limited, evidence for the effectiveness of psychodynamic, psychoanalytic and cognitive-behavioural treatment approaches is considered to be promising with these clients. However, the review of the available evidence in this report is somewhat limited and in places inaccurate. Given the publication date (March 2004), somewhat surprisingly it fails to cite substantive reviews of psychological treatments for people with developmental disabilities and a number of controlled studies published in previous years (e.g. Beail, 2003; Benson, Johnson Rice, & Miranti, 1986; Hatton, 2002; Taylor, 2002a; Taylor et al., 2002; Willner, Jones, Tams, & Green, 2002).

ANGER, AGGRESSION, AND GENERAL WELL-BEING

Anger is a normal human emotion and as such it has a number of positive functions (Novaco & Taylor, in press). Once activated, it can mobilize psychological resources, energize corrective behaviours and facilitate perseverance. Anger can protect self-esteem and communicate negative sentiment. However, there are a number of reasons for considering anger as an emotional dyscontrol problem among people with developmental disabilities requiring therapeutic attention.

First, although anger is neither necessary nor sufficient for the activation of aggression, it is nonetheless closely associated with it. In empirical studies anger has been found to predict aggression by psychiatric and forensic inpatients prior to admission (McNeil et al., 2003), post-admission (Novaco, 1994; Novaco & Renwick, 2003; Wang & Diamond, 1999), and subsequently in the community following discharge (Monahan et al., 2001). More specifically in relation to people with developmental disabilities, Novaco and Taylor (2004) found that anger was strongly associated with and predicted physical assault behaviour among males with developmental disabilities detained in specialist forensic hospital facilities.

Second, in addition to being an important determinant of aggressive behaviour, anger is commonly associated with psychological distress, and it is a feature of a wide range of mental health disturbances including personality, impulse control and conduct disorders, in schizophrenia, bipolar mood and organic brain disorders, and in a variety of conditions resulting from trauma (Novaco & Taylor, in press).

Finally, anger has also been strongly associated with a variety of physical health problems, especially cardiovascular disorders (Chesney & Rosenman, 1985; Dembroski et al., 1985; Diamond, 1982; Siegman & Smith, 1994). Swaffer and Hollin (2001) found that in a detained population of young offenders high levels of self-reported anger were significantly associated with indicators of poorer general health. There is no reason to suppose that people with developmental disabilities are not similarly affected by these psychological and physical correlates of chronic anger problems.

PREVALENCE OF AGGRESSION PROBLEMS AMONG PEOPLE WITH DEVELOPMENTAL DISABILITY

Various surveys of populations of people with developmental disability have found high rates of what has been termed 'challenging behaviour', in which aggression features prominently (see Table 4.1). Harris (1993) conducted a survey of service providers concerning 1,362 children and adults with developmental difficulties in the South-West region of England. The overall prevalence of aggression was found to be 17.6%. The rate for males was 20.6% and 13.4% for females and this difference was significant. Harris' study included

Table 4.1   Studies of prevalence of anger and aggression among people with developmental disabilities (ordered chronologically)

	N	Location	Prevalence (%)		
			Institution	Community	Total
Hill & Bruininks (1984)	2,491	USA	37	16	27
Harris (1993)	1,362	England	38	11	18
Sigafoos et al. (1994)	2,412	Australia	35	10	11
Smith et al. (1996)	2,202	England	40+	–	21
Lindsay & Law (1999)*	161	Scotland	–	66	–
Deb et al. (2001)	101	Wales	–	23	–
Emerson et al. (2001)	2,189	England	–	7	–
Novaco & Taylor (2004)**	129	England	47	–	–
Taylor, Hatton, Gentry, and Wilson (2004)	782	England	–	12	–

Note: *This study involved clients referred because of challenging/offending behaviour. The prevalence pertains to clinically significant *anger* assessed following referral. **This study involved detained male inpatients with offending histories. The prevalence concerns *physical* assaults post-admission.

both hospitals and community day-care facilities. The prevalence of aggressive behaviour in the hospitals (38.2%) was almost four times greater than that found in the community day facilities (9.7%). In a similarly conducted survey regarding a population of children and adults with intellectual disability in Queensland, Australia, Sigafoos, Elkins, Kerr, and Attwood (1994) found that 11% of the total population of 2,412 people were identified by service providers as exhibiting aggressive behaviour, and there was considerable variation as a function of residential setting. The prevalence of aggressive behaviour was 35% for those in institutions, 17% in community-based group homes, and 3% in other community accommodations (giving an average community prevalence rate of 10%). There were no significant differences between males and females in this population in terms of the frequency, severity or chronicity of aggressive behaviour.

Results consistent with these service provider surveys were obtained by Smith, Branford, Collacot, Cooper, and McGrother (1996) in a study involving home interviews with key persons providing care for 2,277 adults with developmental disabilities in Leicestershire, England. From the data reported (ibid., p. 221), it is calculated that across the entire sample 23% of males and 19% of females were reported as being physically aggressive. The prevalence of aggression (40+%) for residents of National Health Service (NHS) institutional settings was described as being significantly higher than that for those residing in the community (ibid., p. 225). In a similar study by Hill and Bruininks (1984), interviews regarding maladaptive behaviour were conducted with direct care staff working with residents with mental retardation. The study involved a representative sample of 236 community and public residential facilities across the USA. From the data presented in Hill and Bruininks' paper (ibid., p. 383), it is calculated that, for the 2,491 residents included in this study, the overall prevalence of behaviour causing injury to others, across all age ranges, was 26.6%. The rate for this behaviour among residents, new admissions, and re-admissions in public facilities averaged 36.9%. For those people residing in community facilities, the prevalence of the same category of behaviour was 16.3%.

In a population-based sample of 101 adults with intellectual disabilities randomly selected from the social services department register in South Wales in the UK, using a questionnaire-based interview procedure with carers and where possible clients, Deb et al. (2001) found that 23% of the participants had histories of severe and/or frequent aggressive behaviour. The percentage of males showing severe physical aggression in this sample was 16% and this compared with 30% of women, but this difference was not statistically significant. A significant difference was detected, however, between those clients receiving anti-psychotic, antidepressant, and epilepsy medication and those who received other or no drugs.

Emerson et al. (2001), in a total population study carried out in two health authority districts in North-West England, used a 'key informant' questionnaire to gather information on personal/demographic characteristics, the presence of a range of challenging behaviours, and the impact and consequences of these behaviours if present. From the 2,189 children and adults with intellectual disabilities screened, 7% were found to have shown serious aggressive behaviour in the past month. In this study aggression was significantly more likely to be shown by people with less severe disabilities (cf. Deb et al., 2001; Harris, 1993; Sigafoos et al., 1994; Smith et al., 1996).

In a single district study in the North-East of England, using a similar approach to classifying challenging behaviour as that utilized by Emerson et al. (2001), Taylor, Hatton, Gentry et al. (2004) found that 12% of the 782 adults with intellectual disabilities living in community settings who were screened were reported as displaying serious aggressive behaviour (verbal and physical). When the criterion is extended to include people who were considered to show a 'lesser' degree aggressive behaviour that still constituted a management concern, the prevalence rate more than doubled to 27%. Table 4.2 shows comparisons of frequencies of serious aggressive and/or destructive behaviour in this population. As can be seen, the proportion of males showing these types of behaviours was much higher than that for females, but this difference was not statistically significant. However, younger people (aged under 40), and those living in NHS Trust or social service commissioned residential care settings were significantly more aggressive and destructive than older people or those living in their own accommodation, or with their families.

Novaco and Taylor (2004) investigated anger and aggression exhibited by male offenders with developmental disabilities detained in specialist forensic hospital facilities in North-East England. They found that 47% of the 129 inpatients assessed had physically assaulted staff or other patients following admission. Importantly, 34% of this population (or 73% of those who had been assaultive) had carried out two or more physical assaults post-admission. As in some previous prevalence studies (e.g. Hill & Bruininks, 1984; Smith et al., 1996), Novaco and Taylor (2004) found that the less able participants were significantly more likely to be physically assaultive.

Anger is rarely an assessment priority outside of specialized services or research studies. It is interesting to note, therefore, that Lindsay and Law (1999) reported that, following assessment, more than 65% of the developmental disabled clients referred to a Scottish community-based service for challenging or offending behaviours had clinically significant anger problems.

The epidemiological research reported above indicates that aggression, and by implication anger, is a significant issue among populations of people with developmental disabilities. In most studies, the rates of aggression are markedly higher for males than for females, although, with the exception of Harris (1993), these gender differences do not reach statistical significance. In the studies by Deb et al. (2001), Emerson et al. (2001),

Table 4.2 Frequencies of adult community clients in a district population reported as showing serious aggressive and/or destructive behaviour

	N	Frequency (%)	χ^2 [df]	p
Gender	781			
Male	432	67 (15.5)		
Female	349	41 (11.7)		
			2.29 [1]	n.s.
Age group	754			
16–25 years	92	17 (18.5)		
26–39 years	245	45 (18.4)		
40–59 years	283	29 (10.2)		
60+ years	134	16 (11.9)		
			9.07 [3]	.028
Age – median split	754			
Below 42 years	369	66 (17.9)		
At or above 42 years	385	41 (10.6)		
			8.10 [1]	.004
Type of residence	781			
Community	421	39 (9.3)		
Residential care	314	58 (18.5)		
NHS Trust home	46	11 (23.9)		
			16.97 [2]	.000

Note: Frequencies relate to clients' aggressive and/or destructive behaviour rated by informants who know the persons well as either 'serious' (in terms of frequency and/or impact), or previously or potentially a challenge, but 'controlled' in the current setting.
Source: Taylor, Hatton, Gentry et al. (2004) Development of an imaginal provocation test to evaluate treatment for anger problems in people with intellectual disabilities. *Clinical Psychology & Psychotherapy, 11*, 233–246.

Harris (1993), and Sigafoos et al. (1994) younger adults were consistently more aggressive than older people, and in the Taylor, Hatton, Gentry, et al. (2004) study this difference was significant.

From Table 4.1 it can be seen that the prevalence of aggression among people with developmental disabilities living in community settings ranged between 7% and 16%, with the exception of the 23% rate reported in the Deb et al. (2001) study. In addition to the Deb et al. being the smallest prevalence study included in this review, with the 101 participant sample being selected from a case register, the criteria used to estimate the degree of aggression shown by individuals were perhaps less stringent than the other studies reporting community rates. For example, individuals were included if they presented 'less severe, but frequent' behavioural problems (ibid., p. 507), whereas most other studies stipulated that 'severe' behaviour problems had to be present. When the criteria were relaxed in the Taylor, Hatton, Gentry et al. (2004) study to include a category of 'lesser' degree of aggressive behaviour, the prevalence increased two-fold to very close to that reported by Deb et al. (2001). The only single figure aggression rate for a community population (7%) was in the Emerson et al. (2001) paper which is the only community prevalence study that appears to include challenging/aggressive behaviour only if it present within a short time period (i.e. within the past month).

The studies by Harris (1993), Hill and Bruininks (1984), Sigafoos et al. (1994), Smith et al. (1996) and Taylor, Hatton, Gentry et al. (2004) show that levels of aggression, and so by association anger, are particularly high for people with developmental disability living in institutional settings. Many people with developmental disability appear to be institutionalized because of their aggressive behaviour. Lakin, Hill, Hauber, Bruininks, and Heal (1983) found that the primary reason for people with developmental disability to be admitted or re-admitted to institutional settings was aggression. Aggression was also the main reason for people in this client group to be prescribed antipsychotic and behavioural control drugs (Aman, Richmond, Stewart, Bell, & Kissell, 1987). On the other hand, many aspects of institutions can elicit feelings of frustration, helplessness, injustice, and anger. They include: little, if any, personal choice; restricted opportunities for the development of mutually supportive or intimate relationships; limited occupational or work-related activities; cramped living conditions and little privacy; over-heated buildings of poor architectural design; and staff who might be inadequately trained, insufficiently supported, or unmotivated (Black, Cullen, & Novaco, 1997; Levey & Howells, 1991).

SYSTEMIC EFFECTS OF ANGER AND AGGRESSION PROBLEMS AMONG PEOPLE WITH DEVELOPMENTAL DISABILITY

As detailed above, anger has been shown to be predictive of physical aggression in psychiatric, forensic and developmental disability hospital inpatients. This is at great cost to the staff working in these settings. In a survey of violence experienced by staff in the National Health Service (NHS) in England and Wales, 10% of respondents reported receiving a minor injury in the previous 12 months and one in six had been threatened verbally (Health and Safety Commission, 1987). High levels of direct care staff injuries have been reported in a number of studies done in secure hospitals in the USA (Carmel & Hunter, 1989; Bensley et al., 1997), in the UK (National Audit Office, 2003), and in Australia (Cheung et al., 1996). The Carmel and Hunter study concerned one of California's primary forensic hospitals, where in one year, 16% of the ward nursing staff sustained serious injuries as a result of patient violence. The Bensley et al. study, involving psychiatric hospital employees in the state of Washington, found that there were 13.8 workers compensation claims due to assault per 100 employees in a one-year period.

There have been comparable findings concerning people with developmental disability living in institutional contexts. In their study of violence faced by staff in a developmental disability service of an NHS Trust in the UK, Kiely and Pankhurst (1998) found that this service recorded nearly five times more incidents of patient-inflicted injury than the Trust's sister psychiatric service. Approximately 80% of respondents in the developmental disability service reported suffering physical assault at the hands of service-users during the previous 12 months.

Bromley and Emerson (1995) found that the emotional responses of developmental disability staff to episodes of service-user aggression included annoyance (41%), anger (24%), and fear (19%). Staff reported the most significant sources of stress were associated with challenging behaviour that was perceived to be chronically wearing, unpredictable, and difficult to deal with and understand. These phenomena are consistent with the process of staff 'burnout' and have clear implications for quality of care provided to patients. Staff in the Kiely and Pankhurst (1998) study reported a range of reactions following a violent incident including ignoring the perpetrator, increased wariness and caution in their contact with the assailant, and loss of confidence in their ability to work competently. Jenkins, Rose, and Lovell (1997) found that staff working with developmentally disabled clients with challenging behaviour (including aggression) were significantly more anxious than staff working with non-challenging clients.

In their review of staff behaviour associated with challenging behaviour, Hastings and Remington (1994) concluded that there is clear evidence that staff respond to challenging behaviours by using strategies that will develop or maintain at least some of the behaviour causing concern. High turnover rates and burnout have been found to be a consequence of exposure to the risk of violence among staff working in developmental disability services (Attwood & Joachim, 1994). In these ways, anger and aggression can be seen to carry heavy costs for the whole system concerned with providing security and rehabilitation for developmentally disabled offenders.

ANGER TREATMENT FOR PEOPLE WITH DEVELOPMENTAL DISABILITIES

INTRODUCTION

The approach to anger treatment developed within the Northgate Anger Treatment Project is cognitive-behavioural. There are two main reasons for this. First, in the non-disability field, these treatment approaches have been found to be effective for a wide range of anger problems across a number of populations (see Chapter 3). Second, with reference to the 'what works' in reducing offending literature, it has been suggested that interventions that adhere to a number of key principles, including use of cognitive-behavioural approaches that are orientated towards skills development, result in significantly improved outcomes (e.g. McGuire, 1995; McGuire, 2002; Skett, 1995) (see Chapter 7).

Despite their widespread use over very many years there is relatively little good quality research available on the use of medications for problems of aggression among people with developmental disabilities. There is, however, a substantial literature on the use of treatment interventions for aggressive behaviour in this population that utilize behavioural approaches. Recently a number of small-scale studies have been reported on the application of cognitive-behavioural approaches to anger and aggression in people with developmental disabilities. Table 5.1 lists a number of papers providing substantive reviews of the treatment of aggression and anger problems in people with learning disability (including cognitive-behavioural approaches). In the following sections the evidence for, and the advantages and limitations of psychopharmacological, behavioural and cognitive-behavioural approaches to the treatment of anger and aggression problems among people with developmental disabilities are discussed in some detail.

PSYCHOPHARMACOLOGICAL TREATMENTS

The use of psychotropic medications with people with developmental disability and various behavioural and psychological difficulties was reviewed by Matson et al. (2000). They reported that despite the very large numbers of people with developmental disability who are prescribed medication for aggression, very little research has been reported in this area over the past ten years. Although Matson et al. reviewed in total 72 studies published

Anger Treatment for People with Developmental Disabilities by J. L. Taylor and R. W. Novaco.
Copyright © 2005 John Wiley & Sons, Ltd.

Table 5.1 Reviews (post-1985) of interventions for aggression and anger problems in people with developmental disabilities (ordered chronologically)

Study	Description of study	Main findings
Lennox, Miltenberger, Spengler, and Erfanian (1988)	Reports on 'decelerative' treatments for behaviour problems published in 7 major developmental disability journals between 1981 and 1985 were reviewed; 162 studies were reviewed involving 548 child and adult subjects with all levels of disability in a wide range of settings; data for 56 subjects with aggression problems across all studies were analysed according to three levels of treatment procedure intrusiveness.	More intrusive interventions, including time-out, aversion techniques and medication, were more likely to be used for behavioural problems than for other types of behaviour problems; less intrusive interventions such as self-management were more effective than intrusive techniques; compared with other types of interventions medication was particularly ineffective in dealing with problems of aggression.
Scotti, Evans, Meyer, and Walker (1991)	Meta-analysis of interventions for problem behaviour published between 1976 and 1987 in 18 major journals in the developmental disability field; 403 studies from 318 articles were included in analyses of treatment effectiveness taking into account type of behaviour problem, severity of the behaviour and degree of intrusiveness of the intervention.	Physical aggression/tantrum behaviours were associated with the lowest overall treatment effects when compared with other classes of behaviour problems; limited evidence is provided for the superiority of less intrusive and constructive interventions such as environmental change and positive practice, over more intrusive techniques, including aversive stimulation, in reducing aggressive behaviour; in general the effectiveness of interventions for problem behaviours is correlated with active programming, generalization, integrated setting and longer follow-up variables.

Whitaker (1993)	Narrative review of psychological methods for reducing aggression; 78 studies categorized into ecological intervention, positive programming and contingency management procedures are included; people with a range of disability levels, from mild to profound, were involved; the studies included children and adults living in staffed and unstaffed settings.	Psychological treatment methods found to be effective were behavioural in nature and concerned mainly with contingency management; little evidence was found for the effectiveness of self-control procedures, particularly with subjects with greater levels of intellectual disability; ecological interventions showed some promise, but difficulties in completing thorough functional analyses may limit the application of these approaches in naturalistic settings; there are great difficulties in successfully implementing behavioural interventions with low frequency aggression and in unstaffed settings.
Baumeister, Sevin, and King (1998)	Narrative review of the efficacy of neuroleptic medication for schizophrenia and aberrant behaviours including aggression; 13 studies on the effects of these drugs on aggression problems published between 1957 and 1995; these studies involved approx. 867 subjects with all levels of mental retardation.	All but three of the 13 studies included were considered to be methodologically unsound; as a result, firm conclusions concerning the effects of these medicines on aggressive behaviour, the evidence for the efficacy of this form of therapy in reducing aberrant behaviour, including aggression, were considered to be weak; individuals' responses to these drugs are highly variable and unpredictable; any effects could be the result of non-specific suppression of behaviour and cognition generally.
Matson et al. (2000)	Narrative review of the use of psychoactive medications for a range of behaviour and psychiatric problems; 72 studies were included in the analysis including 14 that specifically targeted aggression problems; these studies involved a total of 169 child and adult subjects exhibiting all levels of learning disability.	All of the studies aimed at controlling aggression contained serious methodological flaws; 12 of the 14 studies reviewed utilized atypical antipsychotics and their effects are likely to be a consequence of indiscriminate suppression of aggressive and collateral behaviours; the two studies that that evaluated the efficacy of SSRIs were poorly designed and produced confounding results; there is no sound evidence that medications are effective in treating aggression in these client groups.

Continued

Table 5.1 *Continued*

Study	Description of study	Main findings
Brylewski & Duggan (1999)	Cochrane review of RCTs of the effectiveness of antipsychotic medication for challenging behaviour (in the absence of psychiatric disorder) in people with learning disability.	Only three RCTs met the inclusion criteria and were included in the analyses; the analyses provided no evidence for the effectiveness of antipsychotics in reducing challenging behaviour in adults with learning disability.
Carr et al. (2000)	Narrative review of non-contingent reinforcement (NCR) as a treatment for 'aberrant' behaviour in children and adults with learning disability; 33 studies included, the great majority of which were published during the 1990s; 15 of these studies included aggression as a target behaviour involving mainly people with moderate–severe levels of disability.	NCR found to be a promising approach for the treatment of aberrant behaviour, including aggression; has not been evaluated outside of experimental settings; hence issues concerning transferability and generalization of treatment effects are unresolved and the application of this technology in naturalistic settings is in doubt.
Whitaker (2001)	Narrative review of broadly cognitive-behavioural approaches to anger control for people with learning disability; 16 studies published between 1978 and 2000 are included; a total of 88 subjects with mild to moderate levels of disability were involved in these studies; only two of the 16 studies are group comparisons with the rest being case studies or series.	The review indicates that there is limited evidence that cognitive-behavioural anger control packages can be helpful, however, the majority of the studies included produced unclear results and often had poor experimental designs; the non-cognitive components of these packages, including relaxation and self-monitoring, appear to be most effective in increasing anger control; effective use of cognitive techniques with this client group may be hampered by cognitive and language limitations associated with subjects' learning disabilities.

Taylor (2002a)

Narrative review of the assessment and treatment of anger and aggression in people with intellectual disabilities, with a particular focus on those with offending histories. In addition to brief reviews of psychopharmacological and behavioural approaches to anger treatment, 12 primary studies of cognitive behavioural (CBT) approaches to treatment published between 1985 and 2002 were included. Three of these studies involved control group comparisons, two were pre–post group study designs and the remainder were case studies or series.

There is a lack of valid and reliable measures for the diagnosis and formulation of anger problems in this client group, and to evaluate treatment outcome. There is little evidence to support the routine use of psychoactive medications as first-line treatments in reducing anger/aggression problems in people with ID. Behavioural interventions have good evidence to support their use with people with high levels of ID engaged with challenging behaviour services and demonstrating high frequency aggressive behaviour. Cognitive behavioural anger treatment approaches show promise, particularly for high functioning people with low frequency, but high impact aggression (cf. with offenders). The behavioural components of these approaches appear to be most effective, but little direct attention has been given to the cognitive restructuring component of CBT in published studies to date.

between 1990 and 1999, they found only 14 studies that attended specifically to the control of aggression that *partially* met the methodological criteria for inclusion in their review. While most of these studies reported significant reductions in aggression following treatment, all contained serious methodological flaws. The authors suggest that for the 12 studies that utilized antipsychotics, it is likely that their effects are a consequence of indiscriminate suppression of aggressive and other adaptive behaviour that results in serious side-effects. Matson, Bielecki, Mayville, and Matson (2003) detail a number of suggestions for improving the methodology in future psychopharmacological efficacy research among people with developmental disabilities. Matson et al. (2000) concluded from their review that currently there is no sound evidence that medications are effective in treating aggression in people with developmental disability.

Baumeister et al. (1998) briefly reviewed the use of neuroleptic medications for problem behaviour, including aggression, in people with mental retardation. They listed 13 studies investigating the effects of neuroleptics on aggression published between 1957 and 1995. They reported that it was difficult to draw any conclusions from this literature because much of the literature is flawed methodologically. They considered the study method to be sound if it utilized either an experimental design in which the subjects were randomly assigned to concurrently run drug or placebo groups or quasi-experimental within-subject designs in which at least one reversal of the drug effect was demonstrated. Only three of the studies met either criterion. Overall, Baumeister et al. (1998) concluded that the evidence for the efficacy of neuroleptic medication in reducing aberrant behaviour including aggression is weak. The effects of these medicines on individuals with mental retardation are highly variable and unpredictable. They lack specificity with regard to target behaviours and are likely to exert non-specific effects by suppressing behaviour or cognition generally.

Brylewski and Duggan (1999) reviewed 20 randomized controlled trials of antipsychotic medication for challenging behaviour in people with intellectual disability published between 1966 and 1994. They found that only three of these studies met The Cochrane Collaboration (Mulrow & Oxman, 1996) criteria they used for including studies in their analyses. These studies were described as short and poorly reported; they involved small numbers of participants (total $N = 198$) with moderate–profound intellectual disabilities; and they investigated drugs that were not used widely in the UK, using dependent measures of aggression and challenging behaviour with limited reliability and validity. Brylewski and Duggan suggest that the studies included in their review provided no evidence of whether this treatment helps or harms adults with developmental disability and challenging behaviour, and that their continued use without trial-based evidence is ethically questionable.

BEHAVIOURAL TREATMENTS

In their review of 162 studies of 'decelerative' interventions for behaviour problems in people with developmental disability published between 1981 and 1985 Lennox et al. (1988) found that for subjects with aggression problems (total $N = 56$ across studies reviewed) more intrusive interventions such as time-out, aversion techniques and medication were more likely to be used than for other classes of behaviour problems (ibid., p. 495). In terms of treatment effectiveness, less intrusive and more constructive treatment approaches to aggression such as environmental change and contingency management performed slightly better than more intrusive and restrictive techniques (ibid., p. 498, Table 2). The effectiveness of medication was particularly poor for this class of behaviour in comparison to other interventions.

Scotti et al. (1991) sought to improve on the Lennox et al. (1988) review, which was relatively limited in terms of its range and its tolerance of methodological flaws in the studies included, by carrying out a meta-analysis of interventions for problem behaviour in people with developmental disability. In their review, which included 403 studies reported in 18 major journals between 1976 and 1987, Scotti et al. analyzed treatment effectiveness in relation to type of behaviour problem × severity of the behaviour × intrusiveness of the intervention. Compared with other classes of behaviour problems, physical aggression/tantrum behaviours were associated with significantly lower treatment effects (ibid., p. 243). Overall, less intrusive interventions, including environmental change and positive practice, were generally more effective than the most intrusive techniques such as aversive stimulation and restraint (ibid., p. 244, Table 6).

Carr et al. (2000), in a review of non-contingent reinforcement (NCR) as a treatment for 'aberrant' behaviour in people with developmental disability, considered 15 studies published between 1977 and 2000 with aggression as the target behaviour. The great majority of these studies involved people with moderate–severe levels of developmental disability. NCR involves the delivery of the reinforcer for a specific challenging behaviour to the individual on a response-independent basis in order to reduce or extinguish the target behaviour. This approach is thought to be beneficial as it is functional, relatively effective in reducing the frequency of target behaviour, delivers a higher rate of reinforcement than other procedures and is relatively easy to implement. Carr et al. conclude from their review that while NCR is a promising approach for the treatment of problem behaviour, including aggression, it has not yet been evaluated outside of extremely well-controlled experimental settings. Transferability and generalization effects have yet to be explored and the schedule thinning in the studies reported thus far would not be practical in routine clinical or naturalistic settings.

Whitaker (1993) reviewed psychological methods for reducing aggression in people with developmental disability. He found little evidence for the effectiveness of self-control procedures including self-monitoring, contingency control, and self-instruction. This was the case particularly with people with greater levels of disability and associated cognitive and language deficits. While he found some limited evidence for the usefulness of ecological interventions in reducing aggression in subjects with severe and profound levels of developmental disability, the number of studies reporting this approach was small. This was perhaps related to the difficulties involved in doing functional analyses that are necessary for effective ecological interventions.

The bulk of the literature incorporated into Whitaker's (1993) review is concerned with contingency management using behavioural methods with low levels of intellectual functioning. Of the 59 studies reviewed involving contingency management procedures, the level of functioning of study participants could be clearly discerned in 35 of the studies described. In 30 of these studies, participants were either functioning below IQ 50, or were described as having 'moderate', 'severe' or 'profound' levels of disability (Tables 3–12, 1993, pp. 21–36). The findings indicate that for these approaches to be effective in reducing aggression, they need to be delivered consistently and they require high staff ratios. Further, there are great problems in successfully implementing these approaches with low-frequency aggression and in settings without paid-staff support. Whitaker concludes that the most effective psychological approaches to the reduction of aggression in people with developmental disability are behavioural in nature, involving antecedent control, skills training, or contingency management.

COGNITIVE-BEHAVIOURAL ANGER TREATMENTS FOR PEOPLE WITH DEVELOPMENTAL DISABILITIES

In a review of cognitively-based anger control treatments for people with developmental disability, Whitaker (2001) concluded that the experimental evidence for such approaches in effectively reducing aggression with this client group is weak compared with the evidence for behavioural interventions that involve mainly antecedent control and contingency management. Unfortunately behavioural approaches, unlike direct treatment, do not explicitly encourage self-regulation of behaviour, and once the intervention is withdrawn, or the environment is altered so that the same contingencies no longer apply, the aggressive behaviour is likely to recur. On the other hand, self-actualization through the promotion of internalized control of behaviour is intrinsic to the skills training components of cognitive-behavioural approaches developed for use with people with developmental disabilities (e.g. Williams & Jones, 1997). Further, there is evidence from studies in non-disability fields that for a range of psychological problems the effects of cognitive-behavioural treatments do maintain and increase over time compared to control conditions (Barrowclough et al., 2001; Kuipers et al., 1997; Oosterban, van Balkom, Spinhoven, van Oppen, & van Dyck, 2001).

As discussed above, an additional limitation of behavioural procedures is that they are less effective with low-frequency aggression and require high levels of staff input in order to be maintained. Many people with developmental disabilities and severe anger problems associated with a range of offending behaviours are not overtly aggressive on a regular basis. Also, many clients with these types of difficulties do not reside in well-staffed and supervised settings, but are seen in the community by teams with varying levels of expertise and resources. Thus, the efficacy of behavioural interventions directed at aggression is not clear with this particular population. It is important, therefore, for workers in this area to continue to consider the development of better defined treatment approaches for anger problems among people with developmental disability.

Both Whitaker (2001) and Taylor (2002a) provided narrative reviews of studies of cognitively-based anger treatments specifically for people with developmental disabilities. Table 5.2 sets out those studies (post-1985) that have evaluated cognitive-behavioural approaches to anger problems in people with developmental disability. A number of researchers and clinicians have reported studies involving people with developmental disability and histories of aggressive behaviour in in-patient and community settings. For example, Allan, Lindsay, MacLeod, and Smith (2001), Black and Novaco (1993), Lindsay, Allan, MacLeod, Smart, and Smith (2003), Lindsay, Overend, Allan, Williams, and Black (1998), Murphy and Clare (1991), Rose (1996), and Novaco and Taylor (in press) have reported case and case-series studies involving individual and group therapy formats incorporating combinations of cognitive-behavioural techniques including self-monitoring, relaxation and skills training that have yielded reductions in levels of anger and aggression that were maintained at follow-up. In many cases, these treatment gains facilitated community resettlement and integration, and access to occupational opportunities.

Table 5.2 Studies (post-1985) involving cognitive-behavioural treatment of anger in people with developmental disability (ordered chronologically.)

Study	Design*	Participants	Setting (I/C)**	Treatment format/ components	Duration	Dependent variable(s)***	Post-intervention outcome	Follow-up
Benson et al. (1986)	Group study RCT	37 men 17 women mild-moderate ID	C	Group therapy format: self-instruction vs. relaxation vs. problem-solving vs. combined condition	12 weekly 90 min. sessions (Total = 18 hours)	AI (SR) IP (SR) Role-play (OB) Aggression (OB)	Significant pre-post reductions for all conditions on IP, role-play and aggression measures – no significant between group differences	Treatment gains maintained at 4–5 weeks follow-up
Murphy & Clare (1991)	Case study	1 male mild ID	I	Multiple, staged individual and group therapy interventions: self-monitoring; social skills training; coping skills training; relaxation training; token economy	Unclear/ varied over 49-week period	Aggression (OB)	Despite fluctuations during the intervention period, recorded incidents of verbal and physical aggression reduced markedly so that the subject was able to be discharged to a staffed community residential facility	At ten-month follow-up subject continued to make progress and was still living in the same community facility
Black & Novaco (1993)	Case study	1 male mild ID	I	Individual therapy format: self-monitoring; psycho-education; arousal reduction; coping skills training	28 sessions 40 mins. each (Total = 18.7 hours)	Anger diary (SR) Aggression (OB) Pro-social behaviour (CR)	Reduction in frequency of observed aggressive behaviour and increases in pro-social behaviours – self-reported anger increased	Staff-rated improvements maintained during 21-week follow-up

Continued

Table 5.2 *Continued*

Study	Design*	Participants	Setting (I/C)**	Treatment format/ components	Duration	Dependent variable(s)***	Post-intervention outcome	Follow-up
Cullen (1993)	Case series	12 mild–moderate ID	C = 2 I = 10	Group therapy format: self-monitoring; education; relaxation training; behavioural skills training	Up to 100 hours – twice weekly sessions over 1 year	Anger diary (SR) Aggression (OB) Social behaviour ratings (CR)	Mixed results – frequently aggressive subjects showed greatest improvements; no improvements on social behaviour ratings; self-recordings not reported	Unspecified follow-up period; treatment effects unclear
Rose (1996)	Case series	3 men 2 women moderate–severe ID	C	Group therapy format: relaxation training; self-monitoring; identification of triggers; emotional recognition; coping skills training; self-instruction; thought-stopping	16 sessions of 90 min. over 19 weeks (Total = 24 hours)	Anger diary (SR) Anger log (CR)	All subjects were reported by carers as having fewer aggressive incidents per month at the end of treatment than during the three-month baseline period	At three-month follow-up all subjects reported as having fewer incidents than during baseline
Moore, Adams, Elsworth, and Lewis (1997)	Group study	2 men 4 women mild–moderate ID	C	Group therapy format: emotional recognition; self-monitoring; relaxation training; role-play; problem-solving skills	8 weekly 90 min. sessions (Total = 12 hours)	Anger diary (SR) Anger log (CR)	Thirty-nine % reduction in angry/aggressive incidents reported by subjects at the end of treatment over a brief (2-week) baseline; treatment gains corroborated by keyworker staff	Six-month informal follow-up – no data collected but informants suggested that gains were maintained

Study	Design	Subjects		Format/Content	Sessions	Measures	Outcomes	Follow-up
Walker & Chesel-dine (1997)	Case series	4 men ID level unclear	C	Group therapy format: psycho-education; social skills training; relaxation training; self-instruction	8 weekly 90 min. sessions (Total = 12 hours)	PI (SR)	Pre-post PI responses indicate that three subjects reported reduced tendency to respond to provocation in an aggressive manner and increased use of constructive coping strategies	None
Lawrenson & Lindsay (1998)	Case Study	1 male mild ID	C	Group therapy format: psycho-education; relaxation training; problem-solving skills; distraction techniques; self-instruction; role-play	26 weekly 50 min. sessions (Total = 21.7 hours)	AI (SR) PI (SR)	Following intervention subject reported less intense anger reactions in response to a range of situations and more constructive coping, as opposed to aggressive, behavioural responses. Some anecdotal evidence from staff carers to support these improvements.	None
Lindsay et al. (1998)	Case series	3 men 2 mild ID 1 severe ID	C = 1 I = 2	Individual therapy format – differed for each subject: self-monitoring; relaxation training; emotional recognition; psycho-education; role-play	Varied between 50 daily sessions over 10 weeks – weekly sessions for 6 months	Aggression (SR) Aggression (OB) PI (SR) RPP (OB) Anger ratings (SR)	Marked reduction in observed aggression in two subjects treated in institutional settings and reductions in self-reported anger and role-play provocation scores for subject treated in a community setting	Length of follow-up varied from 24 weeks to four years; two patients maintained treatment gains and the third regressed following transfer to another unit

Continued

Table 5.2 *Continued*

Study	Design*	Participants	Setting (I/C)**	Treatment format/ components	Duration	Dependent variable(s)***	Post-intervention outcome	Follow-up
Rossiter, Hunniset, and Pulsford (1998)	Case series	4 men 2 women moderate-severe ID	C = 2 I = 4	Group therapy format: psycho-education; self-monitoring; relaxation training; self-instruction; role-play	8 weekly 90 min. sessions (Total = 12 hours)	None	Unclear as no objective outcome measures were used to establish baseline levels of anger/aggression frequency, intensity or duration; clinical impressions were that all but one subject benefited from the intervention	12 week follow-up indicated that four of the five subjects were less aggressive than before beginning treatment
King, Lancaster, Wynne, Nettleton, and Davis (1999)	Group study A-B	7 men 4 women mild ID	C	Group therapy format: education; relaxation training; self-instruction; problem-solving skills	15 weekly 90 min. sessions (Total = 22.5 hours)	AI (SR) Self-esteem (SR) AI (CR) Behaviour Checklist (CR)	Self-reported anger reactivity was reduced significantly following treatment; caregiver ratings of problem behaviours significantly improved	Anger reaction and self-esteem (SR) & OB effects maintained at 12-week follow-up
Rose & West (1999)	Case series	5 men mild-moderate ID	C	Group therapy format: relaxation training; self-monitoring; identification of triggers; emotional recognition; coping skills training; self-instruction; thought-stopping (in four cases augmented by individual, staff or behavioural interventions)	16 weekly 2 hour sessions (Total = 32 hours)	AI (SR) Aggression (OB)	Mixed and difficult to determine effects of anger management intervention vs. other external factors; in three cases observed challenging behaviour appeared to decrease over time and reductions in self-reported anger inventory scores were observed	Variable follow-up periods for participants; in general, self- and staff-reported improvements maintained

Study	Design	Sample	C	Intervention	Sessions	Measures	Results	
Howells, Roger, and Wilcock (2000)	Case series	3 men 2 women mild ID	C	Group therapy format: emotional recognition; self-monitoring; identification of physical and cognitive triggers; coping skills training; problem solving skills; role-play with video feedback	12 weekly 2 hour sessions (Total = 24 hours over 18 weeks due to break)	Anxiety scale (SR) Self-esteem inventory (SR)	Pre-post changes on the anxiety and self-esteem scales did not provide conclusive evidence of any treatment effect; aggression frequency data from informants not reported due to problems with its reliability; no self-report anger or aggression measures taken.	None
Rose, West, and Clifford (2000)	Group study CT	23 men 2 women mild-moderate ID	C	Group therapy format: relaxation training; self-monitoring; identification of triggers; emotional recognition; coping skills training; self-instruction; thought-stopping; role-play with video feedback	16 weekly 2 hour sessions (Total = 32 hours)	AI (SR) Self-concept scale (SR) Depression Inventory (SR)	Significant reductions in reported anger and depression levels post-treatment; non-significant improvement in self-concept following intervention	Improvements in reported anger levels maintained at 12 months follow-up; improvements in self-concept maintained, but levels of depression increasing during same period

Continued

Table 5.2 Continued

Study	Design*	Participants	Setting (I/C)**	Treatment format/ components	Duration	Dependent variable(s)***	Post-intervention outcome	Follow-up
Allan et al. (2001)	Case series	5 women mild-borderline ID	C	Group therapy format: psycho-education; arousal reduction through relaxation exercises; identification of angry thoughts; role-played problem-solving	Approx. 40 1-hour sessions over 9 months (Total = 40 hours)	AI (SR) Recidivism	Little improvement seen over baseline levels on self-rated anger three months into the treatment – post-treatment scores on this measure had improved significantly for 4 out 5 participants.	Improved scores were maintained for all participants at nine months follow-up. Four of the five clients had not been violent at 15 months follow-up
Taylor et al. (2002)†	Group study CT	20 men mild-borderline ID	I	Individual therapy format: psycho-education; self-monitoring; cognitive re-structuring; relaxation training; self-instruction; stress inoculation; role-play problem solving	18 twice weekly 60 min. sessions (Total = 18 hours)	PI (SR) Anger attributes (CR) Anger coping skills (CR) Recidivism	Post-treatment PI scores were significantly lower for subjects in the treatment condition (TC) compared to the wait-list control subjects; staff reported non-significant improvements for TC subjects on anger attribute and coping skills measures	At one month follow-up staff reported slightly improved anger coping skills for TC patients

Study	Design	Sample		Intervention	Duration	Measures	Results	
Willner et al. (2002)	Group study CT	9 men 5 women mild ID	C	Group therapy format: relaxation training; identification of triggers; behavioural and cognitive coping strategies; assertiveness training; 'brainstorming'; homework tasks; use of anger diaries	9 weekly 2 hour sessions (Total = 18 hours)	AI (SR) AI (CR) PI (SR) PI (CR)	Significant within and between group effects as a result of treatment on self- and carer-rated measures of anger reactivity – with moderate to large effect sizes reported. Improvement was significantly associated with verbal IQ and attendance at group by carers	For the treatment group, self- and carer follow-up assessments at three-months converged and showed continued and significant improvements
Lindsay et al. (2003)	Case series	6 men mild ID	C	Group therapy format: psycho-education; arousal reduction through relaxation exercises and imagery; identification of angry thoughts; role-played problem-solving	Approx. 40 1-hour sessions over 9 months (Total = 40 hours)	AI (SR) Emotion AI (SR) Action RPP (OB) Weekly Anger Diary (SR) Recidivism	All participants' scores fell from baseline levels on self-rated measures of emotional and behavioural reactions to anger provocation, and for weekly anger ratings from clients' diaries. Also, independently rated responses to videotaped provocation role-plays improved during the treatment period	Improved self-rated anger inventory and independently rated provocation role-play scores were maintained at 15-months follow-up. None of the participants had been violent for four years following treatment.

Continued

Table 5.2 Continued

Study	Design*	Participants	Setting (I/C)**	Treatment format/ components	Duration	Dependent variable(s)***	Post-intervention outcome	Follow-up
Lindsay et al. (2004)	Group study CT	33 men 14 women mild ID	C	Group therapy format: psycho-education; arousal reduction through relaxation exercises; identification of angry thoughts; stress inoculation; role-played problem-solving	Approx. 40 1-hour sessions over 9 months (Total = 40 hours)	AI (SR) RPP (OB) Weekly Anger Diary (SR) Assault incidents during treatment period	Post-treatment AI and diary rating scores were significantly lower for subjects in the treatment condition compared to the wait-list control subjects; the treatment group had significant post-treatment reductions on RPP scores and significantly fewer aggressive incidents than controls during the treatment period	The lower post-treatment AI, RRP and diary rating scores were maintained for treatment group subjects for follow-up periods of between three and 30 months; no follow-up comparisons with controls were made
Novaco & Taylor (in press)	Case study	1 man borderline ID	I	Individual therapy format: psycho-education; self-monitoring; cognitive re-structuring; relaxation training; self-instruction; stress inoculation; role-play problem solving	18 twice weekly 60 min. sessions (Total = 18 hours)	AI (SR) PI (SR) IP (SR)	Compared with reference group norms, the client's AI and PI scores reduced following treatment by 3.3 and 2.8 standard deviations respectively. His IP score also fell 50% pre-post treatment. Care staff observations of behaviour were convergent with these findings	AI and PI score improvements were maintained at one and eight months follow-up

Study	Type	Subjects	Setting	Treatment	Sessions	Measures	Results	Follow-up
Taylor et al. (in press)†	Group study CT	40 men mild-borderline ID	I	Individual therapy format: psycho-education; self-monitoring; cognitive re-structuring; relaxation training; self-instruction; stress inoculation; role-play problem solving	18 twice weekly 60 min. sessions (Total = 18 hours)	AI (SR) PI (SR) Anger attributes (CR)	Selected post-treatment AI and PI indices were significantly lower for subjects in the treatment condition (TC) compared to the waiting-list control subjects; staff reported non-significant improvements for TC subjects on an anger attribute measures	TC group's treatment gains on AI and PI indices over controls were maintained at four months follow-up
Taylor, Novaco, Guinan, and Street (2004)†	Group study CT	17 men mild-borderline ID	I	Individual therapy format: psycho-education; self-monitoring; cognitive re-structuring; relaxation training; self-instruction; stress inoculation; role-play problem solving	18 twice weekly 60 min. sessions (Total = 18 hours)	IP (SR)	IP test anger reaction and behavioural reactions indices were significantly lower for subjects in the treatment condition (TC) compared to the waiting-list control subjects. Control subject's scores on these indices improved significantly following treatment	None

Notes: * RCT = randomized controlled trial; CT = controlled trial (without randomization); and A-B = pre-post intervention evaluation (without randomization or comparison group).
** I = institutional setting; and C = community setting.
*** AI = anger inventory; IP = imaginal provocation; PI = provocation inventory; RPP = role-play provocation; (SR) = self-report; (OB) = observed behaviour; and (CR) = carer-rated.
† Taylor et al. (2002, in press) and Taylor, Novaco, Guinan, et al. (2004) studies are concatenated.

The case series studies by Allan et al. (2001) and Lindsay et al. (2003) are noteworthy in that they involved, respectively, five women with developmental disabilities who had been involved with the criminal justice system because of violent assaults and six men with developmental disabilities and criminal convictions for assault. In both studies, following completion of group-based cognitive behavioural interventions delivered over a nine-month period, significant improvements on anger indices were recorded and these were maintained at 15 months follow-up. Just one of the 11 participants was reported to have been violent at follow-up.

Other evaluations of group-based anger management treatments using cognitive-behavioural approaches for people with mild to severe levels of disability have also suggested promising outcomes in spite of substantial flaws and weaknesses in study methods and designs including lack of adequate baseline measures, comparison groups, and robust outcome measures (e.g. Howells et al., 2000; Rossiter et al., 1998; Walker & Cheseldine, 1997).

In addition to these case and case-series studies, which are limited in terms of design, a group study by Moore et al. (1997) using group-based cognitive-behavioural anger treatment resulted in a clinically significant reduction of angry and aggressive incidents reported by six clients with mild–moderate developmental disabilities living in the community. In a methodologically more sophisticated group study using self- and observer-rated outcome measures, King et al. (1999) used a similar group-based cognitive-behavioural package with 11 adults with mild developmental disability residing in community facilities referred because of anger control problems. Pre-post treatment outcome measures showed significant treatment gains on self-report anger and self-esteem inventories, and a carer-rated behaviour inventory, and these gains were maintained at 12-week follow-up. Clinical impressions were that all components of the programme (cognitive, arousal and behavioural) were worthwhile and necessary.

Each of the studies described above have lacked control conditions. However, in recent years there have been a number of small controlled anger treatment studies involving comparison groups in the developmental disabilities field. Using modifications of the Novaco treatment components across four conditions in a group therapy format, Benson et al. (1986) obtained significant treatment effects on self- and staff-rated outcome measures and role-play ratings in a study involving 54 clients with temper control problems living in the community. There were no significant differences between the groups (self-instruction, relaxation training, problem-solving and a combined condition). However, it is not easy to draw clear conclusions from this study as the brevity of the report makes it difficult to discern in any detail the methodology and procedures used.

Rose et al. (2000) described a study in which referrals were invited from community health and social services to take part in a group intervention for problems with expressing anger. Twenty-five people with developmental disabilities who responded to the invitation to take part received the treatment that was delivered in 16 two-hour sessions. The intervention involved education, identification and recognition of emotions, arousal reduction, self-instructional training and problem-solving skills training. The outcomes for the intervention group were compared with those for a group of 19 waiting-list controls who received 'treatment as usual'. An innovation in this study was the active involvement of a direct carer who accompanied each participant to group sessions in order to encourage collaborative working and to facilitate transfer of skills to everyday settings. Results showed that self-reported expressed anger and depression scores reduced significantly as a result of the treatment and these improvements were maintained at 12 months follow-up. Some weaknesses of this study include the use of outcome measures that have only limited reliability and validity data available and a lack of behavioural or observer-rated outcome measures. Further, it appears that the research design resulted in some control group participants also being included in the treatment group, thus violating the independence of the groups for statistical comparison purposes.

Taylor et al. (2002) reported a pilot study involving 20 detained male patients with mild to borderline intellectual disabilities and violent, sexual, and fire-setting offending histories, 50% of whom had carried out physical assaults following their admission to hospital. These patients, all of whom met study inclusion criteria including scores above threshold on a reliable and valid anger measure, were allocated to modified cognitive-behavioural anger treatment or to routine care wait-list control conditions. The same therapist delivered 18 sessions of individual treatment to each participant over a period of approximately 12 weeks.

The treatment protocol for this study was a major re-working of Novaco's (1975, 1993b) treatment approach that was designed specifically for use with people with mild to borderline intellectual disability levels. Following successful completion of six sessions of a broadly psycho-educational 'preparatory phase', study participants moved on to the 12-session 'treatment phase', the core components of which were cognitive re-structuring, arousal reduction, and behavioural skills training. Patients' self-report of anger intensity to provocation was significantly lower following intervention in the treatment condition compared to the waiting-list condition. Some limited evidence for the effectiveness of treatment was provided by staffs' ratings of patients' anger disposition and coping behaviour post-treatment. Taking into account the limitations of this pilot study in terms of small number of participants, the confound of routine care, and so on, it appears nonetheless that detained serious offenders with developmental disability can engage in and benefit from intensive individual cognitive-behavioural anger treatment, at least in terms of self-reported reactions to anger-provoking situations.

In a study involving nine men and five women with mild intellectual disabilities living in the community, Willner et al. (2002) used a nine-session group anger management approach somewhat similar to that employed by Rose et al. (2000), including active involvement of a direct carer in the therapy sessions where possible. As in the Rose et al. study, local community services were invited to refer clients whom they judged might benefit from this intervention. No information is provided on the nature of the participants' anger problems or aggression histories. Although the authors state that the 16 candidates for treatment identified in this way were 'allocated randomly' to treatment and waiting-list control groups (2002, p. 225), in fact, two participants (who subsequently dropped out of the study) were swapped between the conditions due to interpersonal issues with other group members. In the final analysis, therefore, the outcomes on self- and carer-rated anger and provocation indices for seven treatment group participants were compared with those for seven control group members.

The results of this study were that the self- and carer-rated anger indices reduced significantly from pre- to post-treatment for the treated group compared with the scores for the control group. Data available for the treated group only showed further improvement on these participant and caregiver ratings at three-month follow-up. The overall between-group effect size estimates reported for the dependent measures in this study were considered to be large.

Other analyses conducted as part of the study pointed to the benefits of having a carer directly involved in the therapy sessions and higher cognitive abilities as measured by verbal IQ. However, given the small numbers of participants, the reliability and generalizability of these findings are questionable. The authors also suggest that while their intervention is briefer than that reported in many previous studies, there was no apparent reduction in efficacy as a result. However, they also suggest that like previous studies using similar interventions (e.g. Rose et al., 2000), clients in this study responded well to the behavioural components of the intervention, but struggled with the cognitive elements. They conjecture that this may be associated with participants' level of intellectual functioning, but it may also be related to the short intervention period, group therapy format, and lack of a robust psycho-educational preparatory stage of treatment (cf. with Taylor et al., 2002 above).

As part of a study aimed mainly at developing an idiographic and clinically meaningful measure of clients' response to anger treatment, Taylor, Novaco, Guinan et al. (2004) conducted a small controlled study using the same intervention and study procedures described above with reference to Taylor et al. (2002). The first part of this study established the internal reliability and concurrent validity of the *Imaginal Provocation Test* (IPT, see Chapter 6) and its subscales. In order to test whether this newly developed test for people with developmental disabilities was sensitive to change associated with anger treatment, the IPT scores of nine detained offenders allocated to a treatment condition were compared to those of a matched group of eight participants allocated to waiting-list condition.

Between-groups analyses showed that, following intervention, the treatment group's scores were significantly improved compared with those of the control group on the IPT 'anger reaction', 'behavioural reactions', and 'anger composite' (a combination of anger + behavioural reactions) indices. The effect sizes for each measure were firmly in the large range. Although the treatment group did not differ significantly from the control group on the IPT 'anger regulation' index, the effect size was still medium–large. Following anger treatment, the majority of treatment group participant's scores on each of the IPT indices had improved over their pre-treatment scores, while the reverse was the case for control group participants.

Once the waiting-list control group had received anger treatment, they were re-assessed and their pre-post treatment scores improved significantly on the IPT anger reaction, behavioural reactions and anger composite indices. Following treatment, the majority of the control group's scores on the IPT indices had improved over their pre-treatment scores.

The intervention component of this study suffered from small participant numbers, lack of an observer outcome measure and the other limitations of a practice-based study of this nature. However, the results support the findings of the Taylor et al. (2002) study that an intensive individual cognitive-behavioural anger treatment can have a significant impact on the chronic anger problems experienced by incarcerated men with developmental disabilities and significant histories of serious aggression and violence.

In a larger study Lindsay et al. (2004) investigated anger treatment outcome and follow-up for up to 47 men and women with mild intellectual disabilities referred to a specialist community service because of aggressive or destructive behaviour. Thirty-three consecutive referrals were designated as the treatment group and 14 later referrals used a waiting-list comparison group; unfortunately these groups were found to be unbalanced in terms of age and gender. For between-group comparisons a 20-item provocation inventory and weekly anger diary ratings were used. A full dataset was obtained for the provocation inventory measure, but just 50% of study participants provided anger diary ratings that could be used in this analysis. Information was also collected concerning aggressive incidents and offences carried out during the intervention period for the treatment group (nine months) and the waiting-list period (six months) for the control group.

Treatment was group-based and comprised 40-weekly sessions over a period of approximately nine months. It was delivered in several cohorts between 1991 and 2002. Treatment components included psycho-education, arousal reduction through relaxation training, identification of angry thoughts, and problem-solving skills training using role-play. A distinctive feature of the intervention was the inclusion of stress inoculation procedures, albeit utilizing given rather than personal provocation scenes, as suggested by Novaco (1975, 1993).

Results show that treatment group scores on the provocation inventory and anger diary ratings improved significantly as a result of treatment compared to control group scores. For those treatment group participants for whom follow-up data was available, treatment gains on the anger inventory and diary rating scales were maintained for up to 30 months and 9 months respectively. Data were not available for between-group comparisons at follow-up points. Following the waiting-list period, control group participants received the anger treatment and their provocation inventory scores reduced significantly during the treatment interval.

The number of physical assaults carried out by the treatment group during the treatment period was significantly lower than for the number perpetrated by the control group while waiting for treatment. However, baseline rates of assault were not reported, and the assessment intervals were different for the comparison groups (six vs nine months). These limitations, along with the lack of a systematic approach to the collection and collation of incident data, mean that this result needs to be considered carefully.

Lindsay et al. (2004) present a very helpful example of how to carry out treatment outcome research as part of the delivery of routine clinical services using a naturalistic approach. Despite its limitations, the results of the study are consistent with and support the findings of previous studies that cognitive-behavioural anger treatment is effective for people with developmental disabilities who have been referred to services because of significant anger problems.

In an extension of the Taylor et al. (2002) and Taylor, Novaco, Guinan et al. (2004) pilot studies, Taylor et al. (in press) reported on a larger concatenated study with 40 men with mild to borderline intellectual disabilities and histories of offending. All participants were detained in a specialist forensic intellectual disability service under sections of the Mental Health Act 1983, and just seven of the 40 had no prior convictions, although they all had well-documented histories of anti-social and offending behaviours. All participants reached threshold scores on reliable and valid measures of anger.

The study design and procedures were broadly the same as those for the earlier studies, and the intervention was described by the same treatment protocol. The procedures and content of the treatment used this study are elaborated upon in later chapters. However, to summarize, 20 patients were allocated to a treatment condition and 20 to a routine care waiting-list control condition. Four treatment group patients dropped out before follow-up assessments could be completed. The resultant groups were matched on all key variables, with the exception of full-scale IQ which was higher in the control condition and thus was included as a covariate in the outcome analyses. The treatment group received 18 sessions of individual cognitive-behavioural anger treatment from qualified and chartered psychologists; six sessions of a preparatory and motivational nature, followed by 12 sessions of treatment proper based on an individual formulation of each participant's anger problems and needs, and following the classical cognitive-behavioural stages of cognitive preparation, skills acquisition, skills rehearsal, and then practice *in vivo*. The anger disposition, reactivity, and control measures used had been found to be reliable and valid in this population (Novaco & Taylor, 2004), and assessment points were at baseline/screen, pre-treatment, post-treatment, and four-month follow-up.

Scores on self-reported anger disposition and reactivity indices were significantly reduced following intervention in the treatment group compared with scores for the control group, and these differences were maintained at four-month follow-up. The effect sizes for these group × time interaction effects were medium–large. Staff ratings of study participants' anger disposition converged with patient self-reports but did not reach statistical significance. The proportion of participants whose scores improved pre-post treatment by equal to or more than one standard deviation of the treatment sample intake means was calculated for the self-report and staff-rated anger indices. Participants whose scores moved by this degree in the desired direction were consistently higher in the treatment than in the control condition, with rates for anger treatment group being double those for the control group on anger reactivity, anger expression, and staff-rated anger indices.

In order to explore whether treatment responsiveness was a function of IQ level (as suggested by Willner et al., 2002), groupings above and below an IQ median split (full-scale IQ = 69 for the hospital population) were examined for differences in anger measure change scores from pre- to post-treatment and from pre-treatment to follow-up. No significant differences were found in pre- to post-treatment change scores between those in the lower IQ range and those in the higher range. These results suggest that in this study there was no evidence that responsiveness to anger treatment was a function of IQ; in fact, participants in the lower IQ range were equally responsive to treatment, if not more so.

Notwithstanding the limitations of this study by Taylor et al. (in press), e.g., lack of statistical power, the confound of treatment as usual, treatment diffusion effects between treatment and control conditions, the results confirm the findings from earlier pilot studies with this population, and support outcome studies with different samples of clients with developmental disabilities. That is, people with developmental disabilities and significant anger problems associated with aggression can successfully engage in and benefit from cognitive-behavioural interventions focused on the anger emotion construct.

CONCLUSIONS

There appears to be very little evidence from the reviews that have been conducted for the effectiveness of psychoactive medications as first-line treatments in reducing aggression in people with developmental disability (Baumeister et al., 1998; Brylewski & Duggan, 1999; Matson et al., 2000). It would appear that the routine use of these compounds cannot be justified, given their lack of specificity and variable effects on individuals that can include dampening of adaptive behaviour and serious side-effects.

The evidence for cognitive-behavioural treatment approaches to aggression and anger problems with this client group is limited compared with the evidence for behavioural interventions (e.g. Lennox et al., 1988; Scotti et al., 1991). However, most of the studies of the impact of behavioural interventions have involved people with relatively high levels of developmental disability engaged with 'challenging behaviour' services, not high functioning users often referred to specialist community and forensic services (Whitaker, 2001). Also, whereas cognitive-behavioural approaches are aimed at the development of self-control and coping skills that can transfer across a range of dynamic settings, behavioural interventions tend to be situation-specific with regard to contingency management or antecedent control in particular environments. Further, it is clear that the application of relatively non-intrusive and more ethically acceptable behavioural interventions (e.g. non-contingent reinforcement, Carr et al., 2000) have not been proven outside of very controlled and unnatural settings with high staff ratios. Finally, it is questionable how effective these types of interventions can be with low frequency behaviour of the type found more often among higher functioning individuals and clients referred to forensic services. It is important therefore for clinicians and researchers in this area to continue to develop direct treatment approaches that are salient and relevant for anger and aggression problems in people with milder levels of developmental disability and those with forensic backgrounds – and to carry out more methodologically sound evaluations of their effectiveness with these client groups.

A number of commentators have suggested, based on the quite limited outcome research completed to date in this field, that it appears that people with developmental disability and anger problems benefit most from the non-cognitive components of treatment packages including relaxation, self-monitoring, and skills training through role-play (Rose, 1996; Rose et al., 2000; Willner et al., 2002). It has also been suggested that the lack of evidence for the effectiveness of the cognitive components of anger treatments is related to the complexity of these techniques and the difficulties that people with developmental disability have in understanding the cognitive re-structuring concept (Willner et al., 2002). However, many studies that claim to have incorporated cognitive techniques similar to those described by Novaco (1975, 1993) appear to have used cognitive skills training procedures such as self-instruction and inter-personal problem-solving that are aimed at ameliorating cognitive process deficits rather than identifying and modifying cognitive content (faulty beliefs, attributions, and judgements) associated with anger arousal (Beail, 2003). On this basis it is understandable that the available evidence appears to support the effectiveness of the behavioural treatment components that have been delivered in the majority of these group anger management courses.

In studies in which cognitive content techniques (e.g., identification of distorted cognitions, cognitive re-structuring, stress inoculation procedures) have been included as substantive components of the anger treatment, the notion that people with developmental disabilities find these procedures too difficult has been challenged (e.g. Lindsay et al., 2003, 2004; Taylor et al., 2002, in press). Based on the current evidence available it would seem premature, therefore, to downgrade or disregard cognitive procedures that have not been rigorously implemented and evaluated as part of treatment protocols with people with developmental disabilities and anger problems.

Novaco et al. (2000) differentiated between different levels of psychological intervention for anger problems. 'Anger management' provision can be characterized as planned and systematic psycho-educational approaches guided by cognitive-behavioural principles and often delivered in a group format. It is usually less intensive than 'anger treatment' that is driven by analysis and formulation of an individual's anger problems and treatment needs. Most of the studies carried out to date investigating cognitive-behavioural approaches with people with developmental disability and anger problems would fit into the 'anger management' category. The individual, formulation-based treatment protocol developed as part of the Northgate Anger Research Programme emphasizes the importance of cognitive procedures (alongside arousal reduction and skills training techniques) that aim to help modify distorted thoughts and beliefs so that the anger induced by a perceived provocation or threat can be managed effectively. This level of intervention is appropriate for people whose anger difficulties are often chronic, pervasive, and seemingly intractable. It requires the building of therapeutic relationships that can overcome client resistance to and fear of change. These characteristics are often observed in people with developmental disability referred to specialist challenging behaviour and forensic services who may have histories of offending or quasi offending-type behaviour.

6

ISSUES IN ANGER ASSESSMENT AND TREATMENT EVALUATION

INTRODUCTION

Identifying the clinically significant features of a person's anger can be perplexing, and it requires a differentiated assessment scheme. Always bearing in mind the normality of anger, as well as the importance of contextual conditions associated with its activation, designating anger as a problem condition is less than straightforward. There have been calls for a formal designation of 'anger disorders', but it would seem odd to pathologize an emotional state that has important energizing, informational, and potentiating functions and that is a fundamental survival mechanism with extensions to freedom representational symbolic structures. Thus far, advocates of formal diagnostic categories for anger (e.g., Eckhardt & Deffenbacher, 1995; Kassinove & Tafrate, 2003) have put not put forward empirical grounds for their proposition or a coherent nosology. Nor have they addressed potential issues regarding coercion and control associated with such formal diagnoses.

Given that anger is a normal human emotion, ascertaining whether a person's anger experiences and manifestations constitute a problem condition hinges on the defining parameters. Normal emotion is recognizably different from provocation-proneness, but the assessment task is more than merely tagging someone as having an anger problem. Anger assessment should demarcate problem severity and range, and identify the regulatory deficits that treatment might target. Doing this proficiently fundamentally requires engaging the client in the process, and, for persons having developmental disabilities, there are adaptations to be made to facilitate that. Our assessment-based research (Novaco & Taylor, 2004; Taylor, Novaco, Guinan et al., 2004) with patients having developmental disabilities has been successful in achieving reliable and valid measurements of anger that are sensitive to treatment effects.

The association of anger with aggression often provides grounds for treatment service referral, but some clients are referred for anger treatment inappropriately in conjunction with concern about violent or challenging behaviour. At the outset, one must resolve whether the person's problematic behaviour, violent or otherwise, is an anger-regulatory problem and whether the acquisition or augmentation of anger control coping skills would provide a remedy. Not all violent offenders are candidates for anger treatment interventions. Howells (1989) has cogently discussed the issue of suitability of clients for anger management

Anger Treatment for People with Developmental Disabilities by J. L. Taylor and R. W. Novaco. Copyright © 2005 John Wiley & Sons, Ltd.

interventions and provided case illustrations of congruities and incongruities. He stated that anger treatment is not indicated for those whose violent behaviour is not emotionally mediated, whose violent behaviour fits their short-term or long-term goal structure, or whose violence is anger-mediated but not acknowledged.

The conundrums in the calibration of anger problems are not just matters for the mental health professional presented with a referral. There are fundamental quandaries for the client to resolve as well. Anger is often misconceived as a cauldron of tumultuous forces that cannot be moderated and is largely irrational. As Averill (1982) brought to our attention, the classical view of emotion being that of a passion by which we are 'gripped', 'seized' or 'torn', which was quite prevalent among scholars prior to the eighteenth century. Anger is perhaps the prototype of this passion view. Viewing anger as a passion separates it from the intellect, sees only its disturbing qualities, and overemphasizes its association with aggression, by virtue of the intensity, turbulence, and irrational connotations of passion states. An elaboration of the pathology and passion view of anger and its fallacies can be found in Novaco and Welsh (1989).

For a great many clients, anger has come to be an automatic response, akin to the understanding of emotion as a passion that takes control of the personality. Anger reactions are thus subjectively experienced as being uncontrollable and inevitable. This can be unsettling for both clients and the human service professionals who seek to assess and treat them. Anger can easily be mistakenly equated to being out of control or being a bad person. This bears on the issue of reactivity as a threat to validity in anger assessment, which we will discuss in due course. The pertinent matter at this juncture is that, in the assessment of anger, client self-report is a central measurement procedure. This is so not only because anger is a subjective emotion, but also because the factors bearing on anger experiences and control must be uncovered from the client's cognitive processing and symbolic structures. Hence, how clients construe their anger is a pivotal point.

This chapter will address reliability and validity in anger assessment, present an overview of anger assessment instruments and their application to persons with developmental disabilities, and provide guidelines for a multi-modal approach. Assessment will be addressed from both the standpoint of problem identification and of treatment evaluation. At the outset, some general issues bearing on client reports and our understanding of anger will be discussed.

DILEMMAS IN DECIPHERING ANGER

Our ordinary language views of anger have a Janus-faced character in their duality of psychosocial images. The emotional state is depicted as eruptive, destructive, unbridled, savage, venomous, burning, and consuming, but also as energizing, empowering, justifying, signifying, rectifying, and relieving. The metaphors, on the one hand, connote something pressing for expression and utilization; alternatively, they imply something requiring containment and control.

Anger, especially when intense, has semantic ties to concepts of insanity. Becoming 'enraged' suggests being 'rabid', which connotes a diseased state of mind. *Being* angry, *becoming* mad, and *creating* Bedlam are semantically and metaphorically linked. Indeed, the eruption of anger in a syndrome of temporary insanity or even lasting psychosis is common enough in many cultures and is in fact highly systematized in cases of 'wild man' and 'amok' syndromes, as observed by anthropologists in Micronesia and other Pacific Island societies. The Western civilization parallel would be spree murder episodes.

The duality of psychosocial imagery reflects conflicting intuitions about anger, its expression, and its consequences that abound in ordinary language, as well as in scholarly literature and artistic works from the classical period to contemporary times. This mixed sense of anger, along with the semantic links to insanity, foils attempts to understand anger and to therapeutically intervene with recurrently angry individuals. Since the clinician assessing anger will inevitably be dependent on self-report, whether through psychometric instruments or by interview, the assessor should be mindful of these mixed intuitions and help the client feel comfortable with the assessment procedure. Our procedures for anger psychometric testing indeed involve adaptations of use by interview, with wording clarifications to improve understanding of key elements of test items and their intended subtleties.

The judgement of whether someone has an 'anger problem' depends on the consequences of the manifestation, the audience and affected parties, and the decision-making and socio-cultural contexts. Nevertheless, anger frequency, intensity, duration, and mode of expression – how often someone becomes angry, the degree of anger experienced, how long the arousal lasts, and how one behaves when angry – are dimensions by which a person's anger response patterns can be gauged in making judgements about problem status. Because information about anger reactions is very typically obtained from self-report, one must recognize two biases, *proximity* and *reactivity* that bear on how such reports about anger experiences are to be appraised.

Proximity bias

When people report anger experiences, they most typically give accounts of things that have 'happened to them'. For the most part, they describe events physically and temporary proximate to the anger arousal. As a rule, they provide accounts of provocations ascribed to events in the immediate situation of the anger experience. The provocation sources are ordinarily identified as the aversive behaviour of others, such as insults, unfair treatments, or deliberate thwartings. Anger is prototypically experienced as a justified response to some 'wrong' that has been done, portrayed in the telling as being something about which anger is quite fitting. Thus, anger accounts can be seen to have a 'proximity bias' (Novaco, 1993a).

Clinicians and researchers alike have been seduced to attend to anger incident accounts. Clinicians, of course, are pressed with the situational imperative of needing to listen to a client who wants to talk. Indeed, angry people want to be heard. Researchers, particularly when focused on finding main effects rather than higher order interactions, obtain anger self-reports based on daily diary data or classifications of open-ended descriptions, whereby respondents confine their account of the anger instigation to proximate situations. Assigning the causes of anger to discrete occurrences is uniformly the case in the community and student studies by Averill (1982), the autobiographical narrative studies by Baumeister, Stillwell, and Wotman (1990), and the college student questionnaire studies of Ben-Zur and Breznitz (1991) and Harris (1993). Recently, Kassinove, Sukhodolsky, Tsytsarev, and Solovyova (1997) applied this same discrete event, main effects conception in a cross-cultural study. With the exception of Averill, these diary and questionnaire studies were done without knowledge of Hall (1899) and studies in the decades thereafter reviewed in Chapter 1.

The response to the question, 'What makes you angry?' hinges on self-monitoring proficiencies and is often based on intuitions. Precisely because getting angry involves a loss in self-monitoring capacity, people are neither good nor objective observers when they are angry; and because anger is very much a blaming reaction, people are inclined to point. Inspecting any particular episode, the immediate 'causes' of the anger can be identified and ascribed to be the responsible factors. Because the anger is contiguous with situational stimuli that are aversive, it is viewed as being a product of them. People are inclined to attribute the causes of their anger to personal, stable, and controllable aspects of another person's behaviour.

Far less commonly do people disaggregate their anger experiences into multi-causal origins, some of which may originate from prior, remote events and ambient circumstances, rather than from acute, proximal events. Disturbances, which may or may not have involved anger at the outset, leave residues that linger but are not readily recognized. Of relevance here is Zillmann's concept of 'excitation transfer' discussed in Chapter 1. Also, people do not give attentional priority to prevailing contextual conditions, such as worries about residential accommodation, family problems, or job demands that operate as a backdrop for identified provocations. Chronically angry individuals are inclined to perceive malevolent intent in the behaviour of others. Uncovering the backdrop of a client's anger experiences requires probing for possible contextual determinants and supportive, patient listening.

A CBT approach should not be trapped in the head. To be sure, anger is cognitively determined, but anger reactions are primed, shaped, and extended as a function of inter-connected networks of provoking and inhibitory factors *embedded* or nested within overlapping physical and social environments, such as the care setting, the family, placement opportunities, the legal system, and the value structure of the health care system. Anger determinants, anger experiences, and anger sequelae are reciprocally influenced. In a coercive family system, parental anger arises during disciplinary confrontations as an effort to control a child's antagonistic behaviour. The parent's anger display not only can prompt further antagonistic behaviour from the child, but it also models anger as a response to being thwarted, thus reinforcing the coercive character of the milieu. Parental anger episodes that involve abusive behaviour towards the child produce trauma that can lead to anger and aggression problems. In a study with 110 male forensic patients with developmental disabilities, we found that patients' self-reported anger and their documented assaultiveness in hospital were significantly related to parental anger and aggression. That result was obtained in hierarchical regression analyses that controlled for age, IQ, length of stay, violent offence, physical and sexual abuse victimization, and parental and patient alcohol and drug abuse (Novaco & Taylor, 2003). The family environment is a primary context for acquiring anger-proneness, and it should be actively explored in interviews with clients when we seek to understand their anger schemas.

Reactivity bias

In many professional practice and research settings, anger assessment is subject to reactivity as a threat to internal validity. This is particularly the case in the forensic context, but it applies to any setting where the person may be sensitive to audience reaction to anger reports. Reactivity pertains to responses obtained in an assessment procedure that are reactions by the person to his or her inferences about the test situation, rather than to the explicit elements of the testing, i.e., the person is inclined to produce anger reports in anticipation of what those test responses will mean to some audience. People who are in forensic or other custodial settings will have a tendency to 'mask' their anger, as they are unlikely to perceive gain in disclosing it.

For example, in a study purporting to examine anger as a predictor of violent recidivism among Canadian criminal offenders, Loza and Loza-Fanous (1999) administered the *Spielberger State-Trait Anger Expression Inventory* (*STAXI*; Spielberger, 1996) and the *Novaco Anger Scale* (*NAS*; Novaco, 1994). Very low scores on the *STAXI* and *NAS* were reported (their means are 11.6 for *State Anger*, 15.1 for *Trait Anger*, 73.0 for the *NAS*, and 50.5 for the *Provocation Inventory* (*PI*; Novaco, 2003), averaging across the values given in their Table 1). Their means for the *STAXI State* and *Trait Anger* scales are close to the lowest possible score of 10 for each of those scales, which have an upper range of 40. Their *NAS* mean is more than one standard deviation below what we obtained with forensic hospital patients (Novaco & Taylor, 2004). Given the restricted range in their anger assessments, it is not surprising that anger was not found to predict violent recidivism.

There are multiple sources of reactivity bias in anger assessment. People who have long-standing anger difficulties are characteristically suspicious and distrustful, such being the products of troubled life histories. Whoever administers an assessment procedure inquiring about anger may be viewed as representative of a threatening system and thus receive guarded responses. Importantly, the psycho-social symbolism associated with anger (particularly its boiling/eruptive and savage/non-rational aspects) deter respondents from disclosing anger and the actions to which anger might dispose them. Moreover, anger can be a protected part of the person, centrally involving matters of self-worth, and is thus not readily revealed or surrendered. As a patient once commented in reflecting about life in an institution, 'All you've got is your anger.' Disclosing anger may be perceived to carry the psychological cost of losing power and, what may be for that person, the last remaining symbol of personal freedom and self-worth.

This has important implications for assessing anger in conjunction with evaluating the effectiveness of intervention. Because of both reactivity and treatment non-readiness, people having anger difficulties may under-report anger at the outset, thereby making it quite difficult to document treatment gain if an outcome assessment design is only pre-post and has limited measures.

We have discussed these limitations in people's accounts of anger experiences, so as to provide a backdrop for clinical judgement about anger problem severity based on client self-reports. To ascertain the appropriateness of CBT anger treatment, the parameters of frequency, intensity, duration, and mode of expression are briefly described below as useful dimensions (for a fuller account, see Novaco & Jarvis, 2002).

ANGER PARAMETERS

Anger frequency

How often people get angry surely varies culturally, but there is little data in this regard outside of North American samples. As we have discussed, the study of normative patterns of anger began with the research by G. Stanley Hall (1899) and was most extensively undertaken by Averill (1982). On the average in this research, people have reported becoming angry two or three times per week. The data reported in the study by Kassinove et al. (1997), which involved Russian (St Petersburg) and American (New York) participants, show a bi-modal distribution across samples, with 25% reporting anger occurring a few days a week and 33% less than once a week (but more than once a month). The Americans were significantly higher in anger frequency than the Russians, as reflected in 11% of the former reporting getting angry once a day or more, whereas this was the case for only 3% for the latter. Kassinove et al. found no gender differences in anger frequency, which is a common finding. Using the United States General Social Survey (Davis and Smith, 1996) for the question, 'On how many days in the past seven days have you felt angry at someone?' Novaco and Jarvis (2002) found that 63.4% of the sample report that they have become angry in the previous week, with 20.3% stating that they were angry on three or more days. No significant differences were found with regard to gender.

It would seem reasonable then to consider someone who reports becoming angry every day to be high in anger frequency, if these largely American data are a guide. But there are substantial cultural variations to be taken into account. Most generally, it would be safe to say that a client who reports getting angry two or three times a day can be considered high in anger frequency.

Anger intensity

Ratings of anger intensity are a typical feature of anger psychometrics, such as the STAXI (Spielberger, 1996) and the Provocation Inventory (*PI*; Novaco, 2003). It is assumed that higher intensity ratings are indicative of greater disturbance, because the ratings are summed across items. Indeed, the intensity dimension functions as a qualitative discrimination, because we partly judge that we are *angry*, as opposed to being 'upset', 'bothered', or 'annoyed' by virtue of the affect intensity. Unlike frequency, degree of intensity is much more clearly indicative of dysfunction, because physiological arousal is an intrinsic element. It is well established scientifically that high arousal disrupts performance, especially mental processes involved in complex tasks. In addition to having cognitive interference effects, high intensity anger leads to impulsive behaviour, as it over-rides inhibitory controls. People often judge their anger intensity from their behaviour in an anger episode, although this is more the case for men than for women (Frost & Averill, 1982). Kassinove et al. (1997) found no gender differences in anger intensity in either the American or Russian samples, as is the case in many studies. Novaco and Jarvis (2002) did find gender differences, with females reporting higher intensity.

Anger intensity is a very useful parameter for treatment outcome assessment. Adapting the PI for developmental disabilities patients, Taylor, Novaco, Gillmer et al. (2002) obtained significant changes in its anger intensity ratings for patients in an anger treatment condition, compared with those in routine care. Of the provocation categories on that instrument (disrespect, unfairness/injustice, frustration/interruption, annoying traits, and irritations), the highest pre-treatment anger intensity ratings occurred for provocations of unfairness/injustice. This is not surprising, given the unfortunate social exchange circumstances with which persons having developmental disabilities are beset. We also found that the anger treatment effect was strongest in that category.

Duration

For a number of reasons, intensity of anger can be expected to influence anger duration: (1) greater elevation in physiological arousal is associated with longer time for recovery to baseline; (2) circumstances that produce strong anger can escalate and extend as a product of angry behaviour; and (3) high anger results from matters having substantial significance for the person, which are likely to linger and not be resolved promptly; this leads to rumination about the provoking circumstances, which prolongs anger and can re-vivify it.

There is considerable inter-subjective variability in duration of anger episodes, both within and across studies. For example, early research by Gates (1926) and Meltzer (1933) found average durations of 15 to 20 minutes. Several studies in Averill's (1982) monograph found the median duration to be about one hour. In the Kassinove et al.'s (1997) study, 39% of the US sample and 53% of the Russian sample reported anger duration of 30 minutes or less. Curiously, 31% and 20% of the US and Russian samples, respectively, reported anger duration of a full day or more. Similarly, Averill (1982) had found a 25% rate of endorsement for anger duration of one day or more. When people report anger for such long periods, it cannot be interpreted straightforwardly, because it is doubtful that arousal and affect are present continuously throughout the interval. It is more likely that the basis for this duration estimate is that thoughts about the anger incident have re-surfaced throughout the day.

Rumination is a problematic feature of anger reactions. Novaco and Jarvis (2002) found in the US General Social Survey data that women were significantly more likely than men to remain thinking about the anger situation, although there were no differences between genders in the likelihood of giving thought to revenge. Anger duration can be expected to be reciprocally related to violent fantasies. In the study by Grisso et al. (2000) with over 1,100 psychiatric patients in the MacArthur violence risk project, imagined violence was strongly related to anger, indexed by the NAS (Novaco, 1994) Cognitive, Arousal, and Behavioral subscales, especially NAS Cognitive.

The prolongation of anger arousal has several problematic consequences. First, blood pressure is significantly affected by prolonged anger and its non-expression, and this is a substantial factor in essential hypertension, as we have discussed. Second, when anger arousal does not return to baseline, there are likely to be 'excitation transfer' effects, whereby the undissipated arousal adds to arousal activation from new sources and raises the probability of aggressive behaviour (Zillmann & Bryant, 1974). Third, rumination about anger incidents interferes with optimal functioning and lessens positive inputs that are fortifying to the self.

Mode of expression

The behavioural manifestation of anger is the feature having greatest societal import, as anger impels both verbal and physical aggression. Verbal aggression pertains to threatening, abusive, and derogatory statements, the common denominator of which is to produce distress in the target person. Physical aggression, which is overt behaviour intended to produce harm or damage, may be either directed at the provoking person or displaced to a substitute target. Anger can also motivate 'passive' aggression, which is harm-doing behaviour in a disguised form – pretended congeniality, deliberate interpersonal coldness, or neglect, with the intention of producing distress in the target person. In contrast to these harm-intended behaviours, anger may be expressed in constructively minded problem-solving behaviour or be given safe ventilation.

Aggressive behaviour generally has a low base rate, except in the home and in psychiatric and correctional institutions. Domestic violence is a pressing social problem, internationally. The 1996 British Crime Survey estimate for the total number of domestic violence incidents in 1995 was 6.6 million. However, the Home Office definition of domestic violence was broad and included emotional abuse. In the 2001 British Crime Survey (Walby & Allen, 2004), the estimate of total domestic violence incidents (non-sexual threats or force) was 12.9 million against women and 2.5 million against men. With domestic force as the criteria, the estimated number of incidents was 8.28 million for women and 2.24 million for men in the year prior to the interview. For women, the severe force incidents estimate was 4.3 million (Walby & Allen, 2004). In the USA, a survey jointly sponsored by the National Institute for Justice and the Centers for Disease Control found that 5.9 million physical assaults were perpetrated against women in the 12 months preceding the survey for a representative sample of 8,000 women (Tjaden & Thoennes, 1999). The majority of women (64%) who had been victimized by rape, physical assault, or stalking since the age of 18 experienced this at the hands of intimates. Similarly, the Criminal Statistics for England and Wales for 1997 show that 47% of the 224 female homicide victims were killed by partners, whereas only 8% of the 426 male homicide victims were killed by their partners.

It is well recognized that severe psychological adjustment difficulties, such as posttraumatic stress disorder and major depression, are a common consequence to abused women (e.g. Cascardi, O'Leary, Lawrence, & Schlee, 1995; Ham-Rowbottom, Gordon, Jarvis, & Novaco, in press). The detrimental effects on a child of witnessing violence between parents include traumatization and learning violent behaviour as a response to conflict, each of which have long-term consequences for a child's psychological adjustment and well-being, as can be seen in the meta-analysis by Kitzmann, Gaylord, Holt, & Kenny (2003), and the longitudinal studies by Ehrensaft et al. (2003) and Litrownik, Newton, Hunter, English, & Everson (2003). Pertinent to developmental disabilities, the impressive population study of 1,116 5-year-old twin pairs in England by Koenen, Moffitt, Caspi, Taylor, and Purcell (2003) showed that 'the negative effects of domestic violence on IQ (raw scores) increased in a dose-response relationship' (ibid., p. 302). That is, domestic violence suppressed IQ scores; and children who were exposed to high levels of domestic violence were on average 8 points lower than unexposed children. The review by Strickler (2001) provides a cogent discussion of the dynamics of family violence and developmental disabilities, identifying dimensions of risk and impairment and formulating implications for clinical practice and social policy.

While some have questioned the weight that should be given to anger in understanding the behaviour and treatment of batterers (Dobash, 2000), there is sufficient evidence that anger is involved in domestic violence (e.g., Dutton, Saunders, Starzomski, & Bartholomew, 1994; Dutton, Starzomski, & Ryan, 1996). Insufficient attention, however, has been given to anger sequelea that result from the trauma of domestic violence, although there is a modicum of studies in that regard (cf. Novaco & Jarvis, 2002).

In our Northgate Hospital research, we have found that exposure to parental anger and aggression is significantly related to the anger and assaultive behaviour of male forensic patients with developmental disabilities (Novaco & Taylor, 2003). In data obtained from 105 male patients, 51% reported that their parents fought with each other and 27% reported that their parents fought with other people; 82% reported that their parents got angry.

Physical abuse had occurred for 46% of our participants. Having had a history of physical abuse was strongly related to the person's anger level, as rated by the patient himself and by staff. It was also significantly related to the number of assaults by the patient in the hospital. Regarding the witnessing of parental anger and aggression, our more complex findings pertaining to patient anger were rather noteworthy. When we controlled for age, IQ, violence offence, parents' drug or alcohol abuse, patients' alcohol or drug abuse, and whether the patient had been physically abused, the exposure to parental anger and aggression was highly significant in accounting for the patient's anger (as measured by the *NAS* and *STAXI* scales described later in this chapter).

Such findings imply that therapeutic efforts to ameliorate problems of anger and aggression among persons with developmental disabilities ought to give attention to family background experiences that have shaped cognitive structures, arousal dispositions, and behaviour patterns in this clinical population. Trauma-related dyscontrol should also be an agenda in their clinical needs assessment. As Strickler asserted, 'individuals with mental retardation are frequently misdiagnosed with psychiatric or behavioural conditions because abuse issues are not explored' (2001, p. 469).

Among the clinical populations for which anger expression is a substantial problem are institutionalized psychiatric patients, who tend to have substantial histories of violent abuse exposure. For both forensic and civilly committed patients, recurrent anger has been found to be prevalent among 35% of California state hospital patients, replicated across years (Novaco, 1994, 1997). Those data, involving staff observational ratings for over 4,000 patients in each of six years, also show that female patients are significantly more angry and more assaultive in these long-term care hospital than are male patients, and patient self-report data are convergent. High assaultiveness for female patients has been found in a number of studies, including early studies with forensic patients by Fottrell (1980) in England and by Stokman and Heiber (1980) in New York and recent ones with civil commitment patients, such as Krakowski and Czobor (2004) in New York state hospitals. Examining staff injury data over a 10-year period at a short-term inpatient unit in California, Lam, McNeil, and Binder (2000) found that injuries to staff from patient violence were as likely to be caused by female patients as by male patients.

As discussed in Chapter 4 regarding our research with developmental disabilities forensic patients, we have found that the prevalence of physically assaultive behaviour post-admission was 46.5% for our sample of 129 male patients, comprising nearly all of the 137 on the hospital's census. More than a third of the hospital's male forensic population had carried out two or more physical assaults post-admission (Novaco & Taylor, 2004). As given later in this chapter, we have obtained substantial self-reported anger levels in NAS, PI, and STAXI assessments of male patients. The data regarding women reported in Chapter 11 by Alison Robertson show that these female patients are significantly higher than the males in STAXI Trait Anger scores, but across the rest of our STAXI, NAS, and PI assessments, the female patients do not differ significantly from the males.

ANGER AND GENDER

The question of potential gender differences arises partly because anger and aggression have been thought to be differentially socialized for males and females. The social distancing and social support interference effects of anger may have different consequences for men and women as a function of the support resources available to the individual. Anger experiences are likely to vary as a function of contextual and social network conditions. Importantly, anger responding varies with the degree of cultural acceptance for it, including the social rules that define its legitimacy.

The predominant conclusion stated in published studies has been that there is an absence of major differences in anger for gender. Curiously, some research reports that have claimed that there are no major differences have indeed found noteworthy differences, e.g., Frost and Averill (1982), Deffenbacher et al. (1996), and Kopper and Epperson (1996). This is too long a tale for our purposes here. Inspection of the literature on gender differences in anger and aggression does lead to the broad generalization that women do become as angry as men, but the style of anger expression will vary by gender, especially according to the context of the anger activation and its anticipated consequences. The context in which we find the respondent also matters.

Some selected studies serve as examples here. Harris (1993) examined differences in provocations to anger and found that females were more likely than males to become angered by verbal aggression or by insensitive/condescending behaviour, while males were more likely to be angered by behaviour causing harm and by physically aggressive females, and there were gender differences regarding various types of insults. The Kassinove et al. (1997) study in New York and St Petersburg, Russia, as noted earlier, found no gender differences in anger intensity; nor did they find differences in frequency of anger, attributions of intent, day of the week, time of day, or outcome of the episode. However, they did find significant gender differences in location of the anger incident, with males in both countries being more likely to be angered in a public place and females more likely to be angered at home. In parallel to this, women were more likely to be angered by someone they loved, while men were more likely to be angered by someone who was personally disconnected. Also, highly significant gender differences emerged for both nationalities with regard to desired behaviours and reported actions during the anger incident. Men reported more desire for and actual use of physically aggressive behaviour than did women, whereas women reported significantly greater desire for and actual use of verbally aggression behaviours, as well as complaining and resolution-seeking behaviours.

Reviewing studies in the psychosomatic medicine field with regard to potential gender differences in anger, Stoney and Engebretson concluded that 'the literature generally indicates that males and females experience similar levels of experiential anger' (1994, p. 221). Regarding the expression of anger/hostility, these authors stated that with respect to the 'communicative expression' of anger, males are generally found to be more inclined to inhibit the expression of anger relative to females and that females are more outwardly expressive of anger than are males. One might wonder whether such findings are a product of wobbly conceptual frameworks or study procedures, as anger is intrinsically experiential and anger expression is intrinsically communicative.

There is little contrary in the literature to the premise that *men are more physically aggressive than women*, whether angry or not. This is established in the extensive meta-analysis of experimental studies of human aggression by Bettencourt and Miller (1996). Their review is in accord with the prior review by Eagly and Steffen (1986), who had concluded that males are more likely to engage in 'aggressive expression', especially with regard to physical acts. These two reviews are also in accord that women are more likely to fear aggressive retaliation than are men. While Bettencourt and Miller seek to explain gender differences in aggression as partly due to differential appraisals of the danger of retaliation, they miss the elementary point that the difference on this dimension is linked to gender. More importantly, all discussion and interpretation of gender differences in aggression pertaining to the high science of laboratory research must come face to face with the extremely well-established and critical social reality that *approximately 90% of people arrested for all violent crimes are men*, and women account for only 10% of all arrestees for murder and non-negligent manslaughter (Reiss & Roth, 1993). Also, if one examines the traumatic death rate by homicide, decade after decade, the rate of death is three to four times greater for men than for women, regardless of race (cf. Reiss & Roth, 1993). To be sure, it is the case that family violence studies by Straus (e.g. Straus, 1995; Straus & Kantor, 1994), as well as the 2001 British Crime Survey (Walby & Allen, 2004), which have involved large sample surveys, have found women to have comparable rates of physical assault to their partners as men, but the partner assaults by females result in fewer injuries that require medical attention.

What can be said straightforwardly, though, is that there are grounds for asserting that women have anger experiences comparable to those of men, certainly from the standpoint of experienced intensity. Noteworthy findings from an Australian community study by Milovchevich, Howells, Drew, and Day (2001) point to gender role identification, rather than gender itself, as a differentiating factor in anger scores obtained by the STAXI. For both males and females, those having a masculine role identification had higher 'Trait Anger' scores, while those with a feminine role identification had higher 'Anger-In' scores.

Pertinent to clinically distressed clients, female psychiatric patients exhibit higher levels of anger and assaultive behaviour, particularly those in long-term care (Krakowski & Czobor, 2004; Novaco, 1997). Among persons in prison, Suter, Byrne, Byrne, Howells, and Day (2002) found that females scored significantly higher than did males on all STAXI and NAS subscales. Suter et al. conjectured that the higher anger for females was a product of higher levels of psychopathology and trauma. This will be elaborated on in Chapter 11.

There is no clear demarcation of findings across studies regarding gender differences in anger as an experienced emotion, in part because there is no agreed-upon set of parameters, procedures, and conditions of elicitation. As well, variability in observational conditions and characteristics of research participants quite predictably produces disparity in outcomes. To be sure, credence has been given to women's anger, both in the legitimization of their discontent with social inequality and in breaking the social stereotype that anger was a male province. In the latter regard, anger has become an equal opportunity product.

ANGER ASSESSMENT: PRINCIPLES, PROCEDURE, AND INSTRUMENTS

General psychometric principles: reliability and validity

Reliability refers to the reproducibility of test results for a given individual. It pertains to the consistency of observations under maximally similar conditions. It is essential to establish the reliability of a test before questions pertaining to validity can be usefully considered. Reliability sets limits on validity. If one cannot be reasonably assured of obtaining generally reproducible test results, then one cannot safely generalize information gained about the meaning of test results from one situation to another. However, one should bear in mind the points about reactivity in anger assessment, as a reliable test can produce inconsistent scores if the testing situation varies significantly, e.g., differences in privacy associated with the testing occasion or if an event personally important to the respondent occurs prior to the testing or is expected to follow the testing. Our research (Novaco & Taylor, 2004) has shown both internal consistency and test–retest reliability in anger assessments with developmental disabilities patients.

Validity pertains to the meaning of an assessment – its interpretation in a given way, for a given purpose, with a given group of individuals. A test is an operational form of a theoretical concept. To address validity questions, research examines whether a test measures what it purports to measure regarding the focal concept or theoretical term. Such evidence comes from the pattern of relationships among the scores within a test, as well as patterns of correlations between a test's scores and scores from other measures of both similar and differing constructs (construct validity). Anger measures should have high intercorrelations, and they should be significantly related to measures of aggression. As well, respondents scoring high on an anger test, compared to people scoring low, should be more likely to have acted aggressively in the past and to be more likely to be aggressive in the future. In our research at Northgate Hospital, we have found high convergent validity between anger measures and a significant relationship between anger and assaultive behaviour, as will be given in a later section below.

Psychometric testing procedure

To facilitate understanding of the anger assessment process, we provide a synopsis of the anger testing procedure that we have used (for fuller accounts, see Novaco & Taylor, 2004; and Taylor et al., in press). Our research at Northgate Hospital involved 129 male patients, who were mostly forensic. Patients were tested individually in private rooms, either alone with the testing assistant or with the assistant accompanied by a nurse escort, depending on patients' mental state and security status. The assistants introduced themselves and described the purpose of the anger assessment. After carefully checking that the patient understood, he was asked if he would complete a number of questionnaires about anger.

If the patient agreed to the assessment, he was told that he could stop or have a break at any time. For most patients, two or three sessions of up to one hour each were required to complete the anger assessments. Due to patients' literacy problems, the scales were read to everybody. Each patient was told that there were no right or wrong answers, that he could ask questions at any time, and that he should answer questions as carefully as he could. Following completion of the testing, patients were thanked for their co-operation, which they gave without payment, and were given the opportunity to ask further questions about the procedure and how the results would be fed into the hospital's routine case review system. Since several measures were being administered, the order was counterbalanced, to control for any sequencing bias.

Staff involvement in the assessment of patients' anger difficulties was arranged through the unit/ward managers and qualified 'named nurses'. Each member of staff who completed rating scales knew the patient well and had significant contact with him during the period covered by the measures. Completion and collation of staff ratings were organized and supervised by the project assistants, who had briefed nursing colleagues about them at the outset.

In addition to personal, demographic, and diagnostic data, assistants also obtained information from hospital records regarding the number and type of previous convictions and number of physical assaults on staff or other patients since admission. Further, information from routine clinical assessments administered during the first 12 weeks following admission was collated from psychology case notes, including the results of intellectual/cognitive functioning, literacy, and personality psychometrics. Intellectual/cognitive functioning was assessed using the Wechsler Adult Intelligence Scale–Revised UK version (WAIS-R UK). Literacy skills were assessed using the Wechsler Objective Reading Dimensions (WORD).

Anger measures and their modifications

To assess anger with respondents having developmental disabilities, we wanted to use anger measures with established reliability and validity. Therefore adaptations needed to be made in instrument content, as well as in the testing procedure. Test administration was done by interview, as noted above, and the modifications in the instruments are indicated below. Here we provide more details on the psychometric instrument modifications (STAXI, NAS, and PI) than we had space to describe in Novaco and Taylor (2004).[1]

SPIELBERGER STATE-TRAIT ANGER EXPRESSION INVENTORY (STAXI)

The STAXI (Spielberger, 1996) is perhaps the most widely used anger measure in clinical and research settings. It was originally designed to assess those components of anger associated with different personality variables and to measure the impact of anger components on a variety of medical conditions. The STAXI is made up of 44 items organized into scales that give measures of *State Anger*, *Trait Anger*, and *Anger Expression*. The *Anger Expression* scale has sub-scales of *Anger-in*, *Anger-out*, and *Anger Control*. The STAXI has had extensive development and validation with normal, forensic, and medical populations.

A modified version of the STAXI was used as part of this study. Each of the ten State Anger items was prefixed with the temporal anchor 'Right now', and six were modified by a brief elaboration of the key word – for example, 'furious' was elaborated by 'really angry; or in a rage'; 'irritated' was elaborated by 'bad tempered, annoyed, or cross'; 'breaking things' was elaborated by 'smashing stuff up.' Each of the ten Trait Anger items was modified by an elaboration of the key words – for example, 'quick tempered' was elaborated by 'short-tempered, have a short fuse, touchy'; 'fiery temper' was elaborated by 'lose it altogether, go ballistic'; 'fly off the handle' was elaborated by 'lose my temper quickly'. Each of the 24 Anger Expression items were prefixed with 'When I'm angry' as a contextual cue. In addition, nine of these items were altered in order to make the item meaning more explicit to a developmentally disabled patient group. For example, 'I strike out at whatever infuriates me' became 'When I'm angry – I hit out at whatever is making me furious'; 'I keep things in' was elaborated by 'keep things to myself'; 'I keep cool' was elaborated by 'keep calm; stay in control'. Finally, the labelling of two of the four scale points for the State Anger items was modified as follows: 'Not at all' (same), 'A little bit' (in place of 'Somewhat'), 'Quite a bit' (in place of 'Moderately so'), and 'Very much so' (same).

---

[1] The Northgate modifications of the NAS and PI are available from the test publisher, Western Psychological Services, Los Angeles (*www.wpspublish.com*).

NOVACO ANGER SCALE (NAS)

The NAS (Novaco, 1994, 2003) is a self-report instrument containing *Cognitive, Arousal,* and *Behavioral* subscales, which comprise a *Total* score for anger disposition. The subscales relate to the three dispositional domains that are central to the view of anger described by Novaco (1994), as linked to an environmental context. The NAS was developed and validated for use with mentally disordered as well as normal populations. Since its inception, it has received independent validation (Grisso et al., 2000; Jones, Thomas-Peter, & Trout, 1999; McNeil et al., 2003; Mills, Kroner, & Forth, 1998; Monahan et al., 2001). The NAS was subsequently revised (Novaco, 2003) to include an *Anger Regulation* subscale and also to replace four items in the *Cognitive* domain subscale. The full NAS thus contains 60 items rated on three-point scales, including 48 items comprising the NAS Total score, plus the 12-item *Anger Regulation* scale. The NAS Total was found to have internal reliability (alpha) of .95 and a test–retest (two-weeks) reliability of .84 in studies with psychiatric patients in the California state hospital system (Novaco, 1994). In the Mills et al. (1998) study with male offenders in Canada, the alpha for the NAS Total was found to be .95 and test–retest reliability was .89 for a four-week interval.

The NAS was modified for use with developmentally disabled patients for the Northgate project. Of the 48 items comprising the NAS Total, 27 were modified. Of these, 17 were re-worded for clarity or to simplify meaning. Many of these involved a substitution for one word – for example, 'Every week I meet someone I dislike' was changed to 'Every week I meet someone I don't like'; or, the word 'yells' was changed to 'shout', 'muscles' was changed to 'body'. Some entailed slight modifications for simplification of wording, e.g., 'If I don't like someone, it doesn't bother me to hurt their feelings' was changed to 'When I don't like someone, I don't care if I hurt their feelings'; 'When I start to argue with someone, I don't stop until they do' was changed to 'When I argue with someone, I keep going until they stop'. Five of the 17 items involved larger modifications, e.g., 'people act like they are being honest when they really have something to hide' was changed to 'people pretend they are telling the truth, when they are really telling lies'; 'When I get mad at someone, I give them the silent treatment' was changed to 'When I get really angry with someone, I stop talking to them'. Additionally, 12 items were elaborated to make the meaning more concrete and accessible, e.g., 'Once something has made me angry, I keep thinking about it' was elaborated by 'for example, if someone has wound you up, does it stay in your head and you keep going over it'; 'Some people would say I'm a hothead' was elaborated by 'You lose your temper all of a sudden.'

PROVOCATION INVENTORY (PI)

The *PI* is an anger reaction inventory that was developed to accompany the NAS. It is a shortened version of the Novaco Provocation Inventory (Novaco, 1975, 1988) and was first implemented as NAS Part B, but it is now a separate instrument. The PI consists of 25 items providing an index of anger intensity and generality across a range of potentially provocative situations. Research with California state hospital patients found an alpha of .95 and test–retest reliability of .86 (Novaco, 1994). The PI has been independently validated (as NAS Part B) in the studies by Grisso et al. (2000) and Mills et al. (1998). In the latter study with male offenders, the alpha was .96 and the test–retest reliability was .85.

For use in our research, 17 of the 25 items were modified (a) to make the item meaning more accessible; and (b) to increase the relevance of the items to patients living in highly supervised forensic environments. Modifications for two items involved one-word substitutions. Fifteen items were modified with elaborations – e.g., 'Seeing someone bully another person who is smaller or less powerful' was elaborated by 'somebody small is being picked on by somebody big'; 'People who think they are always right' was elaborated by 'someone who thinks they are never wrong'; 'Being singled out for correction, when someone else doing the same thing is ignored' was elaborated by adding, 'for example, everyone in your unit does something silly, but you are the only person who is told-off'.

AGGRESSION QUESTIONNAIRE (AQ)

Another valuable and well-validated self-report measure pertinent to anger assessment is the Buss–Perry Aggression Questionnaire (Buss & Perry, 1992; Buss & Warren, 2000). The first version of this measure was the Buss–Durkee Hostility Inventory (*BDHI*; Buss and Durkee, 1957), but they did not report data from clinical samples; however, Buss (1961) did provide scores from two psychiatric hospitals samples in his book, the landmark volume in the field of human aggression discussed in Chapter 2. Like the original BDHI, the AQ is primarily a hostility and aggression measure, but this newer scale does have a set of seven items that Buss and Perry (1992) designated as anger items. That was established by factor analysis, with the four factors being physical aggression, verbal aggression, anger, and hostility. There have been a number of studies published on the AQ with clinical and with offender samples, including Williams, Boyd, Cascardi, and Poythress (1996), whose factor analysis produced only two factors, 'physical aggression/anger' and 'verbal aggression/hostility'. They also used the NAS in a confirmatory analysis, finding that the first AQ factor correlated most strongly with the NAS Behavioral domain, and the second AQ factor correlated most strongly with the NAS Cognitive domain. The AQ factors had similar correlations with NAS Arousal. Other studies have found empirical linkages between the AQ and anger (e.g., Felsten & Hill, 1999; Morren & Meesters, 2002). As it does identify core dimensions of anger and aggression and its association with problematic behaviour is well established, the *AQ* should be considered as a valuable assessment tool.

OTHER ASSESSMENT INSTRUMENTS

There are many other psychometric instruments that have been constructed for the assessment of anger, hostility, and aggression. Two recent reviews provide valuable coverage. Eckhardt, Norlander, and Deffenbacher's (2004) review gives attention to the range of anger and hostility self-report scales, and a review by Suris et al. (2004) provides coverage of aggressive behaviour measures. The latter article has anger and hostility scale overlap, and its coverage is more overview than analytical; however, it does provide an extensive catalogue of measures and their psychometric properties. One scale not covered in these reviews is the Anger Management Scale by Stith and Hamby (2002), which concerns intimate partner relationships, but these authors do not provide clinical sample data.

Our utilization of the NAS and STAXI measures, as we have indicated, has involved adaptations for developmental disabilities. In addition to these patient self-report measures, which is a crucial mode of anger assessment, we also used a staff-rated measure of anger.

For this measure, a ward staff member who functioned as the patient's 'named nurse' did the ratings.

WARD ANGER RATING SCALE (WARS)

The *WARS* is a two-part scale to be completed by a member of ward staff who knows the patient well and has observed the patient's behaviour during the previous week. It was developed by Novaco (1994) in conjunction with NAS validation testing and is designed for ease of recording in busy clinical settings. Part A consists of 18 dichotomous ratings regarding verbal and physical behaviours associated with anger and aggression. Part B of the instrument consists of seven items regarding 'anger attributes' rated on a five-point scale (not at all, very little, sometimes, fairly often, very often).[2]

Five of the WARS Part A items are summed for an 'antagonistic behavior' index, which concerns overt verbal and physical aggression directed at another person. The items included are 'verbally abused someone', 'verbally threatened to attack a staff member', 'verbally threatened to attack a patient', 'physically attacked a staff member', and 'physically attacked a patient'. The sum of the seven WARS Part B anger attribute ratings produce an Anger index. In a study involving mentally disordered offenders at the maximum security State Hospital in Scotland, the inter-rater reliability (calculated as percentage agreement) for Part A of the WARS was found to be 94.7% and was between 89.7% and 100% for the five items comprising the antagonistic behaviour index (Novaco & Renwick, 2003).

OTHER STAFF-RATED MEASURES

There are a number of staff-rated measures of aggressive behaviour for use in residential settings, which can be found catalogued in Suris et al. (2004). For the most part, these measures attend to aggressive behaviour, to the exclusion or minimization of anger. Even the Patel and Hope (1992) 'Rage' scale gives diminished weight to anger, involving only 3 of its 21 items. Perhaps the best-known staff rating scale is the Staff Observation Aggression Scale (SOAS) by Palmstierna and Wistedt (1987), which has been revised and validated as the SOAS-R (Nijman et al. 1999) to incorporate an improved scoring system, especially with regard to severity. Nijman and Palmstierna (2002) demonstrated further validation of the new measure's severity scoring.

Reliability of anger measures with developmental disabilities patients

The study by Novaco and Taylor (2004) provided the first systematic investigation of anger assessment with persons having developmental disabilities. The psychometric properties of anger assessment devices with this population were unknown. Our clinically focused research led to the selection of the STAXI and the NAS. The internal consistency coefficients (alphas) for the STAXI scales obtained in our research findings were .87 for State Anger,

---

[2] The WARS is published (with permission from its author, Raymond W. Novaco) as an appendix to a published paper by Taylor, DuQueno and Novaco (2004).

.86 for Trait Anger, .92 for NAS Total, and .92 for the PI. For the staff-rated WARS Anger Index, the internal consistency was .95. The results demonstrated high internal reliability for the measures. For a subsample of 44 patients, we also conducted test–retest reliability analyses, which varied over an internal of two to six months. The intra-class correlations obtained were .02 for State Anger, .52 for Trait Anger, .57 for Anger Expression, .52 for NAS Total, and .57 for the PI. Given that the patients were receiving treatment in the hospital during this interval, the results demonstrate good stability for the measures.

Concurrent and predictive validity with developmental disabilities patients

We found a pattern of strong intercorrelations between the anger measures, which were indicative of concurrent validity. For example, Trait Anger is correlated above .70 with each NAS index, except Cognitive (.47). Anger Expression is correlated .78 with NAS Total; among the Anger Expression subscales, Anger-Out is correlated .73 with NAS Behavioral.

Predictive validity was assessed retrospectively, examining patient assaultiveness in the hospital as predicted by patient-rated anger. Controlling for age, length of stay, IQ, violent offence, and Eysenck Personality Questionnaire measures, we found that NAS Total was significantly predictive ($p = .003$) of whether the patient had been physically assaultive in the hospital and the total number of physical assaults. Thus, persons with developmental disabilities will report anger that is predictive of the assaultive behaviour in the hospital. Despite their developmental disabilities, they can tell you about their anger and, in doing so, provide information that is of high clinical and managerial significance.

Comparison with other populations

Benson and Ivins (1992) speculated that developmentally disabled clients might have a social desirability response bias in self-reporting anger or may lack awareness of angry feelings, thereby suppressing anger scores. Those in our research do not appear to be affected in these ways. The anger scores that we obtained for our participants with the STAXI, NAS, and PI measures were generally comparable to those for persons without developmental disability and to patients in other forensic and general psychiatric hospitals. For example, the STAXI State Anger and Trait Anger means of 11.6 and 18.8 are very close to the adult norms of 11.3 and 18.7 for those scales (Spielberger, 1996) and to means of 11.8 and 18.0 on those scales obtained for 119 male forensic patients at the high security hospital in Scotland (Renwick & Novaco, unpublished data). However, the STAXI Anger Expression mean of 30.8 is substantially higher than the adult norm of 19.4 (Spielberger, 1996) and is also higher than the mean of 25.1 for the male patients at Scotland's high security hospital.

The NAS Total and PI means of 92.5 and 62.9 are quite comparable to the means of 90.1 and 65.3 found for California state hospital patients (Novaco, 1994) and the means of 90.2 and 66.0 for civilly committed males at hospital baseline in three US metropolitan areas reported by Grisso et al. (2000) in the 'no imagined violence' category; but they are higher than the means of 82.5 and 56.6 found for the Scotland State Hospital patients, which are in turn comparable to the values found for male offenders in Millhaven Institution, Canada (Mills et al., 1998). While the PI mean is very comparable to the norms ($M = 63.7$, $SD = 14.8$)

for 1,546 normal adolescents and adults in NAS-PI standardization sample (Novaco, 2003), the NAS Total mean is significantly higher than the norms ($M = 83.9, SD = 15.6$).

Since the modified instruments have not yet been demonstrated to be equivalent to the instruments in their original form, we refrain from making any further comparisons across samples in other studies. What we wish to note is that, in our experience and obtained results, the patients who participated in our assessment procedures did not seem to be guarded in disclosure of their anger on these procedurally modified psychometric instruments.

Imaginal Provocation Test (IPT)

Anger psychometric scales are generally 'nomothetic' in nature and are best suited to detecting mean changes following intervention for groups of clients with reference to normative data, rather than highlighting clinically significant changes for individuals. The IPT[3] was designed as an alternative 'idiographic' anger assessment procedure for people with developmental disabilities that is easy to administer, has systematic measurement indices, taps key elements of the experience and expression of anger (emotional reaction, behavioural reactions, and anger control), is sensitive to change associated with anger treatment, and is easily modifiable for idiographic uses. The imaginal provocation procedure (Novaco, 1975) hypothetically has distinct value, because it is easily exportable for use in a variety of settings, has minimal logistical requirements, and the content of the imaginal scenes can be tailored to the modal types of anger-inducing events for a client group or ultimately to the particular circumstances of an individual client's anger control problem.

Taylor, Novaco, Guinan et al. (2004) generated four parallel forms of an IPT that were found to have equal anger-inducing potential for male forensic in-patients, as judged by direct-care nursing staff. The IPT generates four indices relevant to an individual client's experience of anger: (1) the first index concerns the degree of anger actually experienced in imagining the scene and is called 'anger reaction'; (2) the second index concerns subjective estimates of antagonistic 'behavioural reactions' to the provoking situation had it indeed happened; (3) the anger reaction and behavioural reaction index scores are combined to form an 'anger reactions composite' index; and (4) the final index involves ratings of anticipated 'anger regulation'. Analysis following administration of pairs of IPT forms to 48 patients prior to beginning anger treatment showed that the IPT indices had respectable internal reliabilities (Cronabach alpha) of between .70 and .80. The magnitude of the intercorrelations (Pearson) computed for the non-composite IPT indices suggests that they are tapping separate aspects of the anger construct. The concurrent validity of the IPT was examined through the correlation of its indices with the STAXI, NAS, and PI. Overall, the pattern of correlations obtained provided very solid confirmation of concurrent validity for the IPT indices. Having established that the IPT successfully induces anger and that the indices have internal reliability and concurrent validity, Taylor, Novaco, Guinan et al. (2004) then examined whether this procedure for assessing anger is sensitive to change associated with anger treatment. The IPT indices were used as criterion measures in a small controlled trial in which nine male forensic in-patients received the anger treatment protocol developed as part of this programme, and matched controls received treatment as usual. Compared with the control group, the treatment group improved significantly following treatment on the IPT anger reaction, behavioural reactions, and anger composite indices.

---

[3] The IPT can be found as an appendix to Taylor, Novaco, Guinan et al. (2004).

The results of these empirical examinations of the IPT strongly suggest that it has value as a rapid, flexible and idiographic assessment of anger among people with developmental disabilities living in secure and semi-secure settings. Our results indicate that the IPT procedure successfully induces anger, that its indices have internal reliability and concurrent validity with established anger psychometric scales, and that it is sensitive to clinical change in treatment.

ASSESSMENT SCHEME FOR ANGER TREATMENT

At the time of segue to treatment, the therapist should have collated anger assessment data to construct a formulation of the client's anger regulatory problem and the treatment targets. That information should be derived from multiple sources and modes of assessment: (1) clinical interview with the client, significant others, and clinical team or case workers; (2) self-report psychometric scales, such as the NAS-PI, STAXI, and also anger diary recordings, for which there are various formats (see use of 'anger logs' in the anger treatment protocol described in Chapters 8 and 9); (3) behavioural observation ratings, which can be provided by ward staff, such as the Ward Anger Rating Scale (Novaco, 1994; Novaco & Renwick, 2003; Taylor, DuQueno & Novaco, 2004); (4) coding of case files and incident reports (e.g. Novaco & Taylor, 2004); and (5) structured provocation testing, which can be done via imaginal provocation procedures (cf. Novaco, 1975; Taylor, Novaco, Guinan et al., 2004).

General guidelines for anger assessment

For a meaningful assessment of anger, some general principles should be kept in mind:

1 Anger is an *abstract construct* that has many concrete or observable referents and many ways of being measured, none of which constitute a 'pure' index of anger. Accuracy of assessment, therefore, is enhanced by the use of various measurement procedures, seeking convergence or triangulation across different types of measures.

2 Assessment should be conducted with multiple measures and different time points. Because of the reactive nature of anger and fluctuating contextual conditions, it is best to assess anger at different points in time, just as one would want to obtain blood pressure measurement at different times and locations.

3 The timing and test situation in which the anger measures are obtained should be selected with care. Attention should be given to minimizing contextual factors that are likely to induce reactivity and impair the validity of the results obtained. For example, if a person believes that reporting high levels of anger will result in undesirable consequences (such as disapproval, negative reports, loss of privileges, or increased detention), it is then very likely that the level of anger reported will be correspondingly attenuated.

4 High scores on self-report measures of anger are generally less ambiguous than low scores. High scores are those that are one standard deviation above the mean for the specific population. There are many circumstances in which a person might want to report a lower level of anger than is valid for them, but there are few circumstances in which a person would want to report a higher level of anger than is true.

5 Assessment scores for a particular person are most meaningful in relation to the mean for a comparable population and to that person's previous scores.

7

DEVELOPMENT, DELIVERY AND MAINTENANCE OF A COGNITIVE-BEHAVIOURAL ANGER TREATMENT PROTOCOL FOR PEOPLE WITH DEVELOPMENTAL DISABILITIES

BACKGROUND

An Anger Treatment Project was established in the male forensic services at Northgate Hospital, part of a specialist disability NHS Trust in the North-East of England in 1999. The great majority of clients in this service have offending or quasi-offending histories. That is, they have been convicted of carrying out particular offences, or they have well-documented histories of behaviours that for a variety of reasons have not been processed through the criminal justice system, but have placed the individual at risk of becoming a convicted offender.

The major offence categories for this population at Northgate Hospital were, in descending order of frequency, sex offences, violent offences and fire-setting offences. Many clients had convictions or documented histories of behaviour in more than one of these categories. In addition to these offence types, a considerable number of patients have convictions for, or histories of, property-related offences including theft, burglary, criminal damage, and car crime.

Given the forensic backgrounds of this population, the Trust's psychology services had been working over some considerable time to design, develop, and implement offence-specific assessment and intervention programmes aimed at reducing the risk of future offending behaviour and thereby facilitating rehabilitation of clients from in-patient hospital services to community-based facilities. Based on the 'what works' meta-analysis literature concerning recidivism rates for offenders, sex offender, and fire-setter treatment programmes had been developed and implemented with reference to number of key principles (see McGuire, 1995; McGuire, 2002; Skett, 1995). These principles indicated that programmes should be:

Anger Treatment for People with Developmental Disabilities by J. L. Taylor and R. W. Novaco.
Copyright © 2005 John Wiley & Sons, Ltd.

- cognitive-behavioural in nature, multi-faceted in terms of the problem areas targeted and orientated towards skills development;
- responsive to the learning needs, styles and preferences of both clients and therapists;
- focused on the criminogenic aspects of the clients presenting problems that are proximal, rather than distal to offending behaviour(s);
- sensitive to the level of risk presented by clients by increasing the therapeutic 'dosage' proportionately for those judged to be higher risk in terms of recidivism, and;
- attentive to issues of programme integrity by reducing or eliminating 'therapeutic drift', treatment gain reversal and non-compliance with regard to the delivery of programmes by therapists.

It has been estimated that, based on the evidence available for non-developmentally disabled (mainly adolescent) offenders, interventions incorporating these principles and delivered in community settings are likely to be more effective than those that do not, and could reduce recidivism rates by between 12% (McGuire, 1995) and 24% (Skett, 1995).

The issue of programme integrity is thought to be pivotal in delivering successful interventions. Hollin (1995) set out some guidelines to avoid threats to integrity. Suggested ways of safeguarding integrity include:

1 implementation of interventions based on sound theoretical frameworks that have empirical evidence to support them;
2 ensuring that therapists implementing the interventions are well trained in both theory and delivery aspects;
3 use of manuals and protocols to guide the delivery of interventions;
4 provision of clinical and organizational support for therapists, including supervision and access to other resources;
5 the involvement of independent assessors to evaluate the quality and outcomes of the interventions.

Having successfully developed programmes for sexual aggression and fire-setting problems with these principles and issues in mind, attention was turned to anger and aggression in this in-patient population. In addition to the criminogenic/forensic reasons for this, other factors played a part. As well as being closely associated with aggression, anger is known to be a feature of a range of psychological conditions including mood, impulse control, personality and post-traumatic stress disorders (Novaco, 1986; Novaco & Taylor, in press) and has been linked with impaired cardiovascular function and poor general health (see Chapter 1). It was anticipated, therefore, that by helping clients with their anger problems, their general psychological and physical well-being would be improved and they could be more amenable to, and have additional resources to cope with, the demands of offence-specific treatments.

Another reason for giving clinical attention to problems of anger dyscontrol was that many clients were willing to discuss temper control problems early in their rehabilitation, compared with, for example, sexual aggression. Therefore, by beginning with a problem that had salience for the client and was relatively unthreatening, therapeutic relationships and trust could be built that would facilitate more offence-focused work at a later stage.

The Anger Treatment Project involved a range of service development, therapeutic and staff training activities, in addition to evaluative research, concerned with the anger problems experienced by clients in the service. In this context the Project can be viewed as a logical extension of the range of forensic programmes provided by the service. The planning for the development of this project coincided with the NHS publication of *A First Class Service: Quality in the New NHS* (Department of Health, 1998) which set out the government's quality agenda for the NHS. In particular, it describes the importance of gathering evidence for the effectiveness of treatments in order to safeguard and raise standards of care. For this, as well other reasons linked to good practice, it was decided that this clinical service development should take place within a research and development framework. Hence an anger research programme was planned.

The first goal of this programme was to investigate the nature, scope and client needs in relation to anger control problems in the index population. The results of this study linked to this goal are described in detail in Chapter 6 and are reported in a published paper by Novaco and Taylor (2004). The second aim of the research effort was to evaluate the effectiveness of a cognitive-behavioural anger treatment procedure developed specifically for this population using a controlled outcome study design. The method, design, and results of this outcome study are reported by Taylor et al. (in press), but the development of the treatment protocol and issues pertinent to it successful delivery are expanded upon below.

ANGER TREATMENT DEVELOPMENT AND DELIVERY

Anger treatment protocol

The treatment was guided by a new manual, designed specifically for use with people with mild-borderline and moderate intellectual disabilities. This new treatment is based on the cognitive-behavioural approach developed by Novaco (1975, 1993b). Treatment was delivered to individual clients by the same therapist over 18 sessions in a designated therapy room close to or in the client's residential unit. In general, actual treatment sessions involved the therapist and client only. An 18-session treatment package was decided upon for a number of reasons. This approximated the average amount of therapy delivered to participants in the published anger treatment studies involving people with developmental disability (see Table 5.2, Chapter 5). Eighteen one-hour sessions appeared to be about the right amount of time required to deliver the revised and modified content of Novaco's (1993b) most recent anger treatment manual. Finally, this amount of therapy, delivered according to the schedule set out below, had worked well and had been positively received by a small number of clients in a pre-study pilot. The primary clinical focus of each of the 18 sessions of anger treatment making up the protocol is described in Table 7.1.

Due to the security status of some clients, in a few cases a member of the ward nursing staff escorted the client to and from the session and sat outside the therapy room, out of line-sight of the client, during the session. In most cases the client was 'collected' from and returned to their residential unit by the therapist before and following their treatment session.

Whenever possible, treatment was delivered at the rate of two sessions each week, and there was a minimum of one session per week. Previous experience of using psychotherapeutic approaches with this client group suggested that a more intensive treatment schedule would help to overcome fluctuations in individuals' motivation to change by maintaining

Table 7.1   Primary focus of preparatory and treatment phase sessions of anger treatment

	Preparatory phase session focus		Treatment phase session focus
Session 1	Explaining the purpose of anger treatment	Session 7	Introduction to the Treatment Phase sessions
Session 2	Feeling angry is OK – anger as a normal emotion	Session 8	Building an anger hierarchy
Session 3	Understanding our own and other people's feelings	Session 9	Introduction to stress inoculation
		Session 10	Beginning cognitive re-structuring
Session 4	How to control the physical feelings of anger – physiological arousal	Session 11	Developing cognitive re-structuring
		Session 12	Perspective-taking and role-playing
Session 5	Reasons for changing the way we cope with angry feelings	Session 13	Using self-instructions effectively
Session 6	Review of the Preparatory Phase and preview of Treatment Phase	Session 14	Problem-solving through effective communication
		Session 15	Development of problem-solving through effective communication
		Session 16	Dealing with rumination and escalation
		Session 17	Integration of skills and dealing with repeated provocation
		Session 18	Review and evaluation of anger treatment phase

Note: All sessions are guided by a detailed manual, delivered by qualified therapists to individual clients. Each session is of approximately 1 hour duration. Feedback is provided routinely to direct care staff at the end of the each session concerning the client's presentation and progress within the session, and any homework that is to be completed between sessions.

momentum and preventing therapeutic drift. In addition, it was estimated that a higher therapeutic dosage would ameliorate some of the anticipated difficulties with assimilation and recall of information exchanged during the treatment sessions.

Although the treatment sessions routinely involved the therapist and client only, the client's keyworker nurse or a deputy was involved whenever possible at the end of each session to discuss the client's progress and (home) work to be completed between sessions. For example, from the second session onwards the clients were encouraged to complete daily anger logs to record the nature, frequency, duration, and intensity of any angry incidents that occurred. These anger logs were completed, whenever possible, with assistance and support from the client's keyworker nurse or a deputy in order to promote a collaborative approach to treatment through open discussion, shared problem-solving, and mutual reflection concerning anger-provoking incidents.

Engagement and preparation of clients for anger treatment

The special challenges, for both therapists and clients, that anger treatment interventions present has been noted (DiGuiseppe, Tafrate, & Eckhardt, 1994; Novaco, 1995; Novaco & Welsh, 1989). These difficulties are often related to the inherent threat such clients present, their impatience and impulsiveness, and the positive functions and reinforcement that their anger often holds which causes it to be deeply embedded and difficult for them to release. These, and other issues, can create significant difficulties in establishing therapeutic alliances, helping clients to see anger as a legitimate treatment target, and motivating clients to contemplate change with respect to their anger-related difficulties. In addition to these characteristics, many of the participants in the current programme have life histories characterized by trauma and repeated experiences of failure and rejection across a range of health and social care settings.

Ward, Day, Howells, and Birgden (2004) have provided a helpful multifactor model with which to consider the state of 'readiness' of offenders to engage in rehabilitation programmes. This model usefully re-conceptualizes previous notions of treatment-resistant, refractory, and challenging clients in terms of the presence of characteristics within either the client, the therapy, or the therapeutic situation that are likely to promote engagement in therapy. In considering anger treatment specifically, Howells and Day (2003) propose that readiness for therapy is affected by an array of obstacles: the complexity of cases presenting with anger problems, institutional settings, client inferences about their problem, mandatory treatment, the client's personal goals, cultural differences, and gender differences bearing on responsivity to provided programmes. The analysis by Howells and Day is helpful, particularly as it removes the onus of the problem from the dispositional status of the client.

Anger *treatment* is targeted at the modification of cognitive structures that maintain anger, enhancement of self-monitoring, and the development of self-control strategies through the therapeutically guided graded exposure to provocation. It is based on a detailed analysis and formulation of a client's anger problems and requires delivery by trained therapists on an individual basis. Novaco et al. (2000) differentiated this level of intervention from anger *management* approaches that are less intensive, not driven by individual analysis and formulation, and generally involve psycho-educational approaches guided by cognitive-behavioural principles delivered in a group therapy format (see Chapter 2). Anger treatment is recommended for clients with chronic and deep-rooted anger problems that disrupt their interpersonal functioning and psychological and physical well-being. The intensive individualized approach developed as part of this programme was intended to overcome clients' anxieties about change and resistance to engagement in the therapeutic process. Offenders with developmental disabilities can often exhibit such characteristics and the newly developed protocol described in Chapters 8 and 9 was designed specifically for use with this client group.

The personal histories of many of the participants in this programme involved physical, emotional, and sexual abuse, as well as repeated failures across health and social care settings, resulting in perceived rejection by important others and loss of close relationships. Add in impaired intellectual functioning and associated limited psychological/emotional resources, and the scale of the task involved in successfully engaging these clients in anger treatment becomes apparent. Thus, engagement in trusting therapeutic relationships is difficult for these clients (Taylor, Novaco, Gillmer et al., 2004). The need for an introductory phase prior to treatment beginning in earnest for this client group, in order to develop the skills and confidence required to successfully engage in and benefit from anger treatment, and to judge whether the individual can cope with the treatment, was discussed by Black et al. (1997). A similar preparatory phase of treatment was implemented to good effect by Renwick et al. (1997) in the treatment of chronic anger problems in four mentally disordered offenders in a high security hospital setting in Scotland.

For these reasons, and following on from the work of Black et al. (1997), Howells and Day (2003), and Renwick et al. (1997), a broadly psycho-educational 'preparatory phase' of anger treatment was offered which highlighted the normality of anger as a human emotion, but gently introduced the personal costs associated with recurrent maladaptive anger responses. This seems to help psychologically fragile participants form therapeutic relationships and become motivated to maintain them. This stage of treatment enabled participants to gradually engage in the therapy process without feeling threatened.

Given the vulnerability and previous experiences of the programme participants, a cautious and conservative approach to seeking clients' consent was adopted that involved two stages. As well as being ethical, it was considered that this approach would be helpful in engaging clients in what would hopefully become a collaborative therapy process. Before commencing the preparatory phase of treatment, clients were interviewed by the therapist and their named nurse together. They were provided with written information concerning the nature of the research and treatment, confidentiality issues, and their rights to decline involvement without prejudice to their future care and treatment. Each of these areas was discussed with the client and they were told that if they consented to take part in the six-session preparatory phase, they would be asked if they wanted to continue or opt out before the treatment phase began. The named nurse arranged to speak to the client again within 36 hours, answer any questions they might have and seek their written consent. Written consent was sought again following completion of the preparatory phase as, given the educational aspect of this work, it was felt that at this point any consent given would be better informed. Clients retained their own copies of signed consent forms and information leaflets for reference.

Anger treatment protocol delivery and procedure

Detailed session-by-session guidance on the delivery of the anger treatment protocol developed as part of this programme is provided in Chapters 8 and 9. In this section the overall purpose, aims, and goals of the distinctive but sequential preparatory and treatment phases of the 18-session intervention are described. Novaco and Taylor (in press) used a case study to illustrate aspects of this cognitive-behavioural anger treatment procedure. This case example involved Tim, a 25-year-old man with a history of sexual aggression against male and female children. Tim's measured IQ placed him in the mild–borderline range of intellectual disability. He had attended mainstream school until he was 10 years old, after which he was transferred to a special needs school because of his learning difficulties. Tim was reported to have been aggressive and violent from the time he was a young teenager. Following his admission to the low secure area of the specialist forensic service some six years before he started anger treatment, Tim had challenged the service in many ways including numerous absconsions, sexual aggression towards male and female patients, and frequent aggression and violence towards other clients. We will refer to Tim's progress in anger treatment as various elements of the treatment procedure are described below.

PREPARATORY PHASE

In this new treatment manual the preparatory phase comprised six sessions aimed at desensitizing clients to anxieties that they might have about embarking on intensive psychological therapy. The goals of this phase of treatment were:

1 to give the client information on the nature and purpose of anger treatment;
2 to develop some basic skills needed for successful treatment including self-disclosure, emotional awareness, self-monitoring and recording, and basic relaxation techniques;
3 to foster trust and confidence in the therapist and the therapeutic process;
4 to emphasize the collaborative nature of the treatment that is aimed primarily at helping the client achieve better self-control.

A further important goal of this phase of treatment is to encourage motivation to change current unhelpful anger coping responses by identifying the costs of this behaviour. Session 5 of the preparatory phase of anger treatment aims to explore with the client the costs and benefits of anger and aggression, both in the short and longer term. It is designed to help the client to understand that the benefits of developing self-control over anger and aggression outweigh those gained by continuing to be angry and aggressive. A 'decision matrix' exercise is used to facilitate this. In this exercise, our case example Tim referred to a situation that he had recently recorded in his anger logs. This involved a friend (fellow patient) questioning his sexuality. This had made Tim feel angry and he had shouted and swore at his friend and, as a result, ward staff had admonished him. Tim was asked to think about the immediate benefits of being aggressive in this situation. He explained that by reacting in this way 'I got the anger out of my system . . . stopped my mate from taking the mick out of me . . . and showed to the others [patients] that I'm not a soft touch.'

Despite the immediate benefits of becoming aggressive in response to the angry feelings he experienced in this situation, Tim was unable to identify any long-term advantages of behaving in this way. He was, however, able to list many short- and long-term disadvantages of being angry and aggressive. Short-term consequences included getting into trouble with ward staff, losing points on the ward incentive scheme, falling out with his friend, and the possibility of the situation escalating and him and/or his friend getting hurt. In Tim's mind the longer-term problems associated with this style of responding were getting a bad reputation, letting people down (family, friends and staff), feeling ashamed, and losing the trust and concern of carers. Using a worksheet depicting a set of scales, Tim readily weighed the costs of continuing to be aggressive against the costs of attempting to learn to respond to his anger in a calmer and more constructive manner.

This preparatory phase had the added benefit of improving clients' understanding of the treatment process so that they could give more informed consent before moving in to the next phase of treatment.

TREATMENT PHASE

On successful completion of the preparatory phase, and if they renewed their consent to treatment, clients proceeded to the 12-session 'treatment phase', the core components of which are cognitive re-structuring, arousal reduction, and behavioural skills training. These map onto the key domains of the cognitive model of anger proposed by Novaco (1994) and are achieved by building on the therapeutic relationship and skills developed during the preparatory phase. The techniques and procedures utilized in the treatment phase include:

1 more advanced self-monitoring and recording of anger frequency, intensity, duration, and triggers;
2 a detailed analysis and formulation of the individual's anger problems;
3 construction of a personal anger provocation hierarchy from anger log records and recollection of earlier angry situations;
4 cognitive re-structuring by shifting attentional focus, modifying appraisals and challenging expectations;
5 developing arousal reduction techniques including abbreviated progressive muscular relaxation, breathing-focused relaxation and cognitive distraction using calming imagery;
6 training problem-solving approaches through effective communication using role-play rehearsal;
7 development of personalized self-instructions to prompt coping; and
8 use of the stress inoculation approach to practise effective coping while visualizing and role-playing increasingly anger-provoking scenes from the anger hierarchies.

The key components of the treatment including cognitive re-structuring, arousal reduction and behavioural skills training built during therapy in a logical step-wise manner through the classical cognitive preparation, skills acquisition, and skills rehearsal/practice stages so that towards the end of the 18 sessions they are incorporated into practice *in vitro*, and if possible *in vivo*, as a sequential but integrated and comprehensive approach to coping effectively with anger problems.

The treatment protocol developed as part of this programme is considered to be different to approaches described previously in the developmental disability anger treatment literature (see Chapter 5) in two distinct and important ways. First, the treatment is based on an individual analysis of the client's anger problems, from which a formulation is derived that guides the treatment phase of the intervention. During the first two or three sessions of the treatment phase, clients are encouraged to work on an *external events* × *internal processes* × *behavioural responses* analysis of their anger problems in order to reach a shared formulation of their difficulties. Using material from completed anger logs, situations he had described in developing his personal anger hierarchy, and his profile of scores on self-rated Novaco Anger Scale (NAS; Novaco, 2003) and Provocation Inventory (PI; Novaco, 2003) anger measures, Tim and his therapist reached a shared view of the key problems for him in controlling his anger and priorities for treatment. These were organized within a simplified linear cognitive model of anger framework (see Chapter 8, Session 1).

The *situations* that Tim was most sensitive to and likely to react most angrily to included those in which he was accused of doing things he hadn't (unfairness/injustice). The types of *thoughts* that most characterized Tim's cognitive responses to such situations were 'I want to hit him . . . I should hit him . . . he deserves it' (justification) and these thoughts 'go round and round in my head' (rumination). The *feelings* that accompanied this type of situation were typically very strong (intensity) and stayed with Tim for a prolonged period of time (duration). His *behavioural reactions* in these circumstances were typically to swear and shout (verbal aggression) or to grab the other person and threaten him (impulsive confrontation). It was agreed with Tim that in the treatment sessions these areas would be focused on using cognitive re-structuring, arousal reduction, and behavioural skills training approaches.

Second, the treatment protocol has cognitive re-appraisal at its core, along with arousal reduction and skills training (Taylor, Novaco, Gillmer et al., 2004). Therefore, taking into account the intellectual limitations of participants, a description of how this aspect of treatment is covered in the protocol is justified. The putative role of cognitions in the experience of anger is given attention right from the start in Session 1 as part of the presentation of a simplified model of 'How Anger Works'. How cognitions are associated with emotion and behaviour is addressed in detail in Session 3. A detailed exercise considering how thinking differently about events can affect our feelings and reactions is worked through using an example from an anger log completed by the client as homework from Session 2. The work on cognitions is reviewed in the final preparatory phase, Session 6. The role of cognitions in anger is re-introduced during the first anger treatment phase Session 7 as a review of the How Anger Works model. 'Thought catching' as a means of increasing awareness of self-talk is a component part of Session 8 and this is linked to the 'internal processes' aspect of an analysis/formulation of the individual client's anger problems. Thought catching is integrated into anger logs completed as homework at this point. Work on thought catching is developed in Session 9 and is used as the basis of a formal cognitive re-structuring exercise in Session 10 using material collected by clients in their anger logs. These cognitive re-structuring exercises are continued as a formal part of each session from this point on and are developed to incorporate training on cognitive awareness and skills including attentional focus and appraisal processes, perspective-taking, and rumination.

The following excerpt from Session 10 with Tim illustrates how clients are encouraged to try to think differently about anger provocation by, for example, putting themselves in the shoes of the person they were angry with. It shows how this process can begin to work for clients who have had difficulty in the past with disconnecting the threat perception that drives their hostile and aggressive thinking and behavioural styles.

Therapist: Right Tim, tell me what happened in this situation you wrote about in your anger log.

Tim: Well, there was a mix-up about what time my drama session finished. I came back to the ward earlier than I should have 'cause the session finished early. The staff said I was lying.

T: OK. And what were you thinking about when this happened? What thoughts were going through your mind?

Tim: I'm thinking to myself 'I did nothing wrong. Why me? It's always me that gets into bother – no one else. They're always picking on me.'

T: Right. And how were you feeling at this time?

Tim: Raging. I'm furious.

T: Out of ten, how much would you say?

Tim: Ten out of ten!

T: And how were you feeling physically – in your body?

Tim: All tensed up and shaky. Sweaty. Me arms and neck were all tense.

T: Out of ten?

Tim: I'd say seven.

T: And what did you do?

Tim: Ha – I shouted and swore at 'em. Told them to 'eff off'. I argued with them and threatened to make a complaint.

T: So how well do you think you handled this situation?

Tim: Really bad. Not good at all.

T: OK, then, Tim, let's think about how you might have handled this differently. Let's say you're in exactly the same situation. You come back to the ward early because a session has finished early. The staff are suspicious about why you have come back when you shouldn't have. They are asking you why you aren't at your session when you should be. Just the same as what happened to you here. OK?

Tim. Yes.

T: Right. So straight away you start thinking these angry thoughts. Like 'I've done nothing wrong. They're picking on me. It's not fair.' That sort of thing.

Tim: Right.

T: But instead of thinking those thoughts which make you angry straight away, can you think of any other reasons why staff might have behaved like they did?

Tim: Umm.

T: Well, try to put yourself in their shoes – see the situation from their point of view.

Tim: Er, OK . . . .?

T: If you were a member of staff and a patient turns up on the ward when they should be in a session, what are you going to be thinking?

Tim: Yeah, right – well, for one thing I'd be saying to myself 'This guy's maybe trying it on – he shouldn't be leaving sessions early.'

T: OK, well, that sounds possible. Can you think of other any other reasons why staff might be concerned?

Tim: Well, it's their job to be worried about where patients are, isn't it? It's to do with security. You can't have patients just coming and going at all times.

T: So, if you are thinking like that, how are you feeling in this situation?

Tim: I'd be less angry – say five out of ten.

T: And what about your body?

Tim: Oh, I think it wouldn't be as tensed up. Less shaky. Maybe two out of ten.

T: Do you think you would have behaved in a different way?

Tim: I think so.

T: How?

Tim: Maybe I wouldn't have flew off the handle. I'd have tried to explain to the staff what happened with the class finishing early. Calm like.

[During this dialogue the therapist has been using a worksheet with graphics to record two lines: what actually happened (actual), and then what could have happened (possible).]

Therapist: So, if you look at what actually happened, and then look at what might have happened, you had exactly the same situation to begin with, but very different endings. What do you think made the difference?

Tim: Well, maybe thinking about it in a different way helped. Not thinking straight off that they were trying to get me.

Source: Reproduced from Novaco & Taylor (forthcoming) Cognitive-behavioural anger treatment. In Carr & McNulty (Eds), *Handbook of Adult Psychology: An Evidence Based Practice Approach*. London: Brunner-Routledge. Reproduced by permission of Taylor & Francis, Ltd.

This cognitive re-appraisal work is a component part of each session from this point forward. In this way thinking about situations differently is integrated into the behavioural skills repertoire through the stress inoculation imaginal practice procedure, role-play in sessions. From Session 12 onwards clients are asked to do this exercise for themselves, between sessions, each time they record an incident in their anger log so that 'thinking differently' moves temporally closer to actual incidents and is less abstract. Thus, work on the role of cognitions and cognitive processes in anger, and the training of cognitive re-structuring techniques to alter unhelpful cognitions associated with anger problems, is infused in this treatment approach and has equal status with and is given the same amount of attention as arousal reduction and behavioural skills training procedures.

Accommodating individual differences

The manualized treatment is intended to provide a framework within which the therapists and clients can flexibly apply the therapeutic techniques described to meet the needs of individual clients. However, the treatment by nature is collaborative and interactive, and it should, therefore, be applied in a manner that reflects these dynamics. There will be variations in the focus, pace, and emphasis of the therapy delivered by different therapists working with different clients depending on the analysis and formulation of their anger problems. In this way, while the treatment is described in a manual, it is intended to provide a framework within which therapists can flexibly apply the therapeutic techniques described to meet the needs of individual clients. In this sense a clear distinction is made between 'protocol-guided' and 'protocol-driven' treatments. The latter tend to be applied rigidly, are not reflexive to the needs of clients, and do not lead to good outcomes when administered by experienced therapists (see Chapter 10).

Therapists and treatment integrity

In the treatment outcome study the therapy was delivered by four therapists, all of whom were trained and highly experienced clinical and forensic psychologists. To facilitate the integrity of the treatment protocol the therapists met weekly for peer supervision sessions. During these sessions the delivery of the protocol and any deviation from it were discussed, agreed, and noted. At the end of each treatment session therapists were also required to complete a report on the session, including an account of what content from the treatment manual had been covered in the session. This report was then filed with the treatment study research assistant who collated therapist and client session ratings. The principal investigator carried out regular random reviews of therapists' anger treatment files, including session reports and clinical notes, to check on treatment adherence and therapist competence throughout the study period.

The author of the original treatment protocol (RWN) made quarterly on-site visits to provide training through workshops and seminars, clinical supervision, and support to the therapists and to monitor the procedural progress of the treatment project. While these procedures fall short of what might be considered to be a systematic quality assurance system for ensuring treatment integrity (Nezu, 2001), they represented a compromise in attempting to attenuate this internal validity issue. An 'ideal' in monitoring manual adherence and facilitating therapists' supervision, would have involved video or audiotape recording of treatment sessions, a random sample of which would have been reviewed independently.

Since the completion of the treatment outcome study, the anger intervention has become a routine treatment offered within a programmatic framework to clients who might benefit from it. Within this framework peer supervision and protocol adherence checks are carried out. In addition, significant numbers of non-qualified graduate psychologists (assistant psychologists and trainee clinical psychologists) have delivered the protocol under the close supervision of qualified chartered psychologists. Analysis of the outcomes for those clients treated by qualified ($n = 43$) and non-qualified ($n = 27$) psychologists indicate that, with sufficient training, supervision and service support systems, non-qualified personnel can achieve significant treatment gains with anger treatment clients using this protocol. However, it strongly recommended that non-qualified psychologists administer this protocol *only* under the close supervision of appropriately qualified colleagues, and that they stick closely to the guidelines for sessions set out in the manual.

ANGER TREATMENT EVALUATION

The evaluation of the new anger treatment protocol has been described in detail in a series of concatenated and controlled studies (Taylor, Novaco, Guinan et al., 2004; Taylor et al., 2002; Taylor et al., in press) and a case study report (Novaco & Taylor, in press). The main outcome study report can be found in Taylor et al. (in press). However, a summary of this study is provided below.

As it was considered unethical to withhold a potentially effective treatment from those who might benefit from it, a delayed wait-list control design was used in the main study of effectiveness of the new anger treatment protocol. Participants who met the study inclusion criteria were allocated to anger treatment (AT), or routine care (RC) conditions from an anonymized list by a research assistant psychologist. The therapists available for the study could administer the individual anger treatment to a maximum of ten participants at any one time. Therefore, the AT group comprised two sequential cohorts of ten participants. These cohorts provided the treatment ($n = 10$) and comparison ($n = 10$) groups in a pilot study reporting on the impact of anger treatment on a single self-rated anger provocation inventory (Taylor et al., 2002). An important internal validity issue in the current study was whether the two AT group cohorts were sufficiently alike in composition and responses to treatment to be constituted as a single group for comparison with the RC group. Thus, before combining the data from these pilot study treatment cohorts to form a combined AT condition in the main outcome study, potential differences between the cohorts on a range of key variables were examined. No differences were found with regard to the two AT group cohorts in terms of key demographic, clinical, and forensic history characteristics, responses to treatment, or other changes experienced during the treatment period.

Treatment effects were evaluated using analyses of covariance (ANCOVAs) with anger scores as the dependent variables, time of assessment (screen, pre- and post-treatment, and four-month follow-up) as the within-subjects factor and treatment condition (AT versus RC) as the between-subjects factor. Several features of the study design were aimed at maximizing statistical power. These included use of multiple repeated measures, focused contrasts (in the present study, linear trend analysis) and reliable measuring instruments (Hallahan & Rosenthal, 1996). All participants continued to receive treatment as usual.

Blind assessment could not be achieved in this study due to resource limitations. To attenuate this problem, client evaluations were conducted by research assistant psychologists rather than by the therapists themselves.

The participants were administered several criterion anger measures at baseline screening, immediately pre-treatment, following completion of treatment and at four-months follow-up. To measure anger disposition the Novaco Anger Scale (NAS; Novaco, 2003) and the Anger Expression (AX) scale of the Spielberger State-Trait Anger Expression Inventory (STAXI; Spielberger, 1996) were used. The NAS assesses cognitive, arousal and behavioural aspects of anger. The Provocation Inventory (PI; Novaco, 2003) was used to measure anger reactivity across a range of potentially anger-provoking situations. The Anger-Control subscale of the AX was used as an index of participants' capacity to regulate their anger. The NAS, AX and PI are self-report measures and all were modified for use with clients with intellectual disabilities and were administered in the form of structured interviews. The order of presentation of these measures was randomized across participants. The informant-rated Ward Anger Rating Scale (WARS; Novaco, 1994) was completed by a member of the nursing team who knew the client well. The client's behaviour during the previous seven days was rated on scales relating to seven affective-behavioural anger attributes. These ratings are summed to yield an 'Anger Index'.

Novaco and Taylor (2004) investigated the reliability and validity for the modified self- and staff-rated anger measures used in the current study (see Chapter 6). They found that for an inpatient population of offenders with intellectual disabilities, the internal consistency coefficients for the NAS Total, PI Total and WARS Anger Index were good. The Novaco and Taylor study also provided evidence for the concurrent, discriminant and retrospective validity of these modified scales.

The results of the treatment evaluation study showed that the AT group improved significantly following treatment compared with the RC group on measures of anger disposition (NAS) and anger reactivity (the unfairness/injustice scale of the PI), and these improvements were maintained at four-months follow-up. The AT group's score on the STAXI anger control measure just failed to be significantly improved compared to the RC group, but effect sizes for this difference, along with those for the above indices were in the medium–large range. Staff-rated WARS Anger Index scores were not significantly different for the AT and RC groups, although the means on this measure changed in the predicted directions.

In addition to these statistical analyses, the results indicated that in terms of treatment responsiveness, the proportion of participants whose scores improved pre-post treatment by equal to or more than one standard deviation of the treatment sample intake means was consistently higher in the AT than in the RC condition, with rates for AT group being double those for RC on PI Total, STAXI AX and WARS Anger Index. Further, only two of the 20 AT group participants did not complete the treatment, both for reasons clearly not connected with the treatment process. This suggests that the protocol was acceptable to clients with significant anger problems and relatively few psychological resources who often had had difficulty in engaging with rehabilitation programmes in the past. There was also evidence for 'spill-over' or diffusion of treatment programme effects. It seems possible that direct care staff involvement in the treatment project may have led to positive changes in the way that they responded to clients' anger problems, including those of clients in the RC group waiting to enter treatment. In addition, it seems likely that at least some participants in the AT group may have transmitted some of their knowledge and skills to others living in the same clinical areas awaiting treatment. It is also possible that the AT group participants, in receiving the specialized treatment and learning how to cope more effectively with angry situations, became less antagonistic on their residential wards and thereby lowered general levels of hostility in the enclosed living environments that they shared with RC group participants. Thus, it is possible that the treatment approach had an effect at a systemic, as well as at an individual client level.

There are a number of methodological and design limitations to main outcome evaluation study. These include the confound of treatment as usual, diffusion of the treatment group experiences of therapy affecting control group participants, lack of blind evaluation and limited treatment fidelity checks, and low participant numbers reducing the statistical power available to detect treatment effects. However, the results obtained point to the potential benefits of this approach for individual clients receiving the treatment, in terms of anger disposition, reactivity and control, and for the system (staff and organization) supporting these clients and the therapy. Furthermore, the approach appears to be acceptable to clients as an adjunctive treatment, and was successful in engaging them in remedial work aimed at increasing psychological resources and improving the basic skills required to benefit from other types of psychological therapies, e.g., offence-related interventions.

ANGER TREATMENT MAINTENANCE

The notion that psychological interventions alone can produce permanent changes in behaviour and attitudes has long been questioned, and the idea that follow-up or 'booster' sessions can help maintain treatment gains has been advocated for some considerable time (e.g., Eysenck, 1963). There is some evidence available to support the view that maintenance strategies can help in sustaining treatment gains achieved through the implementation of behavioural and cognitive-behavioural interventions. In a comprehensive review of the literature over an 18-year period, Whisman (1990) identified 30 clinical trials of the impact of maintenance sessions on behaviour therapy interventions for a range of clinical problems including alcoholism, smoking, weight loss, headache and depression. From the 26 studies in his review that evaluated the added value of booster/maintenance sessions to standard treatments, Whisman concluded that maintenance sessions significantly enhanced outcomes in 58% of the studies. On the other hand, it seemed that in a number of studies, maintenance sessions served only to delay the onset of relapse. That is, they maintained treatment gains for only as long as they were continued.

In the context of his review, Whisman highlighted a number of difficulties in evaluating the effectiveness of maintenance strategies. Specific process issues identified in the reviewed studies included: (1) the lack of information about, and thus evidence for, particular schedules of maintenance/booster sessions; (2) the lack of information about, and thus evidence regarding, the content of booster sessions; and (3) little attempt to examine the mechanism(s) for change in booster maintenance sessions. Whisman concluded that future studies with improved methodology, particularly in terms of increased statistical power, might usefully identify factors associated with the change process and indicate the optimum content and schedule of delivery of booster sessions to enhance maintenance of treatment-induced behaviour change.

P.H. Wilson (1996) overviewed developments in the area of treatment maintenance following cognitive-behavioural interventions for selected psychological disorders including problem drinking, smoking, obesity, and depression. Wilson suggests that in addition to questions about which strategies are helpful in reducing relapse following successful interventions, there are other important issues concerning how relapse is defined, the natural course (rate) of relapse following particular types of interventions for certain problems, and the causes of relapse.

In his overview, P.H. Wilson distinguishes research on the effectiveness of relapse prevention techniques in the treatment of addictive behaviours (e.g. alcohol abuse, smoking, over-eating) and mood disorders, primarily depression. While the effectiveness of cognitive-behavioural therapy in the treatment of depression is now well established, the relapse rates following successful intervention are reported by P.H. Wilson to be in the region of 20–30% over a 1–2-year period. The value of booster sessions to maintain gains following cognitive-behavioural treatment for depression was not demonstrated in studies by Baker and Wilson (1985) and Kavanagh and Wilson (1989) that compared booster with control groups. However, in a study by Blackburn and Moore (1997) involving patients with major recurring depressions, participants maintained using cognitive-behavioural therapy were significantly less likely to relapse than those maintained on medication.

The framework adopted by P.H. Wilson (1996) in his overview was the 'relapse prevention' model (Marlatt & Gordon, 1985), which is underpinned by social learning theory principles and the self-efficacy concept (Bandura, 1977). The relapse prevention approach was originally developed by Marlatt and Gordon (1985) within the addictive behaviours field and comprises distinct elements including awareness and identification of risks for relapse, coping skills practice and rehearsal, relapse/lapse counselling, and positive lifestyle changes. This approach is distinguished from simply adding booster sessions on to the end of standard treatments in that relapse prevention techniques are a specific and integrated part of the treatment from the outset. That is, relapse prevention approaches have as a central aim of treatment not just the relief of symptoms associated with a disorder, but the development of relapse prevention strategies. In this way clients are prepared for any lapses/relapses in advance of their occurrence through the application of cognitive-behavioural techniques including recognition of and attention to negative cognitions (appraisals and expectations) and environmental cues, self-monitoring, production risk hierarchies, and rehearsal of coping skills in simulated high risk situations.

It can be seen that the integrated approach to preventing relapse developed by Marlatt and Gordon (1985) has many similarities to the cognitive-behavioural anger treatment approach of Novaco (1975, 1993b), further developed for use with developmental disabilities in this programme. The anger treatment protocol described in Chapters 8 and 9 involves development of the awareness of situations and cognitions that are likely to evoke anger responses in individuals, self-monitoring through the use of anger logs, elicitation of an anger hierarchy, and the development of skills to cope with anger hierarchy situations through graded exposure in imagination using a stress inoculation procedure, followed by practice using role-play.

Towards the end of the 18-session treatment protocol, clients work with the therapist, and with supporters outside of the treatment sessions if appropriate, to develop a 'personal reminder sheet' that sets out, in the client's own words, the anger situations he or she is most sensitive to, self-instructions to remain calm in such situations, problem-solving strategies, and an 'escape route' if required (see Chapter 9, Sessions 17 and 18). In the case of our case example, Tim's personal reminder sheet looked like this:

1. *The types of anger situations I am sensitive to are those that involve:*
   (a) People slagging-off my family/girlfriend (Disrespect).
   (b) Me being accused of doing something I didn't do (Unfair).
   (c) Me having to live with 17 other people in a small place with all the noise and fighting (Agitation).
2. *In these types of situations I must try to keep calm and in control by telling myself to:*
   (a) Take deep breaths.
   (b) Tell myself to stay calm and relax.
   (c) Think nice thoughts (calming picture of being on holiday with my family).
   (d) Put myself in the other person's shoes – try to see things through their eyes.
3. *Once I am sure that I am calm and in control, I should try to sort the problem out by doing the following:*
   (a) Think about the situation in a calm way.
   (b) Try to be clear about how I'm going to try to sort things out.
   (c) Be honest about my feelings.
   (d) Try to talk to the person in a reasonable way.
   (e) Give and take so nobody feels they are losing out.
4. *If I can't get calm and in control, or if the other person is getting more angry and aggressive, then I should try the following things:*
   (a) Avoid aggravation/confrontation if possible.
   (b) Walk away and calm myself down – let the other person cool off.
   (c) Discuss things with staff if they are around.

These individual personal reminder sheets form the basis for an anger maintenance programme that is discussed and agreed between the therapist, the client, and their named nurse. Depending on the needs of the individual, their preferences, and the resources available in terms of support, a maintenance plan is drawn up that specifies the frequency with which the client is to meet with their named nurse (or deputy) and/or their therapist for routine maintenance sessions and reviews of progress. It will also set out what should be routinely covered in these sessions. Typically the content of maintenance sessions will include: (1) review and discussion of patient's anger logs that might be completed daily or less frequently by agreement; (2) cognitive re-framing of situations (from anger logs) that appear to have been misinterpreted; (3) rehearsal of awareness, self-instructional and behavioural coping strategies as set down in the client's personal reminder sheet; and (4) either prompts to use arousal reduction techniques regularly, or practice of abbreviated relaxation exercises in the session. Using this general approach, clients are not simply going over material covered in the standard treatment sessions, but are building on the techniques acquired by drawing on here-and-now events in order to consolidate the skills learnt in treatment. This hopefully increases the client's confidence in their ability to cope with provocation and thus increases self-efficacy. Whisman (1990) pointed out other mechanism(s) by which maintenance strategies might have an impact including reducing the client's fear of failure by staying in contact with the therapist, and the extension of the stimulus control of the therapy procedures into the client's everyday environment.

In addition to being unsure about the mechanism(s) by which maintenance approaches might work, we are not yet clear to what extent implementation of anger maintenance programmes has an impact on maintaining treatment gains or reducing the rate of relapse.

Part of the problem with this is that once anger treatment therapists withdraw from individual clients' cases into a review/advisory role, maintenance programmes are frequently not implemented by direct care staff. To date, 70 patients have completed treatment through the Northgate Anger Treatment Project, and 47 of these treatment completers remain in hospital. The mean length of time since completing anger treatment for this hospital sub-group is 2.7 years (range: 2 months–4.5 years). A recent audit showed that just under 25% (11) of these 47 patients were receiving anger treatment maintenance sessions, although just one of this group is recorded as having declined this input.

There is limited evidence from other patient populations and problem types that people who have received cognitive-behavioural interventions continue to improve once standard treatment is finished (e.g. Barrowclough et al., 2001; Kuipers et al., 1997; Oosterban et al., 2001) and there is some indication that maintenance of gains is associated with continued practice of cognitive-behavioural strategies (Westbrook & Hill, 1998). Therefore, while we continue to consider that, on balance, it is probably important to implement maintenance strategies for people with developmental disabilities who have received anger treatment, the processes to ensure that this occurs more consistently require more development, and further research is needed to evaluate the impact of this phase of intervention on anger treatment gains and the mechanisms by which these are achieved.

Detailed session-by-session guidance on the delivery of the treatment protocol developed as part of the Northgate Anger Treatment Project is provided in the next two chapters. It is probable that the principles underpinning this approach to anger treatment, and the procedures incorporated into the protocol, will be applicable to a wide range of people with developmental disabilities. However, putative therapists should keep in mind that the treatment was developed within a clinical research framework, and delivered in a specialist in-patient setting where particular (security) constraints applied. It is likely, therefore, that some minor changes and adjustments will need to be made by therapists in the delivery of the manual materials to clients in different settings and clinical contexts. It is anticipated that experienced therapists can make such variations without altering the overall integrity of the treatment or adversely affecting its clinical effectiveness. Therapists should keep in mind, however, that to deviate radically from the form or content of the protocol described could reduce the effectiveness of the intervention and consequently disadvantage clients in terms of clinical outcomes. A balance is required that can be achieved safely by appropriately trained and experienced psychological therapists who can access regular clinical supervision and support systems (see Chapter 10).

8

ANGER TREATMENT PROTOCOL – PREPARATORY PHASE

SESSION 1 EXPLAINING THE PURPOSE OF ANGER TREATMENT

	Contents	Duration (Approximate)
1	Introduction to preparatory phase of anger treatment	20 minutes
2	Negotiation of general rules and boundaries	15 minutes
3	Introduction to relaxation strategies	15 minutes
4	Reflection and session evaluation	10 minutes

Aims

- To orientate the client to the purpose of anger treatment, and the preparatory phase in particular, in a non-threatening style.
- To encourage the client to discuss the treatment openly and thereby begin to develop a collaborative working relationship.
- To discuss and agree ground rules and boundaries within which this work can take place.
- To introduce the concept of relaxation strategies as a means of reducing anger arousal.
- To introduce the notion of homework exercises as one way of carrying over learning between sessions and beginning to take some personal responsibility.

Session guidelines

1. *Introduction to anger treatment/preparatory phase (20 mins)*
   (a) Outline the purpose of anger treatment referring to the explanatory leaflet 'What is Anger Treatment About?' (see *Handout/Exercise Sheet 1.1*).
   (b) Emphasize the following:
      - the rationale for anger treatment;
      - the importance of developing self-control of angry feelings;

Anger Treatment for People with Developmental Disabilities by J. L. Taylor and R. W. Novaco.
Copyright © 2005 John Wiley & Sons, Ltd.

- collaboration (working together) is the key to success – the therapist is not there just to tell the client what to do.

    (c) Outline in brief the format and content of the Preparatory Phase sessions (see *Handout/Exercise Sheet 1.2*).

2. Negotiation of ground rules and boundaries (15 mins)

Discuss the following issues and complete *Handout/Exercise Sheet 1.3*.

(a) Confidentiality between therapists and clients.
  - The detail of what is said in the session will stay in the session.
  - Clinical reports on the anger treatment will be shown to and discussed with the client.
  - Some information (specify) would have to be passed on for ethical or security reasons.

(b) Trust and respect.
  - This should be built up by the therapist and client, allowing each other to speak.
  - Irrespective of what is being discussed, the therapist and client should not offend or abuse one another.

(c) Opportunities to raise issues.
  - The client is encouraged to ask questions or raise issues at any time.
  - If the client is drifting off task, or is avoiding the work of the session, the therapist will point this out clearly.

(d) Dealing with angry feelings.
  - If the session is becoming too difficult for the client, and if the client is becoming angry, then either the client or the therapist should end the session politely and without offending the other person.

(e) Collaboration and choice.
  - The client is encouraged to see the treatment as a joint effort to solve any problems he has.
  - The client has the choice to withdraw from a session at any time.

3. Introduction to relaxation strategies (15 mins)

It is important at this early stage to engage the client in discussion about their awareness of the differences between being uptight or tense, and calm and relaxed.

- Ask the client about what music they like listening to and why they like it.
- Prompt the client to explain how they feel when they listen to their favourite music.
- Ask the client if they have noticed feeling calmer or more relaxed after listening to their favourite music. The learning point is that attending to/concentrating on particular things can affect the way we feel. That is, we have some choice and can begin to control how we feel.
- Ask the client to complete *Handout/Exercise Sheet 1.4* for homework. Explain what is required and suggest that the client's keyworker might be able to help with this exercise. Agree to liaise with the keyworker as appropriate.

4. Reflection and session evaluation (10 mins)

This slot is to be provided routinely at the end of each session to give clients an opportunity to reflect on the session, to ask questions and to express any concerns that they may have.

Therapists should also work through section C ('Client's Report and Ratings on the Session') of *Handout/Exercise Sheet 1.5* at the end of every session.

Materials for Session 1

- *Handout/Exercise Sheet 1.1* What is Anger Treatment About?
- *Handout/Exercise Sheet 1.2* Outline of Preparatory Phase Sessions of Anger Treatment
- *Handout/Exercise Sheet 1.3* Ground Rules for Anger Treatment Sessions
- *Handout/Exercise Sheet 1.4* Ways of Dealing with Feeling Tense/Uptight
- *Handout/Exercise Sheet 1.5* Anger Treatment (Preparatory Phase) Report on Treatment Session

SESSION 2 FEELING ANGRY IS OK – ANGER AS A NORMAL EMOTION

	Contents	Duration (Approximate)
1	Introduction and review of previous session	10 minutes
2	Anger as a normal emotion	20 minutes
3	Self-monitoring of anger	10 minutes
4	Discussion of relaxation strategies	10 minutes
5	Reflection and session evaluation	10 minutes

Aims

- To explain that anger is a normal emotion, which everybody experiences from time to time.
- To indicate to the client that their feelings of anger are no different to other peoples.
- To explore in a preliminary manner different coping strategies people can use when angry.
- To introduce the concept of self-monitoring of angry feelings and how these can be recorded.
- To explore various relaxation strategies as a means of reducing anger arousal.

Session guidelines

1. *Introduction and review of previous session (10 mins)*
   (a) Briefly review previous session by summarizing the main areas covered including the purpose of anger treatment, general rules, and boundaries for sessions and relaxation through music. Check that the client has completed *Handout/Exercise Sheet 1.4* for homework. Explore any difficulties either with the homework or the content of the previous session.
   (b) Introduce the content of Session 2. Explain that you are going to talk about the angry feelings that everybody has, how to monitor and record feelings of anger, and the

client's ideas about different ways of dealing with feeling tense/uptight from their homework exercise.

2. *Anger as a normal emotion (20 mins)*
   (a) Introduce and describe the Anger-Provoking Scenario described in *Handout/Exercise Sheet 2.1*.
   (b) Explore with the client their understanding of anger by prompting discussion about the scenario in the following areas:
   - *How do you think Bill is likely to be feeling?*
   - *What would cause somebody to get angry in that situation?*
     Explore predisposing vulnerability factors such as learnt behaviour, rigid thinking/attitudes, poor problem-solving skills, etc.; and antecedent triggers including anxiety, distorted thoughts (cognitions), fear, feelings of threat, disrespect, injustice, etc.
   - *What is anger?*
     In relation to the scenario, explore the idea of anger as a reaction to a provocation that includes *thinking* in a particular way, as well as emotional and *physical feelings*. It might be useful to refer back to the 'How Anger Works' section of *Handout/Exercise* Sheet 1.1 at this point.
   - *What purpose does getting angry serve (functions of anger)?*
     Getting angry can be helpful sometimes and unhelpful at other times. Getting angry about something can lead to feeling more in control of a situation, bring about a sense of achievement, give us the energy or momentum to confront a problem. At other times getting angry can lead to a situation escalating, getting out of control, and feelings of failure and helplessness.
   - *Does everyone get angry?*
     Highlight anger as a normal emotion, which everybody feels from time to time. Explain that anger is a problem for people only if it happens too often, lasts too long, or is so strong the person cannot control it.
   - *How do people cope with (handle) feelings of anger?*
     Discuss the coping strategies people can use for anger. Highlight the importance for people of showing (expressing) their anger in socially acceptable ways that are more likely to lead to positive, rather than negative outcomes. Acknowledge that it is sometimes more difficult to deal with anger in a hospital setting and that more opportunities for coping with angry feelings exist outside the hospital.

     During this discussion note any themes that emerge in terms of the client's thoughts and observations on the scenario. For example, it might be that the client clearly indicates that a lack of fairness or respect is important in provoking anger in relation to the scenario. The ability of the client to 'perspective-take' when considering the scenario is also a useful indicator for future treatment sessions.

3. *Self-monitoring of anger (10 mins)*
   (a) Introduce the importance of self-monitoring of angry feelings for the following reasons:
   - To help the client become more aware of the kinds of situations which cause him/her to feel angry and how often this happens.
   - To provide a baseline against which the progress the client makes in treatment can be measured.

- To give the client and his therapist material to work on in the treatment sessions in order to help the client cope with angry feelings better in the future.
- Monitoring a problem in this way can sometimes help in itself by putting it in context.

(b) Introduce Anger Log I (*Handout/Exercise Sheet 2.2*) to the client and work through the log with him/her. Check with the client their ability to read the material in the log, as well as their ability to self-record.

(c) To help with this exercise ask the client to describe the last occasion they felt angry and work through Anger Log I using this as an example.

(d) Ask the client if they are able/willing to complete Anger Logs between this session and the next when what they have recorded can be discussed. Emphasize that, at this stage, this is a learning exercise and we do not expect them to be able to complete the log perfectly.

(e) Discuss with the client whether it would be helpful for their named keyworker to help them with this exercise. Obviously this will be a requirement for those clients who are unable to self-record and require somebody else to scribe for them. In general, collaboration with named keyworkers on this exercise should be encouraged. If the client responds positively to this suggestion agree to liaise with the named keyworker about them helping the client complete the Anger Logs.

4. *Discussion of relaxation strategies (10 mins)*

(a) Discuss with the client their ideas for dealing with feeling tense/uptight listed on *Handout/Exercise Sheet 1.4* completed as homework.

(b) Introduce the use of imagery:
- Refer back to the last part of the session when the client described the last occasion on which he felt angry. Discuss how thoughts or *images/pictures* about what happened made him feel uptight or angry.
- Suggest that in the same way thinking about, or having images/pictures in your mind of pleasant, enjoyable, or relaxing things can help people feel calmer and more relaxed.
- Ask the client to come up with previous experiences which when they think about them make them feel happy and calm. Some prompting might be required with this exercise. These experiences may be recent or from the past. Helpful examples can include memories of an enjoyable holiday, happy and enjoyable family occasions/parties, etc.
- Once a pleasant image or scene has been identified, ask the client to sit quietly for a few moments and concentrate on this image/scene.
- After about 60 seconds discuss with the client if this exercise helped them feel more relaxed and calmer.

5. *Reflection and session evaluation (10 mins)*

See Section 4 of Session 1 above for directions.

Material for Session 2

Handout/Exercise Sheet 2.1 Anger Log I

SESSION 3 UNDERSTANDING OUR OWN AND OTHER PEOPLE'S FEELINGS

	Contents	Duration (Approximate)
1	Introduction and review of previous session	10 minutes
2	Understanding other people's feelings	15 minutes
3	Understanding our own feelings	15 minutes
4	Development of relaxation strategies	10 minutes
5	Reflection and session evaluation	10 minutes

Aims

- To help clients to recognize and identify basic emotional states in other people, including happiness, sadness and anger.
- To increase awareness of the situational/contextual component of the development of various emotional states.
- To introduce the role cognitions play in the induction of different emotions and behavioural responses to situations.
- To explore with the client how thoughts and feelings are linked with reference to their own emotional state.
- To develop relaxation coupled with imagery as a means of reducing anger arousal.

Session guidelines

1. *Introduction and review of previous session (10 mins)*
   (a) Briefly review previous session by summarizing the main areas covered including anger as a normal emotion, the importance of self-monitoring of anger, and the use of imagery to facilitate relaxation. Check that the client has completed at least one Anger Log (*Handout/Exercise Sheet 2.2*) for homework. Explore any difficulties either with the homework or the content of the previous session.
   (b) Introduce the content of Session 3. Explain that you are going to discuss how we recognize how other people are feeling, how the way in which we think about situations affects the way we feel about things, and how imagery ('pictures in the mind') can help with feeling calm and relaxed.

2. *Understanding other people's feelings (15 mins)*
   (a) Introduce this exercise by explaining to the client that making sense of what is going on around us, including how other people are thinking and feeling, is very complicated. However, we are weighing up situations and people all of the time, often without realizing that we are doing it. The purpose of this exercise is to think about and discuss how this happens.
   (b) Present the client with *Handout/Exercise Sheets 3.1, 3.2 and 3.3* which show pictures of situations in which people appear happy, sad and angry respectively. Tell the client that you would like him to look at each of the pictures for a short time after which you will ask him some questions and have a discussion about what they show.

(c) For each picture in turn ask the client the following set of questions:
  - *What do you think is going on in this picture?*
  - *How do you think the person(s) in this picture is feeling?*
  - *What do you think they might be thinking?*
  - *What do you think they are likely to do?*
  - *What is likely to happen to them if they behave in this way?*

(d) Discuss with the client what clues/cues they used to answer these questions, including verbal, non-verbal and contextual clues/cues.

(e) Introduce the idea that cognitions/thoughts affect how we make judgements about what other people are thinking and feeling and *why* they are thinking and feeling this way. Illustrate this by using *Handout/Exercise Sheet 3.2* depicting a sad scene.

(f) Ask the client if they can think of any other reason why the person in this scene appears sad (and is crying). Prompt the idea that the person in the scene may have just been told some extremely important *good* news (for example, they have won millions of pounds on the lottery). If this was the case can the client recognize/identify how the person is feeling? If need be, prompt an alternative explanation; for example, the person is overcome with joy and happiness and is crying as a result.

Reiterate the point that how we look at a situation (what we expect and assume is happening) can greatly affect what we believe other people are thinking and feeling.

3. *Understanding our own feelings (15 mins)*

(a) Review with the client Anger Logs completed between this and the previous session for homework. Briefly give feedback on the logs in terms of the completeness of the information provided, its relevance in relation to the different sections of the log, etc. Ensure that this feedback is as positive and as rewarding as possible.

(b) Select a situation from the client's completed Anger Logs in which they have felt angry to some extent. (If, for whatever reason, the client has not completed an Anger Log use the situation provided by the client during Session 2 to describe the last occasion they felt angry.) Discuss the situation in some detail with the client, translating key elements onto *Handout/Exercise Sheet 3.4*. Place the client's most recent experience of feeling angry in the 'Actual' row highlighting the situation, thoughts about the situation, emotional and physical feelings that accompanied the situation, and the client's reaction to this situation.

(c) Illustrate how thoughts (expectations and assumptions) about a particular situation can affect our emotional and physical feelings by using the 'Possible' row of *Handout/Exercise Sheet 3.4*. That is, retain the situation exactly as it was recorded previously. However, ask the client whether they think there could be another explanation for why this situation arose (why what happened, why the person involved behaved as they did). Should the client have difficulty with this, then an alternative interpretation might be suggested to the client. If they can accept this alternative interpretation as being possible/realistic, ask them how their emotional and physical feelings might be different in this case. Further, do they think that their behavioural reactions to the situation would have been different?

(d) Based on this re-analysis, if appropriate, reiterate how our thoughts about a particular situation can affect how we feel (both emotionally and physically) and how we react and behave.

(e) Ask the client to continue to complete Anger Logs for monitoring purposes.

4. *Development of relaxation strategies (10 mins)*

(a) Briefly remind the client of the work done during the last session to identify an image/picture, which he found calming and relaxing.

(b) Ask the client to think about, and if possible explain how they feel physically (that is, what happens to their body) when they feel wound up and angry. If necessary, prompt the client to think about how their breathing becomes uneven and rapid. This is part of the physical reaction to being angry. On the other hand, when people are feeling calm and relaxed, their breathing tends to be slower, even and more under control.

(c) Ask the client to relax by sitting back, perhaps closing their eyes if they are comfortable with this, and concentrating on breathing in a regular, even and controlled way. Allow the client a few moments (up to 60 seconds) to achieve this.

(d) Whether or not the client appears to have achieved a degree of relaxation by concentrating on breathing, introduce the image/picture they identified during Session 2 and ask them to concentrate on this scene for a few moments (up to 60 seconds) to maintain relaxation.

(e) At the end of this exercise discuss with the client if it helped them, how easy it was for them to form a mental image/scene, and whether they noticed if controlled breathing helped with relaxation.

(f) For homework, ask the client to draw, describe in writing (in detail), or represent in some other way their favourited relaxing, calming image/picture/scene. (If appropriate, they can use *Handout/Exercise Sheet 3.5* to record this.)

5. *Reflection and session evaluation (10 mins)*

As for previous sessions.

Materials for session 3

- *Handout/Exercise Sheet 3.1* Understanding Other People's Feelings 1 (picture showing a happy scene)
- *Handout/Exercise Sheet 3.2* Understanding Other People's Feelings 2 (picture showing a sad scene)
- *Handout/Exercise Sheet 3.3* Understanding Other People's Feelings 3 (picture showing an angry scene)
  (*Note*: The line drawings provided on pages 41 and 42 of the 'Activities and people in relationships' section of Sex and the 3Rs (McCarthy & Thompson, 1992) are useful resources for Handout/Exercise Sheets 3.1, 3.2 and 3.3.)
- *Handout/Exercise Sheet 3.4* How our Feelings and Thoughts are Linked
- *Handout/Exercise Sheet 3.5* Relaxing and Calming Image/Picture

SESSION 4 HOW TO CONTROL THE PHYSICAL FEELINGS OF ANGER – PHYSIOLOGICAL AROUSAL

	Contents	Duration (Approximate)
1	Introduction and review of previous session	10 minutes
2	How high levels of stress affect thinking and behaviour	15 minutes
3	The purpose of relaxation	15 minutes
4	Development of relaxation strategies	10 minutes
5	Reflection and session evaluation	10 minutes

Aims

- To help clients understand how high levels of stress affects thinking and behaviour.
- To discuss and explore the physical response to high levels of stress.
- To consider in detail how relaxation can counteract the physical arousal associated with high levels of stress and so increase self-control.
- To further develop relaxation coupled with imagery as a means of reducing anger associated with a self-recorded incidents.
- To introduce the concept of self-instruction as a means of facilitating self-control

Session guidelines

1. Introduction and review of previous session (10 mins)
   (a) Briefly review the previous session by summarizing the main areas covered including recognition and identification of basic emotional states in other people (including happiness, sadness, and anger), the situational/contextual components of the development of various emotional states, the role cognitions play in the induction of different emotions and behaviours, and the use of imagery to facilitate relaxation. Check that the client has completed the homework tasks set during the last session including at least one Anger Log (*Handout/Exercise Sheet 2.2*), and a pictorial or written representation of a relaxing and calming image (*Handout/Exercise Sheet 3.5.*) Explore any difficulties either with the homework or the content of the previous session.
   (b) Introduce the content of Session 4. Explain that you are going to discuss how high levels of stress can affect the way people think and behave; the physical reactions people experience when they are feeling very stressed; and how relaxation, along with imagery, can help us to manage these physical feelings.

2. How high levels of stress affect thinking and behaviour (15 mins)
   (a) Ask the client what they understand by the term 'stress'. If necessary, prompt with alternative terms such as 'anxiety', 'pressure', feeling 'wound-up', 'tense'.
   (b) Introduce the 'stress/anger thermometer' model using Handout/Exercise Sheet 4.1. Explain to the client that an ordinary thermometer measures temperature (that is, how hot it is), the 'stress/anger thermometer' measures how much stress or anger a person is feeling:
   - At, or below 0 a person is not feeling stressed, is switched off, sleepy, very slow.
   - Between 0–50 people are experiencing normal everyday levels of stress which helps to get things done, gives us our energy and we feel in control of things.
   - Between 50–100, the amount of stress is making us feel very tense or anxious, wound-up, or 'up-a-height'. At these levels things are beginning to feel out of control.
   - 100 is 'boiling point'. Above this the person feels out of control, is unable to think straight, and often cannot control their behaviour. This is when things can go badly wrong.

      It is important for us when stress levels are getting high, and we are at risk of reaching boiling point (when things can get out of control), to reduce the stress to below 50 by exercising self-control. Obviously this is difficult to do and requires us to learn new skills and to practise these.

3. *The purpose of relaxation (15 mins)*
   (a) Discuss with the client the physical signs of stress, that is, the physiological response to stress in terms of physical symptoms. Ask the client if they have noticed particular physical feelings when in the past they have felt either highly stressed, or very angry.
   (b) Relate the client's ideas about the physical feelings, which accompany high levels of stress with common physiological responses shown in *Handout/Exercise Sheet 4.2*. Explain how this physiological response is natural and normal, and serves a clear purpose with respect to the 'fight or flight' response. In the same way that our physical reaction to high levels of arousal is very quick (automatic) to prepare us for a (perceived) threat, our thoughts and feelings react very quickly also (as discussed above) for the same reasons. That is, to protect ourselves. These fast (automatic) responses can lead us to see situations as threatening, frightening, and hostile even when they are not.
   (c) Relaxation can help us to manage highly stressful/angry situations in a number of ways:
     • It can help us to feel better physically (in our bodies). Relate this to the relaxed and calm feelings following brief periods of relaxation during previous anger treatment sessions.
     • By reducing the physical feelings of stress and tension we can begin to think more clearly about what is going on, rather than reacting quickly and seeing the situation as threatening, frightening or hostile. Thinking differently in this way will also make us feel better physically. (Again, relate this to earlier work on how concentrating on/thinking about pleasant things such as favourite music, or a relaxing and calming image, helped to make the client feel calmer, relaxed and happy.)
     • If relaxation can help us to feel better physically, help us think about situations more clearly, then there is a better chance that we will behave (react) in a way that will help the situation rather than make it worse and get us into trouble.

If we can control how we think and feel in stressful/angry situations by learning to relax, we will be able to 'buy time' in order to 'think twice' before we react/behave in a way that causes more trouble. We are then in a better position to choose the best way to behave and sort things out.

4. *Development of relaxation strategies (10 mins)*
   (a) Look at and discuss with the client the pictorial/written representation of a relaxing and calming image completed for homework using *Handout/Exercise Sheet 3.5*.
   (b) Review with the client the Anger Logs completed between this and the last session. If there has been a situation, which has provoked a degree of anger, work through the stages of this incident briefly with the client. (If no angry incidents have been recorded, use an incident from previous logs, or the last angry incident reported by the client during Session 2.)
   (c) Ask the client to concentrate on the situation that made him/her angry and to imagine that this was happening now. If appropriate, the client should be asked to close his/her eyes to concentrate on this situation. After a short time ask the client how well they are able to remember the situation and how angry thinking about it makes them feel (not at all, a little, or very angry).

(d) Then ask the client to relax themselves by sitting back, closing/keeping their eyes closed, and concentrating on breathing in a regular, even and controlled way. Allow the client a few moments (up to 60 seconds) to achieve this.

(e) Whether or not the client appears to have achieved a degree of relaxation by concentrating on breathing, introduce the image/picture they have previously identified and ask them to concentrate on this scene for a short while (up to 60 seconds) to maintain relaxation.

(f) While still relaxed, ask the client how angry they feel now (not at all, a little, very) and ask them how relaxed they feel (not at all, a little, very).

(g) Discuss with the client how relaxation has/has not helped them feel less angry/more relaxed than they were when they were thinking about the anger-provoking situation earlier. Highlight how by relaxing and thinking about/concentrating on something pleasant, they have been able to change how they feel both physically and emotionally.

(h) For homework ask the client to continue to use the Anger Logs to record any situations in which they feel angry. Also, suggest that the client discusses with their named keyworker what they might say to themselves to remind them of their relaxing and calming image, which when they remember and think about it helps them to relax. (Use *Handout/Exercise Sheet 4.3* 'Self-Instructional Statements to Help with Relaxation' for this).

5. Reflection and session evaluation (10 mins)

As for previous sessions.

Materials for Session 4

- *Handout/Exercise Sheet 4.1* Stress/Anger Thermometer
- *Handout/Exercise Sheet 4.2* How our Bodies Feel When We Are Stressed
- *Handout/Exercise Sheet 4.3* Self-Instructional Statements to Help with Relaxation

SESSION 5 REASONS FOR CHANGING THE WAY WE COPE WITH ANGRY FEELINGS

	Contents	Duration (Approximate)
1	Introduction and review of previous session	10 minutes
2	Anger treatment decision matrix	20 minutes
3	Preparedness for therapy assessment	10 minutes
4	Development of relaxation strategies	10 minutes
5	Reflection and session evaluation	10 minutes

Aims

- To encourage the client's commitment to and motivation for anger treatment.
- To explore with the client the costs and benefits of anger and aggression both in the short and longer term.

- To help the client to understand that the benefits of developing self-control over anger and aggression outweigh those gained by continuing to be angry and aggressive.
- To assess the client's preparedness and motivation for anger treatment.
- To further develop relaxation coupled with imagery, using self-instruction, as a means of reducing anger arousal.

Session guidelines

1. *Introduction and review of previous session (10 mins)*
   (a) Briefly review the previous session by summarizing the main areas covered, including how high levels of stress affect thinking and behaviour, the physical response to stress, how relaxation can help to combat the physical response to stress and so help with self-control, and how relaxation coupled with imagery can help to reduce angry feelings. Check that the client has completed the homework tasks set during the last session (*Handout/Exercise Sheet 4.3* 'Self-Instructional Statements to Help with Relaxation') and at least one Anger Log (*Handout/Exercise Sheet 2.2*). Explore any difficulties either with the homework or the content of the previous session.
   (b) Introduce the contents of Session 5. Explain that you are going to discuss the costs (disadvantages/negative consequences) and benefits (advantages) of getting angry and aggressive; help the client weigh up whether it is better for them to develop self-control over anger and aggression, or continue to be angry and aggressive; discuss the client's readiness to continue with anger treatment; and how relaxation coupled with imagery can be facilitated by self-instructions and used to reduce anger arousal.

2. *Anger treatment decision matrix (20 mins)*
   (a) Check the Anger Logs previously completed by the client for any situations that have been recorded involving the client becoming aggressive, as well as feeling angry. If a situation involving aggression has been recorded, explain to the client that you are going to discuss with them with 'pros and cons' of anger/aggression using this as an example. However, if the client has not previously recorded an incident involving them becoming aggressive, ask the client to describe the last occasion on which they behaved aggressively. (For the purposes of this exercise aggressive behaviour can include shouting, swearing, threatening others, damaging property, assaulting, or attempting to assault others, etc.)
   (b) Using the incident identified above, work through (*Handout/Exercise Sheet 5.1* 'Anger Treatment Decision Matrix'. Ask the client what they think the immediate benefits of being angry and aggressive were in this situation. If necessary, the client can be prompted with this exercise by the therapist (who may wish to refer to *Handout/Exercise Sheet 5.2* 'Costs and Benefits of Anger and Aggression'). In addition, the therapist may wish to refer back to the work done in Session 2 ('Feeling Angry is OK') on what purpose does getting angry serve (functions of anger)?
   (c) Ask the client for their ideas about the immediate costs (negative consequences/disadvantages) of being angry/aggressive in this situation. Again, if required, prompt the client with this exercise by reference to *Handout/Exercise Sheet 5.2*.
   (d) Then explore with the client the benefits and costs over time (longer term).
   (e) Using *Handout/Exercise Sheet 5.3* help the client to weigh up the costs and benefits of being angry/aggressive. Use the 'Total number of benefits' and 'Total number of costs' figures from *Handout/Exercise Sheet 5.1* to mark on the scales the relative

number of benefits and costs. Then draw in using the second fulcrum how the scales would be tilted towards costs.

(f) Discuss with the client how continuing to be angry (and aggressive) will cost them dearly both immediately and in the future. Explain how anger treatment is designed to help them to develop *self-control* over their anger and aggression and thereby reduce the costs (disadvantages). Stress that this has to be their own choice, something that they would like to do for themselves and that the therapist, along with other members of the clinical team, can only help and support the client if they want to help themselves.

(g) Explain that giving up some of the immediate benefits of being angry/aggressive (for example, relief of tension) will be difficult for the client to begin with. But reassure them that if they are committed to developing better self-control, then the benefits will be much greater in the long term. Also, because this work is difficult, if the client does not progress, then they will not be blamed or abandoned. They will have the opportunity to try again at a later time when perhaps they are better prepared.

3. Preparedness for therapy assessment (10 mins)

(a) Discuss with the client whether they feel they are prepared and ready to continue with anger treatment to help them develop their self-control over anger and aggression. Explore any difficulties that the client identifies and reassure, or re-frame these as appropriate.

(b) Administer the Preparedness for Therapy Questionnaire (PTQ) on *Handout/Exercise Sheet 5.4*. This is designed to give an indication of the client's preparedness and motivation, for, as well as commitment, to anger treatment. Use the 10 items to prompt and explore any difficulties the client indicates in relation to their preparedness, motivation, and commitment. The questionnaire can be used as a structured interview to facilitate this discussion.

4. Development of relaxation strategies (10 mins)

(a) Look at and discuss with the client their homework from Session 4 on self-instructional statements to help with relaxation (*Handout/Exercise Sheet 4.3*). Identify with the client a self-instructional statement which they think would be most helpful/powerful in prompting them to remember the relaxing and calming image identified during earlier sessions. If, for whatever reason, the client has been unable to complete this homework, briefly carry out this exercise with them at this point to identify a suitable self-instructional statement.

(b) Review with the client Anger Logs completed between this and the last session. If there has been a situation that has provoked a degree of anger, work through the stages of the incident briefly with the client. (If no angry incidents have been recorded, use an incident from previous logs, or the last angry incident reported by the client during Session 2.)

(c) Ask the client to concentrate on the situation that made them angry and to imagine that this is happening now. If appropriate, the client should be asked to close his eyes to facilitate concentration. After a short time ask the client how well they are able to remember the situation and how angry thinking about it makes them feel (not at all, a little, or very).

(d) Ask the client to remember the self-instructional statement and to say it to themselves, either out loud or under their breath, two or three times. Then ask the client to relax by sitting back, closing/keeping their eyes closed, and concentrating on breathing in a regular, even and controlled way. Allow the client a few moments (up to 60 seconds) to achieve this.

(e) Whether or not the client appears to have achieved a degree of relaxation by concentrating on breathing, introduce the image/picture which they have previously identified and ask them to concentrate on this scene for a short while (up to 60 seconds) to maintain relaxation.

(f) While still relaxed, ask the client how angry they feel now (not at all, a little, very) and ask them also how relaxed they feel (not at all, a little, very).

(g) Discuss with the client how relaxation has/has not helped them feel less angry/more relaxed than they were when they were thinking about the anger-provoking situation earlier. Explain how using the self-instructional statement will prompt/cue them to control their breathing and so control the physical response to the stressful/angry situation. Also, by thinking about and concentrating on the happy and pleasant image, they are able to deepen the feeling of relaxation and change how they feel, both physically and emotionally.

(h) For homework ask the client to continue to use the Anger Logs to record any situations in which they feel angry. Also, ask the client to discuss with their named keyworker reasons they should continue with their anger treatment to help themselves have better self-control over anger and aggression. They can use *Handout/Exercise Sheet 5.5* for this.

5. Reflection and session evaluation (10 mins)

As for previous sessions.

Materials for Session 5

- *Handout/Exercise Sheet 5.1* Anger Treatment Decision Matrix
- *Handout/Exercise Sheet 5.2* Examples of the Advantages and Disadvantages of Being Angry and Aggressive
- *Handout/Exercise Sheet 5.3* Weighing up Costs and Benefits of Anger and Aggression
- *Handout/Exercise Sheet 5.4* Preparedness for Therapy Questionnaire (PTQ)
- *Handout/Exercise Sheet 5.5* Reasons to Continue with Anger Treatment

SESSION 6 REVIEW OF THE PREPARATORY STAGE AND PREVIEW OF THE TREATMENT PHASE

	Contents	Duration (Approximate)
1	Introduction and review of previous session	10 minutes
2	Review and evaluation of the preparatory phase sessions	20 minutes
3	Deciding whether to continue with anger treatment	10 minutes
4	Development of relaxation strategies	10 minutes
5	Reflection and session evaluation	10 minutes

Aims

- To review with the client the aims and the content of the preparatory phase sessions.
- To receive feedback on the preparatory phase through client's evaluation of the sessions.
- To discuss with the client whether they wish to continue with anger treatment beyond the preparatory phase.
- To further develop relaxation strategies involving self-instruction, controlled breathing, and use of imagery as a means of reducing anger arousal.
- To assess the client's competencies in a range of areas covered during the preparatory phase sessions.

Session guidelines

1. *Introduction and review of previous session (10 mins)*
   (a) Briefly review the previous session by summarizing the main areas covered including the immediate and long-term costs and benefits of being angry and behaving aggressively; whether it is better for the client to develop self-control over anger and aggression, or to continue to be angry and aggressive; how prepared the client is to continue with anger treatment; and how relaxation coupled with imagery can be facilitated by self-instruction to reduce anger arousal. Check that the client has completed the homework tasks set during the last session including *Handout/Exercise Sheet 5.5* 'Reasons to Continue with Anger Treatment', and at least one Anger Log (*Handout/Exercise Sheet 2.2*). Explore any difficulties either with the homework or the content of the previous session.
   (b) Introduce the content of Session 6. Explain that you are going to review the aims and work done during the previous five sessions; ask the client to give feedback and evaluate the preparatory phase sessions; discuss with the client whether they wish to continue with their anger treatment; and finally, practise relaxation including self-instruction, controlled breathing, and imagery to reduce anger arousal.

2. *Review and evaluation of the preparatory phase sessions (20 mins)*
   (a) Prompt the client to recall the main areas covered during the previous five sessions. This exercise can be facilitated by reference to *Handout/Exercise Sheet 1.2* 'Outline of Preparatory Phase Sessions of Anger Treatment'. Prompt discussion with the client of the main aims of this phase of treatment covered during these sessions and briefly review each area.
   (b) Ask the client to complete (with any assistance they require) the 'Patient's Evaluation of Anger Treatment – Preparatory Phase' (*Handout/Exercise Sheet 6.1*).

3. *Deciding whether to continue with anger treatment (10 mins)*
   (a) Leading on from the review and evaluation exercise above, with the client look at their 'Reasons to Continue with Anger Treatment' completed as homework (*Handout/Exercise Sheet 5.5*).
   (b) Use this material to discuss with the client their willingness to continue with anger treatment beyond completion of the preparatory phase sessions. It may be helpful to guide this discussion by referring back to the work done during Session 5 on the costs

and benefits of continuing to be angry and behave aggressively (*Handout/Exercise Sheets 5.1 and 5.3*).

(c) If the client is indicating clearly that they wish to continue with anger treatment, explain that at the end of this session you will, along with their named keyworker, ask them to look at and sign a consent form for this continuation of treatment.

(d) If the client is either uncertain, or indicating clearly that they do not wish to continue with anger treatment, explore reasons for this in an open, non-challenging or non-judgemental manner. If the client agrees, suggest that he takes some time (a few days if necessary) to think over this decision and discuss it with his named keyworker, or anybody else he wishes to. After that time he will be given another opportunity to indicate whether he wishes to continue with, or stop, treatment.

(e) For those clients indicating their willingness to continue with anger treatment, and if appropriate for those who are uncertain, briefly outline what will happen next procedurally, in terms of the next phase of anger treatment. For those continuing with anger treatment, the programme will involve deepening and developing of their understanding of and skills for *self-control* over the thoughts, emotional feelings, and physical reactions associated with anger. In addition, they will be helped to learn new skills to solve problem situations and to get on better with people.

4. *Development of relaxation strategies (10 mins)*

(a) Review with the client Anger Logs completed between this and the last session. If there has been a situation that has provoked a degree of anger, work through the stages of the incident briefly with the client. (If no angry incidents have been recorded, use an incident from previous logs or the last angry incident reported by the client during Session 2.)

(b) Review with the client the work done during Session 5 on self-instructions to cue/prompt relaxation in stressful/angry situations, and, if appropriate, develop the self-instruction identified with the client during the last session.

(c) Ask the client to concentrate on the situation that made them angry and to imagine that this is happening now. If appropriate, the client should be asked to close his eyes to facilitate concentration. After a short time ask the client how well they are able to remember the situation and how angry thinking about it makes them feel (not at all, a little, or very).

(d) Ask the client to remember the self-instructional statement and to say it to themselves, either out loud or under their breath, two or three times. Then ask the client to relax by sitting back, closing/keeping their eyes closed, and concentrating on breathing in a regular, even and controlled way. Allow the client a few moments (up to 60 seconds) to achieve this.

(e) Whether or not the client appears to have achieved a degree of relaxation by concentrating on breathing, introduce the image/picture which they have previously identified and ask them to concentrate on this scene for a short while (up to 60 seconds) to maintain relaxation.

(f) While still relaxed, ask the client how angry they feel now (not at all, a little, very) and ask them also how relaxed they feel (not at all, a little, very).

(g) Discuss with the client how relaxation has/has not helped them feel less angry/more relaxed than they were when they were thinking about the anger provoking situation earlier. Discuss how use of the self-instructional statement helped to prompt/cue control of breathing and so control the physical response to the stressful/angry situation. Reiterate that by thinking about and concentrating on the happy and pleasant image, they are able to deepen the feeling of relaxation and change how they feel, both physically and emotionally.

5. Reflection and session evaluation (10 mins)

As for previous sessions.

Following completion of this session, the therapist, in collaboration with the client's named keyworker, should complete the 'Patient's Competency Checklist – Preparatory Phase' (*Handout/Exercise Sheet 6.2*) and the 'Goal Attainment Scales for Emotional Awareness and Expression – Post-preparatory' (*Handout/Exercise Sheet 6.3*).

Materials for Session 6

- *Handout/Exercise Sheet 6.1* 'Patient's Evaluation of Anger Treatment – Preparatory Phase'
- *Handout/Exercise Sheet 6.2* 'Patient's Competency Checklist – Preparatory Phase'
- *Handout/Exercise Sheet 6.3* 'Goal Attainment Scales for Emotional Awareness and Expression – Post-preparatory'

9

ANGER TREATMENT PROTOCOL – TREATMENT PHASE

SESSION 7 INTRODUCTION TO TREATMENT PHASE SESSIONS

	Contents	Duration (Approximate)
1	Brief review of preparatory phase of treatment	10 minutes
2	Introduction to treatment phase sessions	10 minutes
3	Anger problem analysis and formulation	20 minutes
4	Review of relaxation strategies	10 minutes
5	Reflection and session evaluation	10 minutes

Aims

- To review briefly the preparatory phase of treatment, focusing on what anger treatment is about and motivation for change.
- To re-orientate the client to the purpose of anger treatment, and the treatment phase in particular, in a non-threatening and collegial style.
- To carry out an analysis of the client's anger problem and reach a shared preliminary formulation of treatment needs.
- To re-introduce self-monitoring of anger problems and relaxation strategies to reduce anger arousal.

Session guidelines

1. *Brief review of preparatory phase of treatment (10 mins)*
   (a) Begin by asking the client to recall the main areas covered during the six preparatory phase sessions. This exercise can be facilitated by reference to *Handout/Exercise Sheet 1.2* 'Outline of Preparatory Phase Sessions of Anger Treatment'.
   (b) Review with the client the work done in preparatory phase Session 5 using the anger treatment decision matrix to look at the costs and benefits of being angry/aggressive and of engaging in anger treatment. Re-emphasize the heavy costs attached to

Anger Treatment for People with Developmental Disabilities by J. L. Taylor and R. W. Novaco.
Copyright © 2005 John Wiley & Sons, Ltd.

continuing to be angry/aggressive both in the short and long term. Remind the client that anger treatment is designed to help them to develop *self-control* over their anger and aggression and thereby reduce the costs (disadvantages or negative consequences). Reiterate that they have indicated that this is something they would like to do for themselves and that the therapist, along with other members of the clinical team, can only help and support the client if they want to help themselves by working hard at their treatment.

(c) Following on from discussion of motivational issues above, review with the client what anger treatment is about in relation to the 'How Anger Works' model described in *Handout/Exercise Sheet 1.1*. Remind the client that anger is a normal emotion and is part of being human. It becomes a problem only when it happens too often, lasts for too long, or is so strong that it gets out of control and leads to aggression/violence. Review the 'How Anger Works' model in relation to the situational/contextual aspect of anger, how thinking in particular ways and certain kinds of feelings (emotional and physical) lead us to be angry and can affect the way we behave (react). In addition, our behaviour when angry leads to a range of consequences, both for us and for others, which can be negative and costly (refer back to the cost–benefit analysis discussed earlier in this session).

2. *Introduction to treatment phase sessions (10 mins)*

(a) Explain that this phase of treatment will be for 12 sessions, and if possible indicate a timescale for this. Explain that the treatment is aimed at helping the client to cope with angry feelings more effectively both now and in the future. This is an important part of the client's rehabilitation so that there is less chance of them behaving in ways which will get them into trouble when they are feeling angry.

(b) Discuss with the client how the treatment sessions will work. Explain that they will build on and develop the understanding and skills acquired during the preparatory phase sessions. That is, the treatment phase will help the client to think differently about the things that make them angry (cognitive re-structuring), it will help them to regulate the levels of cognitive and somatic arousal experienced when angry (relaxation strategies), and it will help them to learn more effective ways of dealing with people and situations which tend to make them angry (task-orientated skills training). Emphasize again that the main point of treatment is to help the client to control their feelings better so that they can choose how to behave in the future. For this to be successful, the clients will have to work together with the therapist and other members of the clinical team.

3. *Anger problem analysis and formulation (20 mins)*

(a) Carry out a preliminary *external events* × *internal processes* × *behavioural responses* analysis of the client's anger problem. Begin by asking the client to describe the sorts of situations (including settings, people, issues, etc.) that tend to provoke anger; the internal processes (thoughts and physical feelings) they associate with feeling angry; and typical behavioural responses (that is how anger is expressed when aroused in particular circumstances).

(b) This exercise can be facilitated by referring the client to the Anger Logs completed during the preparatory phase sessions, and other reports of anger disclosed during these sessions. Prompt the client to look at these incidents in relation to the three main areas of analysis, and ask them if they can identify any patterns or themes that might be emerging.

(c) Develop this analysis by using NAS, PI and STAXI responses as a basis for cross-referencing with any emerging themes, and/or for introducing additional information regarding the determinants of anger arousal in relation to the situational, internal and behavioural components. If themes are emerging in any of these component areas, it might be helpful to map these onto (write into) the relevant sections of the 'How Anger Works' diagrammatic model in *Handout/Exercise Sheet 1.1*.

(d) Regarding any clear themes that emerge from this preliminary analysis of the client's anger problem, it can be agreed with the client that these should become the focus of the anger treatment and can be worked on explicitly during the remaining 11 sessions. Hopefully this will increase the salience of the treatment for the client and motivate them to fully engage in the treatment process.

(e) Clearly this is a preliminary analysis and formulation of the client's anger problem, which might benefit from being carried over into the next session and beyond if necessary. As future sessions unfold, undoubtedly there will be opportunities to return to this analysis and formulation in order to refine it, review it, and, where necessary, modify the agreed treatment targets. Based on this analysis and formulation, the framework provided by the treatment manual can be used flexibly in order to meet the needs and agreed treatment targets for individual client's. That is, more weight can be given to treatment areas that are particularly relevant to identified needs and agreed treatment goals in relation to individual client's anger problems. Reflexive use of the therapeutic techniques described in the manual will result in good treatment outcomes that are relevant to individual clients.

4. *Review of relaxation strategies (10 mins)*

(a) Review briefly with the client previous work done on the development of relaxation strategies including self-instructional statements to prompt self-control in angry situations, breathing control to counteract the physical arousal associated with anger, and use of relaxing images to deepen relaxation and calm the mind.

(b) Discuss with the client any anger-provoking incidents that have occurred since the last preparatory phase session. It would be interesting to note if the client has continued to use the Anger Logs. Ask the client to describe briefly the incident that occurred most recently and provoked the greatest amount of anger.

(c) Ask the client to concentrate on the situation that made them angry and to imagine that this is happening now. If appropriate, the client should be asked to close their eyes to facilitate concentration. After a short time ask the client how well they are able to remember the situation and how angry thinking about it makes them feel (not at all, a little, or very).

(d) Ask the client to remember the self-instructional statement and to say it to themselves, either out loud or under their breath, two or three times. Then ask the client to relax by sitting back, closing/keeping their eyes closed, and concentrating on breathing in a regular, even and controlled way. Allow the client a few moments (up to 60 seconds) to achieve this.

(e) Whether or not the client appears to have achieved a degree of relaxation by concentrating on breathing, introduce the image/picture which they have previously identified and ask them to concentrate on this scene for a short while (up to 60 seconds) to maintain relaxation.

(f) While still relaxed ask the client how angry they feel now (not at all, a little, very) and ask them also how relaxed they feel (not at all, a little, very).

(g) Discuss with the client how relaxation has/has not helped them feel less angry/more relaxed than they were when they were thinking about the anger-provoking situation earlier. Explain how using the self-instructional statement will prompt/cue them to control their breathing and so control the physical response to the stressful/angry situation. Also, by thinking about and concentrating on the happy and pleasant image, they are able to deepen the feeling of relaxation and change how they feel, both physically and emotionally.

(h) Briefly remind the client of the value of self-monitoring of anger using Anger Logs (*Handout/Exercise Sheet 2.2*). For homework ask the client to begin to use the Anger Logs again to record any situations in which they feel angry. Ask the client to complete the logs on a *daily* basis in collaboration with their keyworker.

5. Reflection and session evaluation (10 mins)

Clients are given the opportunity to reflect on the session, to ask questions and express any concerns they may have. The therapist should work through Section C ('Client's Report and Ratings on the Session') of *Handout/Exercise Sheet 7.1*.

Materials for Session 7

• *Handout/Exercise Sheet 7.1* Anger Treatment (Treatment Phase) Report on Treatment Session

SESSION 8 BUILDING AN ANGER HIERARCHY

	Contents	Duration (Approximate)
1	Introduction and review of previous session	10 minutes
2	Building an anger hierarchy	20 minutes
3	Introduction to abbreviated progressive relaxation (APR)	20 minutes
4	Reflection and session evaluation	10 minutes

Aims

• To refine the preliminary '*external events* × *internal processes* × *behavioural responses*' analysis and formulation started in the last session.

• To begin to construct a hierarchy of anger incidents to be used in the stress inoculation procedure in future sessions.

• To introduce the concept of '*thought catching*' as a means of increasing awareness of self-talk (internal dialogue).

• To expose the client to *abbreviated progressive relaxation (APR)* as a technique for deepening the effects of relaxation.

Session guidelines

1. *Introduction and review of previous session (10 mins)*

   (a) Briefly review the previous session by summarizing the main areas covered including the review of the preparatory phase of treatment, the introduction to treatment phase sessions, the preliminary analysis and formulation of anger problems, and the re-introduction to relaxation strategies.

   (b) Introduce the content of Session 8. Explain that you are going to begin to create a list of angry incidents that the client has experienced in the past, and discuss which provokes the least amount, and which provokes the most amount of anger. In addition, you are going to show the clients some new relaxation exercises to build on the skills already acquired in the preparatory phase of treatment.

   (c) Check that the client has completed Anger Logs between this and the last session as requested. Explore any difficulties with completion of this homework. Work through the Anger Logs with the client and use this as the basis for discussion reflecting on, and where relevant, refining the analysis and formulation of the client's anger problems started in the last session. Use a copy of the 'How Anger Works' model from *Handout/Exercise Sheet 1.1* to note any amendments or revisions to the situational, cognitive, arousal, and behavioural domains of the anger problem. From this refined analysis agree with the client the primary targets for treatment (cognitive, arousal, behavioural, problem-solving skills) to be worked on during the remainder of the treatment sessions.

   (d) Introduce to the client the new form for recording angry incidents *Handout/Exercise Sheet 8.1* 'Anger Log II'. Explain that this form is exactly the same as the previous Anger Log, except that there is a new section in which they are to record the thoughts, that is what was going through their minds *as* the incident was taking place. Be clear that we are not asking the client to record what they thought about the situation afterwards, or at the time they were completing the log. What they were thinking about *at the time* is what is important. Discuss with the client how *'thought catching'* is important in learning how to think differently about angry situations. It might be helpful to illustrate this point by referring back to the cognitive re-structuring exercise completed during Session 3 and recorded on *Handout/Exercise Sheet 3.4* 'How our Feelings and Thoughts are Linked'. Impress on the client how thought catching is difficult to do at first, but becomes easier with practice and will be very helpful to the client during future treatment sessions.

2. *Building an anger hierarchy (20 mins)*

   (a) Explain to the client that, if possible, they need to come up with five or six situations relating to previous experiences, which have provoked, at one end of the scale, a little anger or annoyance, and, at the other end of the scale, extreme anger or fury. We will be using these situations in future sessions to learn how to remain calmer, to think things through more effectively, and to deal with situations in ways which will help, instead of making things worse.

   (b) Using *Handout/Exercise Sheet 8.2* ask the client to describe an experience that has made them the most angry/furious that they have ever been. Help the client to develop this description by prompting them to describe clearly, but succinctly, the setting conditions, context, and situational details (where, people present, what was said, etc.). Ideally the situation described should be specific, but not so particular that the circumstances, or an approximation of them, are unlikely to occur in the future. The description *should not* include the client's reactions to the situation. As these items are to be used as imaginal provocation's in future sessions, the client's reactions are left to occur and to be moderated by the therapy.

(c) By contrast, identify a situation experienced by the client, which provoked only a mild degree of anger/annoyance. Develop this description in the same way as described in (b) above. In both cases, once the description has been developed and written down, ask the client to rate the amount of anger the experience provoked. Depending on how well this exercise is progressing continue to develop anger hierarchy descriptions that relate to previous experiences which provoked levels of anger between these extreme points. It is likely that this exercise will need to be carried over into the next session.

(d) If the client is having difficulty in volunteering anger situations for the hierarchy, they can be prompted by reference to previous logs, client records, or an item analysis of the Provocation Inventory. Obviously the more able the client is to volunteer their own ideas and experiences, the better. However, for some clients it may be necessary to suggest ideas based on documentary/assessment information in order to kick-start this part of the treatment procedure. It is important not to be tempted to do therapy during the construction of the anger hierarchy by suggesting alternative appraisals for situations, more adaptive responses, etc. It is to be hoped that during stress inoculation procedures to be implemented in future sessions, the clients will begin to generate more helpful, cognitive, emotional and behavioural responses for themselves.

3. *Introduction to abbreviated progressive relaxation (APR) (20 mins)*
    (a) Remind the client of the importance of reducing and controlling the physical arousal and feelings that accompany anger. Refer back to the key learning points from Session 4 – How to Control the Physical Feelings of Anger. Reiterate how high levels of stress can affect thinking and behaviour and the purpose of relaxation in moderating arousal.
    (b) Review with the client the techniques they have learnt and have begun to practise to help with relaxation, including self-instructions, breathing control, and relaxing images/pictures. Explain that you now want to teach them some new exercises to help them become even better at relaxation and so improve their *self-control* in angry situations.
    (c) Work through with the client the therapist's script for APR on *Handout/Exercise Sheet 8.3*. The therapist will need to model these exercises to the client during initial administrations in order to demystify the exercises, to reduce any anxieties the client might have about doing them, and to facilitate learning.
    (d) Following completion of the APR exercises, discuss with the client how they have/have not helped them feel more relaxed, what they were thinking about during the procedure, and any difficulties that they had with it. Reiterate that by practising these exercises the client will become better (more skilled) at relaxation and this will help them to have more self-control in angry situations in future. Indicate to the client that you will be practising these exercises with them again during the next session, after which they will be asked to practise themselves between sessions using audiotaped instructions.

4. *Reflection and session evaluation (10 mins)*

See section 5 of Session 7 above for directions.

Materials for Session 8

- *Handout/Exercise Sheet 8.1* Anger Log II
- *Handout/Exercise Sheet 8.2* Anger Hierarchy Work Sheet
- *Handout/Exercise Sheet 8.3* Abbreviated Progressive Relaxation (APR) Therapist's Script

SESSION 9 INTRODUCTION TO STRESS INOCULATION PROCEDURE

	Contents	Duration (Approximate)
1	Introduction and review of previous sessions	10 minutes
2	Development of anger hierarchy	15 minutes
3	Introduction to stress inoculation procedure	25 minutes
4	Reflection and session evaluation	10 minutes

Aims

- To complete the construction of the *hierarchy of anger incidents* to be used in the stress inoculation procedures.
- To develop the client's understanding of *thought-catching* as a means of increasing awareness of self-talk (internal dialogue).
- To rehearse the *abbreviated progressive relaxation (APR)* exercises prior to personal practice between sessions.
- To introduce the *stress inoculation procedure* as a means of improving the client's ability to cope with anger situations.

Session guidelines

1. Introduction and review of previous session (10 mins)
  (a) Briefly review the previous session by summarizing the main areas covered including the importance of becoming aware of and recording cognitions in anger situations (thought-catching), the construction of a hierarchy of anger incidents, and new relaxation exercises (APR) to help increase self-control over anger arousal.
  (b) Introduce the content of Session 9. Explain that you are going to discuss with the client how easy/difficult it has been for them to catch their thoughts in anger situations and record these. You will be doing some more work on developing (and hopefully finishing) the anger hierarchy, and you will be beginning to teach them how to see themselves coping more effectively with anger situations in imagination (stress inoculation).
  (c) Check that the client has completed the new logs (Anger Log II) including the section in which they were to record thoughts at the time anger incidents took place. Explore any difficulties with completion of this homework. If the client has been able to record incidents, including contemporaneous thoughts, point out how these cognitions fit

into the 'How Anger Works' model from *Handout/Exercise Sheet 1.1*. If relevant, use this material to confirm or revise the analysis and formulation of the client's anger problems carried out during Sessions 7 and 8.

(d) Be sure to reinforce positively *any* efforts the client has made in attempting to identify and record angry self-talk. If appropriate advice and guidance can be given to the client to sharpen up this procedure by, for example, attempting to get at the thoughts taking place as the anger situation developed, rather than their thoughts about the reactions of others, or the consequences of their own actions afterwards. Reiterate the pivotal role that cognitions have in mediating feelings about and reactions to anger situations.

(e) Ask the client to continue to complete the Anger Logs daily with support from members of the nursing team, and to give particular attention to thought-catching.

2. *Development of the anger hierarchy (15 mins)*

(a) Review with the client the work done during the last session on their anger hierarchy. Ask the client to recall and describe three or four situations they experienced which provoked varying degrees of anger between the 'mild annoyance' example and the 'most angry/furious ever' example described during the last session. As before, help the client to develop these descriptions by prompting them to describe clearly, but succinctly, the setting conditions, context, and situational details associated with these incidents. Try to ensure that the situations described are specific, but not so particular that the circumstances, or a close approximation of them, are unlikely to occur in the future. Avoid discussion of the client's reactions to the situations described and do not be tempted to do therapy at this point by suggesting alternative strategies for more effective coping.

(b) Record the descriptions of the anger-provoking situations using *Handout/Exercise Sheet 8.2*. Once the five or six anger hierarchy items have been elicited, ask the client to rank order them by indicating which situation caused them to feel most angry, which situation comes next in terms of the degree of anger provocation it caused, and so on.

3. *Introduction to stress inoculation procedure (25 mins)*

(a) Review with the client the abbreviated progressive relaxation exercises introduced in the last session. Briefly remind the client of the importance of relaxation in reducing and controlling the physical arousal and feelings which accompany anger. Emphasize how being able to relax will increase the client's self-control in anger situations and so enable them to cope more effectively.

(b) Work through with the client the therapist's script for APR on *Handout/Exercise Sheet 8.3*. Once again model these exercises for the client in order to facilitate learning.

(c) Following the relaxation exercises and visualization of their preferred calming image/picture, present to the client the first anger hierarchy scene describing a situation of mild annoyance. Instruct the client to continue relaxing and then to imagine the scene that you describe. Ask the client to indicate if they are able to visualize the scene as described. If they can, then ask them how angry imagining the scene makes them feel (not at all, a little, or very).

If the client does not signal anger after around 15 seconds, instruct him to switch the picture off and go back to visualizing the relaxing/calming image/picture.

If the client does indicate a degree of anger then give the following instruction:

You are feeling angry imagining this situation, but now see yourself coping with it and handling it well. See yourself staying calm, relaxed and in control. Keep the picture of the situation clear in your mind, but see yourself handling it well.

After around 30 seconds ask the client to go back to thinking about their relaxing image/picture and have them concentrate on this for a further 30 seconds. Then ask the client to slowly take in a deep breath through their nose, hold it momentarily, and then slowly exhale through their mouth before opening their eyes.

(d) Discuss with the client their experiences during this procedure. Ask them how clearly they were able to imagine the first anger hierarchy scene and how they saw themselves coping in this situation (even if they did not need to be prompted to imagine coping). Depending on the outcome of this exercise, modify the anger hierarchy rank order so that, if necessary, another scene which is potentially less anger-provoking becomes the first item in the hierarchy. Explain to the client how you will work through the anger hierarchy so that eventually they will be able to imagine themselves coping effectively with the items at the top.

(e) Explain to the client that for homework, in addition to continuing with their Anger Logs, the client is now required to practise relaxation exercises for themselves. Provide them with a cassette tape with relaxation instructions on it (based on the 'Abbreviated Progressive Relaxation (APR) Therapist's Script' provided in *Handout/Exercise Sheet 8.3*), which they can use to help them practise. Discuss with the client the practicalities of practising relaxation. These will need to be negotiated with their keyworker at the end of the session.

4. Reflection and session evaluation

As for previous sessions.

Materials for Session 9

• *Cassette tape* Anger Treatment – Relaxation Exercises

SESSION 10 BEGINNING OF COGNITIVE RE-STRUCTURING

	Contents	Duration (Approximate)
1	Introduction and review of previous sessions	10 minutes
2	Beginning cognitive re-structuring	20 minutes
3	Stress inoculation procedure	20 minutes
4	Reflection and session evaluation	10 minutes

Aims

• To introduce the concepts of *expectations and appraisals (judgements)* as cognitive processes that can cue anger in certain situations.
• To begin *cognitive re-structuring* using material collected by clients in their Anger Logs.

- To develop the *stress inoculation* procedures begun in the last session.
- To rehearse *abbreviated progressive relaxation (APR)* and review practice of these exercises between sessions.

Session guidelines

1. *Introduction and review of previous session (10 mins)*
   (a) Briefly review the previous session by summarizing the main areas covered including completion of the anger hierarchy, understanding the importance of thought-catching, and the introduction of stress inoculation as a procedure for improving in imagination the ability to cope with anger situations.
   (b) Introduce the content of Session 10. Explain that you are going to look closely at the client's thinking in anger situations in terms of expectations and appraisals that can cue angry feelings. The way in which we think about situations can affect the way we feel and behave and this will be discussed along with how thinking differently can alter our feelings and reactions (cognitive re-structuring). Finally, we will use the stress inoculation procedure to help the client improve their ability to cope, in their imagination, with angry situations.
   (c) Check that the client has completed Anger Logs between this and the last session as requested, including recording the thoughts that they had in anger situations. Learn from the client how they have managed with practising abbreviated progressive relaxation using the relaxation tape. Explore any difficulties with carrying out these homework tasks.

2. *Beginning cognitive re-structuring (20 mins)*
   (a) Briefly go through with the client once more the role that thoughts have in mediating the feelings and behavioural reactions that people have in response to anger situations. Use the 'How Anger Works' model from *Handout/Exercise Sheet 1.1* to illustrate this.
   (b) Select a salient event from the client's Anger Logs in which they have attempted to describe the thoughts that they had at the time of an angry incident. With the client, explore what it was they saw or picked out in this situation that led them to feel angry. If appropriate, explain how previous experiences influence our expectations, and hence what we give attention to in certain situations. Also, our own reactions and those of others in such situations tend to lead to appraisals (judgements), which confirm our expectations. This pattern/cycle in our way of thinking about these situations can lead us to react both in terms of our feelings and behaviour, in an impulsive and unhelpful manner.
   (c) Using the example provocation use *Handout/Exercise Sheet 3.4* to work through the 'Actual' row highlighting key situational factors, the client's thoughts about the situation, the emotional and physical feelings that accompanied the situation, and their behavioural reaction to this situation.
   Then use the 'Possible' row to explore with the client how thinking differently about this situation can change their emotional, physical and behavioural response to it. Ask the client whether they think there could be another explanation for why this situation arose (why what happened, why the person involved behaved as they did, etc.). Should the client have difficulty with this, then an alternative interpretation can be suggested to the client. If they can accept an alternative explanation as being

possible/realistic, explore with them how their emotional and physical responses might have been different. Further, discuss whether their behavioural reaction to the situation might have been different, more helpful, constructive, etc.

Based on this re-structuring and analysis, if appropriate, reiterate how thoughts about a particular situation can affect how we feel (both emotionally and physically) and how we behave. Using this example suggest to the client how in future they can use calm/relaxed self-talk, rather than angry self-talk to be more in control and cope with anger situations.

3. *Stress inoculation procedure (20 mins)*
   (a) Prepare for the inoculation training by reviewing the procedure worked through in the last session. Also, discuss anger hierarchy scene 1 and how the client might successfully cope with this situation were it to occur again. Draw heavily on the cognitive re-structuring work completed in the previous section, and, if appropriate, model and rehearse with the client successful coping in this situation.
   (b) Work through with the client the therapist's script for APR on *Handout/Exercise Sheet 8.3*. If necessary, continue to model these exercises in order to facilitate learning.
   (c) Once the client is relaxed and is concentrating on visualizing their preferred calming image/picture, present anger hierarchy scene 1 describing a situation of mild annoyance. Ask the client to indicate if they are able to visualize the scene as described. If they can, then ask them how angry imagining the scene makes them feel (not at all, a little, or very).

   If the client does not signal anger after around 15 seconds, instruct him to switch the picture off and go back to visualizing the relaxing/calming image/picture.

   If the client does indicate a degree of anger then give the following instruction:

   You are feeling angry imagining this situation, but now see yourself coping with it and handling it well. See yourself staying calm, relaxed and in control. Keep the picture of the situation clear in your mind, but see yourself handling it well.

   After around 30 seconds ask the client to go back to thinking about their relaxing image/picture and have them concentrate on this for a further 30 seconds. Then ask the client to slowly take in a deep breath through their nose, hold it momentarily, and then slowly exhale through their mouth before opening their eyes.

   (d) Discuss with the client their experiences during this procedure. Ask them how clearly they were able to imagine the first anger hierarchy scene and how they saw themselves coping in this situation (even if they did not need to be prompted to imagine coping). Depending on the outcome of this exercise you may need to re-evaluate the position of this item in the anger hierarchy. In addition, if the client has had difficulty with imagining coping effectively you may need to suggest effective coping strategies which they can try to use during re-presentation of the scene.
   (e) For homework ask the client to continue with their Anger Logs and practising relaxation exercises using the relaxation tape.

4. *Reflection and session evaluation (10 mins)*

As for previous sessions.

Materials for Session 10

- *Handout/Exercise Sheet 10.1* Thinking Differently about Anger Situations

SESSION 11 DEVELOPING COGNITIVE RE-STRUCTURING: ATTENTIONAL FOCUS, EXPECTATIONS AND APPRAISALS

	Contents	Duration (Approximate)
1	Introduction and review of previous session	10 minutes
2	Developing cognitive re-structuring	20 minutes
3	Stress inoculation procedure	20 minutes
4	Reflection and session evaluation	10 minutes

Aims

- To work on the concepts of *attentional focus, expectations and appraisals* as cognitive processes that can cue anger in certain situations.
- To develop *cognitive re-structuring* using material collected by clients in their Anger Logs.
- To introduce the concept of *'perspective-taking'* to enhance appraisal modification.
- To develop further *stress inoculation* procedures.

Session guidelines

1. *Introduction and review of previous session (10 mins)*
   (a) Briefly review the previous session by summarizing the main areas covered including the client's Anger Log recordings of their thoughts in anger situations, discuss how thinking in anger situations can affect feelings and behaviour, and how thinking differently can help us to alter feelings and reactions (cognitive re-structuring). In addition, the stress inoculation procedure was used to help the client imagine coping with a low anger situation from their anger hierarchy.
   (b) Introduce the content of Session 11. Explain that you are going to look closely again at the client's thinking in anger situations in terms of attentional focus, expectations and appraisals that can cue angry feelings. Different ways of thinking about situations will be explored as a means of altering feelings and reactions (cognitive re-structuring). We will also begin to talk about perspective-taking as a means of modifying appraisals (judgements) about anger situations. Finally, we will use the stress inoculation procedure to help the client to practise their ability to cope, in imagination, with an angry situation from their anger hierarchy.
   (c) Check that the client has completed Anger Logs between this and the last session as requested, including recording the thoughts that they had in anger situations. Learn from the client how they have managed with practising abbreviated progressive

relaxation using the relaxation tape. Explore any difficulties with compliance with these homework tasks.

2. *Developing cognitive re-structuring (20 mins)*
   (a) Review briefly with the client once more the role that thoughts have in mediating the feelings and behavioural reactions that people experience in response to anger situations. Use the 'How Anger Works' model from *Handout/Exercise Sheet 1.1* to illustrate this as required.
   (b) Review the Anger Logs completed by the client between this and their last session. Discuss and praise situations in which the client has managed to maintain self-control, especially when experiencing intense feelings of anger and tension. Give constructive feedback on the quality of the recordings, giving particular attention to the thoughts/self-talk reported at the time of the incident. Have the client attempt to identify any recurring themes or patterns in these thoughts and, if appropriate, reference these to the analysis and formulation of the client's anger problem carried out during Sessions 7 and 8. For example, it may be possible to highlight to the client that they tend to become more angry and aroused in relation to situations that contain perceived unfairness/injustice, disrespectful treatment, etc. Their responses to such situations might be characterized by, for example, intense feelings of anger and very quick/impulsive reactions.
   (c) Using these, and earlier Anger Log recordings, discuss the *attentional focus, expectation*, and *appraisal* components of their thinking in anger situations. Explain that often, based on previous experiences, people selectively attend to and focus on particular aspect of others' behaviour, which they see as intentionally provocative or threatening. In such situations people attend *only* to these aspects of others' actions and filter out other information.

   This *selective attentional focus* can prime people to *expect* a situation to become unpleasant, confrontational, angry, etc. These *expectations* cue our own reactions in terms of emotional feelings, tension, and the way we behave.

   Because of these *expectations,* and the way in which we and others react, we *appraise* (or *judge*) the other person to be behaving in the way we expected them to. This then confirms the initial attentional focus on those actions perceived as intentionally provocative.
   (d) Select a salient event from the client's Anger Logs in which they have attempted to describe their thoughts at the time of an angry incident. With the client explore, with reference to section (c) above, the attentional focus, expectations, and appraisal components of their thinking in this situation. Illustrate how these cognitive processes influenced their emotional, physical and behavioural responses to this situation. This exercise can be done using the 'Actual' row of *Handout/Exercise Sheet 10.1* 'Thinking Differently About Anger Situations'.

   Then, using the 'Possible' row of *Handout/Exercise Sheet 10.1* explore with the client how thinking differently about the situation can alter their emotional, physical and behavioural responses to it. In particular, have the client consider how shifting their attentional focus, altering their expectations, and modifying their appraisals concerning others can help them think differently about the situation and generate an alternative explanation for why it arose. Should the client have difficulty with this exercise, then an alternative interpretation can be suggested. They should then work out how an alternative explanation can alter the emotional, physical, and behavioural responses to the situation. Have them re-rate their emotional and physical feelings and discuss how their behavioural reaction to the situation might have been different, more helpful and constructive.

(e) Introduce to the client the idea that perspective-taking (empathy, 'putting yourself in the other person's shoes') can be very helpful in modifying appraisals (judgements) about others' behaviour in anger situations. Relate this concept to the situation and example worked through above and ask the client if putting themselves in the other person's shoes helps them to think about the situation in a different way to their initial interpretation.

3. Stress inoculation procedure (20 mins)

(a) Prepare for the inoculation training by reviewing the procedure worked through in the last session. Review the anger hierarchy constructed in previous sessions and discuss whether the hierarchy order needs to be adjusted. Select with the client a second anger hierarchy scene to be worked on during this procedure.

(b) Having selected an anger hierarchy scene, discuss with the client how they might cope successfully with this situation were it to occur again. Draw heavily on the cognitive re-structuring work completed earlier in the session, and verbally rehearse and model with the client successful coping in this situation.

(c) Have the client become as relaxed as possible using the abbreviated progressive relaxation (APR) exercises previously rehearsed and practised by the client. At this stage if the client appears to be successful in using these relaxation techniques, the exercises can be made briefer, to save time. If, however, you judge that the client continues to require coaching in the use of these exercises, work through the therapist's script for APR on *Handout/Exercise Sheet 8.3*.

(d) Once the client is relaxed and is concentrating on visualizing their preferred calming image/picture, present anger hierarchy scene 2 describing a low anger situation. Then follow the procedure described in Session 10, Section 3 (Stress inoculation procedure), paragraphs (c) and (d).

(e) For homework ask the client to continue with their Anger Logs, to practise relaxation exercises using the relaxation tape, and to attempt to perspective-take in angry situations in order to improve their ability to think differently.

4. Reflection and session evaluation (10 mins)

As for previous sessions.

SESSION 12 PERSPECTIVE-TAKING AND ROLE-PLAYING

Contents	Duration (Approximate)
1 Introduction and review of previous session	10 minutes
2 Developing cognitive re-structuring (to include perspective-taking)	20 minutes
3 Developing stress inoculation procedure (to include role-playing)	20 minutes
4 Reflection and session evaluation	10 minutes

Aims

- To enhance cognitive restructuring by developing the concept of *perspective-taking* as an effective means of modifying appraisals.
- To continue to develop further *stress inoculation* procedures to improve imaginal coping in anger situations.
- To introduce *role-playing* as a technique for practising behavioural coping skills previously rehearsed in imagination.

Session guidelines

1. Introduction and review of previous session (10 mins)
   (a) Briefly review the previous session by summarizing the main areas covered, including discussion of attentional focus, expectations and appraisals as cognitive processes that can cue angry feelings, how perspective-taking can help to modify appraisals (judgements) about anger situations, and how the stress inoculation procedure was used to help the client to imagine coping with a second anger situation from their anger hierarchy.
   (b) Introduce the content of Session 12. Explain that you are going to spend some more time thinking about how perspective-taking can help clients to think differently about anger situations, slow things down, and help with self-control. As well as using the stress inoculation procedure to help the client to rehearse coping (in imagination) with an angry situation from their anger hierarchy, you will be helping them to practise these coping strategies using role-play.
   (c) Check that the client has completed Anger Logs between this and the last session as requested, including recording the thoughts that they had in anger situations. Learn from the client how they have managed with practising abbreviated progressive relaxation using the relaxation tape.

2. Developing cognitive re-structuring (to include perspective-taking) (20 mins)
   (a) Review the Anger Logs completed by the clients between this and their last session. Routinely praise the situations in which the client has managed to maintain self-control, especially when experiencing intense feelings of anger and tension. Continue to give constructive feedback on the quality of the recordings, giving particular attention to the thoughts/self-talk reported at the time of the incident. Identify with the client any recurring themes or patterns in these thoughts, and if appropriate, reference these to the analysis and formulation of the client's anger problem carried out in previous sessions.
   (b) Select a salient event from the client's Anger Logs in which they have attempted to describe their thoughts at the time of an angry incident. With the client explore, with reference to the cognitive/re-structuring work carried out during Session 11, the attentional focus, expectations, and appraisal components of their thinking in this situation. As in previous sessions, illustrate how these cognitive processes have influenced their emotional, physical and behavioural responses to this situation using the 'Actual' row of *Handout/Exercise Sheet 10.1* 'Thinking Differently about Anger Situations'.

Remind the client of the discussion during Session 11 about how perspective-taking ('putting yourself in the other person's shoes') can be very useful in helping us to think differently about anger situations. In a deliberate manner, have the client re-consider the anger situation being discussed. Ask them to perspective-take by putting themselves in the other person's shoes and looking at the situation from their point of view, or through their eyes, etc. Then prompt the client to suggest alternative explanations for the other person's behaviour and discuss how realistic or probable these suggestions are. From this perspective-taking exercise help the client to come up with some different thoughts about the anger situation and include these in the 'Possible' row of *Handout/Exercise Sheet 10.1*. Then, as in previous sessions, explore with the client how thinking differently about the situation can alter their emotional, physical and behavioural responses to it. Point out how perspective-taking has helped shift their attention, alter their expectations, and modify their appraisals concerning others' action and can help them to respond in a calmer, more self-controlled way.

(c) Introduce to the client the new form for recording angry incidents *Handout/Exercise Sheet 12.1* 'Anger Log III'. Explain that this form is exactly the same as the previous Anger Log II, except that there is a new section in which they are to record different, or alternative thoughts about angry situations. Encourage the client to use perspective-taking, to help them come up with different thoughts about anger incidents. It might be helpful to illustrate how to complete the new Anger Logs by quickly re-recording the incident worked on above including completion of the new section for alternative/different thoughts.

3. *Developing stress inoculation procedure (to include role-playing) (20 mins)*

(a) Prepare for the inoculation training by reviewing the procedure worked through in the last session. Routinely review the anger hierarchy constructed previously and make any necessary adjustments. Select with the client a third anger hierarchy scene to be worked on in this procedure.

(b) Discuss with the client how they might cope successfully with the selected situation if it were to occur again. Draw on the cognitive re-structuring work completed earlier, and verbally rehearse and model with the client successful coping in this situation.

(c) Have the client become as relaxed as possible using the abbreviated progressive relaxation (APR) exercises. These exercises may be shortened to save time depending on how you judge the client to be progressing with their relaxation training.

(d) Once the client is relaxed and is concentrating on visualizing their preferred calming image/picture, present anger hierarchy scene 3 describing a low/medium anger situation. Then follow the procedure described in Session 10, Section 3 (Stress inoculation procedure) paragraphs (c) and (d).

(e) Following completion of the stress inoculation procedure, conduct a role-play inoculation exposure to anger hierarchy scene 3 (assuming that it involves the behaviour of another person). Carry out a 'dry run' by taking the role of the provoking person and enacting their provocative behaviour. Check with the client that this is a reasonable approximation of the other person's behaviour. Then review with the client the coping strategies that they found to be successful in imaginal rehearsal and encourage them to try these out in role-play. Prompt, as necessary, to use self-instructions, alternative thoughts, breathing control, and calming imagery in order to handle the situation effectively. Discuss with the client the effectiveness of the various coping strategies tried during the role-play and note those components reported as being most helpful.

(f) If required, and if time allows, re-present anger hierarchy scene 3 in imagination to ensure that the client has experienced success in coping with this scene before ending the session.

4. Reflection and session evaluation (10 mins)

As for previous sessions.

Materials for Session 12

• *Handout/Exercise Sheet 12.1* Anger Log III

SESSION 13 USING SELF-INSTRUCTIONS EFFECTIVELY

	Contents	Duration (Approximate)
1	Introduction and review of previous session	10 minutes
2	Further developing cognitive re-structuring	20 minutes
3	Further developing stress inoculation procedure (to include self-instructions and role-playing)	20 minutes
4	Reflection and session evaluation	10 minutes

Aims

• To develop cognitive re-structuring incorporating perspective-taking and re-introducing the notion of *self-instructions.*
• To continue to develop further *stress inoculation* procedures by incorporating and re-hearsing the use of *self-instructions.*
• To develop *role-playing* as a technique for practising behavioural coping skills previously rehearsed in imagination.

Session guidelines

1. Introduction and review of previous session (10 mins)
   (a) Briefly review the previous session by summarizing the main areas covered including how perspective-taking can help clients to think differently about anger situations, slow things down and help with self-control; and how role-play can help them to practise the coping strategies that they have previously rehearsed in imagination.
   (b) Introduce the content of Session 13. Explain that you are going to look again at how to think differently about anger situations by perspective-taking, discuss self-instructions, or things that clients can tell themselves to remind them to keep in control of their thoughts, feelings and behaviour, to use role-play to practise the coping strategies rehearsed in imagination to deal with a situation from their anger hierarchy.

(c) Check that the client has completed the new Anger Logs (Anger Log III) between this and the last session as requested, including recording the thoughts that they had in anger situations, as well as any different thoughts about situations they were able to come up with by perspective-taking. Learn from the clients how they have managed with practising abbreviated progressive relaxation using the relaxation tape. Explore any difficulties that the client has had with completing these homework tasks.

2. *Further developing cognitive re-structuring (20 mins)*

(a) Review the new Anger Logs completed by the clients between this and their last session. Routinely praise situations in which the client has managed to maintain self-control, especially when experiencing intense feelings of anger and tension. Continue to give constructive feedback on the quality of recordings. Identify with the client any recurring themes or patterns in the thoughts/self-talk reported at the time of an incident. If appropriate, reference these thoughts to the analysis and formulation of the client's anger problem carried out in previous sessions.

Give particular attention to the section of the new Anger Logs concerning alternative thoughts that they might have had in anger situations. Discuss with the client their success with this exercise and any difficulties they might have had with it. Explore whether the client has been able to use perspective-taking to help them identify different thoughts about anger incidents.

(b) Select a salient event from the client's Anger Logs in which they have attempted to describe their thoughts at the time of an angry incident. Let the client explore, with reference to the cognitive re-structuring work carried out during previous sessions, the attentional focus, expectations, and appraisal components of their thinking in this situation. As in previous sessions, illustrate how these cognitive processes influenced their emotional, physical and behavioural responses to this situation using the 'Actual' row of *Handout/Exercise Sheet 10.1* 'Thinking Differently about Anger Situations'.

Examine closely with the client the section of the new Anger Log in which they were to record different, or alternative thoughts about the angry situation. Discuss with the client the appropriateness of any alternative thoughts recorded, whether or not they attempted to perspective-take to help them come up with different appraisals about the situation, etc. At this stage, depending on the quality of the client's recording, you may need to prompt or suggest alternative explanations for the other person's behaviour.

Following on from this 'different thinking through perspective-taking' exercise, explore with the client how their emotional, physical, and behavioural responses to the anger situation have changed. Use the 'Possible' row of *Handout/Exercise Sheet 10.1* to facilitate this. Once again, point out how perspective-taking has helped them to shift their attention, alter their expectations, and modify their appraisals concerning others' actions and can help them to respond in a calmer, more self-controlled way.

(c) Discuss with the client how thinking differently through perspective-taking in order to remain calm and in control could be helped by the use of self-instructions. Ask the client 'What could you tell yourself, or what could you say to yourself to remind you to think differently in an angry situation, stay calm and handle things?'.

To help with this exercise have the client consider the anger incident from their Anger Log discussed above. Suggest that they 'talk themselves through' this incident in terms of what they need to remind themselves to do in order to think differently, remain calm and behave appropriately. If possible, from this elicit discreet self-instructions relevant to the type of situation being considered and reflect these back to the client.

3. *Further developing stress inoculation procedure (to include self-instructions and role-playing) (20 mins)*
   (a) Prepare for the inoculation training by reviewing the procedure worked through in the last session. Routinely review the anger hierarchy constructed previously and make any necessary adjustments. Select with the client a fourth anger hierarchy scene to be worked on in this procedure.
   (b) Discuss with the client how they might cope successfully with the selected situation if it were to occur again. Draw on the cognitive re-structuring work completed earlier, incorporating appraisal modification through perspective-taking. In addition, have the client talk themselves through the situation out loud, and by so doing give themselves self-instructions as prompts/reminders for thinking differently/perspective-taking, arousal reduction through breathing control, use of calming imagery, and successful coping with the situation through problem-solving, assertiveness, a dignified retreat, etc. In this way successful coping through the use of self-instruction will have been verbally rehearsed.
   (c) Have the client become as relaxed as possible using the abbreviated progressive relaxation (APR) exercises. These exercises may be shortened to save time depending on how you judge the client to be progressing with their relaxation training.
   (d) Once the client is relaxed and is concentrating on visualizing their preferred calming image/picture, present anger hierarchy scene 4 describing a medium anger situation. Then follow the procedure described in Session 10, Section 3 (Stress inoculation procedure), paragraphs (c) and (d). During the inoculation exposure to the hierarchy scene, encourage the clients to see themselves coping by using self-instructions verbally rehearsed earlier in the sessions.
   (e) Following completion of the stress inoculation procedure, conduct a role-play inoculation exposure to anger hierarchy scene 4 (assuming that it involves the behaviour of another person). Carry out a 'dry run' by taking the role of the provoking person and enacting their provocative behaviour. Check with the client that this is a reasonable approximation of the other person's behaviour. Then review with the client the coping strategies that they found to be successful in imaginal rehearsal and encourage them to try these out in role-play. Prompt, as necessary, the use of self-instructions discussed earlier to cue the use of alternative thoughts, breathing control, and calming imagery in order to handle the situation effectively. Discuss with the client the effectiveness of the various coping strategies tried during the role-play and note those components reported as being most helpful.
   (f) If required, and if time allows, re-present anger hierarchy scene 4 in imagination to ensure that the client has experienced success in coping with this scene before ending the session.

4. *Reflection and session evaluation (10 mins)*

As for previous sessions.

SESSION 14 PROBLEM-SOLVING THROUGH
EFFECTIVE COMMUNICATION

	Contents	Duration (Approximate)
1	Introduction and review of previous session	10 minutes
2	Further development of cognitive re-structuring	15 minutes
3	Problem-solving through effective communication	10 minutes
4	Further development of stress inoculation procedure (to include self-instructions and role-playing)	15 minutes
5	Reflection and session evaluation	10 minutes

Aims

* To further develop *cognitive re-structuring* incorporating *perspective-taking* and *self-instructions*.
* To introduce the idea of dealing with anger situations effectively by *communicating constructively (problem-solving approach)*.
* To continue to develop further *stress inoculation* procedure incorporating *self-instructions* and *effective communication*.
* To develop further *role-playing* as a technique for practising *behavioural coping skills* previously rehearsed in imagination.

Session guidelines

1. Introduction and review of previous session (10 mins)
   (a) Briefly review the previous session by summarizing the main areas covered including how to think differently about anger situations by perspective-taking, how to use self-instructions to remind clients to keep in control of their thoughts, feelings and behaviour; and how role-play can help to practise the coping strategies that they have previously rehearsed in imagination.
   (b) Introduce the content of Session 14. Explain that as in previous sessions you will be looking again at how to think differently about anger situations by perspective-taking; discussing again how self-instructions can help to remind them to keep in control of their thoughts, feelings and behaviour; how anger situations can be dealt with by communicating effectively, and; finally you will use role-play to practise the coping strategies rehearsed in imagination to deal with a situation from their anger hierarchy.
   (c) Check that the client has completed Anger Logs between this and the last session as requested, including recording of the thoughts that they had in anger situations, as well as any different thoughts about situations they were able to come up with by perspective-taking. Learn from the clients how they have managed with abbreviated progressive relaxation using the relaxation tape. Explore any difficulties that the client has had with completing these homework tasks.

2. *Developing Cognitive Re-structuring (20 mins)*

(a) Review the new Anger Logs completed by the client between this and their last session. Routinely praise situations in which the client has managed to maintain self-control, especially when experiencing intense feelings of anger and tension. Continue to give constructive feedback on the quality of recordings. Identify with the client any recurring themes or patterns in the thoughts/self-talk reported at the time of an incident. If appropriate, reference these thoughts to the analysis and formulation of the client's anger problem carried out in previous sessions.

(b) Give particular attention to the section of the new Anger Logs concerning alternative thoughts that they might have had in anger situations. Discuss with the client their success with this exercise and any difficulties they might have had with it. Explore whether the client has been able to use perspective-taking to help them identify different thoughts about anger incidents.

In addition, discuss with the client how able they have been to use self-instructions in anger situations to remind them to control thoughts, feelings and behaviour. Review the self-instructions clients report using and discuss how effective these have been. Help the client to develop and shape self-instructions as appropriate.

(c) Select a salient event from the client's Anger Logs in which they have attempted to describe their thoughts at the time of an angry incident. Let the client explore, with reference to the cognitive re-structuring work carried out during previous sessions, the attentional focus, expectations, and appraisal components of their thinking in this situation. As in previous sessions, illustrate how these cognitive processes influenced their emotional, physical and behavioural responses to this situation using the 'Actual' row of *Handout/Exercise Sheet 10.1* 'Thinking Differently About Anger Situations'.

Examine closely with the client the section of the new Anger Log in which they were to record different, or alternative thoughts about the angry situation. Discuss with the client the appropriateness of any alternative thoughts recorded, whether or not they attempted to perspective-take to help them come up with different appraisals about the situation, etc. At this stage, depending on the quality of the client's recording, you may still need to prompt or suggest alternative explanations for the other person's behaviour.

Following on from this 'different thinking through perspective-taking' exercise, explore with the client how their emotional, physical and behavioural responses to the anger situation have changed. Use the 'Possible' row of *Handout/Exercise Sheet 10.1* to facilitate this. Once again, point out how perspective-taking has helped them to shift their attention, alter their expectations, and modify their appraisals concerning others' actions and can help them to respond in a calmer, more self-controlled way.

(d) Review with the client how thinking differently through perspective-taking in order to remain calm and in control can be helped by the use of self-instructions. Using the anger incident from their Anger Log discussed above, ask the client 'What could you tell yourself, or what could you say to yourself to remind you to think differently in this situation, stay calm and handle things?' As before, help the client to generate discreet self-instructions relevant to the type of situation being considered and suggest that these can be used to good effect in future.

3. *Problem-solving through effective communication (10 mins)*

    (a) Using the Anger Log incident worked on during the cognitive re-structuring exercise above, discuss with the client their behavioural response to this situation and any consequences (positive or negative) that flowed from it. Explain that as the client is getting better at controlling their thinking and feelings in anger situations, they can now begin to concentrate on reacting/behaving in ways that are more likely to help them and others, rather than make things worse. Suggest to the client that the key to coping effectively in anger situations is constructive communication.

    (b) Explain to the client the distinction between being *passive* and *aggressive* in anger situations. It is more likely that by being *assertive* they will be able to communicate their thoughts and feelings in a calm and controlled way and solve problem situations. Referring to *Handout/Exercise Sheet 14.1* 'Effective Communication in Anger Situations' might facilitate this discussion. Be clear with the client that being passive ('a soft touch') or being aggressive (abusive, offensive) will not solve anger situations. Rather, if the client can steer a middle course whereby they are assertive by being firm and clear about their feelings, while at the same time being polite and reasonable, they are more likely to achieve a good outcome with positive consequences.

        Have the client re-consider their behavioural response and the consequences of this to the situation worked on earlier during the cognitive re-structuring exercise. Discuss how a more assertive approach, compared with either a passive or aggressive response, might have improved the outcome of the situation for both the client and others involved.

4. *Developing stress inoculation procedure (15 mins)*

    (a) Prepare for the inoculation training by reviewing the procedure worked through in the last session. Routinely review the anger hierarchy constructed previously and make any necessary adjustments. Select with the client a fifth anger hierarchy scene to be worked on in this procedure.

    (b) Discuss with the client how they might cope successfully with the selected situation if it were to occur again. Draw on the cognitive re-structuring work completed earlier, incorporating appraisal modification through perspective-taking. Also, have the client rehearse self-instructions they would use to remind them to control their thinking and feelings. Finally, discuss with the client how they would attempt to resolve the situation by dealing with it in an assertive manner. In this way, successful coping with the situation through the use of perspective-taking, self-instructions and assertiveness will have been verbally rehearsed.

    (c) Have the client become as relaxed as possible using the abbreviated progressive relaxation (APR) exercises. These exercises may be shortened and abbreviated further to save time depending on how you judge the client to be progressing with their relaxation training.

    (d) Once the client is relaxed and is concentrating on visualizing their preferred calming image/picture, present anger hierarchy scene 5 describing a medium/high anger situation. Then follow the procedure described in Session 10, Section 3 (Stress inoculation procedure) paragraphs (c) and (d). During the inoculation exposure to the hierarchy scene, encourage the clients to see themselves coping by using self-instructions and being assertive as verbally rehearsed earlier in the session.

(e) Following completion of the stress inoculation procedure, conduct a role-play inoculation exposure to anger hierarchy scene 5 (assuming that it involves the behaviour of another person). Carry out a 'dry run' by taking the role of the provoking person and enacting their provocative behaviour. Check with the client that this is a reasonable approximation of the other person's behaviour. Then review with the client the coping strategies that they found to be successful in imaginal rehearsal and encourage them to try these out in role-play. Prompt, as necessary, the use of self-instructions discussed earlier to cue cognitive and emotional control. In addition, guide the client in using an assertive style of communication in an attempt to resolve the anger situation to the mutual satisfaction of the client and others involved. Discuss with the client the effectiveness of the various coping strategies tried during the role-play and note those components reported as being most helpful.

(f) If required, and if time allows, re-present anger hierarchy scene 5 in imagination to ensure that the client has experienced success in coping with this scene before ending the session

5. Reflection and session evaluation (10 mins)

As for previous sessions.

Materials for Session 14

- *Handout/Exercise Sheet 14.1* Effective Communication in Anger Situations

SESSION 15 DEVELOPMENT OF PROBLEM-SOLVING THROUGH EFFECTIVE COMMUNICATION

	Contents	Duration (Approximate)
1	Introduction and review of previous session	10 minutes
2	Further development of cognitive re-structuring	15 minutes
3	Development of problem-solving through effective communication	10 minutes
4	Further development of stress inoculation procedure (to include self-instructions and role-playing)	15 minutes
5	Reflection and session evaluation	10 minutes

Aims

- To further develop *cognitive re-structuring* incorporating *perspective-taking* and *self-instructions*.
- To develop skills in dealing with anger situations effectively by *communicating constructively* (*problem-solving approach*).

- To continue to develop further *stress inoculation* procedure incorporating *self-instructions* and *effective communication*.
- To develop further *role-playing* as a technique for practising *behavioural coping skills* previously rehearsed in imagination.

Session guidelines

1. *Introduction and review of previous session (10 mins)*
   (a) Briefly review the previous session by summarizing the main areas covered including how to think differently about anger situations by perspective-taking; further discussion of how self-instructions can help to keep in control of thoughts, feelings and behaviour; how anger situations can be dealt with by communicating effectively, and use of role-play to practise the coping strategies rehearsed in imagination to deal with a situation from the anger hierarchy.
   (b) Introduce the content of Session 15. Explain that this session will be essentially the same as Session 14. The main aim is to build on the ideas discussed in the last session about how anger situations can be dealt with by communicating effectively. In addition, thinking differently about anger situations by perspective-taking, using self-instructions, relaxation and role-play will be covered as usual.
   (c) Check that the client has completed Anger Logs between this and the last session as requested, including recording of the thoughts that they had in anger situations, as well as any different thoughts about situations they were able to come up with by perspective-taking. Learn from the clients how they have managed with abbreviated progressive relaxation using the relaxation tape. Explore any difficulties that the client has had with completing these homework tasks.

2. *Further developing cognitive re-structuring (20 mins)*
   (a) Follow the procedure described for Session 14, Session Guidelines, section 2, paragraphs (a), (b), and (c).
   (b) In this way you will be reviewing with the client the use of Anger Logs and the development of their skills in more accurately recording thoughts/cognitions at the time of anger incidents, as well as alternative appraisals generated through perspective-taking. In addition, you will have guided them through a cognitive re-structuring exercise using an incident selected from the Anger Logs. During this exercise you will have reviewed with the client the use of self-instructions to cue cognitive and emotional control.

3. *Development of problem-solving through effective communication (10 mins)*
   (a) Using the Anger Log incident worked on during the cognitive re-structuring exercise above, discuss with the client their behavioural response to this situation and any consequences (positive or negative) that flowed from it. Emphasize once again that as the client is now getting better at controlling their thinking and feelings in anger situations, they should be concentrating on responding/behaving in ways that are more likely to help them and others, rather than make things worse. Remind the client that the key to coping effectively in anger situations is through constructive communication.

(b) Review with the client the distinction between being *passive* and *aggressive* in anger situations. That by being *assertive* they will be able to communicate their thoughts and feelings in a calm and controlled way in order to solve problem situations. Refer once again, to *Handout/Exercise Sheet 14.1* 'Effective Communication in Anger Situations' to facilitate this discussion. Reiterate that being passive ('a soft touch' or 'a pushover') or being aggressive (abusive, offensive, etc.) will not solve anger situations. If the client can instead steer a middle course whereby they are assertive by being firm and clear about their feelings, while at the same time being polite and reasonable, they are more likely to achieve a good outcome with positive consequences. If appropriate, relate these points to the role-play inoculation exposure to the anger hierarchy scene covered during Session 14. This role-play exercise may have demonstrated some of the difficulties in communicating effectively by being assertive in anger situations.

(c) Explain to the client that communicating effectively in order to solve problems is a new skill that (like the many other skills they have learned during anger treatment) takes time to acquire and requires practice and training. It is likely that they have got used to a certain style of responding/behaving in anger situations and it will take some time to learn to deal with these situations in a different, but more effective way. For these reasons it is likely that clients will not always 'get it right' when trying to deal with situations by being assertive, communicating effectively and solving problems. However, they should not feel that they have failed, or lose heart if, on occasions, they find this new way of behaving difficult and hard to do. Emphasize once again the benefits of learning to behave and respond in this way in relation to the costs and benefits discussed in previous sessions.

(d) Discuss with the client how being *goal-orientated* will help them to communicate effectively and problem-solve so that no heavy costs are incurred. That is, they need to be clear about how they want the situation to end. Having the last word or attempting to 'win' is unlikely to help. In general a good outcome from an anger situation involves the following:
  - Nobody has been hurt (emotionally or physically).
  - Nobody has 'lost' or 'lost out'
  - Everybody involved is able to accept/feels OK about how things have worked out.

(e) Have the client re-consider their behavioural response and consequences to the anger situation worked on earlier during the cognitive re-structuring exercise. Discuss in detail how a more assertive approach, compared with either a passive or aggressive response, might have improved the outcome of the situation both for the client and others involved.

4. *Developing stress inoculation procedure (15 mins)*
  (a) Work through the stress inoculation procedure in imagination and role-play as de-scribed in Session 14 Session Guidelines, section 4, paragraphs (a), (b), (c), (d), (e) and (f).
  (b) If appropriate, present anger hierarchy scene 6 describing a high anger situation for the imaginal stress inoculation procedure. Both during the imaginal inoculation exposure and the role-play exposure be sure to emphasize the role of effective com-munication through an assertive style in order to problem-solve in anger situations.

5. Reflection and session evaluation (10 mins)

As for previous sessions.

SESSION 16 DEALING WITH RUMINATION AND ESCALATION

	Contents	Duration (Approximate)
1	Introduction and review of previous session	10 minutes
2	Developing cognitive re-structuring and problem-solving	15 minutes
3	Further development of problem-solving through effective communication: dealing with rumination and escalation	10 minutes
4	Development of stress inoculation procedure	15 minutes
5	Reflection and session evaluation	10 minutes

Aims

- To further develop *cognitive re-structuring* incorporating *perspective-taking* and *self-instructions.*
- To further develop skills in dealing with anger situations effectively by *communicating constructively (problem-solving approach).*
- To introduce the concepts of *rumination* and *escalation* which can work against self-control of anger.
- To continue to develop further *stress inoculation* procedures including *imaginal* and *role-play* exposures to anger-provoking situations.

Session guidelines

1. Introduction and review of previous session (10 mins)
   (a) Briefly review the previous session by summarizing the main areas covered, including how to think differently about anger situations by perspective-taking; further discussion of how self-instructions can help to keep control of thoughts, feelings and behaviour; how anger situations can be dealt with by communicating effectively, and use of role-play to practise the coping strategies rehearsed in imagination to deal with a situation from the anger hierarchy.
   (b) Introduce the content of Session 16. Explain that this session will cover most of the work covered during Session 15. In addition, the concept of *rumination* (dwelling on things) and *escalation* (situations getting out of control) will be discussed as threats to self-control of anger.
   (c) Check that the client has completed Anger Logs between this and the last session as requested, including recording of the thoughts that they had in anger situations, as well as any different thoughts about situations they were able to come up with by perspective-taking. Learn from the clients how they have managed with abbreviated

progressive relaxation using the relaxation tape. Review and explore any difficulties that the client has had with completing these homework tasks.

2. *Developing cognitive re-structuring (15 mins)*
   (a) Follow the procedure described for Session 14, Session Guidelines, section 2, paragraphs (a), (b), and (c).
   (b) In this way you will be reviewing with the client the use of Anger Logs and the development of their skills in more accurately recording thoughts/cognitions at the time of anger incidents, as well as alternative appraisals generated through perspective-taking. In addition, you will have guided them through a cognitive re-structuring exercise using an incident selected from the Anger Logs. During this exercise you will have reviewed with the client the use of self-instructions to cue cognitive and emotional control.
   (c) As part of the cognitive re-structuring exercise, discuss with the client their behavioural responses in those situations recorded in their Anger Logs. Explore their use of problem-solving through effective communication with reference to the work carried out during Sessions 14 and 15 on distinguishing between passive, aggressive and assertive styles of communication. Discuss whether they have been able to adopt a 'goal-orientated' approach to problem-solving in order to improve outcomes in anger situations both for themselves and others.

3. *Further development of problem-solving through effective communication: dealing with rumination and escalation (10 mins)*
   (a) Remind the client of the work done in earlier sessions on 'attentional focus'. Referring to the analysis and formulation of the client's anger problems carried out at the beginning of the Treatment Phase sessions (as well as work done on Anger Logs in the meantime), remind the client that they tend to be 'sensitive' to particular types of anger situations which they then focus on; for example, situations involving perceived unfairness, frustration, disrespect, etc.
   (b) Explain how this 'sensitivity' to particular types of situations can continue after the situation has ended so that the client can sometimes dwell on the incident and is unable to put it out of their mind. Discuss how this is unhelpful in that it keeps anger levels 'topped-up' making it easier for new incidents to trigger angry feelings and may encourage the client to spend too much time thinking about (fantasizing) about how to get back at whoever has provoked them. This in turn increases their sensitivity to the types of situations to which they are already sensitized.
   (c) Explore with the client different ways in which rumination might be combated including self-monitoring and recording, discussion of the problem with others (staff, therapists, etc.,) relaxation exercises, use of calming images, and other forms of distraction. Be clear with the client that continued rumination has a potential high cost in that by staying angry they are more likely to lose control and incur costs discussed in earlier sessions.
   (d) From Anger Logs previously completed, or from the client's anger hierarchy, select an anger situation in which there has been an escalation of provocation. Explore with the client how this situation escalated in terms of a discreet series of steps that included increased levels of anger, breakdown in communication, loss of control, etc.
   (e) Explain to the client that while keeping control of thoughts and feelings and attempting to problem-solve is more difficult in an escalating situation, there are

things that they can do to prevent a situation from getting out of control. Ask the client to suggest tactics or techniques that they might use to achieve this. Discuss different possibilities including:

- Attempting to listen and understand the other person's point of view (perspective-taking).
- Staying calm and composed and not reacting to the other person's increasing levels of anger.
- Attempting to reassure the other person that, whatever the problem, it can be sorted out if they can discuss it calmly in a reasonable manner.
- Choosing to walk away or remove oneself from the situation if it is clear the other person is becoming more and more angry ('strategic withdrawal').
- Effective communication through an assertive style, which involves being reasonable, polite and measured.

Explain that if necessary 'strategic withdrawal' is not being weak, a pushover, or losing out. If the client decides that this is the best option, then they are in control and are exercising their own choice. They can take some 'time out' to cool down and allow the other person to cool off, and then decide the best way to sort out the problem (whether with the person directly or by involving others, for example, staff). Discuss with the client how adoption of one or more of these techniques might have helped in the situation identified from their Anger Logs/anger hierarchy.

4. *Developing stress inoculation procedure (15 mins)*
   (a) Work through the stress inoculation procedure in imagination and role-play as described in Session 14, Session Guidelines, section 4, paragraphs (a), (b), (c), (d), (e) and (f).
   (b) Present an Anger Log/hierarchy scene involving escalation for the imaginal stress inoculation procedure. Both during the imaginal inoculation exposure and the role-play exposure, be sure to emphasize the role of effective communication through an assertive style and additional techniques for preventing an escalation of the situation.

5. *Reflection and session evaluation (10 mins)*

As for previous sessions.

SESSION 17 INTEGRATION OF SKILLS AND DEALING WITH REPEATED PROVOCATION

	Contents	Duration (Approximate)
1	Introduction and review of previous session	10 minutes
2	Further development of cognitive re-structuring	15 minutes
3	Development of problem-solving through effective communication	10 minutes
4	Further development of stress inoculation procedure *(to include self-instructions and role-playing)*	15 minutes
5	Reflection and session evaluation	10 minutes

Aims

- To further develop *cognitive re-structuring* incorporating *perspective-taking* and *self-instructions*.
- To discuss how the *sequential skills* involved in dealing with anger situations need to be *integrated* in order to be effective.
- To further develop skills in dealing with anger situations effectively by *communicating constructively (problem-solving approach)*.
- To introduce the concept of *repeated provocation* and how this can be dealt with.
- To continue to develop further *stress inoculation* procedures including *imaginal* and *role-play* exposures to anger-provoking situations.

Session guidelines

1. *Introduction and review of previous session (10 mins)*
   (a) Briefly review the previous session by summarizing the main areas covered, including how to think differently about anger situations by perspective-taking; how self-instructions can help to keep control of thoughts, feelings and behaviour; how anger situations can be dealt with by communicating effectively; how to deal with rumination and escalating situations, and use of role-play to practise the coping strategies rehearsed in imagination to deal with a situation from the anger hierarchy/Anger Logs.
   (b) Introduce the content of Session 17. Explain that this session will go over most of the work covered during Session 16. In addition, how to deal with situations involving repeated provocations will be discussed.
   (c) Check that the client has completed Anger Logs between this and the last session as requested, including recording of the thoughts that they had in anger situations, as well as any different thoughts about the situations they were able to come up with by perspective-taking. Learn from the clients how they have managed with abbreviated progressive relaxation using the relaxation tape. Review and explore any difficulties that the client has had with completing these homework tasks.

2. *Further developing cognitive re-structuring (15 mins)*
   (a) Follow the procedure described for Session 14, Session Guidelines, section 2, paragraphs (a), (b), and (c).
   (b) In this way you will be reviewing with the client the use of Anger Logs and the development of their skills in more accurately recording thoughts/cognitions at the time of anger incidents, as well as alternative appraisals generated through perspective-taking. In addition, you will have guided them through a cognitive re-structuring exercise using an incident selected from the Anger Logs. During this exercise you will have reviewed with the client the use of self-instructions to cue cognitive and emotional control.
   (c) As part of the cognitive re-structuring exercise, discuss with the client their behavioural responses in those situations recorded in their Anger Logs. Explore their use of problem-solving through effective communication with reference to the work carried out during Sessions 14 and 15 on distinguishing between *passive, aggressive,*

and *assertive* styles of communication. Discuss whether they have been able to adopt a 'goal-orientated' approach to problem-solving in order to improve outcomes in anger situations both for themselves and others.

Finally, remind the client of the work done during the last session on rumination and escalation and relate these issues to the anger incident being discussed and analyzed as part of the cognitive re-structuring exercise.

(d) Take this opportunity to review with the client the step-wise, but integrated approach that they have been developing towards dealing with anger problems. Remind them of the different skills that they have been working on in order to be better able to deal effectively with anger situations. These skills involve increased awareness of the types of situations to which they are sensitive (attentional focus), use of self-instructions to cue them to stay calm, relaxed and in control, thinking differently about situations (cognitive re-structuring), arousal control through deep breathing and relaxation exercises, and problem-solving through a goal-orientated approach to effective communication.

Explain that in order to be successful in dealing with anger situations, each of these new skills needs to be used in a sequential step-wise manner so that eventually they will become integrated, natural and automatic. To facilitate understanding of this concept it might be helpful, depending on the abilities of individual clients, to have them work through *Handout/Exercise Sheet 17.1* 'Dealing with Anger Incidents – Personal Reminder Sheet' for homework. It is likely this task will require support from the client's keyworker and will need to be shaped up during Session 18. Depending on how the client responds to this exercise it may be useful to consider miniaturizing the personal reminder sheet (possibly having it laminated) so that the client can carry it with them as a prompt/cue card.

3. *Further development of the problem-solving approach through effective communication: dealing with repeated provocations (10 mins)*

(a) Discuss with the client how they would deal with a situation involving repeated provocation, that is repetitive or continuous aggression and offensive behaviour directed towards them. Select a situation from their anger hierarchy or Anger Logs to illustrate this. If necessary, magnify the provocation described in the hierarchy scene/Anger Log for this exercise.

(b) Guide the client in developing appropriate responses to a situation involving repeated provocation. These might include, for example, attempting to remain calm and in control, use of calming imagery, self-instructions, breathing control, etc. Help them to work out a coping strategy for this type of situation.

(c) Discuss with the client responses that would *not* be effective in coping with a situation involving repeated provocation. That is, identify those types of behaviours that would constitute poor control of anger, including not listening, being threatening, shouting and swearing, being rude, etc. In this way develop a clear understanding of what *not to do* in such a situation. Point out the negative consequences of these poor anger control responses both for the client and others involved. Explore how the more positive coping strategies discussed above are more likely to lead to positive outcomes and consequences for all involved.

(d) Go over once again how 'strategic withdrawal' might on occasion be the most appropriate and effective coping behaviour and response to repeated provocation. If another person is intent on being aggressive and abusive, if the situation is becoming more heated and the client is having difficulty remaining calm and in control, withdrawing, backing off, and walking away are likely to be the best options in order to maintain control and exercise personal choice. Reiterate how this can enable all people involved to have 'time out' to cool down and decide the best way forward. The client may then decide to approach again the other person(s) involved in order to engage in goal-orientated problem-solving, or they may seek help from others, for example, staff. Discuss with the client how adopting one or more of these techniques might have helped in the situation identified from their Anger Log/anger hierarchy.

4. *Further developing stress inoculation procedures (15 mins)*
   (a) Work through the stress inoculation procedure in imagination and role-play as described in Session 14, Session Guidelines, section 4, paragraphs (a), (b), (c), and (d).
   (b) Present an Anger Log/hierarchy scene involving a 'high' anger incident and magnify this to involve repeated provocation. Both during the imaginal inoculation exposure and the role-play exposure be sure to emphasize the role of problem-solving through adoption of the techniques discussed in section 3 above in order to de-escalate the situation or strategically withdraw from repeated provocation.

5. *Reflection and session evaluation (10 mins)*

As for previous sessions.

Materials for Session 17

- *Handout/Exercise Sheet 17.1* Dealing with Anger Incidents – Personal Reminder Sheet
- *Handout/Exercise Sheet 17.2* Dealing with Anger Incidents – Personal Reminder Sheet (Example)

SESSION 18 REVIEW AND EVALUATION OF ANGER TREATMENT

	Contents	Duration (Approximate)
1	Introduction and review of previous session	10 minute
2	Review and evaluation of anger treatment phase	25 minutes
3	Final rehearsal of stress inoculation, use of imagery, relaxation, and self-instruction	15 minutes
4	Reflection and session evaluation	10 minutes

Aims

- To consolidate the client's *personal script* for dealing with anger situations.
- To review with the client the work completed in the anger treatment phase sessions.

- To receive feedback on the anger treatment phase sessions through client's evaluation of their treatment.
- To assess the client's competencies in a large range of areas worked on during the anger treatment phase sessions.

Session guidelines

1. *Introduction and review of previous session (15 mins)*
   (a) Briefly review the previous session by summarizing the main areas covered. In particular, discuss with the client recent work on rumination, escalation, and repeated provocation.
   (b) Introduce the content of Session 18. Explain that this session is the final session and will concentrate on reviewing the anger treatment phase, as well as asking the client to indicate how they think this work has progressed. In addition, some time will be spent on shaping their personal reminder sheets for dealing with anger situations.
   (c) Review with the client any Anger Logs completed between this and the last session. Reinforce successful coping with anger situations through appraisal modification, arousal control, and use of problem-solving approaches. Discuss with clients their progress with relaxation exercises. Discuss their future use of the relaxation tape and the need for continued practice in order to be able to master self-control of anger arousal.
   (d) Look at the client's attempt to develop a personal script for dealing with anger situations using *Handout/Exercise Sheet 17.1* 'Dealing with Anger Incidents – Personal Reminder Sheet'. Develop this personalized reminder sheet with the client reiterating as you go the step-wise, sequential, but *integrated* approach needed in order to maintain calm and control in anger situations so that problem-solving approaches can follow. Discuss with the client whether they would value having the final personal reminder sheet miniaturized as a cue/prompt card for effective coping in future anger situations.

2. *Review and evaluation of the anger treatment phase (25 mins)*
   (a) Prompt the client to recall the main areas of work covered during the 12 anger treatment phase sessions. This exercise will be facilitated by use of *Handout/Exercise Sheet 18.1* 'Patient's Evaluation of Anger Treatment – Treatment Phase'. As you work through the client's evaluation, prompt discussion about the main aims and outcomes of the anger treatment phase work. This exercise can be enhanced by direct reference to the work completed by clients in the key areas being evaluated.

3. *Abbreviated progressive relaxation exercises (15 mins)*
   (a) To close the session positively, suggest working through the abbreviated progressive relaxation exercises together for a final time. Remind the client of the central role relaxation plays in reducing and controlling the physical arousal associated with anger. Reiterate how high levels of stress affect thinking and behaviour and can prevent problem-solving in anger situations.
   (b) Work through with the client the therapist's script for APR on *Handout/Exercise Sheet 8.3*. A shortened version of the script can be used if preferred. Following

successful completion of the exercises suggest to the client that they visualize as clearly as possible their personal relaxing and calming image/picture. Ask them to concentrate on this scene for a few moments (up to 60 seconds) to maintain and deepen relaxation.

(c) Following completion of the APR exercises, discuss their continued use as a means of preventing the build-up of stress and anger.

4. Reflection and session evaluation (5 mins)

As for previous sessions.

Following completion of this session, the therapist, if possible in collaboration with the client's named keyworker, should complete the 'Patient's Competency Checklist – Treatment Phase' (*Handout/Exercise Sheet 18.2*) and the 'Goal Attainment Scales for Emotional Awareness and Expression (Post-Treatment)' (*Handout/Exercise Sheet 18.3*).

Materials for Session 18

- *Handout/Exercise Sheet 18.1* Patients' Evaluation of Anger Treatment – Treatment Phase
- *Handout/Exercise Sheet 18.2* Patients' Competency Checklist – Treatment Phase
- *Handout/Exercise Sheet 18.3* Goal Attainment Scales for Emotional Awareness and Expression (Post-Treatment)

10

THERAPIST TRAINING, SUPERVISION, AND PROCESS CONSIDERATIONS

Bruce T. Gillmer
Northgate and Prudhoe NHS Trust and
University of Newcastle upon Tyne, UK

INTRODUCTION

In order for new evidence-based interventions to have enduring value, there is a reciprocal requirement of training for competency and expert supervision. Such an assertion requires no more justification than those provided by a parent of professional psychology and a champion of manual-based therapy, respectively:

> The survival of our profession requires us to direct our energies towards meeting the most funda-mental needs of our society, often by creating new services, not towards preserving the status quo or enhancing advantages to our own professional establishment. Scientific professional psychology is the only legitimate and acceptable form of professional psychology. Procedures must be likely to offer demonstrable utility in the long run.
>
> (Peterson, 1995, p. 182)

> Therapists must be specifically trained in the use of manual-based treatments ... The more comprehensive and flexible the manual, the greater will be the contribution of the therapist and the greater the corresponding need for appropriate training.
>
> (Wilson, 1998, p. 371)

The foregoing chapters have set out how a protocol-guided treatment can provide a cus-tomized, validated method within which is nested in idiographic case formulation. It is the task of a systematic supervisory structure to ensure that the method is employed to best effect. This chapter is concerned with particular supervisory issues. There are many com-prehensive, practical and authoritative general guides for supervisors and supervisees (e.g. Scaife, 2001).

The supervisory, training and related issues involved in delivering manualized cognitive-behaviour therapy (CBT) for anger to people with developmental disabilities include:

Anger Treatment for People with Developmental Disabilities by J. L. Taylor and R. W. Novaco.
Copyright © 2005 John Wiley & Sons, Ltd.

- the phenomenon of ambivalent disdain for manualized therapy;
- a requirement for special adaptations of CBT with developmental disability populations;
- the entrenched functional value anger can have for people with developmental disabilities;
- personal-professional support in working with this client group.

Then there are the more universal issues of:

- identifying and nurturing the core components of therapeutic skill;
- the nature and extent of expertise/training required;
- awareness of best evidence in supervisory practice.

A LOVE–HATE RELATIONSHIP WITH MANUALIZED THERAPIES

In this cost-conscious climate of time-limited delivery of interventions by differentially skilled therapists, manualized approaches are readily shifted from their research-based origins to the clinical shelf. Where they sit. Then the self-evident truth of individualized wizardry, derived from experience, emerges. Systematic and empirically validated techniques are set aside in favour of personalistic formulations in the belief that any proper therapy demands a flexibility of method that is inherently denied by interventions described by protocol. In any event, manuals which may be suitable for the pre-selected samples of research cohorts are bound to fall short of the needs of the particular patient in ordinary practice.

It is nearly half a century since that rare figure, a rigorous psychoanalyst, bemoaned the 'cultural lag between what the published research shows and what clinicians persist in claiming to do' (Meehl, 1960, p. 26). Yet even researchers describing highly successful structured manual-based therapy (e.g. Hickling & Blanchard, 1997) seem unable to resist a 'clinician's reaction' to justify deviation from protocol, ostensibly based on experience, to critique a strong proponent of manual adherence (G.T. Wilson, 1996), thereby missing the point entirely. In terms of patient outcome we simply have no way of knowing whether a particularly charismatic and experienced therapist using clinical judgement can improve upon adherence to a treatment manual. We do know of evidence that doctoral-level therapists are no more effective, on average, than those with lesser credentials (Christensen & Jacobson, 1994), and that clinicians' confidence in their judgement has been shown to be unrelated to their accuracy (G.T. Wilson, 1996). What is probably far more the case is that, as Lambert and Ogles (1997) found, more experienced therapists make more appropriate use of manuals. This point will be addressed under considerations for competency.

The simple truth is that manual-based therapy is widely misunderstood. In the first place, such interventions span a continuum of flexibility and required skill. These range from the protocol-bound for the novitiate to manualized guides for the competent. This differentiation of treatment intervention levels raises other important questions concerning the capacity available in forensic developmental disability services to deliver high quality anger treatment programmes which are appropriately managed, monitored and evaluated (Taylor, 2002a). Novaco et al. (2000) helpfully differentiated between several levels of psychological intervention for anger problems:

Anger management provision can be characterized as planned and systematic psychoeducational approaches, guided by cognitive-behavioural principles, and often delivered in a group format. A range of health care workers can be adequately trained to deliver such programmes. The content of this intervention type is structured, but can vary considerably.

It is less intensive than anger treatment provision, and is not driven by analysis and formulation of an individual's anger problems and treatment needs.

Cognitively-based *anger treatments*, on the other hand, aim to help to modify thoughts and beliefs so that the level of anger intensity induced by provocation remains at a level that allows the individual to cope with such situations effectively. This level of intervention is appropriate for high-anger people whose difficulties are often deep-rooted and chronic. It requires delivery by trained and supervised therapists on an individual basis, in order to promote a therapeutic relationship that can overcome client resistance to and fear of change.

In cognitive-behavioural anger treatment there is variation in the focus, pace, and emphasis of the therapy delivered by different therapists working with different patients, depending on the analysis and formulation of their anger problems. The treatment is by nature collaborative and interactive. It is therefore applied in a manner that reflects these dynamics. Thus, while it is a manualized intervention, cognitive-behavioural anger treatment is intended to provide a framework within which the therapist and patient can flexibly apply the therapeutic techniques described to meet individual needs. In this sense Taylor, Novaco, Gillmer, and Robertson (2004) draw a clear distinction between *protocol-guided* and *protocol-driven* treatment. The latter tend to be applied rigidly, are not reflexive to the needs of clients and tend not to lead to good outcomes when administered by experienced therapists. This raises the issue of fit between patient, therapeutic approach, and expertise.

There is often an assumption that manualized interventions and individual formulations are mutually exclusive. Clinical psychologists trained in Britain tend to put great store by 'formulation', holding a special value for practice and, indeed, hold that psychological formulation is that profession's most distinctive domain. There is an odd tension between the arid high ground of the evidence-based scientist practitioner and the ambiguity characterizing the swampy terrain readily traversed by the reflective practitioner (Schon, 1983). This phenomenon is well illustrated by Huey and Britton's (2002) attempt, in a review of the dominant profile of clinical psychology in the UK, to reconcile these positions. The two core features of the profession that emerge are:

1 Level 3 skills: 'A flexible and generic knowledge of psychology which facilitates the ability to draw from a range of theories, in order to devise individually tailored strategies for complex presenting problems' (ibid., p. 70);
2 'The clinical attitude . . . conceptualised as the tendency to integrate deductive and inductive approaches (the general with the particular) . . . with its requisite sceptical, openminded and flexible approach to psychological problems, can be viewed as a necessary determinant of the implementation of so-called "level 3 skills"' (ibid., p. 70).

Thus a fully-fledged professional is envisaged as one who is skilled in individual assessment, formulation, and intervention, yet is tolerant of ambiguity and equipped for clinical decision-making. It is as if there are, on the one hand, manuals that are created by level 3 research clinicians for level 2 practitioners to deliver in a static, standardized and unreflective way and, on the other hand, highly individualized and flexible therapies within the ambit of professional expertise, with no middle ground. Yet in the cognitive-behavioural anger treatment protocol described in this book (see Chapters 8 and 9) individual formulation is fundamental to the protocol.

Wilson (1998) argued that, far from curtailing therapeutic flair and innovation, we should welcome what he termed 'manualised therapeutic autonomy' as a crucial step in the evolution of evidenced-based therapy. Protocols should be used as guides, not scripts.

It is a crucial element of the supervisory role to understand, be alive to and correct the ambivalence or even cognitive bias of clinicians who overtly embrace the ethos of evidence-based intervention, yet eschew its application in practice. Nisbett and Ross's (1980) classical work on human inference provides a compelling and parsimonious explanation of this phenomenon with the concept of the 'availability heuristic'. The clinician thereby tends to notice any immediate therapeutic success at the expense of reflecting on failures; this cognitive selectivity exerts more influence than does probative research data which is, by its nature, comparatively remote. In this all too human way plausible anecdotal case studies have had a completely disproportionate influence on the science and practice of psychotherapy (Wilson, G.T., 1996). The 'availability heuristic phenomenon' may also help to explain the obscene plethora of unproven therapies that grow like untrammelled weeds in the advertising pages of professional guild journals.

THE MYTHICAL SUPERIORITY OF CLINICAL JUDGEMENT

Disregard of the relevant scientific findings helps maintain the illusion that clinical judgement is superior to actuarial prediction when if anything the opposite is true (Dawes, 1994; Meehl, 1960; Peterson, 1995; Wilson, 1997). The supervisory task is to maintain therapist integrity to conceptual model and intervention method, and to alert the supervisee to the 'non-specifics' of the therapeutic alliance, such as constructive engagement and ambivalence about change (Addis, 1997).

A particularly important therapist skill, in implementing manual-based treatment, irrespective of conceptual model, is the ability to maintain a consistent focus on explicit therapeutic goals while remaining responsive to what may be the patient's changing emotional needs. In other words, facilitating focal therapy. The supervisor needs to remain alert to therapists who have difficulty meticulously following manual guidelines at the expense of attention to the ubiquitous attractions of the therapeutic alliance. In clinical practice, which addresses the needs of the individual patient, greater flexibility is possible than in the rigorous world of research trial. The supervisory challenge of modifying empirically based treatments for use with individual patients can be seen as an example of the more general problem of what has elsewhere been termed 'the paradox of guideline implementation' (Brown, Shye, & McFarland, 1995). This notion holds that, while the value of treatment guidelines resides in their grounding in the best research and in being implemented in accord with underlying science, if practitioners are not allowed to modify empirically derived guidelines to meet local conditions, then the guidelines are less likely to be followed.

The successful implementation of protocol-guided treatment programmes, far from being simplistic derivations of the 'real thing', require a systemic management, in common with all good training structures (Salas & Cannon-Bowers, 2001). To this end, a pyramidal arrangement of supervision and intervention maintenance is advocated (see Figure 10.1).

The Supervisory Formula:

Therapy Competence = Adherence + Skill + Interpersonal Effectiveness

Whether working cognitively (James, Blackburn, Milne, & Reichfelt, 2001), psychodynamically (Krasner, Howard, & Brown, 1998), or interpersonally (Fairburn, Marcus, & Wilson, 1993), the three core features of therapeutic competence lie in:

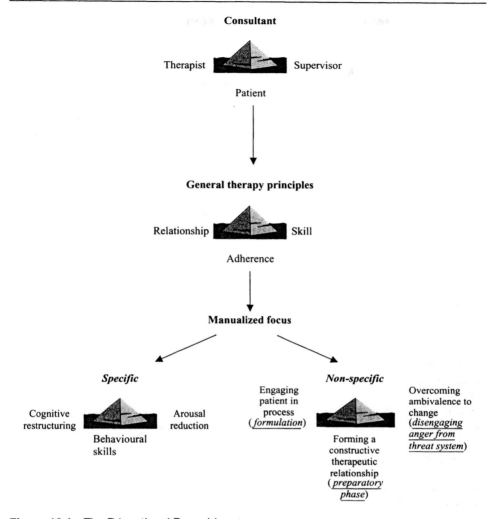

Figure 10.1 The Educational Pyramid

- adherence to the therapeutic model;
- skill in applying the given techniques; and
- interpersonal effectiveness with the patient.

Therapist adherence has been shown to be particularly predictive of positive treatment outcome in a variety of manualized approaches (Wilson, 1998). This is precisely what is required for successful application of this manualized therapy – protocol-guided adherence to the anger treatment model, basic technical competence and a positive therapeutic alliance. What manuals add to the general rubric is a sustained focus on therapeutic goals that demand considerable therapist discipline (G.T. Wilson, 1996). The supervisor's role is to hold the supervisee to task, which is not easy given the natural cognitive bias in favour of clinical judgement, or what is often seductively termed 'clinical artistry' (Huey & Britton, 2002). The greatest true artists are inordinately disciplined and are surrounded by dedicated apprentices and this is often overlooked.

COGNITIVE-BEHAVIOURAL THERAPY SUPERVISION ISSUES

Supervision provides the cornerstone of training and support for psychological therapists and is an essential prerequisite for the practice of psychotherapy (Roth & Fonagy, 1996) – yet little specific attention has been directed to the training of supervisors (James et al., 2001). The work of Derek Milne, Ian James, and their associates provides a rare exception. Because most of the systematic research in this area has come from the developmental disability field (Milne & James, 2000) and their concern is with cognitive therapy supervision (James et al., 2001), it behoves us to draw heavily on their research findings (Milne & James, 2002) in clinical application (Milne, Pilkington, Gracie, & James, 2003).

A pyramidal supervisory structure

The systematic use of a tiered triadic supervisory arrangement is strongly advocated both for measured therapist competence and its generalization to therapy outcome. Milne and James (2000) have undertaken one of very few empirical studies of the conceptual structure known as the 'educational pyramid' whose facets comprise: (1) Consultant-Supervisor; (2) Supervisor-Supervisee; and (3) Supervisee-Patient (see Figure 10.1). Clinical supervision is an intensive and interpersonally focused relationship (Scaife, 2001) in which one person – the supervisor – is designated to facilitate the development of therapeutic competence in the supervisee. The functions that are presumed to be served by such supervision include facilitating the supervisee's experiential learning, establishing the fitness of the supervisee to practice, maintenance of competency standards, and promotion of general professional development.

Supervision can occur at a number of levels and not just at the level of clinical supervisor and therapist. The *Consultant* is normally instrumental in teaching and monitoring the work of the supervisor, principally by observationally auditing and thereby ensuring adherence and application of appropriate techniques by the supervisee. The logic underlying these relationships is reflected in the metaphor of the educational pyramid. The use of training manuals is advocated to systematize the preparation of therapists. It is uncommon to find this methodology applied to the preparation of supervisors or consultants. Competence does not develop automatically and more experienced therapists make more appropriate use of manuals (Lambert & Ogles, 1997). There appears to be a 'dilution' effect as one proceeds down the pyramid with supervisors most directly benefiting from consultancy, followed by supervisees, and then patients (Milne & James, 2000), which is as it should be.

Consultancy, especially when based on feedback, improves supervisor competence especially in guided experiential learning with predictable changes in associated supervisees' learning. Following the well-known experiential learning cycle (Kolb, 1984), the supervisors' use of guided learning very closely mirrors a quadrupling in supervisees' actual use of the experimenting, conceptualizing, and experiencing modes of learning (Milne & James, 2000). It does, however, take time to socialize both supervisors and supervisees to new learning styles especially in the use of direct feedback of competencies. The use of video recording and role-play can foster supervision competencies. It is well established that behaviour role modelling emphasizing practice and performance feedback is significantly superior to didactic or demonstration teaching (Salas & Cannon-Bowers, 2001).

In setting up a programme it is recommended that, based on our experience, a consultant to the programme oversees the identified supervisors and takes them through the first cycle of treatment as the lead clinicians. Thereafter, they can be used to take on the more complex cases, whilst supervising the next cohort of therapists. The consultant remains the supervisors' overseer. In addition to individual supervision, there is much to be gained by scheduled group supervision where all the therapists can bring issues to a forum, again supervised by the consultant. The value of a shared protocol brings a clear focus to such a diversified and layered arrangement.

Issues of therapist experience and competence

Training is necessary to develop expertise, which in turn predicts therapeutic success but surprisingly little is known about professional training. It is generally assumed that competence is an acquired skill which is influenced by situational moderators such as therapist training experience (James et al., 2001).

It will be recalled that the three core features of therapeutic competence lie in adherence to the therapeutic model, level of skill in applying the given techniques, and interpersonal effectiveness with the patient. Prior CBT experience facilitates the acquisition of competence in CBT, but prior general experience of the therapist does not (James et al., 2001). These findings suggest that at the outset a trainee may only be able to apply the CBT model by following a standard and somewhat rigid format. Hence, in the presence of a suitable case, the trainee therapist is more readily able to demonstrate competence. However, with a less standard presentation the neophyte cognitive-behavioural therapist struggles to adhere to the model and to demonstrate skilfulness. Nevertheless with specific experience in CBT the more expert therapist may be able to be flexible and adaptable with respect to their approach and thus successfully apply effective therapy to more complex (and less suitable) cases. Put differently, more experienced therapists make more appropriate use of manuals (Lambert & Ogles, 1997). There is a strong association between suitability and competence or patient–therapist fit. A recent naturalistic study (Trepka, Rees, Shapiro, Hardy, & Barkham, 2004) supported the common-sense prediction of a connection between competent therapy and good outcomes. This effect was most pronounced in those patients who received the full 'dose' of therapy. It may be that with less suitable patients, less competent or inexperienced cognitive-behavioural therapists adhere too closely to methods, thus losing flexibility and flair, with negative consequences on outcome. Such findings about suitability may also help to explain the equivocal results within the therapeutic literature relating therapist experience to patient outcome (Dawes, 1994). Indeed, previous findings that could not differentiate novice from expert may have been confounded by the fact that more experienced therapists took on more difficult and less suitable patients. Certainly this was our experience in the Northgate Anger Treatment Project as we moved from the research trial to clinical roll-out, hence the advocacy of a diverse and layered supervisory structure.

There has been an important shift in the size of therapist effect from earlier to more recent manual-based treatments. Provided therapists are trained to a reasonable criterion level of competence, so that they can reliably administer a standardized treatment protocol, there is no significant therapist effect (Wilson, 1998). This frees specialist clinicians to manage more complex and resistant patients and, more importantly, to break new ground in intervention development.

It is in this spirit of fitness-for-purpose that, by systematically yoking expertise via the educational pyramid of consultant–supervisor–therapist–patient, one can ensure therapeutic competency most economically. For example, the supervisor's primary focus on adherence to the model, technical skill and therapeutic relationship can be audited by the consultant while the supervisor steps in to assist the less experienced therapist to grapple with the patient's formulation of anger.

THE SYSTEMIC PICTURE OF PRACTICE AND TREATMENT-GAIN MAINTENANCE

Although anger treatment sessions within the Northgate Project routinely involve only therapist and patient, the patient's keyworker nurse or a deputy should be involved whenever possible at the end of each session to discuss the patient's progress and any homework to be completed between sessions. Patients are encouraged to complete daily Anger Logs to record the nature, frequency, and intensity of any angry incidents. These are completed with assistance and support from the patient's keyworker nurse in order to promote a collaborative approach to treatment through open discussion, shared problem-solving, and mutual reflection concerning anger-provoking incidents (Taylor et al., 2002; Taylor, Novaco, Gillmer et al., 2004). Nursing staff involved in supporting patients undergoing treatment indicated that they acquire a greater awareness of anger-related issues such as individual differences in the experience of anger and why some patients might not choose to use the anger-coping techniques they had learnt in treatment. Support staff also gained a better general knowledge about anger-coping strategies, including relaxation, effective communication and use of self-instructions. The positive experiences reported by nursing staff are closely associated with having learned something about anger treatment. In this way, there is an ownership across the treatment milieu which more securely anchors the patient's therapeutic gains. Most nurses believed that their involvement in the anger treatment had had a more general impact on the way in which they dealt with patients' anger and aggression problems, particularly in encouraging patients to adopt the anger-coping strategies that had been identified. Generally they had increased awareness of anger-related problems and there was a spill-over effect in that nurses had noticed that patients receiving anger treatment quite commonly passed on information about their treatment to others. This potential confound in research work can be a salutary clinical phenomenon systemically. Supervision therefore needs to be extended to support staff.

SPECIAL SUPERVISORY CONSIDERATIONS FOR INTERVENTIONS WITH THIS CLIENT GROUP

Little is known about the emotional lives of that socially excluded and marginalized group of people with developmental disabilities. Therapists are avoidant of engaging at an intensive and intimate level with people perceived as unattractive (Bender, 1993) and emotional difficulties are often attributed to the disability rather than to emotional state or need

(Hollins & Sinason, 2000). Anger and aggression carry heavy costs both for the institutionalized person with developmental disabilities and for the whole system concerned with providing security and rehabilitation, especially for offenders with developmental disabilities (Taylor et al., 2002). 'Challenging behaviour', in which aggression features prominently, is frequently reported, but this is commonly located behaviourally rather than in making any connections with an internal world. Little systemic attribution is made to the institutional life and its necessarily associated frustration, helplessness, and injustice; environments that for anyone would be constraining, depersonalized, alien in character and stressful (Black et al., 1997).

The ideological implications of working cognitively with people who have developmental disabilities are well known (Stenfert Kroese, Dagnan, & Loumidis, 1997). It is hard to set aside the anticipation that IQ is an insuperable barrier to CBT and the reality is that there are some problems. These include:

- a learning history of failure;
- a lifetime of dependency;
- less intrinsic motivation;
- generally unreflective of self–other attributions;
- acquiescence;
- lack of confidence;
- poor self-regulation;
- little transfer of learning; and
- restricted receptive and expressive language.

All therapeutic interventions for anger present special challenges for both therapists and patients (DiGuiseppe et al., 1994). These difficulties are related to the inherent threats such patients present, their impatience and impulsiveness, and the positive functions and reinforcements that their anger often holds, causing it to be deeply embedded and difficult to relinquish. Such issues create significant obstacles to the establishment of therapeutic alliances, to help patients to see anger as a legitimate treatment target and to motivate clients to contemplate change with respect to their anger-related difficulties. People with developmental disabilities and anger problems typically have life histories characterized by trauma and repeated experience of failure and rejection across a range of health and social care settings. Given their impaired intellectual functioning and associated limited psychological/emotional resources, the scale of the task involved in successfully engaging these patients in anger treatment becomes apparent. Nonetheless, despite these difficulties, the therapy can be made acceptable to patients who have expressed high levels of satisfaction with it and found it to be helpful (Taylor, Novaco, Gillmer et al., 2004).

The key task in the *preparatory phase* highlights the normality of anger while introducing the personal costs associated with recurrent maladaptive anger reactions. This strategy appears to be successful in helping psychologically fragile participants form therapeutic relationships and become motivated to maintain them. Even wary and suspicious patients generally choose to go beyond the preparatory phase. Very little additional work is required from therapists in supplementary sessions outside of the protocol. Therapists occasionally report in peer supervision sessions that particular patients appear to be engaging in treatment at a superficial level – the concern being that they are 'playing along'. However, almost without exception, for those patients who complete treatment, therapists report that at some point during the therapeutic process they begin to respond in a meaningful and beneficial way to the content and process. Patient feedback provides evidence to support these clinical observations (Taylor, Novaco, Gillmer, et al., 2004). That is, while the percentage of patients reporting enjoyment reduced slightly from post-preparatory to post-treatment (94% to 83%,) the percentage of those indicating that the sessions have been helpful remain much the same (78% to 83%) and increased markedly (from 22% to 67%) for patients' own estimates of positive change following the treatment phase. This is not to say that it is always the case that individuals either engage in treatment effortlessly or quickly become motivated to change their maladaptive anger-coping responses. It may well prove necessary for therapy to be offered repeatedly despite patient decision to terminate at various points. The functional value of such refusals may well disclose attempts by a patient to have some control over a system perceived as indifferent to his or her needs and unjustly constraining. This could be in response to seemingly unrelated events such as an unsatisfying Mental Health Act Tribunal or a personal loss. Therapists therefore need to be systemically aware when applying the treatment protocol. The value of supervision in this regard is obvious. Patients may also have a vested interest in maintaining an aggressive persona as a response to threat so that an aggressive style is a survival strategy.

THE 'SALIENT GATEWAY': A SUMMARY FOR SUPERVISORS

The somatic aspects of anger arousal, marked by activation of the autonomic nervous system, is possibly the most obvious and identifiable aspect of the experience of anger for many people. This seems in our experience to be particularly so for people with more limited intellectual abilities. Therefore, increasing understanding and self-awareness of the concrete noticeable elements of anger experience (dry mouth, palpitations, churning stomach, sweating, breathlessness, muscular tension) is likely to be more achievable than for more abstract concepts such as subjective affect or cognitive labelling of emotional states. Supervision can direct the therapist to this characteristic somatization of emotional experience.

The arousal aspect of anger is particularly salient and of more interest to younger men who are often concerned about and preoccupied with their physicality and self-image. As a consequence, they might be particularly motivated to develop a greater control over the anger arousal that they experience. Learning how to relax in order to reduce the physiological arousal associated with anger is a frequently endorsed item in terms of helpfulness and usefulness (Taylor, 2002b).

In an early paper Novaco (1976) identified anger as a subjective affect that works in favour of the physiological characteristics of arousal in the face of threat. The common folk-psychology conflation of anger with aggression and hostility has blurred the recognition of anger's adaptive functions. Anger is often equated with destructive forces and its energizing, expressive, discriminative and potentiating functions are accordingly overlooked. A primary difficulty in the treatment of people with chronic anger problems is that they may enjoy getting angry. In considering the functionality of anger, Novaco points to a spectrum of adaptive and maladaptive functions. It is crucial to attune the patient to the discriminative functions of anger. The Anger Logs, in requiring a reflective stance, promote awareness especially of somatic cues (the salient gateway) as well as the use of relaxation in stress inoculation.

A distinctive characteristic of cognitive-behavioural anger treatment is the modification of perceptual schemas and entrenched beliefs that maintain anger problems. A basic premise of CBT approaches is that psychological distress is a derivative of distortions in processing information about oneself in environmental demands, and this assumptive framework has certainly been articulated with regard to anger (Beck, 1999). Attentional biases and cognitive processing distortions associated with threat perception, as well as memory biases for distressing experiences, are quite intrinsic to problems of anger and aggression. CBT strives to shift attentional focus, modify appraisals of events, restructure belief systems and self-schemas, and develop effective emotional regulation and behavioural coping skills. It is predicated on the human tendency to behave as guided by symbols, to seek meaning, and to formulate strategies to optimize quality of life.

Disconnecting the anger from threat perception and instilling self-control is central to anger treatment. People having serious anger difficulties have lost the capacity to self-regulate and are quick to perceive malevolence. Elementary CBT language encourages the patient to recognize that consequences are closely linked to thoughts and beliefs about activating events, and not directly related to the events themselves. In anger treatment the process begins by creating space and safety and, in normalizing the patient's experience of anger, with constant support and validation of personal worth, anger intensity moderation is encouraged. With this firmly based alliance, self-monitoring can be shaped and self-control augmented. The putative role of cognitions and the experience of anger are given attention right from the start as part of the presentation of a simplified linear model of 'How Anger Works' in Session 1 of the preparatory phase of anger treatment. Cognitive restructuring techniques are infused in this treatment approach and are given the same amount of attention as arousal reduction and behavioural skills training. Sessions 10 through to 17 of the treatment protocol are concerned with *cognitive restructuring*.

This defining feature of CBT is the hardest part of the process to communicate to clients with developmental disabilities and can deter many therapists from using a CBT framework. CBT pivots on symbolic representation and language: the precise area this group has difficulty with. Cognitive restructuring processes require special adaptations and structures. A cardinal component of CBT procedures involves conveying and making the link between beliefs (about the activating events) and the consequences. This link is very difficult to convey, because it is counter-intuitive: it always *feels* as if the activating event caused the consequential reaction, rather than any interpretations or judgemental beliefs about that event. People with developmental disabilities are usually going to foreground feelings over cognitions and are especially likely to feel as if the triggering *event* (e.g. 'I see my friend/with whom I had an argument/cross the road/ without so much as a glance at me') caused the *consequence* ('I feel hurt/because *I know* that she is avoiding me'). Whereas, in fact, you *thought* you saw her crossing the road to avoid you, because when you spotted her you remembered that you had had an argument. In fact you don't know whether she saw you at all. In fact, she didn't even glance in your direction. Could it be that she hadn't seen you? Could it be that it is your interpretation of events that has caused your feeling, rather than what happened? You *believed* that she avoided you, and that's what made you feel bad. A great deal for anyone to take in.

So, in the case of an actual patient, Joe is furious because his girlfriend is late for the social club. In his experience lateness means she couldn't give a damn, because women (sooner or later) don't. This core belief has to be brought to the surface and examined. Only then, from taking up her perspective (*'Maybe she got held back at the ward ... maybe she's upset for keeping me waiting'*), can the therapist begin to challenge the feeling-based assumption that late means neglect or rejection.

Having ever so briefly disconnected Joe from his characteristic anger-signature, the therapist tries to put him in touch with alternative emotions.

Now he feels: *'I dunno, heavy'*.

And what could he do instead of being angry? Could he comfort her, if she's upset? Could he put his arm around her and check how she is? Joe mutters: *'I never done that'*, and looks sad.

Urged to 'stay with that for a while', Joe begins to cry softly. *'I got to protect meself, somehow.'*

Joe has a measured IQ of 60. After an early history of abuse and neglect, he becomes an angry substance-misusing vagrant. Under the dual influence of a more able person and solvents he rapes a woman who has allowed him to sleep rough in an outhouse. His co-accused sets the victim's hair aflame with lighter fuel. Joe douses the fire and, pathetically, tries to apologize to her.

Through individual and group supervision the therapist/s can learn a great deal from patients like Joe about the 'non-specifics' of working cognitively with people who have an ID.

Motivation arises in and through learning rules (if ... then). As Vygotsky (1978) put it, people must learn in order to be motivated, rather than the other way around. The shift from the successes of behaviour modification to cognitive-behavioural work with this developmental disability population involves a fundamental move from a cognitive deficit to a cognitive distortion model. That is, from:

- problems of cognitive processing to cognitive content (*'maybe this ... maybe that'*);
- from a therapy that is simple to one that is elegant (*'let's think about how she might be feeling'*);
- requiring rote-learning to meta-cognition and personal meaning (*'stay with that for a while, Joe'*);
- patients who are cognitively passive to being active and explicit (*'I got to defend meself, somehow'*);
- a values base of an environmental ideology to one of self-determination (*'I've never done that'*).

There is a centrality of nurturing inner speech. The supervisor's credo needs to be that 'rules are exciting discoveries and lead to control over one's life'.

INTERNAL RULES AND META-COGNITION

The process of developing *verbal* rules is crucial. Describing behaviour by monitoring (e.g. through Anger Logs) and evaluating accuracy is less important than learning the process: self-monitoring is potently reinforcing and extinguishes negative automatic thoughts and associated behaviours. Rule formation ('if ... then') has intrinsic reinforcement.

CBT requires the patient to think about their thinking. This kind of meta-cognition can be conveyed to the patient with developmental disability by teaching self-talk which, with self-reflection, constitutes self-regulation. Ceding regulation from others to oneself results in inner speech ('when I feel like that, then this follows'). To remain deficit-focused is a self-fulfilling prophesy. For the therapist to try and sidestep language, due to deficit, is fatal because it is within and through language that inner speech and transformational learning occur (the kind of learning that is mine and unique to my experience).

There are some practical ways for the supervisor to help the therapist to overcome some of these problems that are experienced by patients with developmental disabilities (from Gillmer, 2003). These include:

- emphasizing procedural above declarative language, which sidesteps but does not avoid fundamental intellectual deficits (e.g. by using role-plays, exercises and examples from own experiences);
- making language visible (by using props like the 'anger thermometer' and the 'how anger works' model; having the patient make drawings of their relaxation imagery);
- using high dosage interventions to create therapeutic momentum in order to offset cognitive and memory deficits; ensuring, wherever possible, twice-weekly sessions to avoid 'drift';
- encouraging collaborative scaffolds that triangulate nurse–patient–therapist and help to consolidate gains and enhance ecological validity. These interpersonal structures facilitate involvement, ownership, and systemic awareness.
- highlighting treatment components that are strong on visualized bodily experience can provide the 'salient gateway' to the patient owning and dealing with their anger.

PROCESS AND STRUCTURE ISSUES: THE SPECIFICS OF 'NON-SPECIFICS'

This concluding section bears on what Addis (1997) referred to as the 'non-specifics' of treatment. Irrespective of therapy modality, the universal features of these factors involve the forming of a constructive therapeutic relationship, engaging the patient in the active process of treatment, and overcoming patient ambivalence about change (Wilson, 1998). In manual-based anger treatment, these three non-specific factors can be found in:

(i) Forming a constructive therapeutic relationship:
  - Preparatory treatment phase.
(ii) Engaging the patient in the active process of treatment:
  - Formulation of individual anger characteristics
  - Self-monitoring (Anger Logs)
  - Reflective perspective-taking.
(iii) Overcoming patient ambivalence about change:
  - Costs and benefits of excessive anger
  - Disengaging the anger from the perceived-threat system.

The main concern for supervisors should lie in identifying and naming or 'specifying the non-specifics'. For example, helping the therapist to learn to confidently use the new-found constructive treatment relationship robustly enough for the patient to risk disengaging from the long-standing and exquisitely sensitive perceptions that arm the threat system. After all, anger works: it distances, and the arousal switch is always 'ON'. The task of the supervisor is to hold the therapist to their task which is, first and foremost, to adhere to the guiding protocol. This in turn requires the therapist to lead the patient through the intervention specifics of cognitive restructuring, arousal reduction, and behavioural rehearsal. The therapeutic alliance is as much a function of mutual confidence in knowing what is going on from therapeutic step-to-step, as being some kind of alchemy that non-specifically engenders a positive outcome. Skilful supervision is the indispensable element in socializing therapists into what may be termed an unapologetic argument for manualized therapeutic autonomy.

Lest this suggests a straying, at the end of this chapter, into oxymoron territory: the supervisor must ensure that the protocol is used as a guide, not a script; that it is clear why and how manual-based interventions provide a crucial step in the evolution of evidence-based therapy; and that the very structure of this type of treatment feeds the process. Far from being restrictive, properly administered manual-based treatment promotes a customizing validated method, which nests an ideographic case formulation. It is a natural meeting place between the high ground of technical certainty and the swamp of the individual case. As Wilson (1998, p. 371) put it, 'the more comprehensive and flexible the manual, the greater will be the contribution of the therapist and the greater the corresponding need for appropriate training'.

11

ANGER TREATMENT FOR WOMEN WITH DEVELOPMENTAL DISABILITIES

Alison Robertson
Northgate and Prudhoe NHS Trust and
University of Newcastle upon Tyne, UK

INTRODUCTION

What is presented in this book on the assessment and treatment of anger for persons with developmental disabilities is primarily based on work that has been done with men. Anger, of course, is not exclusively a male province, and indeed female psychiatric patients often present with significant problems of anger and aggressive behaviour (Krakowski and Czobor, 2004; Novaco, 1997). For female clients seeking mental health care, the following quotes from Thomas (1995) and from our project involving women with developmental disabilities are illustrative:

> I don't talk to my husband at all when I'm mad at him. I just do what my mother did. I ice up. He never even knows I'm mad, even if it is something important.
> > (tape-recorded quotation, Thomas, 1995)

> It takes me a long time to get angry – too long because by the time I decide I'm mad the incident is past and the offender is out of reach.
> > (tape-recorded quotation, Thomas, 1995)

> My doctor has forgotten to write that letter for me again. But I don't want to say anything, he might get upset.
> > (Northgate Women's Anger Treatment Project)

A pervasive role for women is that of 'stroking' (Bernard, 1981) by which is meant helping, agreeing, complying, and passively accepting. Outwardly expressed anger does not conform to the feminine (but not *feminist*) ideal of the self-less, ever-nurturing woman. However, from Medusa to Lady Macbeth to Aileen Carol Wournos, the serial killer, there are ample images of female anger run amok. Alternatively, in the history of social movements, one

Anger Treatment for People with Developmental Disabilities by J. L. Taylor and R. W. Novaco.
Copyright © 2005 John Wiley & Sons, Ltd.

can find female anger that has energized significant social change, as occurred with suffrage and the expansion of employment opportunities.

Just as it does for men, unregulated anger among women has adverse effects on their well-being. In the field of behavioural medicine and heart disease (which was overviewed in Chapter 1), despite the higher prevalence of heart disease among males, females have often been included in research on anger and hostility as risk factors (e.g., Barefoot et al. 1987; Barefoot et al. 1991; Kneip et al., 1993; Iribarren et al. 2000). Various efforts have been made to understand gender differences in cardiovascular disease in terms of anger dimensions with regard to both coronary artery disease and hypertension (e.g., Haynes, Feinleib, & Kannel, 1980; Helmers, Baker, O'Kelly, & Tobe, 2000; Stoney & Engebretson, 1994). In the field of human aggression, women have been included both in laboratory and in questionnaire studies, as well as in psychiatric patient studies on violence, as discussed in Chapter 4. This background will be elaborated here as a prelude to presenting our early work with female patients having developmental disabilities.

Overall, the anger difficulties experienced by women have not received sufficient attention. A notable exception has been the volume by Thomas (1993), the contributors to which presented empirical studies regarding anger determinants, patterns of anger expression, associated clinical factors (e.g. depression, eating disorders, and substance use), moderating variables (e.g. self-esteem and social support), and approaches to treatment. Thomas and her colleagues presented data on women's anger from a broad-based community sample, finding variations by age, education, and ethnicity, and exercise levels. While several structured psychometric tests were used to assess anger, Thomas and her colleagues found in open-ended questionnaires that women often reported modes of anger expression not captured by the structured tests. '*Crying* was the most frequently reported experience' (Thomas, 1993, p. 65). This emotional behaviour perhaps deserves special attention for women in conjunction with the dynamics of anger episodes and their resolution.

There are a few women-focused anger management studies, each of which has been conducted in forensic settings (Fitzharding, 1997; Kendall, 2001; Smith, Smith, & Beckner, 1994). These studies have been limited in depth of treatment application and have lacked rigour in design and measurement. The Fitzharding (1997) project involved ten women prisoners who received seven sessions, six of which occurred on three consecutive days, and their interview responses were contrasted with that of ten other women whose comparability was not established. More new anger management techniques were found for the intervention group. Smith et al. conducted a three-session series of two-hour workshops with 11 women in a medium security prison and found significant reductions in anger inventory scores and mood diary ratings in a pre-post evaluative design. Their intervention involved education about anger, self-monitoring, relaxation techniques, cognitive review of anger events, and strategies to escape from conflict. In the volume by Thomas (1993), anger treatment is discussed in a chapter by Wilt (1993), who presents six cases chosen from her private practice; the women received weekly or biweekly psychodynamic therapy sessions for an average of one and a half years. This is not an approach that lends itself to treatment with our clinical population.

While the argument for conducting research into treatment of anger problems for people with developmental disabilities has already been made, there may be additional reasons to suppose that women have a specific claim on research priorities. A recent survey of psychiatric symptomatology in a large sample of people with developmental disabilities found that women were more likely than men to suffer from neurotic and affective disorders

(Taylor, Hatton, Dixon et al., 2004). Criminological research over recent decades indicates that women offend at far lower rates than men, but those who do offend have far higher rates of psychiatric disorder (Harvey, Burnham, Kendall, & Pease, 1992; Maden, Swinton, & Gunn, 1994).

Group treatment studies in the developmental disability field have included women among the small samples used, and one study (Allan et al., 2001) reported on women only, though treatment had in fact been delivered in mixed sex groups. Individual cognitive behavioural treatment studies so far have only included men. Forensic settings tend to favour group work, and the priorities in such services have been men, who are present in far greater numbers.

While this book has described a treatment approach based on Novaco's model of anger, which is intended to be gender-neutral, the main research programme involved a population of men. This chapter attempts to give some gender balance to the assessment and treatment evidence base, as this is an area with a paucity of research involving women as subjects (Stanko, 1995). While there have been a number of studies concerning differences between men and women in the experience and expression of anger, there has been little work considering whether the application of treatment approaches largely developed for men are effective also for women. Thus this chapter will (1) summarize differences in the experience of anger between men and women that have emerged in general research; (2) compare the men and women in the screening samples of the in-patient developmental disabilities service; and (3) utilize case material and outcomes from a small project ($N = 9$) based in the same setting, extending the individual cognitive behavioural anger treatment programme to the women's service.

DIFFERENCES BETWEEN MEN AND WOMEN IN THE EXPERIENCE OF ANGER

Apart from obvious physiological differences between men and women in height, weight, and hormones, each of which may bear on the experience and expression of anger, there are other gender-based differences that may also have an impact. This section will briefly consider sociological factors, obtained differences in expression and experience of anger in community samples, and differences in anger and aggression in clinical in-patient populations.

Sociological factors

At the societal level, there is important gender variation in financial and occupational status, as well as in physical and sexual victimization. These have been considered at length in the sociological and criminological literature (Carlen, 1988; Cook, 1987; Faragher, 1981; Walklate, 2000). Walklate points out that the criminal justice system is mainly peopled by men, although in the past 20 years change has occurred towards balancing the sexes in this domain. There may be criminological features particularly pertinent to women and their anger expression that result in involvement with either mental health or criminal justice systems (Hedderman & Gelsthorpe, 1997; Jackson, Glass, & Hope, 1987). Hedderman and Gelsthorpe use a phrase to capture the way in which magistrates in England view women defendants: 'more troubled than troublesome'.

Differences in expression and experience of anger

Research into the development of anger indicates that boys' games continue through frequent quarrels, while girls' games end when quarrels occur (Lever, 1976). A study of 100 girls through childhood to teenage years indicated that young girls are willing to express their anger, but by adolescence most girls suppressed feelings, especially anger, in order to be more popular (Brown & Gilligan, 1992). In her community sample study, Thomas (1993, 1995) utilized both quantitative and qualitative methodology. She suggested that there may be reasons to expect differences in anger expression in adult women.

Thomas described the development of the concept of anger expression, with its accompanying concepts of inwardly expressed and outwardly expressed anger, and anger control, and she added anger discussion (getting anger off one's chest by talking), and anger symptoms (expression of anger via somatic symptoms such as headaches). She suggests that women are more likely to discuss their anger. Research has consistently shown that men are more likely to behave aggressively (Bettencourt & Millen, 1996; Campbell, 1994). Campbell stated that aggression feels good to men as it asserts control and power. Thomas asserts that aggression does not feel good to women because it means loss of self-control and guilt regarding distress to others, as well as greater fear of getting hurt through retaliation from their victim.

Thomas' study focused on anger, rather than hostility or aggression, with some interesting findings. The precipitants of anger in women were located in the interpersonal realm, mainly within a small circle of close relations. Thus, the women seldom described impersonal triggers of anger, such as being stuck in a queue, or bumped by a stranger, which commonly feature in anger questionnaires. Anger was much more likely to be provoked by someone close letting them down, or when someone tried to take advantage of their friendship. Younger women were more likely to overtly express anger, while older women scored highly on inwardly expressed anger. Clearly this difference could be explained by societal shifts in expected gender roles and feminine behaviours, or by a 'mellowing' among the older women. Longitudinal data would be required to address this question. Women with less education scored higher on anger suppression and anger symptoms. Trait anger was highest in all groups of women with children under 18 years, with women with elementary school children scoring highest on outwardly expressed anger. Stress was strongly related to trait anger, cognitive anger, and somatic anger, with vicarious stress being the greatest source for women. Examples related to other people's problems e.g. son's divorce, nephew's car accident, daughter's breast cancer, ageing parents' changing mental capacity. An inverse relationship was found between anger and self-esteem, an important finding given that women tend to have lower self-esteem than men (Rosenberg & Simmons, 1975). Thomas concludes:

> Despite a widely circulated myth that women do not even know when they are angry, only six women in the study failed to complete the 'typical anger experience' page of the questionnaire ... evidence from this study indicates that for some women anger expression is still inhibited especially those whose lack of education and power keeps them in positions of low status and power. They are seething inside whilst maintaining the façade of 'nice lady'... Much of women's anger seems to be reality based and justifiable ... It arises from interpersonal interactions within which other people deny them power and resources, treat them unjustly or behave irresponsibly towards them.

Thomas acknowledges the need for a matched in-depth examination of men's anger, involving qualitative as well as quantitative data.

In other studies, the absence of gender differences has been a common result. In a study of 361 city dwellers in Australia (Milovchevich et al., 2001), there were no gender differences in trait anger, anger expression, inwardly expressed anger, outwardly expressed anger, or anger control, as measured by the Spielberger State-Trait Anger Expression Inventory (STAXI). The only main effect found was for gender role (masculine, feminine, androgynous or undifferentiated). This absence of gender differences is in accord with previous findings by Kopper (Kopper, 1993; Kopper & Epperson, 1996). As well, one finds comparability between genders in standardization data for anger psychometric scales. Spielberger (1991) reports minimal differences between males and females on the STAXI scales.

For the Novaco Anger Scale and Provocation Inventory (NAS-PI; Novaco, 2003) the non-clinical standardization sample was composed of 1,546 adults and children, and the means across subscales are quite comparable. The primary gender difference occurs in the NAS Behavioral subscale, where men score significantly higher than women (3.1 T score units). However, a recent study by Suter et al. (2002) compared 50 women and 121 men in various prisons in Australia with regard to their STAXI and NAS-PI scores. The female prisoners scored significantly higher on all of the STAXI and NAS subscales; they were not significantly different on the PI, except with regard to provocations of unfairness. Suter et al. conjectured that the higher anger levels for the female prisoners was due to the higher incidence of psychopathology and trauma exposure in that group.

The review by Kring (1999) emphasizes the need for studies to consider the more specific conditions under which the experience and expression of anger may differ for men and women. Although she acknowledges that research results for gender differences are inconclusive, she reports that women react with greater levels of anger in the context of a close or trusting relationship. In addition, she reports the consistent finding that men are more likely to hit or throw something when angry, whereas women are much more likely to cry.

Clinical studies of anger which include women would not fail to note the issues of sexual abuse, prostitution, sexual exploitation, pregnancy and childbirth, often involving children being taken into care by the state (Allan, Lindsay, McLeod, & Smith, 2001) . Provision of care for anger should therefore give attention to issues of disempowerment that have been noted in the feminist and criminological literature. Indeed, Allan et al. propose that the anger and aggression are a manifestation of the abuse experienced in earlier life. Concerns are on occasion expressed that treatment of anger might be done in a way that devalues or minimizes the experiences of vulnerable individuals (Jahoda, Trower, Pert, & Finn, 2001; Kendall, 2001). The male samples in similar clinical studies of men with developmental disabilities and anger problems might have comparable levels of abuse and disempowerment (Novaco & Taylor, 2003). Cognitive-behavioural treatment, of course, emphasizes the normality and functionality of anger, and aims for more adaptive expression and control, with client and therapist working in collaboration.

ANGER AND AGGRESSION IN WOMEN IN-PATIENTS

It is commonly known in secure or forensic services that women's units occasion higher frequencies of disturbances and serious incidents of aggression towards others. This is contrary to what is observed in the normal population, where men aggress and come into contact with the law more frequently. Several studies of in-patient populations have attempted to find reasons for this difference. This section will describe some of this work and report on results from our own project.

Novaco and Thacker's study analyzed archival data in each of six years of an eight-year period for adult psychiatric patients in five institutions and consistently found that women committed more physical assaults and were treated as more dangerous towards others (Novaco & Thacker, 1990; see also Novaco, 1997). The women in this sample were older than the men, yet for the whole sample, they found age to be inversely related to assaults. The highest percentage of assaults occurred for single women. Non-English speakers were not more likely to be aggressive, but those who had not graduated from high school were. The gender differences they found across the whole sample in the study – women were older, more likely to be married and more likely to be high school graduates – would suggest they should have committed less assaults, rather than more. Several other studies found that there were higher levels of aggression in women in-patients (Convit, Isay, & Volavka, 1990; Larkin, Murtagh, & Jones, 1988; Ionno, 1983). It is unclear whether the differences should be attributed to social construction (e.g., differential processing and disposal by the legal system, or differential sensitivity to violence in women by society) or to real differences in levels or expression of anger. However, the results of these studies suggest that study of gender differences in this field should continue. These should include clarification of the stage of development at which higher rates of aggression in females is first observed; clarification of differences in court disposal; and studies of differences in treatment and management of in-patients which may account for the higher frequency aggression observed in women patients.

Our own study was carried out in the women's low secure units in the same hospital for people with developmental disability described in Chapters 3 and 5. The service comprised two wards and a bungalow housing 18, 6 and 4 women respectively. Two of the units were single sex and one utilized half of a ward and staff group, the other half of which was utilized by male patients. All patients are assessed within three months of admission and a range of demographic and clinical data routinely collected. A needs assessment was completed to ascertain how many might benefit from anger treatment and this allowed us to compare 27 of the women with the male population which had been studied earlier. We compared populations on a number of variables and identified some similarities and some differences (See Table 11.1).

These differences included higher levels of diagnosed mental illness, personality disorder, and history of abuse. Women were slightly older and stayed longer. In our own sample, 56% of the women were convicted of a violent offence, by comparison with only 36% of the men. Clearly, one of the factors contributing to this difference, when described for the percentage of the whole population in this forensic in-patient service, is the high frequency of conviction of sex offences in men, but none for women. Data collected by the nursing staff studied for administrative purposes in the hospital would suggest that there are a higher number of incidents in the women's service where patients have to be restrained for their own or others' safety, or *pro re nata* medication is administered. This would suggest higher levels of aggression, supporting reports in the literature elsewhere, but could this equally be explained by differences in the service as by differences between the populations.

Our own data, given in Table 11.2, indicate that there were very few differences indeed between the men and the women in terms of their scores on a variety of self-report measures of anger. The only significant differences were on the State Trait Anger Expression Inventory Trait and T-Ang-T subscales, along with the Disrespect items subscale on the Provocation

Table 11.1   Male and female patient demographic, clinical and forensic characteristics and anger screening data

	Men N = 129		Women N = 30	
Mean age	33.2	(11.6)	38.0	(10.4)
Mean length of stay (years)	3.7	(3.5)	5.2	(4.8)
Mean FSIQ	67.5	(8.0)	65.5	(7.8)
Mean reading age (years)	8.3	(3.7)	9.1	(1.5)
Mental illness	34	(26.4%)	11	(36.7%)
Personality disorder	24	(18.6%)	16	(64%)
Sexual offender	55	(43%)	0	
Arsonist	26	(20%)	8	(26.7%)
Convicted for violence	46	(36%)	17	(56.6%)
History of violence (including prior conviction)	49	(38%)	11	(36.6%)
Detained patients	121	(94%)	30	(100%)
Detained under criminal sections of MHA 1983	81	(67%)	16	(53.4%)
Mean NAS Total	92.4 (16.6)		92.2 (17.5)	
Mean PI Total	62.9 (16.2)		69.0 (17.0)	

Note: Standard deviations are given in parentheses for mean values. Mental illness and personality disorder pertain to 28 and 25 women respectively.

Table 11.2   Anger scores and differences for men and women in the northgate screening samples

	Men N = 112		Women N = 27		t
NAS Total	92.4 (16.6)		92.2 (17.5)		.04
PI Total	62.9 (16.2)		69.0 (16.9)		−1.70
STAXI					
State Anger	11.6	(3.7)	12.5	(4.6)	−1.06
Trait Anger	18.8	(6.3)	22.2	(7.7)	−2.11*
Ax In	17.8	(4.1)	18.0	(5.0)	−.191
Ax Out	16.8	(5.1)	17.7	(6.1)	−.74
Ax Con	19.7	(5.9)	20.0	(6.2)	−.22
Ax Ex	30.8 (11.2)		31.2 (13.6)		−.15

Inventory. Means and standard deviations for the Novaco Anger Scale, Provocation Inventory, and the other STAXI sub-scales were all quite close to those of the men. The author has hypothesized that some of the commonly reported disadvantages experienced by women, and purported to explain their anger and aggression, may be equally experienced by men and women with developmental disabilities (Robertson, 2002).

ANGER TREATMENT OUTCOME FOR WOMEN

The literature on the treatment of anger in people with a developmental disability has been reviewed in Chapter 4, and as mentioned above, there has only been one published study focused on women with a developmental disability (Allan et al., 2001). Other treatment outcome studies involving clients with developmental disabilities have included women (Benson et al., 1986; Howells et al., 2000; King et al., 1999; Moore et al., 1997; Rose, 1996; Rose et al., 2000; Rossiter, Hunniset, & Pulsford, 1998). These studies have focused on effective elements of treatment rather than on gender differences. In a recent meta-analysis of anger treatment outcome studies DiGuiseppe and Tafrate (2003) compared effect sizes on a variety of outcome measures, as well as a variety of elements or types of treatment. Analysis of various moderator variables showed that gender did not predict the effect size of any type of dependent variable, whereas other variables such as use of a treatment manual and inclusion of treatment fidelity checks did. However, just under 50% of the 57 studies included in that review (total $N = 1{,}841$ participants) involved clinical samples, not all of which were drawn from mental health populations.

THE WOMEN'S ANGER PROJECT

Having ascertained that women have been somewhat neglected in the clinical samples used in anger research and that there may be some differences in the way women experience and deal with their anger, this section describes our own women's anger treatment project. This project for the women followed that for the men as an extension of that work and an opportunity for discovery.

The success of the men's anger treatment project prompted clinicians within the women's service to demand a similar treatment programme for the women. The literature described earlier certainly supports the need for anger treatment for women in-patients, given their higher levels of assault and aggression and given what has been mapped regarding the anger–aggression relationship in Chapters 2 and 3. Rather than assume what worked for the men would also work for the women, agreement was reached that this programme development should be evaluated as rigorously as would be possible, given the small overall population ($N = 27$). Routine clinical post-admission assessment data suggested a potential of 15 candidates suitable for treatment, using as an inclusion criterion having a NAS score above the hospital mean. However, when additional inclusion criteria were taken into consideration (IQ over 55; age under 60; Provocation Inventory scores above the mean), it became apparent that numbers would be smaller than hoped. Thus, the inclusion criteria were adjusted slightly (age under 65; PI over 55) and an initial sample of 13 women were identified.

The much smaller population suggested a multiple baseline case series design where subjects acted as their own controls, rather than a controlled group comparison. All subjects were assessed at the same baseline point, and the 18-session treatment programme was delivered as therapist resources allowed over a two-year period thereafter. Treatment was not delivered in random order, but was determined to some extent by clinical priority, as determined in consultation with medical and nursing staff. Consent was sought in the same way as has been described for the men. Treatment was delivered as it was for the men, using the treatment manual without any adaptations.

Unlike the men's project, the therapists were not all qualified applied psychologists, but included trainees and assistants, all with first degrees in Psychology. Previous evaluation, following the men's project, had ascertained that graduates in Psychology could achieve positive outcomes (see Chapter 7 for further discussion). DiGuiseppe and Tafrate's meta-analysis (2003) suggests that greater effect sizes were achieved in those studies that included use of a manual and addressed treatment integrity. The main researcher, who also delivered therapy, arranged weekly supervision for therapists. In addition, therapists were expected to complete session ratings of engagement, patient ratings of helpfulness, learning and enjoyment, as well as hand-written notes on a session record sheet. Patient files and reports were checked from time to time, and protocols were discussed at a monthly anger steering group meeting. Thus, treatment integrity was enhanced.

Outcome measures

Outcome data for all those who remained as in-patients were collected at baseline, pre- and post-treatment, and at four months and 12 months follow-up, using the NAS, PI and STAXI as self-report anger measures. One woman was discharged immediately following treatment but remained locally, and thus follow-up data were collected from her community placement. For five subjects, IPT data was also collected, once it had been confirmed by analysis of data from the men's project that this is a valid and reliable measure. In addition, staff completed the Ward Anger Rating Scale weekly for a month at all data points, as well as weekly throughout treatment as a measure of staff observed anger and aggression.

In addition, the measurement of potential changes in patient care that might have had an effect on anger were monitored to a greater degree than had taken place with the men's project. Staff completed the same Index of Change on a monthly basis, not just at the end of the study period, but at assessment points, and after every month during treatment. Changes such as new admissions, transfer between units, changes of medication, key staff, and family events were monitored.

WOMEN'S RESPONSES TO ANGER TREATMENT

Thirteen women were identified as meeting criteria for inclusion and nine of them completed treatment. Two withheld consent prior to starting treatment, one withheld consent after the preparatory phase, and one completed treatment but absconded before post-treatment assessments had been administered.

The nine who went through the treatment seemed to have no more difficulty relating to the materials provided in the manual than the men did. Analysis of the session ratings of communication, engagement, enjoyment, and learning suggested the majority worked well and appreciated the programme. In the completion of Anger Logs, when asked what they did when they got angry, many of the women said that they cried, but this option was not explicit on the log (though it could be recorded under an 'other' category). Future adaptations to the programme might incorporate this option.

The Patient's Evaluation of Treatment Questionnaire suggested that the elements the women found most helpful were talking to psychologist and/or staff about their anger; understanding how their anger worked; using Anger Logs; doing homework tasks; and using relaxation (although there were several who did not find this helpful). Results from this questionnaire seemed to represent a range of responses, rather than a compliant response set, and patients seemed able to express themselves regarding the areas they did not like or did not find helpful. When asked if they thought they had changed since completing treatment, or if they were any less angry, responses were realistic with the majority indicating

Table 11.3 Numbers of women (N = 9) who improved at post-treatment, 4 and 12 months follow-up

	Assessment points compared	Improved	Deteriorated/ no change
Anger Disposition			
NAS Total	Pre-post	7	2
	Pre-4m	8	1
	Pre-12m	6	3
STAXI Ax/Ex	Pre-post	9	0
	Pre-4m	6	3
	Pre-12m	7	2
Anger Reactivity			
PI Total	Pre-post	7	2
	Pre-4m	6	3
	Pre-12m	7	2
IPT Reactivity (N = 5)	Pre-post	4	1
	Pre-4m	4	1
	Pre-12m	4	1
Anger Control			
NAS Regulation	Pre-post	9	0
	Pre-4m	7	2
	Pre-12m	8	1
STAXI Ax/Control	Pre-post	9	0
	Pre-4m	6	3
	Pre-12m	6	3
WARS Anger Index			
	Pre-post	5	4
	Pre-4m	8	1
	Pre-12m	5	4

improvement, but about a third claiming they were no less angry, and one claiming she had not changed at all. Two-thirds of them thought they had had just about the right amount of support from staff.

Analysis of outcomes was achieved by allocating cases into two categories – 'improved' or 'deteriorated/ no change'. As indicated in Table 11.3, the majority of women improved on most self-report scores from pre- to post-treatment, but several who had improved on STAXI, NAS, and WARS criteria deteriorated during the follow-up period.

Simply examining the shift closer to or below the mean, most women improved immediately post-treatment as measured by the Regulation subscale on the NAS, the STAXI Anger Control, STAXI Anger Expression and the Imaginal Provocation Test. On the staff-reported WARS anger attributes, approximately half of the women improved. Effect sizes for change from pre- to post-treatment ranged from large to medium, which is consistent with other anger interventions (DiGuiseppe & Tafrate, 2003) and would be expected given the use of a manual and attention to treatment integrity.

The total scores for minor and major changes in patients' lives during the course of the project were examined using Index of Change scores. These displayed little variance throughout the project, with the exception of the 12-month follow-up when there seemed to be a higher level of changes. Perhaps the deterioration at follow-up may be due to these changes in the women's lives and care provision.

Case vignette

The following case vignette illustrates some of the process and the outcomes observed.

Trish was a 56-year old woman who had spent many years in both high and low security, with an attempt at discharge in-between. She had been detained originally for a serious assault on a member of staff in a local hospital for people with developmental disabilities. She had been readmitted after discharge back to her home area after she assaulted a vulnerable fellow patient. She was diagnosed as having psychopathy, as well as a mild developmental disability (IQ = 63). Trish had some hearing loss and was not always keen to wear her hearing aid, just as she was unwilling to acknowledge her need for a walking aid caused by lifelong mobility problems. Trish is a proud woman.

Although she held a belief that she would never get out of hospital and was perceived as 'top dog' by others, she seemed highly motivated to complete anger treatment, whether because she genuinely wanted things to change or because she valued the one-to-one sessions it involved. Trish had done work with psychologists in the past and often seemed to form strong relationships with them. She had good literacy skills and was proud of this, and she had attempted to write her own life story.

Prior to treatment she had had a particularly aggressive spell, and staff were keen to see treatment start. She was waiting for an important operation, which may have increased her irritability. At this time, staff introduced a more person-centred programme offering her choices that took her age and deteriorating physical condition into account and involved an individualized reward scheme which she helped to design. During the course of treatment, ward anger rating scales indicated a considerable improvement in aggressive incidents. Scores remained at similar levels between baseline and pre-treatment, with a considerable reduction post-treatment, a rise at four month follow-up and a further reduction at 12 month follow-up, perhaps as discharge plans became clearer. As presented in Figure 11.1, her self-reported PI Total scores and IPT Reactivity scores showed reduction in anger reactions to provocation stimuli.

Trish found the relaxation work particularly challenging, as she was very uncomfortable about closing her eyes in the sessions. It was suggested that she look at a blank area of the therapy room wall instead, but this was equally difficult for her. It transpired that this anxiety was not attributable to embarrassment, as might commonly be the case, but to a posttraumatic response to experiences in a seclusion room in a high security hospital. It was therefore agreed that relaxation could take place facing the therapist, but with her eyes open. Previous formulations of this lady's responses would have interpreted this as simple uncooperative behaviour, but the detailed nature of the relaxation training and the incremental steps involved, as well as the collaborative nature of the cognitive behavioural approach, allowed the therapist to identify an alternative cause of this difficulty with the client.

Treatment gains on the STAXI and NAS scales are presented in Figure 11.1. It can be also seen that STAXI Anger Expression and NAS Total decrease over the course of treatment and at the four month follow-up, but at the 12 month follow-up there is some loss of the achieved improvement. NAS Regulation scores, however, continue to increase through the second follow-up. During the course of treatment this lady was able to identify and challenge dysfunctional cognitions to good effect. Most of the gains made on the cognitive sub-scale of the NAS were made during follow-up. The therapist bore in mind the diagnosis of psychopathy, considering whether Trish might be able to comply with treatment in a

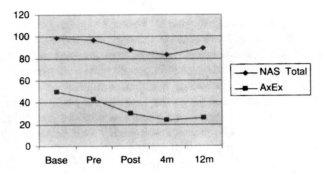

Anger Disposition - Trish

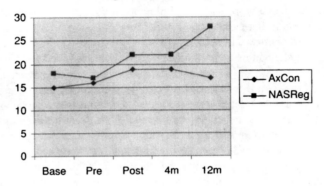

Anger Control - Trish

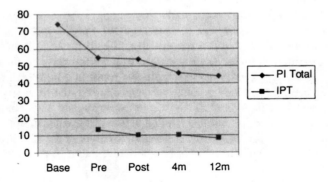

Anger Reactivity - Trish

Figure 11.1   Case vignette – Trish's anger scores over time

procedural way, while perhaps being unable or unwilling to follow through behaviourally. However, her psychometric results at post-treatment and follow-up assessments, as well as clinical reports, suggested that real gains had been made. This was aided by identifying a suitable location to which this very challenging lady could be discharged from hospital.

Staff views of anger treatment

Named nurses had completed two structured interviews during the course of the project, one immediately after their 'named patient' completed treatment, and another at the end of the treatment phase of the whole project. At this latter phase, the two Ward Managers and Clinical Co-ordinators were also interviewed to gain an understanding of their views about what had been gained and suggestions for improvement. The first interview asked more detailed questions relating to the possibility of a generalized or systemic effect. It had been hypothesized that the project intervention might effect change in patients who were not yet receiving anger treatment. This hypothesis had been generated by results of the men's project in which patients in the control group also improved, prior to receiving the specialised anger treatment. Those control group gains, coupled with clinical observations, prompted the conjecture that there may have been a systemic effect or a diffusion of the treatment intervention across the whole service.

Nursing staff are an extremely important part of the patients' environment in this kind of setting. The Staff Questionnaires were an attempt to consider how much such a project might have impacted on staff behaviour, and whether support for patients in understanding and controlling their anger increased over time. A different Staff Survey was completed at the end of the 12-month follow-up that ascertained staff views of the project and any benefits they anticipated. Interestingly, as occurred with the male patients, perceptions of the potential benefits of the project were influenced by staff length of service, with those serving longer as nurses demonstrating a more pessimistic view of the benefits of anger treatment.

Did staff support increase over time?

In the women's project, the nine women were grouped into three cohorts. Graphing the data for the three cohorts did not indicate that there was a 'generalization' phenomenon. The cohorts either remained at the same level between baseline and pre-treatment, or got worse as measured by the NAS Total scores. Patients receiving treatment later in the course of the project did not seem to improve their scores between baseline and pre-treatment, unlike the men. Thus, routine clinical care did not seem to be adequately addressing their anger problems, and nor did the existence of the anger research project add value to their routine care while waiting. Scores on the Staff Questionnaire indicated that those Named Nurses working with the last patients to go through treatment offered no more help than those involved at the beginning of the project. Thus, it does not seem that an ongoing research project in the female in-patient setting incrementally increased the amount of support staff offered to patients in understanding and controlling their anger problems.

CONCLUSIONS

This case series adds to the paucity of literature on cognitive behavioural treatment for anger in women. Several authors in the fields of criminology and elsewhere urge caution in using models of understanding human behaviour and developing interventions based solely on research involving males. The women in the in-patient service studied had similar levels of anger to the men. Although proportionally more met the criteria for treatment, proportionally more withheld consent, making it difficult to establish a sample large enough for rigorous analysis. Few differences were found between the anger experienced by the women and that experienced by the men. Further analysis may reveal qualitative differences in the nature of provocation or the kinds of cognitions experienced by women.

The majority of the women clearly benefited from anger treatment, but gains that were maintained or boosted at four month follow-up fell away for some at one year. There were no indications that this treatment programme, developed mainly for use with men, was inappropriate for application to women. However, further research, including both carefully planned single case studies and larger surveys of clinical populations of women, is needed to ascertain the efficacy of this anger treatment for women with developmental disabilities and whether refinements should be made in the assessment tools.

APPENDICES

These handouts are also available online at www.wiley.com/go/angertreatment

Anger Treatment for People with Developmental Disabilities by J. L. Taylor and R. W. Novaco.
Copyright © 2005 John Wiley & Sons, Ltd.

Handout/Exercise Sheet 1.1

WHAT IS ANGER TREATMENT ABOUT?

INTRODUCTION

The assessments you have done with the psychologists recently tell us that you have had some problems with becoming angry either in the past or now. This doesn't mean you are the kind of person who goes around shouting and swearing, smashing things up, threatening other people, or hitting out. Sometimes when people get angry they bottle it up inside, become sad and depressed, or even hurt themselves. Angry feelings are also often part of the reason people have behaved badly in the past and got themselves into trouble.

Everybody gets angry from time to time. It is a natural feeling and is part of being human. Anger is a problem if it happens too often, lasts too long, or is so strong the person can't control it. Sometimes when this happens, it can lead to people being aggressive or violent, or doing other things which might harm themselves or others.

HOW ANGER WORKS

The figure at the end of this handout shows how angry feelings happen and what can happen as a result. The "*situation*" is what is going on around you at the time. The sorts of situations which can lead to angry feelings include feeling insulted, threatened, frustrated, annoyed or being treated unfairly.

Usually this leads to a person *thinking* that the situation is unfair, threatening or whatever. Often we think that the person who is causing the situation is doing it on purpose to 'wind' us up, or make us angry. Depending on how bad the situation is, we might then *feel* a little angry, quite angry, or very angry/furious.

People *behave* in different ways when they feel angry. Some people ignore whatever or whoever is making them angry. Other people might become aggressive and confront or 'square up' to the person creating the situation. Others might churn it over and over inside for a while and then show their anger in another way, for example, by smashing a window.

Depending on how we behave different things will happen to us *afterwards*. If we react aggressively and hit out, we are likely to get into trouble, lose some privileges, or maybe get locked up. If we think we have handled the situation well, we might feel good about it, but if we have handled the situation badly we could feel upset and unhappy.

Anger Treatment for People with Developmental Disabilities by J. L. Taylor and R. W. Novaco.
Copyright © 2005 John Wiley & Sons, Ltd.

HOW DOES ANGER TREATMENT WORK?

The treatment is geared up to helping you cope with and handle angry feelings better both now and in the future. This is very important so that when you eventually leave the hospital and live in the community there is less chance of you behaving in a way that will get you into trouble when you feel angry.

The treatment works by helping you to think differently about the things and people who make you feel angry. It also helps you to cope with angry feelings better when they happen. The treatment also teaches you how to handle people better and situations that make you angry.

The main point of the treatment is to help you to control your feelings better so that you can choose how to behave in the future. The therapist is here to help you and guide you through the treatment, but it will only work if you want it to and work at it. In this way, you and the therapist, along with your named keyworker and other staff, are working together as a team to help you get better at coping with angry feelings.

PREPARATORY PHASE SESSIONS

The therapist is planning to see you to begin with for six preparation sessions. These sessions are to help you understand better what the anger treatment is about, discuss your own problems and what help you would like with these. What is involved in each of these sessions is explained briefly on *Handout/Exercise Sheet 1.2 'Outline of Preparatory Phase Sessions of Anger Treatment'*.

HOW ANGER WORKS

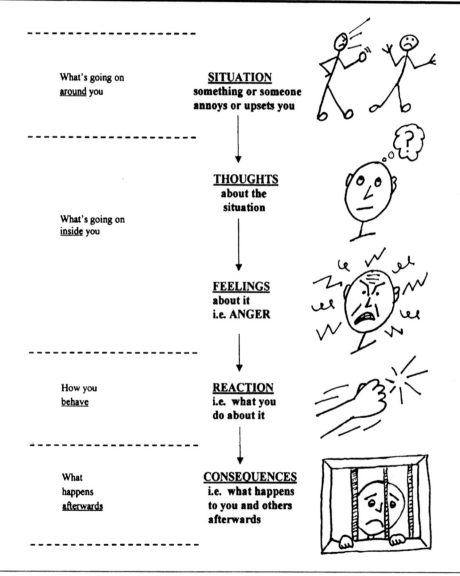

What's going on
<u>around</u> you

SITUATION
something or someone
annoys or upsets you

THOUGHTS
about the
situation

What's going on
<u>inside</u> you

FEELINGS
about it
i.e. ANGER

How you
<u>behave</u>

REACTION
i.e. what you
do about it

What
happens
<u>afterwards</u>

CONSEQUENCES
i.e. what happens
to you and others
afterwards

Anger Treatment for People with Developmental Disabilities by J. L. Taylor and R. W. Novaco.
Copyright © 2005 John Wiley & Sons, Ltd.

Handout/Exercise Sheet 1.2

OUTLINE OF PREPARATORY PHASE SESSIONS OF ANGER TREATMENT

Session 1   Explaining the purpose of anger treatment

Session 2   Feeling angry is OK

Session 3   Understanding our own and other people's feelings

Session 4   How to control the physical feelings of anger

Session 5   Reasons for changing the way we cope with feeling angry

Session 6   Looking back at the preparatory sessions and looking forward to what comes next (Review)

Note: Each session will last around 1 hour (60 minutes). Where possible, two sessions will be delivered each week. One session will be delivered per week as a minimum (excluding periods of holiday and sickness). Frequency, timing and venues for sessions to be discussed and agreed with the client's keyworker as appropriate.

Anger Treatment for People with Developmental Disabilities by J. L. Taylor and R. W. Novaco.
Copyright © 2005 John Wiley & Sons, Ltd.

Handout/Exercise Sheet 1.3

GROUND RULES FOR ANGER
TREATMENT SESSIONS

I have dicussed and agreed with my therapist ....
the following ground rules for our anger treatment sessions.

1. **Confidentiality.**

2. **Respect and good manners.**

3. **Getting the job done.**

4. **Angry feelings.**

5. **Working together.**

6. **Other(s).**

Signed:................................. **Date:**................................

Anger Treatment for People with Developmental Disabilities by J. L. Taylor and R. W. Novaco.
Copyright © 2005 John Wiley & Sons, Ltd.

Handout/Exercise Sheet 1.4

WAYS OF DEALING WITH FEELING TENSE/UPTIGHT

INTRODUCTION

Everyone feels tense or uptight from time to time. These feelings are natural and are part of being human. They are only a problem if they happen too often, go on for too long or are too strong. One way of making sure this doesn't happen is to relax and calm ourselves down from time to time.

In your first anger treatment session you talked about how listening to your favourite music can make you feel better, calmer or relaxed. Can you think of some other ways of relaxing and handling feeling tense and uptight? Write your ideas down below, or ask your keyworker to write them down for you. Your ideas will be discussed in your next anger treatment session.

WAYS OF DEALING WITH FEELING TENSE/UPTIGHT

1. Listening to my favourite music.

2.

3.

4.

5.

6.

7.

8.

Name: . . . .   **Date:** . . . .

Anger Treatment for People with Developmental Disabilities by J. L. Taylor and R. W. Novaco.
Copyright © 2005 John Wiley & Sons, Ltd.

Handout/Exercise Sheet 1.5

ANGER TREATMENT
(PREPARATORY PHASE)

REPORT ON TREATMENT SESSION

Client's Name: .... Session No.: ....
Venue of Session: .... Date of Session: ....
Objective(s) of Session:

....
....
....

A. THERAPIST'S REPORT ON CLIENT'S RESPONSE TO SESSION

Signed: .... Date: ....

Anger Treatment for People with Developmental Disabilities by J. L. Taylor and R. W. Novaco.
Copyright © 2005 John Wiley & Sons, Ltd.

B.   THERAPIST'S RATINGS ON CLIENT DURING SESSION

Communication

1	2	3	4	5
Irrelevant or no contribution to discussion	A few relevant contributions to discussion	Contributions generally relevant to discussion	Good contributions relevant to discussion	Consistently good contributions relevant to discussion

Engagement

1	2	3	4	5
Did not engage even when prompted	Engaged in session but only when prompted	Satisfactory engagement in session	Good level of engagement in session	Active participation relating issues beyond limit of session

Comprehension

1	2	3	4	5
Did not comprehend purpose of session	Limited comprehension of purpose of session	Good comprehension of some parts of the session	Good comprehension of all parts of the session	Complete understanding of the purpose of the session

C.   CLIENT'S REPORT AND RATINGS ON THE SESSION

• Was there anything good about today's session? (i.e. did you learn anything or find out something helpful or useful?)

  ....
  ....

• Was there anything bad about today's session? (i.e. did anything annoy you or wind you up?)

  ....
  ....

• What was the best bit/part of today's session?

  ....
  ....

• Did you enjoy today's session?

  1. No, not at all.   2. Some of it.   3. Yes, all of it.

• Are you learning anything from the sessions?

  1. No, nothing at all   2. A bit/some things   3. Yes, lots of things

• Are the sessions helping you?

  1. No, not at all   2. A bit   3. Yes, in lots of ways

• Any other comments?

  ....
  ....
  ....

Handout/Exercise Sheet 2.1

ANGER-PROVOKING SCENARIO

Bill is standing in a queue in a shop waiting to be served. He has been in the queue for a long time; it is a long queue and isn't moving very quickly.

Another man comes into the shop, looks at the queue and says, "I'm not going to stand around here all day." He then pushes into the queue in front of Bill, barging him as he does so.

When Bill points out to this man that he has been standing in queue for ages, he grins at Bill and says loudly, "So, what are you going to do about it!?"

Anger Treatment for People with Developmental Disabilities by J. L. Taylor and R. W. Novaco.
Copyright © 2005 John Wiley & Sons, Ltd.

Handout/Exercise Sheet 2.2

ANGER LOG I

Name: .... Date: .... Time: ....

Where were you? ....

What happened?

- ❏ Somebody was taking the mick
- ❏ Somebody criticized me
- ❏ Somebody told me to do something
- ❏ Somebody did something I didn't like
- ❏ Somebody stole something of mine

- ❏ Somebody started rowing with me
- ❏ Somebody started fighting with me
- ❏ I did something wrong
- ❏ Other (specify)

Who was that somebody?

❏ Client/Patient   ❏ Friend   ❏ Staff   ❏ Relative   ❏ Other (specify)

How angry were you?

Not angry at all	A little angry	Fairly angry	Very angry	Furious
1	2	3	4	5

What did you do?

- ❏ Shouted/Swore
- ❏ Ran off
- ❏ Smashed/broke something
- ❏ Tried to hit someone
- ❏ Actually hit someone

- ❏ Walked away calmly
- ❏ Talked it over
- ❏ Told someone else
- ❏ Ignored it
- ❏ Other (specify)

How well do you think you handled this situation/problem?

Badly	Not very well	OK	Well	Very well
1	2	3	4	5

Other comments

Anger Treatment for People with Developmental Disabilities by J. L. Taylor and R. W. Novaco.
Copyright © 2005 John Wiley & Sons, Ltd.

Handout/Exercise Sheet 3.1

UNDERSTANDING OTHER PEOPLE'S FEELINGS 1

Source: Reproduced from McCarthy & Thompson (1992) *Sex and the 3Rs: Rights, Responsibilities and Risks – A Sex Education Package for Working with People with Learning Difficulties.* Brighton: Pavilion.

Anger Treatment for People with Developmental Disabilities by J. L. Taylor and R. W. Novaco.
Copyright © 2005 John Wiley & Sons, Ltd.

Handout/Exercise Sheet 3.2

UNDERSTANDING OTHER
PEOPLE'S FEELINGS 2

Source: Reproduced from McCarthy & Thompson (1992) *Sex and the 3Rs: Rights, Responsibilities and Risks – A Sex Education Package for Working with People with Learning Difficulties.* Brighton: Pavilion.

Anger Treatment for People with Developmental Disabilities by J. L. Taylor and R. W. Novaco.
Copyright © 2005 John Wiley & Sons, Ltd.

Handout/Exercise Sheet 3.3

UNDERSTANDING OTHER PEOPLE'S FEELINGS 3

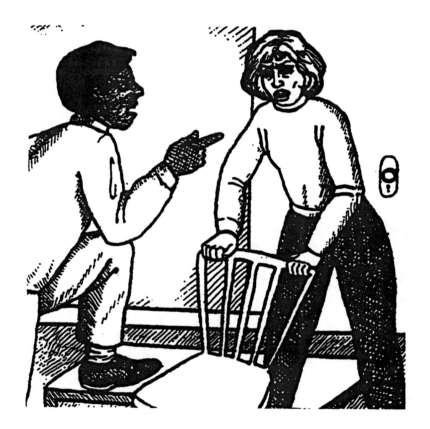

Source: Reproduced from McCarthy & Thompson (1992) *Sex and the 3Rs: Rights, Responsibilities and Risks – A Sex Education Package for Working with People with Learning Difficulties.* Brighton: Pavilion.

Anger Treatment for People with Developmental Disabilities by J. L. Taylor and R. W. Novaco.
Copyright © 2005 John Wiley & Sons, Ltd.

Cog. Emo, Phys. Behav

Handout/Exercise Sheet 3.4

HOW OUR FEELINGS AND THOUGHTS ARE LINKED

	SITUATION Where? What? Who?	THOUGHTS About the Situation	EMOTIONAL FEELINGS	PHYSICAL FEELINGS	REACTION What did you do?
A C T U A L					
P O S S I B L E					

Anger Treatment for People with Developmental Disabilities by J. L. Taylor and R. W. Novaco.
Copyright © 2005 John Wiley & Sons, Ltd.

Handout/Exercise Sheet 3.5

RELAXING AND CALMING IMAGE/PICTURE

Anger Treatment for People with Developmental Disabilities by J. L. Taylor and R. W. Novaco.
Copyright © 2005 John Wiley & Sons, Ltd.

Handout/Exercise Sheet 4.1

STRESS/ANGER THERMOMETER

Ordinary thermometers measure temperature (how hot it is). The stress thermometer measures how much stress or anger a person is feeling.

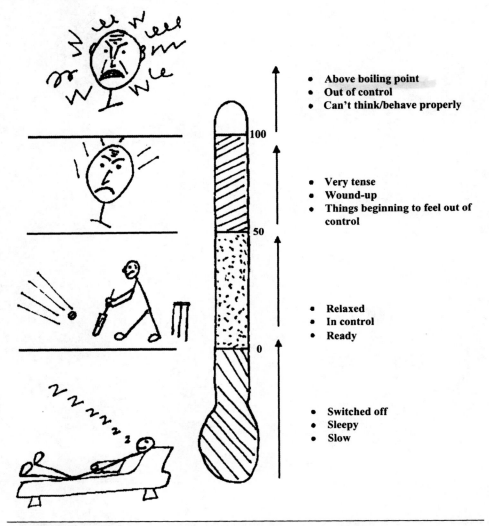

- Above boiling point
- Out of control
- Can't think/behave properly

100

- Very tense
- Wound-up
- Things beginning to feel out of control

50

- Relaxed
- In control
- Ready

0

- Switched off
- Sleepy
- Slow

Anger Treatment for People with Developmental Disabilities by J. L. Taylor and R. W. Novaco.
Copyright © 2005 John Wiley & Sons, Ltd.

Mayait   Swim
Rocio Agua Frio

Handout/Exercise Sheet 4.2

HOW OUR BODIES FEEL WHEN WE ARE STRESSED

Hackles

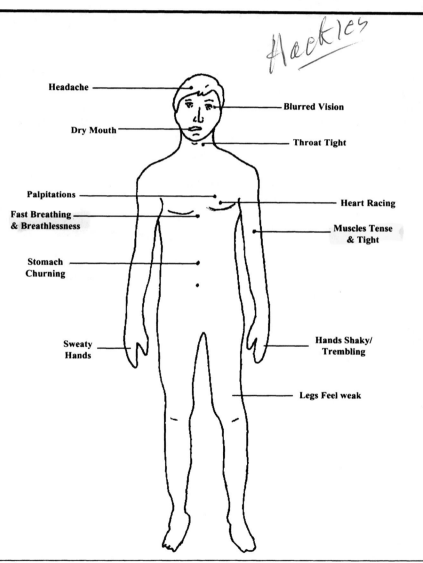

Headache

Blurred Vision

Dry Mouth

Throat Tight

Palpitations

Heart Racing

Fast Breathing & Breathlessness

Muscles Tense & Tight

Stomach Churning

Sweaty Hands

Hands Shaky/ Trembling

Legs Feel weak

Anger Treatment for People with Developmental Disabilities by J. L. Taylor and R. W. Novaco.
Copyright © 2005 John Wiley & Sons, Ltd.

Handout/Exercise Sheet 4.3

SELF-INSTRUCTIONAL STATEMENTS TO HELP WITH RELAXATION

When you are in a situation that can make you feel stressed or angry it would be good if you could keep in control of your feelings and behaviour if you could calm yourself down.

To help with this you should try to remember the relaxing and calming image (picture in the mind) you have been talking to your therapist about in your anger treatment sessions.

Can you think of some things you might say to yourself (under your breath or in your head) that would remind you of this image/picture, help you to feel more relaxed, and keep in control of yourself?

Write down any ideas you have below and then discuss these with your therapist in your next session.

Things I can say to myself to remind me of my relaxing and calming image/picture:

(1)

(2)

(3)

(4)

(5)

Signed:............................. **Date:**..................................

Anger Treatment for People with Developmental Disabilities by J. L. Taylor and R. W. Novaco.
Copyright © 2005 John Wiley & Sons, Ltd.

Handout/Exercise Sheet 5.1

ANGER TREATMENT DECISION MATRIX

Name: . . . .   Date: . . . .

Brief description of angry/aggressive situation

Advantages of or Good Things about being Angry/Aggressive	Disadvantages of or Bad Things about being Angry/Aggressive
Immediate:	Immediate:
Long-term:	Long-term:

Total number of benefits = _____   Total number of costs = _____

Anger Treatment for People with Developmental Disabilities by J. L. Taylor and R. W. Novaco.
Copyright © 2005 John Wiley & Sons, Ltd.

Handout/Exercise Sheet 5.2

EXAMPLES OF THE ADVANTAGES AND DISADVANTAGES OF BEING ANGRY AND AGGRESSIVE

Advantages of or good things about being angry/aggressive	Disadvantages of or bad things about being angry/aggressive
Immediate: • Feel powerful/big man/hard man (self-image) • Feel in control • Not seen by others as 'soft' or an 'easy touch' • Release of anger/tension • Don't feel threatened/vulnerable	**Immediate:** • Getting into trouble/lose privileges/locked up • Injury (physical) to self • Injury (physical) to others • Problems are not helped, but made worse • Feeling bad about failing again (to control self)
Long-term: • None *Motiva.* *Cancer* *di ab*	**Long-term:** • Get a bad reputation • Feel no good, a 'failure' • Poor relationships with staff and other clients (no real friends) • People don't respect you, but are frightened by your behaviour • Get more convictions, locked up for longer • Family are worried and upset about me • People (including family) eventually give up on me • Feel hopeless, useless, can't change

Anger Treatment for People with Developmental Disabilities by J. L. Taylor and R. W. Novaco.
Copyright © 2005 John Wiley & Sons, Ltd.

Handout/Exercise Sheet 5.3

WEIGHING UP COSTS AND BENEFITS OF ANGER AND AGGRESSION

**Benefits of being
angry/aggressive**

**Costs of being
angry/aggressive**

Anger Treatment for People with Developmental Disabilities by J. L. Taylor and R. W. Novaco.
Copyright © 2005 John Wiley & Sons, Ltd.

Handout/Exercise Sheet 5.4

PREPAREDNESS FOR THERAPY QUESTIONNAIRE (PTQ)

Name:..................................... Date:...............................

I am going to ask you some questions about how prepared you think you are for anger treatment. There are no right or wrong answers – this is not a test. I would like to know what *you* think or feel about these questions.

1. **Would you try anything to get rid of your anger problems?**

No – Definitely Not	Maybe	Probably	Yes – Definitely
1	2	3	4

2. **Do you need some help urgently to sort your anger problems out?**

No – Definitely Not	Maybe	Probably	Yes – Definitely
1	2	3	4

3. **Do you think that anger treatment work will help more if you try hard and work at it?**

No – Definitely Not	Maybe	Probably	Yes – Definitely
1	2	3	4

4. **Are you sure that you will be able to do the homework between treatment sessions to practise the things you have learnt?**

No – Definitely Not	Maybe	Probably	Yes – Definitely
1	2	3	4

5. **Would you rather *not* go to work, education, or other things so that you can come to the anger treatment sessions?**

No – Definitely Not	Maybe	Probably	Yes – Definitely
1	2	3	4

6. **Have you made the right decision to do the (anger) treatment?**

No – Definitely Not	Maybe	Probably	Yes – Definitely
1	2	3	4

Anger Treatment for People with Developmental Disabilities by J. L. Taylor and R. W. Novaco.
Copyright © 2005 John Wiley & Sons, Ltd.

7. **Are you prepared (ready) to do some work on your anger problems for a while?**

No – Definitely Not	Maybe	Probably	Yes – Definitely
1	2	3	4

8. **Will you come to all your anger treatment sessions no matter how you are feeling?**

No – Definitely Not	Maybe	Probably	Yes – Definitely
1	2	3	4

9. **Do you think that this treatment will help you to get rid of (solve) your anger problems?**

No – Definitely Not	Maybe	Probably	Yes – Definitely
1	2	3	4

10. **Do you think of yourself as someone who doesn't give up once you've started something?**

No – Definitely Not	Maybe	Probably	Yes – Definitely
1	2	3	4

Note. Questionnaire items adapted from Keijsers et al. (1999). The "preparedness" factor of the Nijmegen Motivation List 2 (NML2). *Behavioural and Cognitive Psychotherapy*, 27, 165–179.

Handout/Exercise Sheet 5.5

REASONS TO CONTINUE WITH ANGER TREATMENT

During your last anger treatment session you discussed with your therapist the advantages (benefits) and disadvantages (costs) of being angry and behaving aggressively; and whether anger treatment might help you in the future.

With your named keyworker, try to think of some of your own reasons for continuing with your anger treatment, or deciding to stop after the six preparation sessions. Write these down below so that you can discuss them in your next (final) anger treatment preparation session with your therapist.

Reasons for me to continue with my anger treatment:

(1)

(2)

(3)

(4)

(5)

Reasons for me to stop anger treatment:

(1)

(2)

(3)

(4)

(5)

Name: . . . .   **Date:** . . . .

Anger Treatment for People with Developmental Disabilities by J. L. Taylor and R. W. Novaco.
Copyright © 2005 John Wiley & Sons, Ltd.

Handout/Exercise Sheet 6.1

PATIENT'S EVALUATION OF ANGER TREATMENT – PREPARATORY PHASE (PEAT-PP)

Name: .... **Date:** ....

In the six preparation sessions we have tried to give you an idea of what anger treatment is all about.

1. Overall, was it worthwhile for you to attend the sessions?

None of the sessions	Some of the sessions	Yes, most of the sessions
1	2	3

2. Have you enjoyed the sessions?

No, not at all	Some of them	Yes, most of them
1	2	3

3. Have the sessions been helpful/useful to you?

No, not at all	A little	Yes, in lots of ways
1	2	3

4. Which bits (parts) of the sessions have been most useful, interesting or helpful?

   (i) ....

   (ii) ....

   (iii) ....

5. Which bits (parts) of the sessions have you disliked, found unhelpful or not useful?

   (i) ....

   (ii) ....

   (iii) ....

Anger Treatment for People with Developmental Disabilities by J. L. Taylor and R. W. Novaco.
Copyright © 2005 John Wiley & Sons, Ltd.

How helpful did you find the following bits?	Unhelpful	A little helpful	Very helpful
	1	2	3
6. Finding out what anger treatment is all about	☐	☐	☐
7. Finding out how anger works (situations/thoughts/feelings/reactions/consequences)	☐	☐	☐
8. Learning that anger is normal and that everybody feels it sometimes	☐	☐	☐
9. Learning that our thoughts affect the way we feel and behave in angry situations	☐	☐	☐
10. Understanding the difference between happy, sad and angry feelings	☐	☐	☐
11. Finding out about how stress affects us ('Stress Thermometer' and physical reactions)	☐	☐	☐
12. Working out the costs (negative consequences) and benefits (advantages) of being angry and aggressive	☐	☐	☐
13. Talking about my feelings/problems	☐	☐	☐
14. Learning how to relax myself (self-instruction/breathing control/relaxing images)	☐	☐	☐
15. Recording angry situations using the Anger Logs	☐	☐	☐
16. Homework exercises	☐	☐	☐

17. Do you think you have changed since you started these sessions?

No, not at all	A little, for the better	Yes, a lot, for the better
1	2	3

Explain: ....
....

18. How could we improve these treatment sessions?
....
....

19. Finally, is there anything that you feel that you are unsure about or would like to discuss?

Handout/Exercise Sheet 6.2

PATIENTS' COMPETENCY CHECKLIST – PREPARATORY PHASE (PCC-PP)

Name: .... Date: ....

The therapist, along with the client/patient's named keyworker, should consider the evidence (hard or clinical) to reach a judgement about the client/patient's competence in each of the areas described below.

(The information in parentheses indicates if the area of competence relates to a specific preparatory phase session, or is general to this phase of treatment.)

	Not competent	Limited competence	Competent
1. Understands how anger works – relationship between thoughts, feelings and behaviour (Session 1)	☐	☐	☐
2. Understands the purpose of anger treatment (Session 1)	☐	☐	☐
3. Aware of the functions of anger as a normal emotion (Session 2)	☐	☐	☐
4. Understands the importance of self-monitoring of angry feelings (Session 2)	☐	☐	☐
5. Aware of basic emotional states in others using a range of contextual cues (Session 3)	☐	☐	☐

Anger Treatment for People with Developmental Disabilities by J. L. Taylor and R. W. Novaco.
Copyright © 2005 John Wiley & Sons, Ltd.

	Not competent	Limited competence	Competent
6. Understands the role cognitions play in the induction of emotions – specifically anger (Session 3)	☐	☐	☐
7. Understands how stress affects thinking and behaviour (Session 4)	☐	☐	☐
8. Aware of the physiological/physical reaction to stress (Session 4)	☐	☐	☐
9. Is able to weigh the costs and benefits of anger and aggression (Session 5)	☐	☐	☐
10. Is prepared to continue with anger treatment – PTQ (Session 5)	☐	☐	☐
11. Ability to communicate appropriately in therapy context (General)	☐	☐	☐
12. Ability to engage appropriately in therapy context (General)	☐	☐	☐
13. Ability to comprehend the therapy process (General)	☐	☐	☐
14. Demonstrates motivation and enthusiasm for therapy (General)	☐	☐	☐
15. Ability to complete assigned homework tasks (General)	☐	☐	☐
16. Ability to complete Anger Logs appropriately (General)	☐	☐	☐
17. Ability to use basic relaxation strategies including controlled breathing, imagery and self-instruction (General)	☐	☐	☐
18. Ability to liaise appropriately with nursing staff to facilitate anger treatment (General)	☐	☐	☐

Handout/Exercise Sheet 6.3

GOAL ATTAINMENT SCALES FOR EMOTIONAL AWARENESS AND EXPRESSION (POST-PREPARATORY)

Name: .... Date: ....

	Guide for Rating Goal Attainments		
Outcome Levels	(1) Ability to identify and describe emotional states in self and others	(2) Ability to demonstrate emotional expression appropriately	(3) Knowledge of emotional coping strategies
Very poor (1)	Little or no evidence of being able to identify or describe emotional states in self and others	No apparent ability to demonstrate emotional expression appropriately (i.e. withdrawn in sessions) and/or disproportionate or inappropriate expression to an event	No apparent ideas or suggestions re. appropriate coping strategies.
Poor (2)	Some ability to identify and describe emotional states in self and understanding of others, and/or evidence of confusion between states, i.e. confusing anger with anxiety, sadness with stress, etc.	Limited ability to demonstrate emotional expression but only on a superficial level (i.e. happy with smiling, sad with tears etc.) and/or tendency to express disproportionate reaction to event.	Only able to make superficial/limited suggestions re. appropriate coping strategies.
Satisfactory (3)	Ability to identify, describe and differentiate between common emotional states, i.e. anxiety, anger, sadness, disgust, etc. in self and others	Evidence of understanding and using appropriate expression to an emotional event, without disproportionate reaction to emotional event.	Some ability to be able to identify or suggest appropriate emotional coping strategies in a range of scenarios.
Good (4)	Good ability to identify, describe and differentiate between common emotional states in self and others. No evidence of confusing different emotional states.	Good ability to express emotion correctly (indicating increasing vocabulary pool) and attach emotional expression appropriately to events both within and outside of treatment sessions.	Good ability to be able to identify appropriate emotional coping strategies *and* some evidence of actual use.
Very good (5)	Very good ability to be able to identify and discuss emotional states in self and others, without confusion.	Consistently good ability to describe and attach an appropriate emotional expression to an event within and beyond the boundaries of the treatment sessions.	Very good understanding of appropriate emotional coping strategies and evidence of consistent use in a range of situations

Outcome Level = _____   _____   _____

Signed (Therapist): ....

Anger Treatment for People with Developmental Disabilities by J. L. Taylor and R. W. Novaco.
Copyright © 2005 John Wiley & Sons, Ltd.

Handout/Exercise Sheet 7.1

ANGER TREATMENT (TREATMENT PHASE)

REPORT ON TREATMENT SESSION

Client's Name: .... **Session No.:** ....

Venue of Session: .... **Date of Session:** ....

Objective(s) of Session:

....

....

....

A. THERAPIST'S REPORT ON CLIENT'S RESPONSE TO SESSION

Signed: .... **Date:** ....

Anger Treatment for People with Developmental Disabilities by J. L. Taylor and R. W. Novaco.
Copyright © 2005 John Wiley & Sons, Ltd.

B. THERAPIST'S RATINGS ON CLIENT DURING SESSION

Communication

1	2	3	4	5
Irrelevant or no contribution to discussion	A few relevant contributions to discussion	Contributions generally relevant to discussion	Good contributions relevant to discussion	Consistently good contributions relevant to discussion

Engagement

1	2	3	4	5
Did not engage even when prompted	Engaged in session but only when prompted	Satisfactory engagement in session	Good level of engagement in session	Active participation relating issues beyond limit of session

Comprehension

1	2	3	4	5
Did not comprehend purpose of session	Limited comprehension of purpose of session	Good comprehension of some parts of the session	Good comprehension of all parts of the session	Complete understanding of the purpose of the session

C. CLIENT'S REPORT AND RATINGS ON THE SESSION

• Was there anything good about today's session? (i.e. did you learn anything or find out something helpful or useful?)

....
....

• Was there anything bad about today's session? (i.e. did anything annoy you or wind you up?)

....
....

• What was the best bit/part of today's session?

....
....

• Did you enjoy today's session?

  1. No, not at all.   2. Some of it.   3. Yes, all of it.

• Are you learning anything from the sessions?

  1. No, nothing at all   2. A bit/some things   3. Yes, lots of things

• Are the sessions helping you?

  1. No, not at all   2. A bit   3. Yes, in lots of ways

• Any other comments

....
....

Handout/Exercise Sheet 8.1

ANGER LOG II

Name: .... **Date:** .... **Time:** ....

Where were you? ....

What happened?

- ❏ Somebody was taking the mick
- ❏ Somebody criticized me
- ❏ Somebody told me to do something
- ❏ Somebody did something I didn't like
- ❏ Somebody stole something of mine

- ❏ Somebody started rowing with me
- ❏ Somebody started fighting with me
- ❏ I did something wrong
- ❏ Other (specify)

Who was that somebody?

❏ Client/Patient   ❏ Friend   ❏ Staff   ❏ Relative   ❏ Other (specify)

What were you thinking about when this happened?

How angry were you?

Not angry at all	A little angry	Fairly Angry	Very Angry	Furious
1	2	3	4	5

What did you do?

- ❏ Shouted/Swore
- ❏ Ran off
- ❏ Smashed/broke something
- ❏ Tried to hit someone
- ❏ Actually hit someone

- ❏ Walked away calmly
- ❏ Talked it over
- ❏ Told someone else
- ❏ Ignored it
- ❏ Other (specify)

How well do you think you handled this situation/problem?

Badly	Not very well	OK	Well	Very well
1	2	3	4	5

Anger Treatment for People with Developmental Disabilities by J. L. Taylor and R. W. Novaco.
Copyright © 2005 John Wiley & Sons, Ltd.

Handout/Exercise Sheet 8.2

ANGER HIERARCHY WORKSHEET

Name: ....

SCENE 1   **Rank No.** = ...
Description of situation (place, people, trigger, own mood, etc.):

How angry were you?

Not angry at all	A little angry	Fairly angry	Very angry	Furious
1	2	3	4	5

SCENE 2   **Rank No.** = ...
Description of situation (place, people, trigger, own mood, etc.):

How angry were you?

Not angry at all	A little angry	Fairly angry	Very angry	Furious
1	2	3	4	5

SCENE 3   **Rank No.** = ...
Description of situation (place, people, trigger, own mood, etc.):

How angry were you?

Not angry at all	A little angry	Fairly angry	Very angry	Furious
1	2	3	4	5

Anger Treatment for People with Developmental Disabilities by J. L. Taylor and R. W. Novaco.
Copyright © 2005 John Wiley & Sons, Ltd.

SCENE 4   **Rank No. =** ....

Description of situation (place, people, trigger, own mood, etc.):

How angry were you?

Not angry at all	A little angry	Fairly angry	Very angry	Furious
1	2	3	4	5

SCENE 5   **Rank No. =** ....

Description of situation (place, people, trigger, own mood, etc.):

How angry were you?

Not angry at all	A little angry	Fairly angry	Very angry	Furious
1	2	3	4	5

SCENE 6   **Rank No. =** ....

Description of situation (place, people, trigger, own mood, etc.):

How angry were you?

Not angry at all	A little angry	Fairly angry	Very angry	Furious
1	2	3	4	5

Handout/Exercise Sheet 8.3

ABBREVIATED PROGRESSIVE RELAXATION (APR) THERAPIST'S SCRIPT

INTRODUCTION

Remind the client that relaxation is to help them get better self-control over the thoughts and feelings that they have in their body when they are angry. Explain that relaxation is a skill that has to be learnt like any other, and becoming good at relaxation involves practice. These exercises involve tensing and then relaxing different muscles in the body and noticing the different feelings. Also they will be asked to think about breathing in a slow, even and controlled way as they go through the exercises. Towards the end of the exercises they will be asked to remember and visualise the relaxing image/scene that they have used in earlier treatment sessions.

INSTRUCTIONS

1. Begin by asking the client to get as comfortable as they can and relaxing their body by letting their muscles go floppy. Prompt them to close their eyes and concentrate on their breathing in a regular, slow, even and controlled way.
2. *Hands*: Ask the client to clench both fists tightly and then slowly open their fingers out and let their hands flop. Prompt the client to concentrate on the difference between the tension and relaxation in the muscles. *Repeat this exercise.*
   Prompt the client to concentrate on regular, slow breathing for a few moments.
3. *Arms*: Ask the client to tense the muscles at the top of the arms by putting their hands up to their shoulders and then slowly letting the arms drop down. Prompt them to concentrate on the difference between the tension and relaxation in their muscles. *Repeat this exercise.*
   Prompt the client to concentrate on regular, slow breathing for a few moments.
4. *Shoulders*: Ask the client to hunch their shoulders up towards their ears and then slowly let the shoulders drop and relax. Prompt the client to concentrate on the difference between the tension and relaxation in the muscles. *Repeat this exercise.*
   Prompt the client to concentrate on regular, slow breathing for a few moments.

Anger Treatment for People with Developmental Disabilities by J. L. Taylor and R. W. Novaco.
Copyright © 2005 John Wiley & Sons, Ltd.

5. *Face*: Ask the client to press their lips together tightly and close their eyes tightly, then slowly relax their mouth and eyes. Prompt the client to concentrate on the difference between tension and relaxation in the muscles. *Repeat this exercise.*
   Prompt the client to concentrate on regular, slow breathing for a few moments.
6. *Stomach*: Ask the client to pull their stomach muscles in (as if they were about to be punched in the stomach) and then slowly let the muscles relax and sit comfortably. Prompt the client to concentrate on the difference between the tension and relaxation in the muscles. *Repeat this exercise.*
   Prompt the client to concentrate on regular, slow breathing for a few moments.
7. *Legs*: Ask the client to lift their feet off the ground a little way and point their toes down. Then slowly let their feet go back to the floor and let their legs relax. Concentrate on the difference between the tension and relaxation in the muscles. *Repeat this exercise.*
   Prompt the client to concentrate on regular, slow breathing for a few moments.
8. Ask the client to spend a little time (still with their eyes closed) enjoying the feeling of relaxation. Ask them to imagine that they are sitting on a bed of cotton wool and sinking deeper and deeper into the cotton wool. As they sink deeper, their body feels heavier and they feel more relaxed.
9. While in this relaxed state ask the client to remember and visualize the relaxing and calming image/picture which they have previously identified. Suggest that they concentrate on this scene for a few moments (up to 60 seconds) to maintain and deepen the relaxation.
10. Ask the client to slowly take in a deep breath through their nose, hold it momentarily, and then slowly exhale through their mouth before opening their eyes.

NOTES

• During early administrations of these exercises the therapists may wish to check with the client as the exercises progress what they are experiencing somatically, cognitively, etc and how relaxed the client is feeling at different stages.

• Throughout this procedure the therapist can develop the suggestions for relaxation by referring to tingling sensations, feelings of heaviness, etc. in the muscle groups as they are relaxed. In addition, it might be suggested to the client when they are concentrating on breathing between tensing muscle groups, that the feeling of relaxation is getting stronger, deeper, etc.

Handout/Exercise Sheet 10.1

THINKING DIFFERENTLY ABOUT ANGER SITUATIONS

Name: ....   Date: ....

	Situation Where? What? Who?	Thoughts About the Situation	Emotional Feelings 0–5	Physical Feelings 0–5	Reaction What did you do?
A C T U A L					
P O S S I B L E					

Anger Treatment for People with Developmental Disabilities by J. L. Taylor and R. W. Novaco. Copyright © 2005 John Wiley & Sons, Ltd.

Handout/Exercise Sheet 12.1

ANGER LOG III

Name: .... **Date:** .... **Time:** ....

Where were you? ....

What happened?

Who was that somebody?

❑ Client/Patient ❑ Friend ❑ Staff ❑ Relative ❑ Other (specify)

What were you thinking about when this happened?

How angry were you?

Not angry at all	A little angry	Fairly angry	Very angry	Furious
1	2	3	4	5

What did you do?/How did you react?

❑	Shouted/Swore	❑ Walked away calmly
❑	Ran off	❑ Talked it over
❑	Smashed/broke something	❑ Told someone else
❑	Tried to hit someone	❑ Ignored it
❑	Actually hit someone	❑ Other (specify)

What other thoughts could you have had in this situation? (Try to put yourself in the other person's shoes.)

How well do you think you handled this situation/problem?

Badly	Not very well	OK	Well	Very well
1	2	3	4	5

Anger Treatment for People with Developmental Disabilities by J. L. Taylor and R. W. Novaco.
Copyright © 2005 John Wiley & Sons, Ltd.

Handout/Exercise Sheet 14.1

EFFECTIVE COMMUNICATION IN ANGER SITUATIONS

To handle anger situations well by sorting out the problem(s) causing the incident, it is important for people to communicate their thoughts, feelings and needs in an effective and constructive manner. This style of communicating is often described as *assertive* and is different from being *passive* or *aggressive*.

Being *Assertive* involves:

- Being calm and clear thinking.
- Saying what you think in a clear, firm way.
- Being polite and reasonable.
- Listening to what others are saying.
- Being honest about your feelings.
- Discussing issues and problems in an adult, grown-up way.
- Being prepared to 'give and take' (compromise).
- Knowing what you want to achieve (have a clear goal in mind).
- Wanting to solve the problem to everybody's satisfaction.

Being *Passive* involves:

- Not being clear and honest about your thoughts and feelings.
- Not saying what you want.
- Avoiding sorting out issues and problems.
- Letting others tell you what you want or need.
- Taking the blame for things that are not your fault.
- Blaming yourself for things that are not your fault.
- Seeing yourself as a victim who things just happen to.

Anger Treatment for People with Developmental Disabilities by J. L. Taylor and R. W. Novaco.
Copyright © 2005 John Wiley & Sons, Ltd.

Being *Aggressive* involves:

- Not listening to what others are saying.
- Wanting to win the argument at all costs.
- Bullying others into agreeing with you.
- Being rude and offensive to others.
- Being unreasonable and demanding things others can't give.
- Being uninterested or not caring about others' needs or wishes
- Always having the last word.

Source: After Williams, E. and Barlow, R. (1998) *Anger Control Training*, Vol 3, part 4. Chesterfield: Winslow Press.

Handout/Exercise Sheet 17.1

DEALING WITH ANGER INCIDENTS
PERSONAL REMINDER SHEET

Name: ....

To handle angry situations well I must remember the following things:

1. The sorts of situations that make me angry easily are:

   (a)

   (b)

   (c)

2. In these sorts of situations I must try to keep calm by telling myself to:

   (a)

   (b)

   (c)

   (d)

3. Once I am sure that I am calm and in control, I should try to sort the situation out ('problem-solve') by:

   (a)

   (b)

   (c)

   (d)

4. If I can't get calm, or if the other person involved is getting more angry and aggressive, I should:

   (a)

   (b)

   (c)

Anger Treatment for People with Developmental Disabilities by J. L. Taylor and R. W. Novaco.
Copyright © 2005 John Wiley & Sons, Ltd.

Handout/Exercise Sheet 17.2

DEALING WITH ANGER INCIDENTS
PERSONAL REMINDER SHEET

EXAMPLE

Name: JIM SMITH

To handle angry situations well I must remember the following things.

1. The sorts of situations that make me angry easily are:
   (a) People being unfair.
   (b) People being rude.
   (c) People being ignorant (disrespectful).

2. In these sorts of situations I must try to keep calm by telling myself to:
   (a) Slow down.
   (b) Take a deep breath.
   (c) Think differently about things.
   (d) Think of my calming image/picture.

3. Once I am sure that I am calm and in control, I should try to sort the situation out ('problem-solve') by:
   (a) Trying to listen and understand what he/she is saying.
   (b) Telling them what I think in an honest and reasonable way.
   (c) Being clear about how I want this situation to end.
   (d) Being prepared to give and take.

4. If I can't get calm, or if the other person involved is getting more angry and aggressive, I should:
   (a) Back off, walk away from it.
   (b) Calm down, cool off.
   (c) Think about how to sort the problem out calmly.

Anger Treatment for People with Developmental Disabilities by J. L. Taylor and R. W. Novaco.
Copyright © 2005 John Wiley & Sons, Ltd.

Handout/Exercise Sheet 18.1

PATIENT'S EVALUATION OF ANGER TREATMENT – TREATMENT PHASE (PEAT-TP)

Name:................................   Date:...............................

You have now completed your anger treatment sessions, 6 preparation and 12 treatment proper sessions.

1. Overall, was it worthwhile for you to attend the sessions?

None of the sessions	Some of the sessions	Yes, most of the sessions
1	2	3

2. Have you enjoyed the sessions?

No, not at all	Some of them	Yes, most of them
1	2	3

3. Have the sessions been helpful/useful to you?

No, not all	A little	Yes, in lots of ways
1	2	3

4. Which bits (parts) of the sessions have been most useful, interesting or helpful?

(i) ....

(ii) ....

(iii) ....

5. Which bits (parts) of the sessions have you disliked, found unhelpful or not useful?

(i) ....

(ii) ....

(iii) ....

Anger Treatment for People with Developmental Disabilities by J. L. Taylor and R. W. Novaco.
Copyright © 2005 John Wiley & Sons, Ltd.

How helpful did you find the following bits?	Unhelpful 1	A little helpful 2	Very helpful 3
6. Working out the kinds of situations that make you angry and how these affect you	☐	☐	☐
7. Learning how to do relaxation exercises	☐	☐	☐
8. Learning how to 'catch your thoughts' during anger incidents	☐	☐	☐
9. Doing an anger hierarchy of situations in the past that have made you angry	☐	☐	☐
10. Practising coping well with anger situations (from your anger hierarchy) in your imagination while relaxed	☐	☐	☐
11. Using a cassette tape to practise relaxation exercises	☐	☐	☐
12. Learning to think differently (putting yourself in the other person's shoes) in anger situations	☐	☐	☐
13. Understanding that you are 'sensitive' to certain kinds of anger situations that make you angry	☐	☐	☐
14. Working out what you can tell yourself (self-instructions) to remind you how to stay calm and in control in angry situations	☐	☐	☐
15. Role-playing (acting out) how to handle well and cope with angry situations	☐	☐	☐
16. Learning how to sort out (problem-solve) in angry situations by being reasonable and talking to people in the right way	☐	☐	☐
17. Understanding that dwelling on anger situations can make things worse	☐	☐	☐

How helpful did you find the following bits?	Unhelpful 1	A little helpful 2	Very helpful 3
18. Learning how to deal with situations that are getting out of control (escalating) by backing-off or taking time-out	☐	☐	☐
19. Having a personal reminder sheet to remind you of what to do in anger situations	☐	☐	☐
20. Being able to talk about your problems/feelings	☐	☐	☐
21. Recording your thoughts and feelings in your Anger Logs	☐	☐	☐
22. Doing the homework exercises	☐	☐	☐
23. Talking to and working with nursing staff on your anger treatment	☐	☐	☐

24. Do you think you have changed since you started your anger treatment?

No, not at all	A little, for the better	Yes, a lot for the better
1	2	3

Explain: _____

_____

_____

25. Are you a more or a less angry person now compared with when you started your anger treatment?

More angry	About the same	Less angry
1	2	3

26. How much help/support do you think you have had from staff on the ward with your anger treatment?

None	A bit	Just about the right amount
1	2	3

27. How could the anger treatment be made better for other clients/patients in the future?

_____

_____

_____

_____

_____

28. Is there anything else that you are unsure about or would like to discuss?

_____

_____

_____

_____

_____

Handout/Exercise Sheet 18.2

PATIENT'S COMPETENCY CHECKLIST – TREATMENT PHASE (PCC-TP)

Client's Name............................. Date...............................

The therapist, if possible in collaboration with the client's keyworker, should consider the evidence (hard or clinical) to reach a judgement about the client's competence in each of the areas described below. (The information in parentheses indicates if the area of competence relates to a specific treatment phase session, or is general to this phase of treatment.)

	Not competent 1	Limited competence 2	Competent 3
1. Understands how anger works – relationship between thoughts, feelings and behaviour (Session 7)	☐	☐	☐
2. Is able to understand the dimensions of their own anger problem – analysis and formulation (Sessions 7 and 8)	☐	☐	☐
3. Understands the concept of 'thought-catching' (Session 8)	☐	☐	☐
4. Is able to construct meaningfully a useful anger hierarchy (Sessions 8 and 9)	☐	☐	☐
5. Is able to understand the rationale for the use and practice of APR exercises (Session 8)	☐	☐	☐

Anger Treatment for People with Developmental Disabilities by J. L. Taylor and R. W. Novaco.
Copyright © 2005 John Wiley & Sons, Ltd.

	Not competent 1	Limited competence 2	Competent 3
6. Understands the rationale for cognitive re-structuring (Session 10)	☐	☐	☐
7. Is able to understand the concept of perspective-taking (Session 11)	☐	☐	☐
8. Comprehends the notions of attentional focus, expectations and appraisals (Session 11)	☐	☐	☐
9. Is able to generate useful self-instructions to cue anger control (Session 13)	☐	☐	☐
10. Understands the importance of effective communication in problem-solving (Sessions 14 and 15)	☐	☐	☐
11. Understands how rumination, escalation and repeated provocation can be threats to self-control (Sessions 16 and 17)	☐	☐	☐
12. Is able to construct a realistic personal script for prompting anger control (Sessions 17 and 18)	☐	☐	☐
13. Is aware of the sequential and integrated nature of anger control skills (Session 17)	☐	☐	☐
14. Understands the importance of 'strategic withdrawal' in some situations (Session 17)	☐	☐	☐
15. Ability to use and benefit from APR exercises (General)	☐	☐	☐
16. Ability to complete Anger Log II appropriately (General)	☐	☐	☐
17. Ability to complete Anger Log III appropriately (General)	☐	☐	☐

	Not competent 1	Limited competence 2	Competent 3
18. Ability to 'thought-catch' (General)	☐	☐	☐
19. Ability to modify appraisals through perspective-taking (General)	☐	☐	☐
20. Ability to use self-instructions (General)	☐	☐	☐
21. Awareness of personal 'anger-sensitive' types of situations (General)	☐	☐	☐
22. Ability to maintain anger control in imagination (Stress inoculation) (General)	☐	☐	☐
23. Ability to role-play successful anger coping skills (General)	☐	☐	☐
24. Ability to communicate effectively in order to problem solve (General)	☐	☐	☐
25. Ability to communicate appropriately in therapy context (General)	☐	☐	☐
26. Ability to engage appropriately in therapy context (General)	☐	☐	☐
27. Ability to comprehend therapy process (General)	☐	☐	☐
28. Demonstrates motivation and enthusiasm for therapy (General)	☐	☐	☐
29. Ability to complete assigned homework tasks (General)	☐	☐	☐

	Not competent 1	Limited competence 2	Competent 3
30. Demonstrates regular use of APR and cassette tape (General)	☐	☐	☐
31. Ability to liaise appropriately with nursing staff to facilitate anger treatment (General)	☐	☐	☐

32. How much help/support did the client receive from staff on the ward with their anger treatment?

None	Limited/variable	About the right amount
1	2	3

33. Punctuality and availability for treatment sessions.

Poor	Satisfactory	Good
1	2	3

34. Did the client complete their anger treatment?   Yes/No

35. Number of Anger Logs completed during anger treatment phase of treatment   N =

36. Other comments on client's competence

_____

_____

_____

_____

_____

Signed: . . . .   Date . . . .

Designation: . . . .

Handout/Exercise Sheet 18.3

GOAL ATTAINMENT SCALES FOR EMOTIONAL AWARENESS AND EXPRESSION (Post-Treatment)

Name:.................................... Date:...............................

	Guide for Rating Goal Attainments		
Outcome Levels	(1) Ability to identify and describe emotional states in self and others	(2) Ability to demonstrate emotional expression appropriately	(3) Knowledge of emotional coping strategies
Very poor (1)	Little or no evidence of being able to identify or describe emotional states in self and others	No apparent ability to demonstrate emotional expression appropriately (i.e. withdrawn in sessions) and/or disproportionate or inappropriate expression to an event	No apparent ideas or suggestions re. appropriate coping strategies.
Poor (2)	Some ability to identify and describe emotional states in self and understanding of others, and/or evidence of confusion between states, i.e. confusing anger with anxiety, sadness with stress, etc.	Limited ability to demonstrate emotional expression but only on a superficial level (i.e. happy with smiling, sad with tears, etc.) and/or tendency to express disproportionate reaction to event.	Only able to make superficial/limited suggestions re. appropriate coping strategies.
Satisfactory (3)	Ability to identify, describe and differentiate between common emotional states, i.e. anxiety, anger, sadness, disgust, etc. in self and others	Evidence of understanding and using appropriate expression to an emotional event, without disproportionate reaction to emotional event.	Some ability to be able to identify or suggest appropriate emotional coping strategies in a range of scenarios.
Good (4)	Good ability to identify, describe and differentiate between common emotional states in self and others. No evidence of confusing different emotional states.	Good ability to express emotion correctly (indicating increasing vocabulary pool) and attach emotional expression appropriately to events both within and outside of treatment sessions.	Good ability to be able to identify appropriate emotional coping strategies *and* some evidence of actual use.
Very good (5)	Very good ability to be able to identify and discuss emotional states in self and others, without confusion.	Consistently good ability to describe and attach an appropriate emotional expression to an event within and beyond the boundaries of the treatment sessions.	Very good understanding of appropriate emotional coping strategies and evidence of consistent use in a range of situations

Outcome Level = _____   _____   _____

Signed (Therapist):...

Anger Treatment for People with Developmental Disabilities by J. L. Taylor and R. W. Novaco.
Copyright © 2005 John Wiley & Sons, Ltd.

REFERENCES

Addis, M.E. (1997). Evaluating the treatment manual as a means of disseminating empirically validated psychotherapies. *Clinical Psychology Science and Practice, 4,* 1–11.

Aggleton, J.P. & Mishkin, M. (1986). The amygdala: sensory gateway to the emotions. In R. Plutchik & H. Kellerman (Eds), *Emotion: Theory, Research and Experience.* Vol. 3 (pp. 281–299). Orlando, FL: Academic Press.

Alexander, F. (1939). Emotional factors in essential hypertension. *Psychosomatic Medicine, 1,* 173–179.

Allan, R., Lindsay, W.R., MacLeod, F., & Smith, A.H.W. (2001). Treatment of women with intellectual disabilities who have been involved with the criminal justice system for reasons of aggression. *Journal of Applied Research in Intellectual Disabilities, 14,* 340–347.

Aman, M.G., Richmond, G., Stewart, A.W., Bell, J.C., & Kissell, R. (1987). The Aberrant Behavior Checklist: Factor structure and the effect of subject variables in American and New Zealand facilities. *American Journal on Mental Deficiency, 91,* 570–578.

American Psychiatric Association (1994). *Diagnostic and Statistical Manual of Mental Disorders* (4th edn). Washington, DC: American Psychiatric Association.

Anastasi, A., Cohen, N., & Spatz, D. (1948). A study of fear and anger in college students through the controlled diary method. *Journal of Genetic Psychology, 73,* 243–249.

Anderson, K. & Silver, J.M. (1998). Modulation of anger and aggression. *Seminars in Clinical Neuropsychiatry, 3,* 232–241.

Arnold, M.B. (1960). *Emotion and Personality.* New York: Columbia University Press.

Arthur, A.R. (1999). Emotions and people with learning disability: Are clinical psychologists doing enough? *Clinical Psychology Forum, 132,* 39–43.

Arthur, A.R. (2003). The emotional lives of people with learning disability. *British Journal of Learning Disabilities, 31,* 25–30.

Attwood, T. & Joachim, R. (1994). The prevention and management of seriously disruptive behavior in Australia. In N. Bouras (Ed.), *Mental Health in Mental Retardation: Recent Advances and Practices.* Cambridge: Cambridge University Press.

Averill, J.R. (1973). Personal control over aversive stimuli and its relationship to stress. *Psychological Bulletin, 80,* 286–303.

Averill, J.R. (1982). *Anger and Aggression: An Essay on Emotion.* New York: Springer-Verlag.

Averill, J.R. (1983). Studies on anger and aggression: Implication for theories of emotion. *American Psychologist, 38,* 1145–1160.

Ax, A.F. (1953). The physiological differentiation between fear and anger in humans. *Psychosomatic Medicine, 15,* 433–442.

Baker, A.L. & Wilson, P.H. (1985). Cognitive-behaviour therapy for depression: The effects of booster sessions on relapse. *Behavior Therapy, 16,* 335–344.

Bandura, A. (1973). *Aggression: A social learning analysis.* Englewood Cliffs, NJ: Prentice Hall.

Bandura, A. (1977). *Social Learning Theory.* Englewood Cliffs, NJ: Prentice Hall.

Bandura, A. (1983). Psychological mechanisms in aggression. In R. Geen & E. Donnerstein (Eds), *Aggression: Theoretical and Empirical Reviews* (pp. 1–40). New York: Academic Press.

Barefoot, J.C., Dahlstrom, G., & Williams, R.B. (1982). Hostility, CHD incidence, and total mortality: A 25-year follow-up study of 255 physicians. *Psychosomatic Medicine, 55,* 59–64.

Barefoot, J.C., Peterson, B.L., Dahlstrom, W.G., Siegler, I.L., Anderson, N.B., & Williams, R.B. (1991). Hostility patterns and health implications: Correlates of Cook-Medley Hostility Scale scores in a national survey. *Health Psychology, 10,* 18–24.

Barefoot, J.C., Siegler, I.L., Nowlin, J.B., Peterson, B.L., Haney, T.L., & Williams, R.B. (1987). Suspiciousness, health, and mortality: A follow-up study of 500 older adults. *Psychosomatic Medicine, 49,* 450–457.

Barrowclough, C., King, P., Colville, J., Russell, E., Burns, A., & Tarrier, N. (2001). A randomized trial of the effectiveness of cognitive-behavioral therapy and supportive counseling for anxiety symptoms in older adults. *Journal of Consulting and Clinical Psychology, 69,* 756–762.

Baumeister, A.A., Sevin, J.A., & King, B.H. (1998). Neuroleptics. In S. Reiss & M.G. Aman (Eds), *Psychotropic Medications and Developmental Disabilities: The International Consensus Handbook.* Columbus, OH: Ohio State University.

Baumeister, R.F., Stillwell, A., & Wotman, S.R. (1990). Victim and perpetrator accounts of interpersonal conflict: Autobiographical narratives about anger. *Journal of Personality and Social Psychology, 59,* 994–1005.

Beail, N. (2003). What works for people with mental retardation? Critical commentary on cognitive-behavioural and psychodynamic psychotherapy research. *Mental Retardation, 41,* 468–472.

Beck, A.T. (1976). *Cognitive Therapy and the Emotional Disorders.* New York: International Universities Press.

Beck, A.T. (1999). *Prisoners of Hate: The Cognitive Basis of Anger, Hostility, and Violence.* New York: HarperCollins Perennial.

Beck, R. & Fernandez, E. (1998). Cognitive-behavioral therapy in the treatment of anger: A meta-analysis. *Cognitive Therapy and Research, 22,* 63–74.

Beers. C.W. (1908). *A Mind that Found Itself.* Garden City, NY: Doubleday.

Bender, M. (1993). The unoffered chair: The history of therapeutic disdain towards people with a learning difficulty. *Clinical Psychology Forum, 54,* 7–12.

Bensley, L., Nelson, N., Kaufman, J., Silverstein, B., Kalat, J., & Shields, J.W. (1997). Injuries due to assaults on psychiatric hospital employees in Washington State. *American Journal of Industrial Medicine, 31,* 92–99.

Benson, B.A. & Ivins, J. (1992). Anger, depression and self-concept in adults with mental retardation. *Journal of Intellectual Disability Research, 36,* 169–175.

Benson, B.A. Johnson Rice, C., & Miranti, S.V. (1986). Effects of anger management training with mentally retarded adults in group treatment. *Journal of Consulting and Clinical Psychology, 54,* 728–729.

Ben-Zur, H. & Breznitz, S. (1991). What makes people angry: Dimensions of anger-evoking events. *Journal of Research in Personality, 25,* 1–22.

Berkowitz, L. (1962). *Aggression: A Social Psychological Analysis.* New York: McGraw-Hill.

Berkowitz, L. (1990). On the formation and regulation of anger and aggression. *American Psychologist, 45,* 494–503.

Berkowitz, L. (1993). *Aggression: Its Causes, Consequences, and Control.* New York: McGraw-Hill.

Bernard, J. (1981). *The Female World.* New York: The Free Press.

Bettencourt, B.A. & Miller, N. (1996). Gender differences in aggression as a function of provocation: A meta-analysis. *Psychological Bulletin, 119,* 422–447.

Black, L., Cullen, C., & Novaco, R.W. (1997). Anger assessment for people with mild learning disabilities in secure settings. In B. Stenfert Kroese, D. Dagnan, & K. Loumidis (Eds), *Cognitive Behaviour-Therapy for People with Learning Disabilities.* London: Routledge.

Black, L. & Novaco. R.W. (1993). Treatment of anger with a developmentally disabled man. In R.A. Wells & V.J. Giannetti (Eds), *Casebook of the Brief Psychotherapies.* New York: Plenum Press.

Blackburn, I-M. & Moore, R.G. (1997). Controlled acute and follow-up trial of cognitive therapy and pharmacotherapy in out-patients with recurrent depression. *British Journal of Psychiatry, 171,* 328–334.

Blunden, R. & Allen, D. (1987). *Facing the Challenge: An Ordinary Life for People with Learning Disabilities and Challenging Behaviour.* London: Kings Fund Project Paper, Number 74.

Bornstein, P.H., Weisser, C.E., & Balleweg, B.J. (1985). Anger and violent behaviour. In M. Hersen & A.S. Bellack (Eds), *Handbook of Clinical Behaviour Therapy with Adults.* New York: Plenum.

Bowlby, J. (1969). *Attachment and loss.* Vol I. *Attachment.* New York: Basic Books.

Bowlby, J. (1973). *Attachment and Loss*. Vol II. *Separation: Anxiety and Anger*. New York: Basic Books.

Braund, S. & Most, G.W. (2003). *Ancient Anger: Perspectives from Homer to Galen*. Yale Classical Studies. Volume XXXII. Cambridge: Cambridge University Press.

Bromley, J. & Emerson, E. (1995). Beliefs and emotional reactions of care staff working with people with challenging behavior. *Journal of Intellectual Disability Research, 39*, 341–352.

Brown, J., Shye, A., & McFarland, E.W. (1995). The paradox of guideline implementation. *Journal on Quality Improvement, 21*, 5–12.

Brown, L.M. & Gilligan, C. (1992). *Meeting at the Crossroads: Women's Psychology and Girls' Development*. Cambridge, MA: Harvard University Press.

Brylewski, J. & Duggan, L. (1999). Antipsychotic medication for challenging behaviour in people with learning disability. *Journal of Intellectual Disability Research, 43*, 360–371.

Bushman, B.J. & Anderson, C.A. (2001). Is it time to pull the plug on the hostile versus instrumental aggression dichotomy? *Psychological Review, 108*, 273–279.

Buss, A.H. (1961). *The Psychology of Aggression*. New York: John Wiley and Sons.

Buss, A.H. (1966). Instrumentality of aggression, feedback, and frustration as determinants of physical aggression. *Journal of Personality and Social Psychology, 3*, 153–162.

Buss, A.H. & Durkee, A. (1957). An inventory for assessing different kinds of hostility. *Journal of Consulting Psychology, 21*, 343–349.

Buss, A.H. & Perry, M. (1992). The Aggression Questionnaire. *Journal of Personality and Social Psychology, 63*, 452–459.

Buss, A.H. & Warren, W.L. (2000). *The Aggression Questionnaire (AQ): Manual*. Los Angeles: Western Psychological Services.

Butz, M.R., Bowling, J.B. & Bliss, C.A. (2000). Psychotherapy with the mentally retarded: a review of the literature and the implications. *Professional Psychology: Research and Practice, 31*, 42–47.

Cahill, L. & McGaugh, J. (1990). Amygdaloid complex lesions differentially affect retention of tasks using appetitive and aversive reinforcement. *Behavioral Neuroscience, 104*, 523–534.

Cahill, L., Roozendaal, B., & McGaugh, J. (1997). The neurobiology of memory for aversive emotional events. In M.E. Bouton & M.S. Fanselow (Eds), *Learning, Motivation, and Cognition: The Functional Behaviorism of Robert C. Bolles* (pp. 369–384). Washington, DC: American Psychological Association.

Campbell, A. (1994). *Men, Women and Aggression*. New York: Basic Books.

Campos, J.J., Frankel, C.B., & Camras, L. (2004). On the nature of emotion regulation. *Child Development, 75*, 377–394.

Cannon, W.B. (1915). *Bodily Changes in Pain, Hunger, Fear, and Rage*. New York: Appleton.

Cannon, W.B. (1931). Again the James-Lange and the thalamic theories of emotion. *Psychological Review, 38*, 281–295.

Carlen, P. (1988). *Women, Crime and Poverty*. Milton Keynes: Open University Press.

Carmel, H. & Hunter, M. (1989). Staff injuries from patient violence. *Hospital and Community Psychiatry, 40*, 41–46.

Carr, J.E., Coriaty, S., Wilder, D.A., Gaunt, B.T., Dozier, C.L., Britton, L.N., Avina, C., & Reed, C.L. (2000). A review of 'noncontingent' reinforcement as treatment for the aberrant behavior of individuals with developmental disabilities. *Research in Developmental Disabilities, 21*, 377–391.

Carter, L. (2003). *The Anger Trap: Free Yourself from the Frustrations that Sabotage your Life*. San Francisco, CA: Jossey-Bass.

Carver, C.S. & Scheier, M.F. (1990). Origins and functions of positive and negative affect: A control-process view. *Psychological Review, 97*, 19–35.

Cascardi, M., O'Leary, K.D., Lawrence, E.E., & Schlee, K.A. (1995). Characteristics of women physically abused by their spouses and who seek treatment regarding marital conflict. *Journal of Consulting and Clinical Psychology, 63*, 616–623.

Catalano, R., Novaco, R., & McConnell, W. (1997). A model of the net effect of job loss on violence. *Journal of Personality and Social Psychology, 72*, 1440–1447.

Catalano, R., Novaco, R.W., & McConnell, W. (2002). Layoffs and violence revisited. *Aggressive Behavior, 28*, 233–247.

Chang, P.P., Ford, D.E., Meoni, L.A., Wang, N., & Klag, M.J. (2002). Anger in young men and subsequent premature cardiovascular disease. *Archives of Internal Medicine, 162*, 901–906.

Chemtob, C.M., Novaco, R.W., Hamada, R.S., & Gross, D.M. (1997b). Cognitive-behavioral treatment for severe anger in posttraumatic stress disorder. *Journal of Consulting and Clinical Psychology, 65*, 184–189.

Chemtob, C.M., Novaco, R.W., Hamada, R.S., Gross, D.M., & Smith, G. (1997a). Anger regulation deficits in combat-related posttraumatic stress disorder. *Journal of Traumatic Stress, 10*, 17–36.

Chesney, M.A. & Rosenman, R.H. (Eds) (1985). *Anger and Hostility in Cardiovascular and Behavioral Disorders*. Washington, DC: Hemisphere.

Cheung, P., Schweitzer, I., Tuckwell, V., & Crowley, K.C. (1996). A prospective study of aggression among psychiatric patients in rehabilitation wards. *Australian and New Zealand Journal of Psychiatry, 30*, 257–262.

Christensen, A. & Jacobson, N.S., (1994). Who (or What) can do psychotherapy?: The status of challenge of non professional therapy. *Psychological Science, 5*, 8–14.

Cohen, A.R. (1955). Social norms, arbitrariness of frustration, and status of agent of frustration in the frustration-aggression hypothesis. *Journal of Abnormal and Social Psychology, 51*, 222–226.

Cohen, J. (1992). The power primer. *Psychological Bulletin, 112*, 155–159.

Colbert, D. (2003). *Deadly Emotions: Understand the Mind-Body-Spirit Connection that Can Heal or Destroy You*. Nashville, TN: Thomas Nelson.

Cole, P.M. & Zahn-Waxler, C. (1992). Emotion dysregulation in disruptive behavior disorders. In D. Cicchetti & S.L. Toth (Eds), *Developmental Perspectives on Depression*. Rochester, NY: University of Rochester Press.

Convit, A., Isay, D., & Volavka, J. (1990). Characteristics of repeatedly assaultive psychiatric inpatients. *Hospital and Community Psychiatry, 41*, 1112–1115.

Cook, D. (1987). Women on welfare: In crime or injustice? In P. Carlen (Ed.), *Gender, Crime and Justice*. Milton Keynes: Open University Press.

Craig, T.J. (1982). An epidemiological study of problems associated with violence among psychiatric patients. *American Journal of Psychiatry, 139*, 1262–1266.

Crocker, D. (1955). The study of a problem of aggression. *The Psychoanalytic Study of the Child, X*, 330–335.

Cullen, C. (1993). The treatment of people with learning disabilities who offend. In K. Howells & C. Hollin (Eds), *Clinical Approaches to the Mentally Disordered Offender*. Chichester: Wiley.

Cullen, M. & Freeman-Longo, R.E. (1995). *Men & Anger: Understanding and Managing your Anger for a Much Better Life*. Brandon, VT: The Safer Society Press.

Darwin, C. (1859). *The Origin of Species*. London:

Darwin, C. (1872/1998). *The Expression of Emotions in Animals and Man*. (3rd edn). London: Harper-Collins.

Davidson, R.J., Putnam, K.M., & Larson, C.L. (2000). Dysfunction in the neural circuitry of emotion regulation: A possible prelude to violence. *Science, 289*, 591–594.

Davies, W. (2000). *Overcoming Anger and Irritability: A Self-Help Guide Using Cognitive-Behavioural Techniques*. London: Constable & Robinson.

Davis, J.A. & Smith, T.W. (1996). General Social Survey [Electronic data file]. Chicago, IL: National Opinion Research Center (Producer); Bellevue, WA: MicroCase Corporation (Distributor).

Dawes, R.M. (1994). *House of Cards*. New York: Free Press.

Deb, S., Thomas, M. & Bright, C. (2001). Mental disorder in adults with intellectual disability. 2: The rate of behaviour disorders among a community-based population aged between 14 and 64 years. *Journal of Intellectual Disability Research, 45*, 506–514.

Deffenbacher, J.L., Dahlen, E.R., Lynch, R.S., Morris, C.D., & Gowensmith, W.N. (2000). An application of Beck's cognitive therapy to general anger reduction. *Cognitive Therapy and Research, 24*, 689–697.

Deffenbacher, J.L., Oetting, E.R., Thwaites, G.A., Lynch, R.S., Baker, D.A., Stark, R.S., Thacker, S., & Eiswerth-Cox, L. (1996). State-Trait anger theory and the utility of the Trait Anger Scale. *Journal of Counseling Psychology, 43*, 131–148.

Deffenbacher, J.L., Story, D.A., Stark, R.S., Hogg, J.A., & Brandon, A.D. (1987). Cognitive-relaxation and social skills interventions in the treatment of general anger. *Journal of Counseling Psychology, 34*, 171–176.

Del Vecchio, T. & O'Leary, K.D. (2004). Effectiveness of treatments for specific anger problems: A meta-analytic review. *Clinical Psychology Review, 24*, 15–24.

Dembroski, T.M., MacDougall, J.M., Williams, R.B., Jr., Haney, T.L., & Blumenthal, J.A. (1985). Components of Type A, hostility, and anger-in: Relationship to angiographic findings. *Psychosomatic Medicine, 47*, 219–233.

Department of Health (1998). *A First Class Service: Quality in the New NHS*. London: Department of Health.

Department of Health (1999). *Clinical Governance: Quality in the New NHS (HSC 1999/065)*. London: Department of Health.

Diamond, E.L. (1982). The role of anger and hostility in essential hypertension and coronary heart disease. *Psychological Bulletin, 92*, 410–433.

DiGuiseppe, R. & Tafrate, R.C. (2003). Anger treatments for adults: A meta-analytic review. *Clinical Psychology: Science and Practice, 10*, 70–84.

DiGuiseppe, R., Tafrate, R., & Eckhardt, C. (1994). Critical issues in the treatment of anger. *Cognitive & Behavioural Practice, 1*, 111–132.

Dobash, R.E. (2000). *Changing Violent Men*. Los Angeles: Sage.

Dodge, K.A. (1989). Coordinating responses to aversive stimuli: Introduction to a special section on the development of emotion regulation. *Developmental Psychology, 25*, 339–342.

Dollard, J., Doob, L.W., Miller, N.E., Mowrer, O.H., & Sears, R.R. (1939). *Frustration and Aggression*. New Haven, CT: Yale University Press.

Dutton, D.G., Saunders, K., Starzomski, A., & Bartholomew, K. (1994). Intimacy-anger and insecure attachment as precursors of abuse in intimate relationships. *Journal of Applied Social Psychology, 24*, 1367–1386.

Dutton, D.G., Starzomski, A., & Ryan, L. (1996). Antecedents of abusive personality and abusive behavior in wife assaulters. *Journal of Family Violence, 11*, 113–132.

Eagly, A.H. & Steffen, V.J. (1986). Gender and aggressive behavior: A meta-analytic review of the social psychological literature. *Psychological Bulletin, 100*, 309–330.

Eaker, E.D., Sullivan, L.M., Kelly-Hayes, M., D'Agostino, R.B., & Benjamin, E.J. (2004). Anger and hostility predict the development of atrial fibrillation in men in the Framingham Offspring Study. *Circulation, 109*, 1267–1271.

Eamon, K.C., Munchua, M.M., & Reddon, J.R. (2001). Effectiveness of an anger management program for women inmates. *Journal of Offender Rehabilitation, 34*, 45–60.

Eckhardt, C.I. & Deffenbacher, J.L. (1995). Diagnosis of anger disorders. In H. Kassinove (Ed.). *Anger Disorders: Definition, Diagnosis, and Treatment* (pp. 27–48). Washington, DC: Taylor & Francis.

Eckhardt, C., Norlander, B. & Deffenbacher, J. (2004). The assessment of anger and hostility: a critical review. *Aggression and Violent Behavior, 9*, 17–43.

Edmondson, C.B. & Conger, J.C. (1996). A review of treatment efficacy for individuals with anger problems: Conceptual, assessment and methodological issues. *Clinical Psychology Review, 16*, 251–275.

Ehrensaft, M.K., Cohen, P., Brown, J., Smailes, E., Chen, H., & Johnson, J.G. (2003). Intergenerational transmission of partner violence: A 20-year prospective study. *Journal of Consulting and Clinical Psychology, 71*, 741–753.

Eigen, M. (2002). *Rage*. Middletown, CT: Wesleyan University Press.

Eisenberg, N. & Fabes, R.A. (1992). Emotion, regulation, and the development of social competence. In M.S. Clark (Ed.), *Review of Personality and Social Psychology: Vol. 14. Emotion and Social Behavior* (pp. 119–150). Newbury Park, CA: Sage.

Ekman, P. (2003). *Emotions Revealed: Recognizing Faces and Feelings to Improve Communication and Emotional Life*. New York: Times Books.

Ekman, P., Friesen, W.V., & Ancoli, S. (1980). Facial signs of emotional expression. *Journal of Personality and Social Psychology, 39*, 1125–1134.

Ellis, A. (1977). *How to Live With and Without Anger*. New York: Readers' Digest Press.

Emerson, E., Kiernan, C., Alborz, A., Reeves, D., Mason, H., Swarbrick, R., Mason, L., & Hatton, C. (2001). The prevalence of challenging behaviours: A total population study. *Research in Developmental Disabilities, 22*, 77–93.

Eysenck, H.J. (1963). Behavior therapy, extinction and relapse in neurosis. *British Journal of Psychiatry, 109*, 12–18.

Fairburn, C.G., Marcus, M.D., & Wilson G.T. (1993). *Cognitive Behaviour Therapy for Binge Eating and Bulimia Nervosa: A Comprehensive Treatment Manual*. New York: Guilford Press.

Faragher, T. (1981). The police response to violence against women in the home. In J. Pahl (Ed.) *Private Violence and Public Policy*. London: Routledge.

Feindler, E.L. & Ecton, R.B. (1986). *Adolescent Anger Control: Cognitive Therapy Techniques*. New York: Pergamon Press.

Feindler, E.L., Ecton, R.B., Kingsley, R.B., & Dubey, D.R. (1986). Group anger-control training for institutionalized psychiatric male adolescents. *Behavior Therapy, 17*, 109–123.

Felsten, G. & Hill, V. (1999). Aggression Questionnaire hostility scale predicts anger in response to mistreatment. *Behaviour Research and Therapy, 37*, 87–97.

Feshbach, S. (1964). The function of aggression and the regulation of aggressive drive. *Psychological Review, 71*, 257–272.

Feshbach, S. (1971). Dynamics and morality of violence and aggression. *American Psychologist, 26*, 281–292.

Fitzharding, S. (1997). Anger management groupwork with women prisoners. *Forensic Update, 48*, 3–7.

Ford, R.D. (1991). Anger and irrational beliefs in violent inmates. *Personality and Individual Differences, 12*, 211–215.

Fottrell, E. (1980). A study of violent behaviour among patients in psychiatric hospitals. *British Journal of Psychiatry, 136*, 216–221.

Frankish, P. (1989). Meeting the emotional needs of handicapped people: a psycho-dynamic approach. *Journal of Mental Deficiency Research, 33*, 407–414.

Freud, A. (1949). Aggression in relation to emotional development; normal and pathological. *The Psychoanalytic Study of the Child, III/IV*, 37–42.

Freud, S. (1930/1961). *Civilization and its Discontents*. New York: W.W. Norton.

Friedman, H.S. (1992). *Hostility, Coping, and Health*. Washington, DC: American Psychological Association.

Friedman, M. & Rosenman, R.H. (1974). *Type A Behavior and Your Heart*. Greenwich, CT: Fawcett.

Frost, W.D. & Averill, J.R. (1982). Differences between men and women in the everyday experience of anger. In J. Averill, *Anger and Aggression: An Essay on Emotion* (pp. 281–316). New York: Springer-Verlag.

Frijda, N.H. (1986). *The Emotions*. Cambridge: Cambridge University Press.

Frijda, N.H. (1988). The laws of emotions. *American Psychologist, 43*, 349–358.

Funkenstein, D.H., King, S.H., & Drolette, M. (1954). The direction of anger during a laboratory stress-inducing situation. *Psychosomatic Medicine, 16*, 404–413.

Gates, G.S. (1926). On observational study of anger. *Journal of Experimental Psychology, 9*, 325–331.

Geen, R.G. (1968). Effects of frustration, attack, and prior training in aggressiveness upon aggressive behavior. *Journal of Personality and Social Psychology, 4*, 316–321.

Geen, R.G. & O'Neal, E.C. (1969). Activation of cue-elicited aggression by general arousal. *Journal of Personality and Social Psychology, 11*, 289–292.

Gilliom, M., Shaw, D.S., Beck, J.E., Schonberg, M.A., & Lukon, J.L. (2002). Anger regulation in disadvantaged preschool boys: Strategies, antecedents, and the development of self-control. *Developmental Psychology*, 222–235.

Gillmer, B.T. (2003). Process and structure issues in cognitive treatment for offenders with developmental disabilities. Paper delivered to the BPS Division of Forensic Psychology Annual Conference, Cambridge University, March 2003.

Glass, D. & Singer, J. (1972). *Urban Stress: Psychological Experiments on Noise and Social Stressors*. New York: Academic Press.

Goldstein, A.P. & Keller, H.R. (1987). *Aggressive Behavior: Assessment and Intervention*. Oxford: Pergamon Press.

Goldstein, A.P., Nensen, R., Daleflod, B., & Kalt, M. (2004). *New Perspectives on Aggression Replacement Training*. Chichester: John Wiley & Sons.

Goodenough, F. (1931/1975). *Anger in Young Children*. Westport, CT: Greenwood Press.

Gray, J.S. (1935). An objective theory of emotion. *Psychological Review, 42*, 108–116.

Grisso, T., Davis, J., Vesselinov, R., Appelbaum, P.S., & Monahan, J. (2000). Violent thoughts and violent behavior following hospitalization for mental disorder. *Journal of Consulting and Clinical Psychology, 68*, 388–398.

Gross, J.J. (1998). The emerging field of emotion regulation: An integrative review. *Review of General Psychology, 2,* 271–299.

Gross, J.J. (2002). Emotion regulation: Affective, cognitive, and social consequences. *Psychophysiology, 39,* 281–291.

Gross, J.J. & Oliver, O.P. (2003). Individual differences in two emotion regulation processes: Implications for affect, relationships, and well-being. *Personality and Social Psychology, 85,* 348–362.

Hall, G.S. (1899). A study of anger. *American Journal of Psychology, 10,* 516–591.

Hall, G.S. (1915). Anger as a primary emotion, and the application of Freudian mechanisms to its phenomena. *Journal of Abnormal Psychology, 10,* 81–87.

Hall, J. & Firth-Cozens, J. (2000). *Clinical Governance in the NHS: A Briefing.* Division of Clinical Psychology Information Leaflet No. 4. Leicester: The British Psychological Society.

Hallahan, M. & Rosenthal, R. (1996). Statistical power: Concepts, procedures, and applications. *Behavior Research and Therapy, 34,* 489–499.

Ham-Rowbottom, K.A., Gordon, E.E., Jarvis, K.L., & Novaco, R.W. (in press). Life constraints and psychological well-being of domestic violence shelter graduates. *Journal of Family Violence.*

Harbin, T.J. (2000). *Beyond Anger: How to Free Yourself from the Grip of Anger and Get More out of Life.* New York: Marlowe and Company.

Harburg, E., Blakelock, E., & Roeper, P. (1979). Resentful and reflective coping with arbitrary authority and blood pressure: Detroit. *Psychosomatic Medicine, 41,* 189–202.

Harburg, E., Erfurt, J.C., Hauenstein, L.S., Chape, C., Schull, W.J., & Schork, M.A. (1973). Socio-ecological stress, suppressed hostility, skin color, and Black-White male blood pressure: Detroit. *Psychosomatic Medicine, 35,* 276–296.

Harmon-Jones, E. (2004). Contributions from research on anger and cognitive dissonance to understanding the motivational functions of asymmetrical frontal brain activity. *Biological Psychology, 67,* 51–76.

Harmon-Jones, E. & Allen, J.J.B. (1998). Anger and frontal brain activity: EEG asymmetry consistent with approach motivation despite negative affective valence. *Journal of Personality and Social Psychology, 74,* 1310–1316.

Harmon-Jones, E. & Sigelman, J. (2001). State anger and prefrontal brain activity: Evidence that insult-related relative left-prefrontal activation is associated with experienced anger and aggression. *Journal of Personality and Social Psychology, 80,* 797–803.

Harris, M.B. (1993). How provoking! What makes men and women angry. *Aggressive Behavior, 19,* 199–211.

Harris, P. (1993). The nature and extent of aggressive behaviour amongst people with learning difficulties (mental handicap) in a single health district. *Journal of Intellectual Disability Research, 37,* 221–242.

Harris, W.V. (2001). *Restraining Rage: The Ideology of Anger Control in Classical Antiquity.* Cambridge, MA: Harvard University Press.

Hartmann, H., Kris, E., & Loewenstein, R.M. (1949). Notes on the theory of aggression. *The Psychoanalytic Study of the Child, III/IV,* 9–36.

Harvey, L., Burnham, R.W., Kendall, K., & Pease, K. (1992). Gender differences in criminal justice: an international comparison. *British Journal of Criminology, 32,* 208–217.

Hastings, R.P. & Remington, B. (1994). Staff behavior and its implications for people with learning disabilities and challenging behaviours. *British Journal of Clinical Psychology, 33,* 423–438.

Hatton, C. (2002). Psychosocial interventions for adults with intellectual disabilities and mental health problems. *Journal of Mental Health, 11,* 357–373.

Haynes, S.G., Feinleib, M., & Kannel, W.B. (1980). The relationship of psychosocial factors to coronary disease in the Framingham Study: III. Eight-year incidence of coronary heart disease. *American Journal of Epidemiology, 111,* 37–58.

Hazaleus, S.L. & Deffenbacher, J.L. (1986). Relaxation and cognitive treatments of anger. *Journal of Consulting and Clinical Psychology, 54,* 222–226.

Health and Safety Commission (1987). *Violence to Staff in the Health Services.* Health & Safety Executive, London: HMSO.

Hebb, D.O. (1946). Emotion in man and animal: An analysis of the intuitive processes of recognition. *Psychological Review, 53,* 88–106.

Hedderman, C. & Gelsthorpe, L. (1997). *Understanding the Sentencing of Women*. Home Office Research Study, *170*. London: HMSO.

Helmers, K., Baker, B., O'Kelly, B., & Tobe, S. (2000). Anger expression, gender, and ambulatory blood pressure in mild, unmedicated adults with hypertension. *Annals of Behavioral Medicine, 22*, 60–64.

Hill, B.K. & Bruininks, R.H. (1984). Maladaptive behavior of mentally retarded individuals in residential facilities. *American Journal of Mental Deficiency, 88*, 380–387.

Hickling, E.J. & Blanchard, E.B. (1997). The private practice psychologist and manual-based treatments. *Behaviour Research and Therapy, 35*, 191–204.

Hodgins, S. & Muller-Isberner, R. (2000). *Violence, Crime and Mentally Disordered Offenders*. Chichester: John Wiley & Sons.

Hokanson, J.E. (1961a). Vascular and psychogalvanic effects of experimentally aroused anger. *Journal of Personality, 29*, 30–39.

Hokanson, J.E. (1961b). The effects of frustration and anxiety on overt aggression. *Journal of Abnormal and Social Psychology, 62*, 346–351.

Hollin, C. (1995). The meaning and implications of programme integrity. In J. McGuire (Ed.), *What Works: Effective Methods to Reduce Reoffending: Guidelines from Research and Practice*. Chichester: Wiley.

Hollins, S. & Sinason, V. (2000). Psychotherapy, learning disabilities and trauma: new perspectives. *British Journal of Psychiatry, 176*, 32–36.

Horney, K. (1939). *New Ways in Psychoanalysis*. New York: Norton.

Howells, K. (1989). Anger-management methods in relation to the prevention of violent behaviour. In J. Archer & K. Brown (Eds), *Human Aggression: Naturalistic Accounts*. (pp. 153–181) London: Routledge.

Howells, K. & Day, A. (2003). Readiness for anger management: clinical and theoretical issues. *Clinical Psychology Review, 23*, 319–337.

Howells, P.M., Rogers, C., & Wilcock, S. (2000). Evaluating a cognitive/behavioural approach to anger management skills in adults with learning disabilities. *British Journal of Learning Disabilities, 28*, 137–142.

Huesmann, L.R. (1998). The role of social information processing and cognitive schema in the acquisition and maintenance of habitual aggressive behavior. In R.G. Geen & E. Donnerstein (Eds), *Human Aggression: Theories, Research, and Implications for Social Policy*. San Diego, CA: Academic Press.

Huey, D.A. & Britton P.G. (2002). A portrait of clinical psychology. *Journal of Inter-Professional Care, 16*, 69–78.

Ionno, J.A. (1983). A prospective study of assaultive behaviour in female psychiatric patients. In J.R. Lion & W.H. Reid (Eds). *Assaults within Psychiatric Facilities* (pp. 71–79). New York: Grune & Stratton.

Iribarren, C., Sidney, S., Bild, D.E., Liu, K., Markovitz, J.H., Roseman, J.M., & Matthews, K. (2000). Association of hostility with coronary artery calcification in young adults. *Journal of the American Medical Association, 283*, 2546–2551.

Izard, C.E. (1977). *Human Emotions*. New York: Plenum.

Jackson, H.F., Glass, C., & Hope S. (1987). A functional analysis of recidivistic arson. *British Journal of Clinical Psychology, 26*, 175–185.

Jahoda, A., Trower, P., Pert, C. & Finn, D. (2001). Contingent reinforcement or defending the self? A review of evolving models of aggression in people with mild learning disabilities. *British Journal of Medical Psychology, 74*, 305–321.

James, I.A., Blackburn, I.M., Milne, D.L., & Reichfelt, F.K. (2001). Moderators of trainee competence in cognitive therapy. *British Journal of Clinical Psychology, 40*, 131–141.

James, W. (1890). *Principles of Psychology*. New York: Holt.

Jenkins, C.D. (1978). Components of the coronary-prone behavior pattern: Their relation to silent myocardial infarction and blood lipids. *Journal of Chronic Diseases, 19*, 599–609.

Jenkins, R., Rose, J., & Lovell, C. (1997). Psychological well-being of staff working with people who have challenging behaviour. *Journal of Intellectual Disability Research, 41*, 502–511.

Johnson, E.H. (1990). *The Deadly Emotions: The Role of Anger, Hostility, and Aggression in Health and Emotional Well-Being*. New York: Praeger.

Johnson, E.H., Gentry, W.D., & Julius, S. (1992). *Personality, Elevated Blood Pressure, and Essential Hypertension*. Washington, DC: Hemisphere.

Johnson, R.N. (1972). *Aggression in Man and Animals*. Philadelphia: W.B. Saunders.

Jones, J.P., Thomas-Peter, B.A., & Trout, A. (1999). Normative data for the Novaco Anger Scale from a non-clinical sample and implications for clinical use. *British Journal of Clinical Psychology, 38*, 417–424.

Kannel, W.B., Neaton, J.D., Wentworth, H.D. et al. (1986). Overall and coronary heart disease mortality rates in relation to major risk factors in 325,348 men screened for the MRFIT (Multiple Risk Factor Intervention Trial). *American Heart Journal, 112*, 825–836.

Kassinove, H., Sukhodolsky, D.G., Tsytsarev, S.V., & Solovyova, S. (1997). Self-reported anger episodes in Russia and America. *Journal of Social Behavior and Personality, 12*, 301–324.

Kasssinove, H. & Tafrate, R.C. (2003). *Anger Management: The Complete Treatment Guidebook for Practitioners*. Atascadero, CA: Impact Publishers.

Kavanagh, D.J. & Wilson, P.H. (1989). Prediction of outcome with a group version of cognitive therapy for depression. *Behaviour Research and Therapy, 27*, 333–343.

Keijsers, G.P.J., Schaap, C.P.D.R., Hoogduin, C.A.L., Hoogsteyns, B., & de-Kemp, E.C.M. (1999). Preliminary results of a new instrument to assess patient motivation for treatment in cognitive-behaviour therapy. *Behavioural & Cognitive Psychotherapy, 27*, 165–179.

Kendall, K. (2001). Anger management with women in coercive environments. *Issues in Forensic Psychology, 2*, 35–41.

Kendall, P.C., Chu, B., Gifford, A., Hayes, C., & Nauta, M. (1998). Breathing life into a manual: Flexibility and creativity with manual-based treatments. *Cognitive and Behavioral Practice, 5*, 177–198.

Kiely, J. & Pankhurst, H. (1998). Violence faced by staff in a learning disability service. *Disability and Rehabilitation, 20*, 81–89.

King, N., Lancaster, N., Wynne, G., Nettleton, N., & Davis, R. (1999). Cognitive behavioural anger management training for adults with mild intellectual disability. *Scandinavian Journal of Behavioural Therapy, 28*, 19–22.

Kitzmann, K.M., Gaylord, N.K., Holt, A.R., & Kenny, E.D. (2003). Child witnesses to domestic violence: A meta-analytic review. *Journal of Consulting and Clinical Psychology, 71*, 339–352.

Kneip, R.C., Delamater, A., Ismond, T., Milford, C., Salvia, L., & Schwartz, D. (1993). Self- and spouse ratings of anger and hostility as predictors of coronary disease. *Health Psychology, 12*, 301–307.

Koenen, K.C., Moffitt, T.E., Caspi, A., Taylor, A., & Purcell, S. (2003). Domestic violence is associated with environmental suppression of IQ in young children. *Development and Psychopathology, 15*, 297–311.

Kolb, D.A. (1984). *Experiential Learning: Experience as the Source of Learning and Development*. Englewood Cliffs, NJ: Prentice-Hall.

Konecni, V.J. (1975a). Annoyance, type, and duration of postannoyance activity, and aggression: "The cathartic effect". *Journal of Experimental Psychology: General, 104*, 76–102.

Konecni, V.J. (1975b). The mediation of aggressive behavior: Arousal level versus anger and cognitive labeling. *Journal of Personality and Social Psychology, 32*, 706–712.

Kopper, B.A. (1993). Role of gender, sex role identity, and type A behaviour in anger expression and mental health functioning. *Journal of Counselling Psychology, 40*, 232–237.

Kopper, B.A. & Epperson, D.I. (1996). The experience and expression of anger: Relationships with gender, gender role socialization, depression, and mental health functioning. *Journal of Counseling Psychology, 43*, 158–165.

Krakowski, M. & Czobor, P. (2004). Gender differences in violent behaviors: Relationship to clinical symptoms and psychosocial factors. *American Journal of Psychiatry, 161*, 459–465.

Krantz, D.S., Contrada, R.J., Hill, D.R., & Friedler, E. (1988). Environmental stress and biobehavioral antecedents of coronary hear disease. *Journal of Consulting and Clinical Psychology, 56*, 333–341.

Krasner, F.R., Howard, K.I., & Brown A.S. (1998). The acquisition of psychotherapeutic skill. *Journal of Clinical Psychology, 54*, 895–903.

Kring, A. (1999). Gender and anger. In A.H. Fischer (Ed.), *Gender and Emotion: Social and Psychological Perspectives*. Cambridge: Cambridge University Press.

Kuipers, E., Garety, P., Fowler, D., Dunn, G., Bebbington, P., Freeman, D., & Hadley, C. (1997). London – East Anglia randomised controlled trial of cognitive-behavioural therapy for psychosis. *British Journal of Psychiatry, 171*, 319–327.

Lakin, K.C., Hill, B.K., Hauber, F.A., Bruininks, R.H., & Heal, L.W. (1983). New admissions to a national sample of public residential facilities. *American Journal on Mental Retardation, 88*, 13–20.

Lam, J.N., McNeil, D.E., & Binder, R.L. (2000). The relationship between patients' gender and violence leading to staff injuries. *Psychiatric Services, 51*, 1167–1170.

Lambert, M.J. & Ogles, B.M. (1997). The effectiveness of psychotherapy supervision. In E. Watkins (Ed.), *Handbook of Psychotherapy Supervision*. New York: Wiley.

Landis, C., Ferrall, S., & Page, J. (1936). Fear, anger, and disease: Their inter-correlations in normal and abnormal people. *The American Journal of Psychology, 48*, 585–597.

Lang, P.J. (1995). The emotion probe: Studies of motivation and attention. *American Psychologist, 50*, 372–385.

Larkin, E., Murtagh, S., & Jones, S. (1988). A preliminary study of violent incidents in a special hospital (Rampton). *British Journal of Psychiatry, 153*, 226–231.

Lawrenson, H. & Lindsay, W.R. (1998). The treatment of anger in individuals with learning disabilities. In W. Fraser, D. Sines, & M. Kerr (Eds), *Hallas' the care of people with intellectual disabilities* (9th edn). Oxford: Butterworth-Heinemann.

Lazarus, R. (1994). Appraisal: The long and the short of it. In P. Ekman & R.J. Davidson (Eds), *The Nature of Emotion* (pp. 208–215). New York: Oxford University Press.

Lazarus, R.S. (1966). *Psychological Stress and the Coping Process*. New York: McGraw-Hill.

Lazarus, R.S. (1967). Cognitive and personality factors underlying threat and coping. In M.H. Appley & R. Trumbull (Eds), *Psychological Stress*. New York: Appleton-Century-Crofts.

Lazarus, R.S. (1968). Emotions and adaptation: Conceptual and empirical relations. In W.J. Arnold (Ed.), *Nebraska Symposium on Motivation*. Lincoln, NE: University of Nebraska Press.

Lazarus, R.S. (1982). On the primacy of cognition. *American Psychologist, 39*, 124–129.

Lazarus, R.S., & Folkman, S. (1984). *Stress, Appraisal, and Coping*. New York: Springer.

LeDoux, J.E. (1984). Cognition and emotion: Processing functions and brain systems. In M.S. Gazzaniga (Ed.), *Handbook of Cognitive Neuroscience* (pp. 357–368). New York: Plenum.

LeDoux, J.E. (1989). Cognitive-emotional interactions in the brain. *Cognition and Emotion, 3*, 267–289.

Leeper, R.W. (1948). A motivational theory of emotion to replace 'emotion as disorganized response'. *Psychological Review, 55*, 5–21.

Lennox, D.B., Miltenberger, R.G., Spengler, P., & Erfanian, N. (1988). Decelerative treatment practices with persons who have mental retardation: A review of five years of the literature. *American Journal on Mental Retardation, 92*, 492–501.

Lever, J. (1976). Sex differences in the games people play. *Social Problems, 23*, 478–487.

Levey, S. & Howells, K. (1991). Anger and its management. *Journal of Forensic Psychiatry, 1*, 305–327.

Lindsay, W.R., Allan, R., MacLeod, F., Smart, N., & Smith, A.H.W. (2003). Long-term treatment and management of violent tendencies in men with intellectual disabilities convicted of assault. *Mental Retardation, 41*, 47–56.

Lindsay, W.R., Allan, R., Parry, C., MacLeod, F., Cottrell, J., Overend, H., et al. (2004). Anger and aggression in people with intellectual disabilities: Treatment and follow-up of consecutive referrals and a waiting list comparison. *Clinical Psychology and Psychotherapy, 11*, 255–264.

Lindsay, W.R. & Law, J. (1999). Outcome evaluation of 161 people with learning disabilities in Tayside who have offending or challenging behavior. Presentation to the BABCP 27th Annual Conference, University of Bristol, July.

Lindsay, W.R., Overend, H., Allan, R., Williams, C., & Black, L. (1998). Using specific approaches for individual problems in the management of anger and aggression. *British Journal of Learning Disabilities, 26*, 44–50.

Lindsay, W.R. & Smith, A.H.W. (1998). Responses to treatment of sex offenders with intellectual disability: A comparison of men with 1- and 2-year probation sentences. *Journal of Intellectual Disability Research, 42*, 346–353.

Lion, J.R. & Reid, W.H. (1983). *Assaults within Psychiatric Facilities*. New York: Grune & Stratton.

Litrownik, A.J., Newton, R., Hunter, W.M., English, D., & Everson, M.D. (2003). Exposure to family violence in young at-risk children: A longitudinal look at the effects of victimization and witnessed physical and psychological aggression. *Journal of Family Violence, 18*, 59–73.

Loza, W. & Loza-Fanous, A. (1999). Anger and prediction of violent and non-violent offender's recidivism. *Journal of Interpersonal Violence, 14*, 1014–1029.

Maden, A., Swinton, M., & Gunn, J. (1994). A criminological and psychiatric survey of women serving a prison sentence. *British Journal of Criminology, 34*, 172–191.

Madow, L. (1972). *Anger*. New York: Charles Scribner's Sons.

Maes, M. & Coccaro, E.F. (1998). *Neurobiology and Clinical Views on Aggression and Impulsivity*. Chichester: John Wiley & Sons.

Mandler, G. (1975). *Mind and Body: The Psychology of Emotion and Stress*. New York: Norton.

Marcus, B.A., Vollmer, T.R., Swanson, V., Roane, H.R., and Ringdahl, J.E. (2001), An experimental analysis of aggression. *Behavior Modification, 25*, 189–213.

Marlatt, G.A. & Gordon, J.R. (1985). *Relapse Prevention: Maintenance Strategies in the Treatment of Addictive Behaviours*. New York: Guilford Press.

Matson, J.L., Bamburg, J.W., Mayville, E.A., Pinkston, J., Bielecki, J., Kuhn, D., Smalls, Y., & Logan, J. R. (2000). Psychopharmacology and mental retardation: A 10 year review (1990–1999). *Research in Developmental Disabilities, 21*, 263–296.

Matson, J.L., Bielecki, J., Mayville, S.B., & Matson, M.L. (2003). Psychopharmacological research for individuals with mental retardation: Methodological issues and suggestions. *Research in Developmental Disabilities, 24*, 149–157.

McCarthy, M. & Thompson, D. (1992). *Sex and the 3Rs: Rights, Responsibilities and Risks – A Sex Education Package for Working with People with Learning Difficulties*. Brighton: Pavilion.

McDougall, C., Boddis, S., Dawson, K. & Hayes, R. (1990). Developments in anger control training. *Issues in Criminological and Legal Psychology, 15*, 39–44.

McGaugh, J.L. (1995). Emotional activation, neuromodulatory systems, and memory. In D.L. Schacter (Ed.), *Memory Distortion: How Minds, Brains, and Societies Reconstruct the Past* (pp. 255–273). Cambridge, MA: Harvard University Press.

McGaugh, J.L. (2003). *Memory and Emotion: The Making of Lasting Memories*. New York: Columbia University Press.

McGuire, J. (1995). *What Works: Reducing Reoffending Guidelines from Research and Practice*. Chichester: Wiley.

McGuire, J. (Ed.) (2002). *Offender Rehabilitation and Treatment: Effective Programmes and Policies to Reduce Re-offending*. Chichester: Wiley.

McKay, M., Rogers, P.D., & McKay, J. (1989). *When Anger Hurts: Quieting the Storm Within*. Oakland, CA: New Harbinger.

McKellar, P. (1948). The emotion of anger in the expression of human aggressiveness. *British Journal of Psychology, 39*, 148–155.

McKellar, P. (1949). Provocation to anger and the development of attitudes of hostility. *British Journal of Psychology, 40*, 104–114.

McNeil, D.E., Eisner, J.P., & Binder, R.L. (2003). The relationship between aggressive attributional style and violence by psychiatric patients. *Journal of Consulting and Clinical Psychology. 71*, 399–403.

Meehl, P.E. (1960). The cognitive activity of the clinician. *American Psychologist, 15*, 19–27.

Meichenbaum, D. (1977). *Cognitive Behavior Modification*. New York: Plenum Press.

Meichenbaum, D. (1985). *Stress Inoculation Training*. Oxford: Pergamon Press.

Meichenbam, D., & Novaco, R.W. (1978). Stress inoculation: A preventative approach. In C. Spielberger & I. Sarason (Eds), *Stress and Anxiety, Vol. 5*. (pp. 419–435). New York: Halstead Press.

Meltzer, H. (1933). Students' adjustments in anger. *Journal of Social Psychology, 4*, 285–309.

Menninger, K. (1938). *Man against Himself*. New York: Harcourt.

Menninger, K. (1942). *Love against Hate*. New York: Harcourt.

Mikulincer, M., Shaver, P.R., & Pereg, D. (2003). Attachment theory and affect regulation: The dynamics, development, and cognitive consequences of attachment-related strategies. *Motivation and Emotion, 27*, 77–102.

Miller, M.L. (1939). Blood pressure in relation to inhibited aggression in psychotics. *Psychosomatic Medicine, 1*, 162–172.

Miller, T.Q., Smith, T.W., Turner, C.W., Guijarro, M.L., & Hallet, A.J. (1996). A meta-analytic review of research on hostility and physical health. *Psychological Bulletin, 119*, 322–348.

Mills, J.F., Kroner, D.G., & Forth, A.E. (1998). Novaco Anger Scale: Reliability and validity within an adult criminal sample. *Assessment, 5*, 237–248.

Milne, D. & James, I. (2000). A systematic review of effective cognitive behavioural supervision. *British Journal of Clinical Psychology, 39*, 111–127.

Milne, D.L. & James, I.A. (2002). The observed impact of training on competence in clinical supervision. *British Journal of Clinical Psychology, 41*, 55–72.

Milne, D.L., Pilkington, J., Gracie, J., & James, I. (2003). Transferring skills from supervision to therapy. *Behavioural & Cognitive Psychotherapy, 31*, 193–202.

Milovchevich, D., Howells, K., Drew. N., & Day. A. (2001). Sex and gender role differences in anger: An Australian community study. *Personality & Individual Differences, 31*, 117–127.

Monahan, J. (1981). *The Clinical Prediction of Violent Behavior*. Washington, DC: Government Printing Office.

Monahan, J. (1992). Mental disorder and violent behavior: Perspectives and evidence. *American Psychologist, 47*, 511–512.

Monahan, J. & Steadman, H.J. (Eds) (1994). *Violence and Mental Disorder: Developments in Risk Assessment*. Chicago: University of Chicago Press.

Monahan, J., Steadman, H.J., Silver, E., Appelbaum, P.S., Robbins, P.C., Mulvey, E.P., Roth, L.H., Grisso, T., & Banks, S. (2001). *Rethinking Risk Assessment: The MacArthur Study of Mental Disorder and Violence*. Oxford: Oxford University Press.

Moore, E., Adams, R., Elsworth, J., & Lewis, J. (1997). An anger management group for people with a learning disability. *British Journal of Learning Disabilities, 25*, 53–57.

Morren, M. & Meesters, C. (2002). Validation of the Dutch version of the Aggression Questionnaire in adolescent male offenders. *Aggressive Behavior, 28*, 87–96.

Moss, S. (1999). Assessment: conceptual issues. In N. Bouras (ed.), *Psychiatric and Behavioural Disorders in Developmental Disabilities and Mental Retardation* (pp. 18–37). Cambridge: Cambridge University Press.

Mulrow, C.D & Oxman, A.D. (Eds) (1996). Cochrane Collaboration Handbook. In The Cochrane Collaboration, *The Cochrane Library [Database on Disk and CDROM]*. Oxford: Update Software.

Muraven, M. & Baumeister, R.F. (2000). Self-regulation and depletion of limited resources: Does self-control resemble a muscle? *Psychological Bulletin, 126*, 247–259.

Murphy, G. & Clare, I. (1991). MIETS: A service option for people with mild mental handicap and challenging behaviour or psychiatric problems. 2. Assessment, treatment, and outcome for service users and service effectiveness. *Mental Handicap Research, 4*, 180–206.

National Audit Office (2003). *A Safer Place to Work: Protecting NHS Hospital and Ambulance Staff from Violence and Aggression*. Report by the Comptroller and Auditor General (HC 527), London.

Nezu, A. (2001). Are we doing what we say we are doing? The importance of assessing treatment integrity. Keynote address to the World Congress of Behavioral and Cognitive Therapies, July 17–21, 2001, Vancouver, BC, Canada. CD-ROM Abstracts. New York: AABT.

Nijman, H.L.I., Muris, P., Merckelbach, H.L.G.J., Palmstierna, T., Wistedt, B., Vos, A.M., van Rixtel, A., & Allertz, W. (1999). The staff observation scale – revised (SOAS-R). *Aggressive Behavior, 25*, 197–209.

Nijman, H. & Palmstierna, T. (2002). Measuring aggression with the staff observation aggression scale – revised. *Acta Psychiatrica Scandinavica, 106*, 101–102.

Nisbett, R. & Ross L. (1980). *Human Inference*. Englewood Cliffs, NJ: Prentice-Hall.

Novaco, R.W. (1975). *Anger Control: The Development and Evaluation of an Experimental Treatment*. Lexington, MA: D. C. Heath.

Novaco, R.W. (1976). The function and regulation of the arousal of anger. *American Journal of Psychiatry, 133*, 1124–1128.

Novaco, R.W. (1977a). Stress inoculation: A cognitive therapy for anger and its application to a case of depression. *Journal of Consulting and Clinical Psychology, 45*, 600–608.

Novaco, R.W. (1977b). A stress inoculation approach to anger management in the training of law enforcement officers. *American Journal of Community Psychology, 5*, 327–346.

Novaco, R.W. (1979). The cognitive regulation of anger and stress. In P. Kendall & S. Hollon (Eds), *Cognitive Behavioral Interventions: Theory, Research, and Procedures* (pp. 241–285). New York: Academic Press.

Novaco, R.W. (1986). Anger as a clinical and social problem. In R. Blanchard and C. Blanchard (Eds), *Advances in the Study of Aggression*. Vol. 2. (pp. 1–67). New York: Academic Press.

Novaco, R.W. (1988). Novaco Provocation Inventory. In M. Hersen & A.S. Bellack (Eds), *Dictionary of Behavioral Assessment Techniques*. New York: Pergamon.

Novaco, R.W. (1993a). Clinicians ought to view anger contextually. *Behaviour Change, 10*, 208–218.

Novaco, R.W. (1993b). Stress inoculation therapy for anger control: A manual for therapists. Unpublished manuscript, University of California, Irvine.

Novaco, R.W. (1994). Anger as a risk factor for violence among the mentally disordered. In J. Monahan & H. Steadman (Eds), *Violence and Mental Disorder: Developments in Risk Assessment*. (pp. 21–59). Chicago: University of Chicago Press.

Novaco, R.W. (1995). Clinical problems of anger and its assessment and regulation through a stress coping skills approach. In W. O'Donohue & L. Krasner (Eds), *Handbook of Psychological Skills Training: Training and Applications*. Boston: Allyn & Bacon.

Novaco, R.W. (1997). Remediating anger and aggression with violent offenders. *Legal and Criminological Psychology, 2*, 77–88.

Novaco, R.W. (2000). Anger. In A.E. Kazdin (Ed.), *Encyclopedia of Psychology* (pp. 170–174). Washington, DC: American Psychological Association and Oxford University Press.

Novaco, R.W. (2003). *The Novaco Anger Scale and Provocation Inventory Manual (NAS-PI)*. Los Angeles: Western Psychological Services.

Novaco, R.W. & Chemtob, C.M. (1998). Anger and trauma: Conceptualization, assessment, and treatment. In V.M. Follette, J.I. Ruzek, and F. Abueg (Eds). *Cognitive-Behavioral Therapies for Trauma* (pp. 162–190). New York: Guilford.

Novaco, R.W. & Chemtob, C.M. (2002). Anger and combat-related posttraumatic stress disorder. *Journal of Traumatic Stress, 15*, 123–132.

Novaco, R.W. & Jarvis, K.L. (2002). Brief cognitive behavioral intervention for anger. In F. Bond & W. Dryden (Eds), *Handbook of Brief Cognitive Behavioural Therapy* (pp. 77–100). London: John Wiley.

Novaco, R.W., Ramm, M., & Black, L. (2000). Anger treatment with offenders. In C. Hollin (Ed.), *Handbook of Offender Assessment and Treatment*. London: John Wiley.

Novaco, R.W. & Renwick, S.J. (1998). Anger predictors of assaultiveness of forensic hospital patients. In E. Sanavio (Ed.), *Behaviour and Cognitive Therapy Today: Essays in Honour of Hans. J. Eysenck* (pp. 213–222). Amsterdam: Elsevier Science.

Novaco, R.W. & Renwick, S.J. (2003). Anger predictors and the validation of a ward behavior scale for anger and aggression. Unpublished manuscript.

Novaco, R.W. & Taylor, J.L. (2003). Family environment links to patient anger and aggression: Effects of volatile parents. Paper presented at the annual conference of the British Association of Behavioural Psychotherapy, York University, UK, July.

Novaco, R.W. & Taylor, J.L. (2004). Assessment of anger and aggression in male offenders with developmental disabilities. *Psychological Assessment, 16*, 42–50.

Novaco, R.W. & Taylor, J.L. (in press). Cognitive-behavioural anger treatment. In M. McNulty & A. Carr (Eds.), *Handbook of Adult Clinical Psychology: An Evidence Based Practice Approach*. London: Routledge.

Novaco, R.W. & Thacker, S. (1990). Anger and assaultive behavior among psychiatric hospital patients. Unpublished manuscript, University of California, Irvine.

Novaco, R.W. & Welsh, W. N. (1989). Anger disturbances: Cognitive mediation and clinical prescriptions. In K. Howells & C.R. Hollin (Eds), *Clinical Approaches to Violence*. Chichester: John Wiley & Sons.

Ohira, T., Iso, H., Tanigawa, T. et al. (2002). The relation of anger expression with blood pressure levels and hypertension in rural and urban Japanese communities. *Journal of Hypertension, 20*, 21–27.

Oken, D. (1960). An experimental study of suppressed anger and blood pressure. *Archives of General Psychiatry, 2*, 441–456.

Oosterban, D.B., van Balkom, A.J.L.M., Spinhoven, P., van Oppen, P., & van Dyck, R. (2001). Cognitive therapy versus moclobemide in social phobia: A controlled study. *Clinical Psychology and Psychotherapy, 8*, 263–273.

Ortony, A., Clore, G.L., & Collins, A. (1988). *The Cognitive Structure of Emotions*. Cambridge: Cambridge University Press.

Osler, W. (1910). The Lumleian Lectures on angina pectoris. Lecture III. *The Lancet, 175* (Issue 4519), 973–977.

Palmstierna, T. & Wistedt, B. (1987). Staff observation aggression scale: presentation and evaluation. *Acta Psychiatrica Scandinavica, 76*, 657–663.

Pastore, N. (1952). The role of arbitrariness in the frustration-aggression hypothesis. *Journal of Abnormal and Social Psychology, 47*, 728–731.

Patel, P., Goldberg, D.P., & Moss, S. (1993). Psychiatric morbidity in older people with moderate and severe learning disability (mental retardation). Part II: The prevalence study. *British Journal of Psychiatry, 163*, 481–491.

Patel, V. & Hope, R.A. (1992). A rating scale for aggressive behaviour in the elderly – the RAGE. *Psychological Medicine, 22*, 211–221.

Peterson, D.R. (1995). The reflective educator. *American Psychologist. 50*, 175–183.

Plutchik, R. (1980). *Emotion: A Psychoevolutionary Synthesis*. New York: Harper & Row.

Prout, H.T., Chard, K.M., Nowak-Drabik, K.M., & Johnson, D.M. (2000). Determining the effectiveness of psychotherapy with persons with mental retardation: the need to move toward empirically based research. *The NADD Bulletin, 3*, 83–86.

Prout, H.T. & Nowak-Drabik, K.M. (2003). Psychotherapy with persons who have mental retardation. *American Journal on Mental Retardation, 108*, 82–93.

Redl, F. & Wineman, D. (1951). *Children who Hate*. New York: Free Press.

Redl, F. & Wineman, D. (1952). *Controls from Within*. New York: Free Press.

Reiss, S., Levitan, G., & Szyszko, J. (1982). Emotional disturbance and mental retardation: diagnostic overshadowing. *American Journal of Mental Deficiency, 86*, 567–574.

Reiss, A.J. & Roth, J.A. (1993). *Understanding and Preventing Violence*. Washington, DC: National Academy Press.

Renwick, S., Black, L., Ramm, M., & Novaco, R.W. (1997). Anger treatment with forensic hospital patients. *Legal and Criminological Psychology, 2*, 103–116.

Rice, M.E., Harris, G.T., Varney, G.W., & Quinsey, V.L. (1989). *Violence in Institutions: Understanding, Prevention, and Control*. Toronto: Hogrefe & Huber.

Richardson, R.F. (1918). *The Psychology and Pedagogy of Anger*. Baltimore, MD: Warwick and York, Inc.

Robertson, A. (2002). Women with learning disabilities detained in hospital: a description of anger and aggression. Paper presented at a conference on A Safer Society: Perspectives on Violence and Aggression, Glasgow Caledonian University, UK.

Rochlin, G. (1973). *Man's Aggression: The Defense of the Self*. Boston: Gambit.

Rose, J. (1996). Anger management: a group treatment program for people with mental retardation. *Journal of Developmental and Physical Disabilities, 8*, 133–149.

Rose, J. & West, C. (1999). Assessment of anger in people with intellectual disabilities. *Journal of Applied Research in Intellectual Disabilities, 12*, 211–224.

Rose, J., West, C., & Clifford, D. (2000). Group interventions for anger in people with intellectual disabilities. *Research in Developmental Disabilities, 21*, 171–181.

Rosenberg, E.L., Ekman, P., Jiang, W., Babyak, M., Coleman, R.E., Hanson, M., O'Conner, C., Waugh, R., & Blumenthal, J.A. (2001). Linkages between facial expressions of anger and transient myocardial ischemia in men with coronary artery disease. *Emotion, 1*, 105–115.

Rosenberg, F. & Simmons, R. (1975). Sex differences in the self-concept of adolescence. *Sex Roles, 1*, 147–159.

Rossiter, R., Hunniset, E., & Pulsford, M. (1998). Anger management training and people with moderate learning disabilities. *British Journal of Learning Disabilities, 26*, 67–74.

Roth, A. & Fonagy, P. (1996). *What Works for Whom?* London: Guildford.

Royal College of Psychiatrists (2004). *Psychotherapy and Learning Disability*. Council Report CR116. London: Royal College of Psychiatrists.

Rubin, T.I. (1969). *The Angry Book*. London: Macmillan.

Russell, J.A. (1991). Culture and the categorization of emotions. *Psychological Bulletin, 110*, 426–450.

Salas, E. and Cannon-Bowers, J.A. (2001). The science of training: A decade of progress. *Annual Review of Psychology, 51*, 471–499.

Saul, L.J. (1939). Hostility in cases of essential hypertension. *Psychosomatic Medicine, 1*, 153–161.

Saul, L.J. (1956). *The Hostile Mind*. New York: Random House.

Scaife, J. (2001). *Supervision in the Mental Health Professions: A Practitioner's Guide*. Hove, Sussex: Brunner-Routledge.

Schacter, J. (1957). Pain, fear, and anger in hypertensives and normotensives: A psychophysiological study. *Psychosomatic Medicine, 19*, 17–29.

Schlichter, K.J. & Horan, J. J. (1981). Effects of stress inoculation on the anger and aggression management skills of institutionalized juvenile delinquents. *Cognitive Therapy and Research, 5*, 359–365.

Schon, D.A. (1983). *The Reflective Practitioner*. New York: Basic Books.

Schum, J.L., Jorgensen, R.S., Verhaeghen, P., Sauro, M., & Thibodeau, R. (2003). Trait anger, anger expression, and ambulatory blood pressure: A meta-analytic review. *Journal of Behavioral Medicine, 26*, 395–415.

Scotti, J.R., Evans, I.M., Meyer, L.H., & Walker, P. (1991). A meta-analysis of intervention research with problem behavior: Treatment validity and standards of practice. *American Journal on Mental Retardation, 96*, 233–256.

Seneca, L. (44/1817). *Seneca's Morals*. New York: Harper & Brothers.

Siegman, A.W. (1994). Cardiovascular consequences of expressing and repressing anger. In A.W. Siegman & T.W. Smith (Eds), *Anger, Hostility, and the Heart*. Hillsdale, NJ: Lawrence Erlbaum.

Siegman, A.W., & Smith, T.W. (1994). *Anger, Hostility, and the Heart*. Hillsdale, NJ: Lawrence Erlbaum.

Sigafoos, J., Elkins, J., Kerr, M., & Attwood, T. (1994). A survey of aggressive behavior among a population of persons with intellectual disability in Queensland. *Journal of Intellectual Disability Research, 38*, 369–381.

Skett, S. (1995). What works in the reduction of offending behaviour? *Forensic Update, 42*, 20–27.

Smith, L.L., Smith, J.N., & Beckner, B.M. (1994). An anger-management workshop for women inmates. *Families in Society: The Journal of Contemporary Human Services, 75*, 431–441.

Smith, S., Branford, D., Collacott, R.A., Cooper, S.-A., & McGrother, C. (1996). Prevalence and cluster typology of maladaptive behaviours in a geographically defined population of adults with learning disabilities. *British Journal of Psychiatry, 169*, 219–227.

Spielberger, C.D. (1991). *State-Trait Anger Expression Inventory: STAXI Professional Manual*. Tampa, FL: Psychological Assessment Resources.

Spielberger, C.D. (1996) *State–Trait Anger Expression Inventory Professional Manual*. Florida: Psychological Assessment Resources, Inc.

Stanko, E.A. (1995). Dancing with denial: Researching women and questioning men. In M. Maynard & J. Purvis (Eds). *Researching Women's Lives from a Feminist Perspective*. London: Taylor & Francis.

Stenfert Kroese, B. (1998). Cognitive-behavioural therapy for people with learning disabilities. *Behavioural and Cognitive Psychotherapy, 26*, 315–322.

Stenfert Kroese, B., Dagnan, D., & Loumidis, K. (1997). *Cognitive-Behaviour Therapy for People with Learning Disabilities*. London: Routledge.

Stermac, L.E. (1986). Anger control treatment for forensic patients. *Journal of Interpersonal Violence, 1*, 446–457.

Stith, S.M. & Hamby, S.L. (2002). The anger management scale: Development and preliminary psychometric properties. *Violence and Victims, 17*, 383–402.

Stokman, C.L.J. & Heiber, P. (1980). Incidents in hospitalized forensic patients. *Victimology: An International Journal, 5*, 175–192.

Stoney, C.M. & Engebretson, T.O. (1994). Anger and hostility: Potential mediators of the gender difference in coronary heart disease. In A.W. Siegman & T.W. Smith (Eds), *Anger, Hostility, and the Heart* (pp. 215–237). Hillsdale, NJ: Lawrence Erlbaum.

Stratton, G.M. (1926). Emotion and the incidence of disease. *Journal of Abnormal and Social Psychology, 21*, 19–23.

Stratton, G.M. (1927). Anger and fear: Their probable relation to each other, to intellectual work, and to primogeniture. *American Journal of Psychology, 39*, 125–140.

Straus, M.A. (1995). Trends in cultural norms and rates of partner violence: An update to 1992. In S.M. Stith & M.A. Straus (Eds), *Understanding Partner Violence* (pp. 30–33). Minneapolis: National Council on Family Relations.

Straus, M.A. & Kantor, G.K. (1994). Corporal punishment of adolescents by parents: A risk factor in the epidemiology of depression, suicide, alcohol abuse, child abuse, and wife beating. *Adolescence, 29,* 543–561.

Strike, P.C. & Steptoe, A. (2004). Psychosocial factors in the development of coronary artery disease. *Progress in Cardiovascular Disease, 46,* 337–347.

Strickler, H. (2001). Interaction between family violence and mental retardation. *Mental Retardation, 39,* 461–471.

Strongman, K.T. (1985). Emotion in mentally retarded people. *Australia and New Zealand Journal of Developmental Disabilities, 10,* 201–213.

Suinn, R.M. (2001). The terrible twos – anger and anxiety: Hazardous to your health. *American Psychologist, 56,* 27–36.

Sukhodolsky, D.G., Kassinove, H., & Gorman, B.S. (2004). Cognitive-behavioral therapy for anger in children and adolescents: A meta-analysis. *Aggression and Violent Behavior, 9,* 247–269.

Suls, J., Wan, C.K., & Costa, P.T. (1995). Relationship of trait anger to resting blood pressure: A meta-analysis. *Health Psychology, 14,* 444–456.

Suris, A., Lind, L., Emmett, G., Borman, P.D., Kashner, M., & Barratt, E.S. (2004). Measures of aggressive behavior: Overview of clinical and research instruments. *Aggression and Violent Behavior, 9,* 165–227.

Suter, J.M., Byrne, M.K., Byrne, S., Howells, K., & Day, A. (2002). Anger in prisoners: women *are* different from men. *Personality and Individual Differences, 32,* 1087–1100.

Swaffer, T. & Hollin, C.R. (2001). Anger and general health in young offenders. *Journal of Forensic Psychiatry, 12,* 90–103.

Tafrate, R.C. (1995). Evaluation of treatment strategies for adult anger disorders. In H. Kassinove, *Anger Disorders.* Washington, DC: Taylor & Francis.

Taylor, J.L. (2002a). A review of the assessment and treatment of anger and aggression in offenders with intellectual disability. *Journal of Intellectual Disability Research, 46,* 57–73.

Taylor, J.L. (2002b). Assessment and treatment of anger in offenders with developmental disability. Unpublished doctoral thesis. University of Edinburgh.

Taylor, J.L., DuQueno, L., & Novaco, R.W. (2004). Piloting a ward anger rating scale for older adults with mental health problems. *Behavioural & Cognitive Psychotherapy, 32,* 467–479.

Taylor, J.L., Hatton, C., Dixon, L., & Douglas, C. (2004). Screening for psychiatric symptoms: PAS-ADD Checklist norms for adults with intellectual disabilities. *Journal of Intellectual Disability Research, 48,* 37–41.

Taylor, J.L., Hatton, C., Gentry, M., & Wilson, D. (2004). Prevalence, severity and impact of challenging behaviour and associated psychiatric symptoms in a community district population of adults with intellectual disabilities. Unpublished manuscript.

Taylor, J.L., Novaco, R.W., Gillmer, B.T. & Robertson, A. (2004). Treatment of anger and aggression. In W.R. Lindsay, J.L. Taylor, & P. Sturmey (Eds), *Offenders with Developmental Disabilities.* Chichester: John Wiley & Sons, Ltd.

Taylor, J.L., Novaco, R.W., Gillmer, B.T., Robertson, A., & Thorne, I. (in press). A controlled trial of individual cognitive-behavioural anger treatment for people with intellectual disabilities and histories of aggression. *British Journal of Clinical Psychology.*

Taylor, J.L., Novaco, R.W., Gillmer, B., & Thorne, I. (2002). Cognitive-behavioural treatment of anger intensity among offenders with intellectual disabilities. *Journal of Applied Research in Intellectual Disabilities, 15,* 151–165.

Taylor, J.L., Novaco, R.W., Guinan, C., & Street, N. (2004). Development of an imaginal provocation test to evaluate treatment for anger problems in people with intellectual disabilities. *Clinical Psychology & Psychotherapy, 11,* 233–246.

Thomas, S.P. (1993). *Women and Anger.* New York: Springer Publishing Company.

Thomas, S.P. (1995). Women's anger: causes, manifestations, and correlates. *Stress and Emotion: Anxiety, Anger and Curiosity, 15,* 53–74.

Tjaden, P. & Thoennes, N. (1999). Prevalence and incidence of violence against women: Findings from the National Violence Against Women Survey. *The Criminologist, 24,* 1–19.

Tomkins, S. (1963). *Affect, Imagery, and Consciousness.* Vol. II: *The Negative Affects.* New York: Springer.

Trepka, C., Rees, A., Shapiro, D.A., Hardy, G.E. & Barkham, M. (2004). Therapist competence and outcome of cognitive therapy for depression. *Cognitive Therapy and Research, 28*, 143–157.

Volavka, J. (2002). *Neurobiology of Violence.* 2nd edn. Washington, DC: American Psychiatric Association.

Vygotsky, L.S. (1978). *Mind in Society: The Development of Higher Psychological Processes.* Cambridge, MA: Harvard University Press.

Walby, S. & Allen, J. (2004). *Domestic violence, sexual assault and stalking: Findings from the British Crime Survey.* Home Office Research Study 276. London: The Stationery Office.

Walker, T. & Cheseldine, S. (1997). Towards outcome measurements: monitoring effectiveness of anger management and assertiveness training in a group setting. *British Journal of Learning Disabilities, 25*, 134–137.

Walklate, S. (2000). *Gender, Crime and Criminal Justice.* Devon: Willner Publishing.

Wang, E.W. & Diamond, P.M. (1999). Empirically identifying factors related to violence risk in corrections. *Behavioral Sciences and the Law, 17*, 377–389.

Ward, T., Day, A., Howells, K., & Birgden, A. (2004). The multifactor offender readiness model. *Aggression and Violent Behavior, 9*, 645–673.

Watt, B.D. & Howells, K. (1999). Skills training for aggression control: Evaluation of an anger management programme for violent offenders. *Legal and Criminological Psychology, 4*, 285–300.

Wechsler, D. (1925). What constitutes an emotion? *Psychological Review, 32*, 235–240.

Westbrook, D. & Hill, L. (1998). The long-term outcome of cognitive behaviour therapy for adults in routine clinical practice. *Behaviour Research and Therapy, 36*, 635–643.

Whisman, M.A. (1990). The efficacy of booster maintenance sessions in behaviour therapy: Review and methodological critique. *Clinical Psychology Review, 10*, 155–170.

Whitaker, S. (1993). The reduction of aggression in people with learning difficulties: A review of psychological methods. *British Journal of Clinical Psychology, 32*, 1–37.

Whitaker, S. (2001). Anger control for people with learning disabilities: A critical review. *Behavioural and Cognitive Psychotherapy, 29*, 277–293.

Williams, E. & Barlow, R. (1998). *Anger Control Training.* Chesterfield: Winslow Press.

Williams, H. & Jones, R.S.P. (1997). Teaching cognitive self-regulation of independence and emotion control skills. In B. Stenfert Kroese, D. Dagnan, & K. Loumidis (Eds), *Cognitive-Behaviour Therapy for People with Learning Disabilities* (pp. 67–85). London: Routledge.

Williams, J.E., Paton, C.C., Siegler, I.C., Eigenbrodt, M.L., Nieto, F.J., & Tyroler, H.A. (2000). Anger proneness predicts coronary heart disease risk: Prospective analysis from the Atherosclerosis Risk in Communities (ARIC) study. *Circulation, 101*, 2034–2039.

Williams, J.E., Nieto, F.J., Sanford, C.P., & Tyroler, H.A. (2001). Effects of an angry temperament on coronary heart disease: The Atherosclerosis Risk in Communities Study. *American Journal of Epidemiology, 154*, 230–235.

Williams, R. & Williams, V. (1993). *Anger Kills.* New York: HarperCollins Perennial.

Williams, T.Y., Boyd, J.C., Cascardi, M.A., & Poythress, N. (1996). Factor structure and convergent validity of the aggression questionnaire in an offender population. *Psychological Assessment, 8*, 398–403.

Willner, P., Jones, J., Tams, R., & Green, G. (2002). A randomised controlled trial of the efficacy of a cognitive-behavioural anger management group for clients with learning disabilities. *Journal of Applied Research in Intellectual Disabilities, 15*, 224–235.

Wilson, G.T. (1996). Manual-based treatments: The clinical application of research findings. *Behavior Research Therapy, 34*, 295–314.

Wilson, G.T. (1997). Treatment manuals in clinical practice. *Behavior Research Therapy, 35*, 205–210.

Wilson, G.T. (1998). Manual-based treatment and clinical practice. *Clinical Psychology: Science and Practice, 5*, 363–375.

Wilson, P.H. (1996). Relapse prevention: Overview of research findings in the treatment of problem drinking, smoking, obesity and depression. *Clinical Psychology and Psychotherapy, 3*, 231–248.

Wilt, D. (1993). Treatment of anger. In S.P. Thomas (Ed.), *Women and Anger* (pp. 233–257). New York: Springer.

World Health Organisation (1992). *ICD-10, Classification of Mental and Behavioural Disorders*. Geneva: World Health Organisation.

Wykes, T. (1994). *Violence and Health Care Professionals*. London: Chapman & Hall.

Zajonc, R.B. (1984). On the primacy of affect. *American Psychologist, 39*, 117–123.

Zangwill, O.L. (1948). The theory of emotion: A correspondence between J.T. MacCurdy and Morton Prince. *British Journal of Psychology, 39*, 1–11.

Zillmann, D. (1971). Excitation transfer in communication-mediated aggressive behavior. *Journal of Experimental Social Psychology, 7*, 419–434.

Zillmann, D. (1979). *Hostility and Aggression*. Hillsdale, NJ: Lawrence Erlbaum.

Zillmann, D. (1988). Cognition and excitation interdependencies in aggressive behavior. *Aggressive Behavior, 14*, 51–64.

Zillmann, D. & Bryant, J. (1974). Effect of residual excitation on the emotional response to provocation and delayed aggressive behavior. *Journal of Personality and Social Psychology, 30*, 782–791.

Zillmann, D., Katcher, A.H., & Milavsky, B. (1972). Excitation transfer from physical exercise to subsequent aggressive behavior. *Journal of Experimental Social Psychology, 8*, 247–259.

INDEX

Gunther Fla.

Not/500 mill

CPS   3⁵
                yrs
Abuse   ea
     5 yr. ?

C. B-
Colonoscopy

H. 2 De. escala

CPSIA information can be obtained at www.ICGtesting.com
Printed in the USA
BVOW01s1937191014

371327BV00015B/75/P

9 780470 870051